T0268095

Title 27
Alcohol, Tobacco Products and Firearms

Part 400 to End

Revised as of April 1, 2023

Containing a codification of documents
of general applicability and future effect

As of April 1, 2023

Published by the Office of the Federal Register
National Archives and Records Administration
as a Special Edition of the Federal Register

Table of Contents

	Page
Explanation	v

Title 27:

| Chapter II—Bureau of Alcohol, Tobacco, Firearms, and Explosives, Department of Justice .... | 3 |

Finding Aids:

Table of CFR Titles and Chapters	215
Alphabetical List of Agencies Appearing in the CFR	235
List of CFR Sections Affected	245

Cite this Code: CFR

To cite the regulations in this volume use title, part and section number. Thus, 27 CFR 447.1 *refers to title 27, part 447, section 1.*

Explanation

The Code of Federal Regulations is a codification of the general and permanent rules published in the Federal Register by the Executive departments and agencies of the Federal Government. The Code is divided into 50 titles which represent broad areas subject to Federal regulation. Each title is divided into chapters which usually bear the name of the issuing agency. Each chapter is further subdivided into parts covering specific regulatory areas.

Each volume of the Code is revised at least once each calendar year and issued on a quarterly basis approximately as follows:

Title 1 through Title 16..as of January 1
Title 17 through Title 27 ....as of April 1
Title 28 through Title 41 ....as of July 1
Title 42 through Title 50 ....as of October 1

The appropriate revision date is printed on the cover of each volume.

LEGAL STATUS

The contents of the Federal Register are required to be judicially noticed (44 U.S.C. 1507). The Code of Federal Regulations is prima facie evidence of the text of the original documents (44 U.S.C. 1510).

HOW TO USE THE CODE OF FEDERAL REGULATIONS

The Code of Federal Regulations is kept up to date by the individual issues of the Federal Register. These two publications must be used together to determine the latest version of any given rule.

To determine whether a Code volume has been amended since its revision date (in this case, April 1, 2023), consult the "List of CFR Sections Affected (LSA)," which is issued monthly, and the "Cumulative List of Parts Affected," which appears in the Reader Aids section of the daily Federal Register. These two lists will identify the Federal Register page number of the latest amendment of any given rule.

EFFECTIVE AND EXPIRATION DATES

Each volume of the Code contains amendments published in the Federal Register since the last revision of that volume of the Code. Source citations for the regulations are referred to by volume number and page number of the Federal Register and date of publication. Publication dates and effective dates are usually not the same and care must be exercised by the user in determining the actual effective date. In instances where the effective date is beyond the cut-off date for the Code a note has been inserted to reflect the future effective date. In those instances where a regulation published in the Federal Register states a date certain for expiration, an appropriate note will be inserted following the text.

OMB CONTROL NUMBERS

The Paperwork Reduction Act of 1980 (Pub. L. 96–511) requires Federal agencies to display an OMB control number with their information collection request.

Many agencies have begun publishing numerous OMB control numbers as amendments to existing regulations in the CFR. These OMB numbers are placed as close as possible to the applicable recordkeeping or reporting requirements.

PAST PROVISIONS OF THE CODE

Provisions of the Code that are no longer in force and effect as of the revision date stated on the cover of each volume are not carried. Code users may find the text of provisions in effect on any given date in the past by using the appropriate List of CFR Sections Affected (LSA). For the convenience of the reader, a "List of CFR Sections Affected" is published at the end of each CFR volume. For changes to the Code prior to the LSA listings at the end of the volume, consult previous annual editions of the LSA. For changes to the Code prior to 2001, consult the List of CFR Sections Affected compilations, published for 1949-1963, 1964-1972, 1973-1985, and 1986-2000.

"[RESERVED]" TERMINOLOGY

The term "[Reserved]" is used as a place holder within the Code of Federal Regulations. An agency may add regulatory information at a "[Reserved]" location at any time. Occasionally "[Reserved]" is used editorially to indicate that a portion of the CFR was left vacant and not dropped in error.

INCORPORATION BY REFERENCE

What is incorporation by reference? Incorporation by reference was established by statute and allows Federal agencies to meet the requirement to publish regulations in the Federal Register by referring to materials already published elsewhere. For an incorporation to be valid, the Director of the Federal Register must approve it. The legal effect of incorporation by reference is that the material is treated as if it were published in full in the Federal Register (5 U.S.C. 552(a)). This material, like any other properly issued regulation, has the force of law.

What is a proper incorporation by reference? The Director of the Federal Register will approve an incorporation by reference only when the requirements of 1 CFR part 51 are met. Some of the elements on which approval is based are:

(a) The incorporation will substantially reduce the volume of material published in the Federal Register.

(b) The matter incorporated is in fact available to the extent necessary to afford fairness and uniformity in the administrative process.

(c) The incorporating document is drafted and submitted for publication in accordance with 1 CFR part 51.

What if the material incorporated by reference cannot be found? If you have any problem locating or obtaining a copy of material listed as an approved incorporation by reference, please contact the agency that issued the regulation containing that incorporation. If, after contacting the agency, you find the material is not available, please notify the Director of the Federal Register, National Archives and Records Administration, 8601 Adelphi Road, College Park, MD 20740-6001, or call 202-741-6010.

CFR INDEXES AND TABULAR GUIDES

A subject index to the Code of Federal Regulations is contained in a separate volume, revised annually as of January 1, entitled CFR INDEX AND FINDING AIDS. This volume contains the Parallel Table of Authorities and Rules. A list of CFR titles, chapters, subchapters, and parts and an alphabetical list of agencies publishing in the CFR are also included in this volume.

An index to the text of "Title 3—The President" is carried within that volume.

The Federal Register Index is issued monthly in cumulative form. This index is based on a consolidation of the "Contents" entries in the daily Federal Register.

A List of CFR Sections Affected (LSA) is published monthly, keyed to the revision dates of the 50 CFR titles.

REPUBLICATION OF MATERIAL

There are no restrictions on the republication of material appearing in the Code of Federal Regulations.

INQUIRIES

For a legal interpretation or explanation of any regulation in this volume, contact the issuing agency. The issuing agency's name appears at the top of odd-numbered pages.

For inquiries concerning CFR reference assistance, call 202–741–6000 or write to the Director, Office of the Federal Register, National Archives and Records Administration, 8601 Adelphi Road, College Park, MD 20740-6001 or e-mail *fedreg.info@nara.gov.*

THIS TITLE

Title 27—ALCOHOL, TOBACCO PRODUCTS AND FIREARMS is composed of three volumes: Parts 1–39, parts 40–399, and part 400 to end. The contents of these volumes represent all current regulations issued by the Alcohol and Tobacco Tax and Trade Bureau, Department of the Treasury, and the Bureau of Alcohol, Tobacco, Firearms, and Explosives, Department of Justice, as of April 1, 2023.

For this volume, Gabrielle E. Burns was Chief Editor. The Code of Federal Regulations publication program is under the direction of John Hyrum Martinez, assisted by Stephen J. Frattini.

Title 27—Alcohol, Tobacco Products, and Firearms

(This book contains part 400 to end)

Part

CHAPTER II—Bureau of Alcohol, Tobacco, Firearms, and Explosives, Department of Justice 447

ABBREVIATIONS USED IN THIS CHAPTER:
ATF = *Alcohol, Tobacco and Firearms.*
TD = *Treasury Decision.*
TTB = *Alcohol and Tobacco Tax and Trade Bureau.*

CHAPTER II—BUREAU OF ALCOHOL, TOBACCO, FIREARMS, AND EXPLOSIVES, DEPARTMENT OF JUSTICE

SUBCHAPTER A [RESERVED]

SUBCHAPTER B—FIREARMS AND AMMUNITION

Part		Page
400–446	[Reserved]	
447	Importation of arms, ammunition and implements of war	5
478	Commerce in firearms and ammunition	18
479	Machine guns, destructive devices, and certain other firearms	101

SUBCHAPTER C—EXPLOSIVES

555	Commerce in explosives	136

SUBCHAPTER D—MISCELLANEOUS REGULATIONS RELATING TO ALCOHOL AND TOBACCO

646	Contraband cigarettes	192
647–699	[Reserved]	

SUBCHAPTER E—EXPLOSIVE LICENSE AND PERMIT PROCEEDINGS

700–770	[Reserved]	
771	Rules of practice in explosive license and permit proceedings	195
772–799	[Reserved]	

SUBCHAPTER A [RESERVED]
SUBCHAPTER B—FIREARMS AND AMMUNITION

PARTS 400–446 [RESERVED]

PART 447—IMPORTATION OF ARMS, AMMUNITION AND IMPLEMENTS OF WAR

Subpart A—Scope

Sec.
447.1 General.
447.2 Relation to other laws and regulations.

Subpart B—Definitions

447.11 Meaning of terms.

Subpart C—The U.S. Munitions Import List

447.21 The U.S. Munitions Import List.
447.22 Forgings, castings, and machined bodies.

Subpart D—Registration

447.31 Registration requirement.
447.32 Application for registration and refund of fee.
447.33 Notification of changes in information furnished by registrants.
447.34 Maintenance of records by persons required to register as importers of Import List articles.
447.35 Forms prescribed.

Subpart E—Permits

447.41 Permit requirement.
447.42 Application for permit.
447.43 Terms of permit.
447.44 Permit denial, revocation or suspension.
447.45 Importation.
447.46 Articles in transit.

Subpart F—Miscellaneous Provisions

447.51 Import certification and delivery verification.
447.52 Import restrictions applicable to certain countries.
447.53 Exemptions.
447.54 Administrative procedures inapplicable.
447.55 Departments of State and Defense consulted.
447.56 Authority of Customs officers.
447.57 U.S. military defense articles.
447.58 Delegations of the Director.

Subpart G—Penalties, Seizures and Forfeitures

447.61 Unlawful importation.
447.62 False statements or concealment of facts.
447.63 Seizure and forfeiture.

AUTHORITY: 22 U.S.C. 2778; E.O. 13637, 78 FR 16129 (Mar. 8, 2013).

SOURCE: T.D. ATF–8, 39 FR 3251, Jan. 25, 1974, unless otherwise noted. Redesignated by T.D. ATF–487, 68 FR 3747, Jan. 24, 2003.

EDITORIAL NOTE: Nomenclature changes to part 447 appear by T.D. ATF–487, 68 FR 3748, Jan. 24, 2003.

Subpart A—Scope

§ 447.1 General.

The regulations in this part relate to that portion of section 38 of the Arms Export Control Act of 1976, as amended, authorizing the President to designate defense articles and defense services as part of the United States Munitions List (USML) for purposes of import and export controls. To distinguish the list of defense articles and defense services controlled in this part for purposes of permanent import from the list of defense articles and defense services controlled by the Secretary of State for purposes of export and temporary import, this part shall refer to the defense articles and defense services controlled for purposes of permanent import as the U.S. Munitions Import List (USMIL) and shall refer to the export and temporary import control list set out by the Department of State in its International Traffic in Arms Regulations as the USML. Part 447 contains the USMIL and includes procedural and administrative requirements relating to registration of importers, permits, articles in transit, import certification, delivery verification, import restrictions applicable to certain countries, exemptions, U.S. military firearms and ammunition, penalties, seizures, and forfeitures. The President's delegation of permanent import control authorities to the Attorney General provides the Attorney General the authority to assess whether controls are justified, but in designating the defense articles and defense services set out in the USMIL the Attorney General shall be guided by the views of the Secretary of State on matters affecting world peace and the external security and foreign policy of the United States. All designations and changes in designations of defense articles and defense services subject to permanent import control under this part must have the concurrence of the Secretary of State and the Secretary of Defense, with notice given to the Secretary of Commerce.

[ATF–50F, 78 FR 23676, Apr. 22, 2013]

§ 447.2   Relation to other laws and regulations.

(a) All of those items on the U.S. Munitions Import List (see § 447.21) which are "firearms" or "ammunition" as defined in 18 U.S.C. 921(a) are subject to the interstate and foreign commerce controls contained in Chapter 44 of Title 18 U.S.C. and 27 CFR Part 478 and if they are "firearms" within the definition set out in 26 U.S.C. 5845(a) are also subject to the provisions of 27 CFR Part 479. Any person engaged in the business of importing firearms or ammunition as defined in 18 U.S.C. 921(a) must obtain a license under the provisions of 27 CFR Part 478, and if he imports firearms which fall within the definition of 26 U.S.C. 5845(a) must also register and pay special tax pursuant to the provisions of 27 CFR Part 479. Such licensing, registration and special tax requirements are in addition to registration under subpart D of this part.

(b) The permit procedures of subpart E of this part are applicable to all importations of articles on the U.S. Munitions Import List not subject to controls under 27 CFR Part 478 or 479. U.S. Munitions Import List articles subject to controls under 27 CFR Part 478 or 27 CFR Part 479 are subject to the import permit procedures of those regulations if imported into the United States (within the meaning of 27 CFR Parts 478 and 479).

(c) Articles on the U.S. Munitions Import List imported for the United States or any State or political subdivision thereof are exempt from the import controls of 27 CFR Part 478 but are not exempt from control under Section 38, Arms Export Control Act of 1976, unless imported by the United States or any agency thereof. All such importations not imported by the United States or any agency thereof shall be subject to the import permit procedures of subpart E of this part.

(d) For provisions requiring the registration of persons engaged in the business of brokering activities with respect to the importation of any defense article or defense service, see Department of State regulations in 22 CFR part 129.

[T.D. ATF–215, 50 FR 42158, Oct. 18, 1985, as amended by T.D. ATF–426, 65 FR 38197, June 20, 2000]

Subpart B—Definitions

§ 447.11   Meaning of terms.

When used in this part and in forms prescribed under this part, where not otherwise distinctly expressed or manifestly incompatible with the intent thereof, terms shall have the meanings ascribed in this section. Words in the plural form shall include the singular, and vice versa, and words imparting the masculine gender shall include the feminine. The terms "includes" and "including" do not exclude other things not enumerated which are in the same general class or are otherwise within the scope thereof.

Appropriate ATF officer. An officer or employee of the Bureau of Alcohol, Tobacco, Firearms, and Explosives (ATF) specified by ATF Order 1130.34, Delegation of the Director's Authorities in 27 CFR Part 447, Importation of Arms, Ammunition and Implements of War.

Article. Any of the defense articles enumerated in the U.S. Munitions Import List (USMIL).

Bureau. Bureau of Alcohol, Tobacco, Firearms, and Explosives, the Department of Justice.

Carbine. A short-barrelled rifle whose barrel is generally not longer than 22 inches and is characterized by light weight.

CFR. The Code of Federal Regulations.

Chemical agent. A substance useful in war which, by its ordinary and direct chemical action, produces a powerful physiological effect.

Defense articles. Any item designated in §447.21 or §447.22. This term includes models, mockups, and other such items which reveal technical data directly relating to §447.21 or §447.22.

Defense services. (a) The furnishing of assistance, including training, to foreign persons in the design, engineering, development, production, processing, manufacture, use, operation, overhaul, repair, maintenance, modification, or reconstruction of defense articles, whether in the United States or abroad; or

(b) The furnishing to foreign persons of any technical data, whether in the United States or abroad.

Director. The Director, Bureau of Alcohol, Tobacco, Firearms, and Explosives, the Department of Justice, Washington, DC 20226.

Executed under the penalties of perjury. Signed with the prescribed declaration under the penalties of perjury as provided on or with respect to the application, form, or other document or, where no form of declaration is prescribed, with the declaration: "I declare under the penalties of perjury that this _____ (insert type of document such as statement, certificate, application, or other document), including the documents submitted in support thereof, has been examined by me and, to best of my knowledge and belief, is true, correct, and complete."

Firearms. A weapon, and all components and parts therefor, not over .50 caliber which will or is designed to or may be readily converted to expel a projectile by the action of an explosive, but shall not include BB and pellet guns, and muzzle loading (black powder) firearms (including any firearm with a matchlock, flintlock, percussion cap, or similar type of ignition system) or firearms covered by Category I(a) established to have been manufactured in or before 1898.

Frame or receiver. The term "frame or receiver" shall have the same meaning as in 27 CFR 478.12.

Import or importation. Bringing into the United States from a foreign country any of the articles on the Import List, but shall not include intransit, temporary import or temporary export

transactions subject to Department of State controls under Title 22, Code of Federal Regulations.

Import List. The list of articles contained in §447.21 and identified therein as "The U.S. Munitions Import List".

Machinegun. A "machinegun", "machine pistol", "submachinegun", or "automatic rifle" is a firearm which shoots, is designed to shoot, or can be readily restored to shoot, automatically more than one shot, without manual reloading, by a single function of the trigger. The term shall also include the frame or receiver of any such weapon, any part designed and intended solely and exclusively, or combination of parts designed and intended, for use in converting a weapon into a machinegun, and any combination of parts from which a machinegun can be assembled if such parts are in the possession or under the control of a person. For purposes of this definition, the term "automatically" as it modifies "shoots, is designed to shoot, or can be readily restored to shoot," means functioning as the result of a self-acting or self-regulating mechanism that allows the firing of multiple rounds through a single function of the trigger; and "single function of the trigger" means a single pull of the trigger and analogous motions. The term "machinegun" includes a bump-stock-type device, *i.e.*, a device that allows a semi-automatic firearm to shoot more than one shot with a single pull of the trigger by harnessing the recoil energy of the semi-automatic firearm to which it is affixed so that the trigger resets and continues firing without additional physical manipulation of the trigger by the shooter.

Permit. The same as "license" for purposes of 22 U.S.C. 1934(c).

Person. A partnership, company, association, or corporation, as well as a natural person.

Pistol. A hand-operated firearm having a chamber integral with, or permanently aligned with, the bore.

Privately made firearm. The term "privately made firearm" shall have the same meaning as in 27 CFR 478.11.

Revolver. A hand-operated firearm with a revolving cylinder containing chambers for individual cartridges.

Rifle. A shoulder firearm discharging bullets through a rifled barrel at least 16 inches in length, including combination and drilling guns.

Sporting type sight including optical. A telescopic sight suitable for daylight use on a rifle, shotgun, pistol, or revolver for hunting or target shooting.

This chapter. Title 27, Code of Federal Regulations, Chapter II (27 CFR Chapter II).

United States. When used in the geographical sense, includes the several States, the Commonwealth of Puerto Rico, the insular possessions of the United States, the District of Columbia, and any territory over which the United States exercises any powers of administration, legislation, and jurisdiction.

(26 U.S.C. 7805 (68A Stat. 917), 27 U.S.C. 205 (49 Stat. 981 as amended), 18 U.S.C. 926 (82 Stat. 959), and sec. 38, Arms Export Control Act (22 U.S.C. 2778, 90 Stat. 744))

[T.D. ATF–48, 43 FR 13535, Mar. 31, 1978; 44 FR 55840, Sept. 28, 1979, as amended by T.D. ATF–202, 50 FR 14382, Apr. 12, 1985; T.D. ATF–215, 50 FR 42158, Oct. 18, 1985; T.D. ATF–484, 67 FR 64526, Oct. 21, 2002; ATF–9F, 72 FR 72938, Dec. 26, 2007; ATF–50F, 78 FR 23677, Apr. 22, 2013; ATF 2013R–9F, 79 FR 46692, Aug. 11, 2014; ATF 2018R–22F, 83 FR 66553, Dec. 26, 2018; ATF–2021R–05F, 87 FR 24734, Apr. 26, 2022]

Subpart C—The U.S. Munitions Import List

§ 447.21   The   U.S.   Munitions   Import List.

The following defense articles and defense services, designated pursuant to section 38(a) of the Arms Export Control Act, 22 U.S.C. 2778(a), and E.O. 13637 are subject to controls under this part. For purposes of this part, the list shall be known as the U.S. Munitions Import List (USMIL):

THE U.S. MUNITIONS IMPORT LIST

CATEGORY I—FIREARMS

(a) Nonautomatic and semiautomatic firearms, to caliber .50 inclusive, combat shotguns, and shotguns with barrels less than 18 inches in length, and all components and parts for such firearms.

(b) Automatic firearms and all components and parts for such firearms to caliber .50 inclusive.

(c) Insurgency-counterinsurgency type firearms of other weapons having a special military application (e.g. close assault weapons systems) regardless of caliber and all components and parts for such firearms.

(d) Firearms silencers and suppressors, including flash suppressors.

(e) [Reserved]

NOTE: Rifles, carbines, revolvers, and pistols, to caliber .50 inclusive, combat shotguns, and shotguns with barrels less than 18 inches in length are included under Category I(a). Machineguns, submachineguns, machine pistols and fully automatic rifles to caliber .50 inclusive are included under Category I(b).

CATEGORY II—ARTILLERY PROJECTORS

(a) Guns over caliber .50, howitzers, mortars, and recoiless rifles.

(b) Military flamethrowers and projectors.

(c) Components, parts, accessories, and attachments for the articles in paragraphs (a) and (b) of this category, including but not limited to mounts and carriages for these articles.

CATEGORY III—AMMUNITION

(a) Ammunition for the arms in Categories I and II of this section.

(b) Components, parts, accessories, and attachments for articles in paragraph (a) of this category, including but not limited to cartridge cases, powder bags, bullets, jackets, cores, shells (excluding shotgun shells), projectiles, boosters, fuzes and components therefor, primers, and other detonating devices for such ammunition.

(c)–(d) [Reserved]

NOTE: Cartridge and shell casings are included under Category III unless, prior to their importation, they have been rendered useless beyond the possibility of restoration for use as a cartridge or shell casing by means of heating, flame treatment, mangling, crushing, cutting, or popping.

CATEGORY IV—LAUNCH VEHICLES, GUIDED MISSILES, BALLISTIC MISSILES, ROCKETS, TORPEDOES, BOMBS AND MINES

(a) Rockets (including but not limited to meteorological and other sounding rockets), bombs, grenades, torpedoes, depth charges, land and naval mines, as well as launchers for such defense articles, and demolition blocks and blasting caps.

(b) Launch vehicles and missile and antimissile systems including but not limited to guided, tactical and strategic missiles, launchers, and systems.

(c) Apparatus, devices, and materials for the handling, control, activation, monitoring, detection, protection, discharge, or detonation of the articles in paragraphs (a) and (b) of this category. Articles in this category include, but are not limited to, the following: Fuses and components for the items in this category, bomb racks and shackles, bomb shackle release units, bomb ejectors, torpedo tubes, torpedo and guided missile boosters, guidance system equipment and parts, launching racks and projectors, pistols (exploders), igniters, fuze arming devices, intervalometers, guided missile launchers and specialized handling equipment, and hardened missile launching facilities.

(d) Missile and space vehicle powerplants.

(e) Military explosive excavating devices.

(f) [Reserved]

(g) Non/nuclear warheads for rockets and guided missiles.

(h) All specifically designed components or modified components, parts, accessories, attachments, and associated equipment for the articles in this category.

NOTE: Military demolition blocks and blasting caps referred to in Category IV(a) do not include the following articles:

(a) Electric squibs.

(b) No. 6 and No. 8 blasting caps, including electric ones.

(c) Delay electric blasting caps (including No. 6 and No. 8 millisecond ones).

(d) Seismograph electric blasting caps (including SSS, Static-Master, Vibrocap SR, and SEISMO SR).

(e) Oil well perforating devices.

CATEGORY V [Reserved]

CATEGORY VI—VESSELS OF WAR AND SPECIAL NAVAL EQUIPMENT

(a) Vessels of War, if they are armed and equipped with offensive or defensive weapon systems, including but not limited to amphibious warfare vessels, landing craft, mine warfare vessels, patrol vessels, auxiliary vessels, service craft, experimental types of naval ships, and any vessels specifically designed or modified for military purposes or other surface vessels equipped with offensive or defensive military systems.

(b) Turrets and gun mounts, special weapons systems, protective systems, and other components, parts, attachments, and accessories specifically designed or modified for such articles on combatant vessels.

(c)–(d) [Reserved]

(e) Naval nuclear propulsion plants, their land prototypes and special facilities for their construction, support and maintenance. This includes any machinery, device, component, or equipment specifically developed or designed or modified for use in such plants or facilities.

NOTE: The term "vessels of war" includes, but is not limited to, the following, if armed and equipped with offensive or defensive weapons systems:".

(a) Combatant vessels:

(1) Warships (including nuclear-powered versions):

(i) Aircraft carriers (CV, CVN)

(ii) Battleships (BB)

(iii) Cruisers (CA, CG, CGN)

(iv) Destroyers (DD, DDG)

(v) Frigates (FF, FFG)

(vi) Submarines (SS, SSN, SSBN, SSG, SSAG).

(2) Other Combatant Classifications:

(i) Patrol Combatants (PC, PHM)

(ii) Amphibious Helicopter/Landing Craft Carriers (LHA, LPD, LPH)

(iii) Amphibious Landing Craft Carriers (LKA, LPA, LSD, LST)

(iv) Amphibious Command Ships (LCC)

(v) Mine Warfare Ships (MSO).

(b) Auxiliaries:

(1) Mobile Logistics Support:

(i) Under way Replenishment (AD, AF, AFS, AO, AOE, AOR)

(ii) Material Support (AD, AR, AS).

(2) Support Ships:

(i) Fleet Support Ships (ARS, ASR, ATA, ATF, ATS)

(ii) Other Auxiliaries (AG, AGDS, AGF, AGM, AGOR, AGOS, AGS, AH, AK, AKR, AOG, AOT, AP, APB, ARC, ARL, AVM, AVT).

(c) Combatant Craft:

(1) Patrol Craft:

(i) Coastal Patrol Combatants (PB, PCF, PCH, PTF)

(ii) River, Roadstead Craft (ATC, PBR).

(2) Amphibious Warfare Craft:

(i) Landing Craft (AALC, LCAC, LCM, LCPL, LCPR, LCU, LWT, SLWT)

(ii) Special Warfare Craft (LSSC, MSSC, SDV, SWCL, SWCM).

(3) Mine Warfare Craft:

(i) Mine Countermeasures Craft (MSB, MSD, MSI, MSM, MSR).

(d) Support and Service Craft:

(1) Tugs (YTB, YTL, YTM)

(2) Tankers (YO, YOG, YW)

(3) Lighters (YC, YCF, YCV, YF, YFN, YFNB, YFNX, YFR, YFRN, YFU, YG, YGN, YOGN, YON, YOS, YSR, YWN)

(4) Floating Dry Docks (AFDB, AFDL, AFDM, ARD, ARDM, YFD)

(5) Miscellaneous (APL, DSRV, DSV, IX, NR, YAG, YD, YDT, YFB, YFND, YEP, YFRT, YHLC, YM, YNG, YP, YPD, YR, YRB, YRBN, YRDH, YRDM, YRR, YRST, YSD).

(e) Coast Guard Patrol and Service Vessels and Craft:

(1) Coast Guard Cutters (CGC, WHEC, WMEC)

(2) Patrol Craft (WPB)

(3) Icebreakers (WAGB)

(4) Oceanography Vessels (WAGO)

(5) Special Vessels (WIX)

(6) Buoy Tenders (WLB, WLM, WLI, WLR, WLIC)

(7) Tugs (WYTM, WYTL)

(8) Light Ships (WLV).

CATEGORY VII—TANKS AND MILITARY VEHICLES

(a) Military type armed or armored vehicles, military railway trains, and vehicles specifically designed or modified to accommodate mountings for arms or other specialized military equipment or fitted with such items.

(b) Military tanks, combat engineer vehicles, bridge launching vehicles, halftracks and gun carriers.

(c) Self-propelled guns and howitzers.

(d)–(e) [Reserved]

(f) Amphibious vehicles.

(g) [Reserved]

(h) Tank and military vehicle parts, components, accessories, attachments, and associated equipment for offensive or defensive systems for the articles in this category, as follows:

(1) Armored hulls, armored turrets and turret support rings;

(2) Active protection systems (i.e., defensive systems that actively detect and track incoming threats and launch a ballistic, explosive, energy or electromagnetic countermeasure(s) to neutralize the threat prior to contact with a vehicle);

(3) Composite armor parts and components;

(4) Spaced armor components and parts, including slat armor parts and components;

(5) Reactive armor and components;

(6) Electromagnetic armor parts and components, including pulsed power;

(7) Gun mount, stabilization, turret drive, and automatic elevating systems;

(8) Kits specifically designed to convert a vehicle in this category into either an unmanned or a driver-optional vehicle. For a kit to be controlled by this paragraph it must include all of the following:

(i) Remote or autonomous steering;

(ii) Acceleration and braking; and

(iii) A control system;

(9) Fire control computers, stored management systems, armaments control processors, vehicle weapon interface units and computers;

(10) Electro-optical sighting systems; and

(11) Laser rangefinder or target designating devices.

(i) Other ground vehicles having all of the following:

(1) Manufactured or fitted with materials or components to provide ballistic protection to level III (NIJ 0108.01, September 1985) or better;

(2) A transmission to provide drive to both front and rear wheels simultaneously, including those vehicles having additional wheels for load bearing purposes whether driven or not;

(3) Gross Vehicle Weight Rating (GVWR) greater than 4,500 kg; and

(4) Designed or modified for off-road use.

NOTE: An "amphibious vehicle" in Category VII(f) is a vehicle or chassis that is equipped to meet special military requirements, and that is designed or adapted for operation on or under water, as well as on land.

NOTE: Engines and engine parts are not included in paragraph (h) of Category VII.

NOTE: Paragraph (i) of Category VII does not apply to civil vehicles designed or modified for transporting money or valuables.

CATEGORY VIII—AIRCRAFT AND ASSOCIATED EQUIPMENT

(a) Aircraft, including but not limited to helicopters, non-expansive balloons, drones and lighter-than-air aircraft, which are specifically designed, modified, or equipped for military purposes. This includes but is not limited to the following military purposes: gunnery, bombing, rocket or missile launching, electronic and other surveillance, reconnaissance, refueling, aerial mapping, military liaison, cargo carrying or dropping, personnel dropping, airborne warning and control, and military training.

(b) [Reserved]

NOTE: In Category VIII, "aircraft" means aircraft designed, modified, or equipped for a military purpose, including aircraft described as "demilitarized." All aircraft bearing an original military designation are included in Category VIII. However, the following aircraft are not so included so long as they have not been specifically equipped, re-equipped, or modified for military operations:

(a) Cargo aircraft bearing "C" designations and numbered C–45 through C–118 inclusive, and C–121 through C–125 inclusive, and C–131, using reciprocating engines only.

(b) Trainer aircraft bearing "T" designations and using reciprocating engines or turboprop engines with less than 600 horsepower (s.h.p.).

(c) Utility aircraft bearing "U" designations and using reciprocating engines only.

(d) All liaison aircraft bearing an "L" designation.

(e) All observation aircraft bearing "O" designations and using reciprocating engines.

CATEGORIES IX–XIII [Reserved]

CATEGORY XIV—TOXICOLOGICAL AGENTS AND EQUIPMENT AND RADIOLOGICAL EQUIPMENT

(a) Chemical agents, including but not limited to lung irritants, vesicants, lachrymators, and tear gases (except tear gas formulations containing 1% or less CN or CS), sternutators and irritant smoke, and nerve gases and incapacitating agents.

(b) [Reserved]

(c) All specifically designed or modified equipment, including components, parts, accessories, and attachments for disseminating the articles in paragraph (a) of this category.

10

(d)–(e)[Reserved]

NOTE: A chemical agent in Category XIV(a) is a substance having military application which by its ordinary and direct chemical action produces a powerful physiological effect. The term "chemical agent" includes, but is not limited to, the following chemical compounds:

(a) Lung irritants:

(1) Diphenylcyanoarsine (DC).

(2) Fluorine (but not fluorene).

(3) Trichloronitro methane (chloropicrin PS).

(b) Vesicants:

(1) B-Chlorovinyldichloroarsine (Lewisite, L).

(2) Bis(dichlorethyl) sulphide (Mustard Gas, HD or H).

(3) Ethyldichloroarsine (ED).

(4) Methyldichloroarsine (MD).

(c) Lachrymators and tear gases:

(1) A-Brombenzyl cyanide (BBC).

(2) Chloroacetophenone (CN).

(3) Dibromodimethyl ether.

(4) Dichlorodimethyl ether (ClCi).

(5) Ethyldibromoarsine.

(6) Phenylcarbylamine chloride.

(7) Tear gas solutions (CNB and CNS).

(8) Tear gas orthochlorobenzalmalononitrile (CS).

(d) Sternutators and irritant smokes:

(1) Diphenylamine chloroarsine (Adamsite, DM).

(2) Diphenylchloroarsine (BA).

(3) Liquid pepper.

(e) Nerve agents, gases, and aerosols. These are toxic compounds which affect the nervous system, such as:

(1) Dimethylaminoethoxycyanophosphine oxide (GA).

(2) Methylisopropoxyfluorophosphine oxide (GB).

(3) Methylpinacolyloxyfluoriphosphine oxide (GD).

(f) Antiplant chemicals, such as: Butyl 2-chloro-4-fluorophenoxyacetate (LNF).

CATEGORY XV [Reserved]

CATEGORY XVI—NUCLEAR WEAPONS DESIGN AND TEST EQUIPMENT

(a)[Reserved]

(b) Modeling or simulation tools that model or simulate the environments generated by nuclear detonations or the effects of these environments on systems, subsystems, components, structures, or humans.

NOTE: Category XVI does not include equipment, technical data, or services controlled by the Department of Energy pursuant to the Atomic Energy Act of 1954, as amended, and the Nuclear Non-Proliferation Act of 1978, as amended, or are government transfers authorized pursuant to these Acts.

CATEGORY XVII–XIX [Reserved]

CATEGORY XX—SUBMERSIBLE VESSELS, OCEANOGRAPHIC AND ASSOCIATED EQUIPMENT

(a) Submersible vessels, manned and unmanned, designed or modified for military purposes or having independent capability to maneuver vertically or horizontally at depths below 1,000 feet, or powered by nuclear propulsion plants.

(b) Submersible vessels, manned or unmanned, designed or modified in whole or in part from technology developed by or for the U.S. Armed Forces.

(c) Any of the articles in Category VI and elsewhere in this part specifically designed or modified for use with submersible vessels, and oceanographic or associated equipment assigned a military designation.

(d) Equipment, components, parts, accessories, and attachments specifically designed for any of the articles in paragraphs (a) and (b) of this category.

CATEGORY XXI—MISCELLANEOUS ARTICLES

Any defense article or defense service not specifically enumerated in the other categories of the USMIL that has substantial military applicability and that has been specifically designed or modified for military purposes. The decision as to whether any article may be included in this category shall be made by the Attorney General with the concurrence of the Secretary of State and the Secretary of Defense.

[T.D. ATF–215, 50 FR 42158, Oct. 18, 1985; 50 FR 46647, Nov. 12, 1985, as amended by T.D. ATF–426, 65 FR 38197, June 20, 2000; ATF–9F, 72 FR 72938, Dec. 26, 2007; ATF–50F, 78 FR 23677, Apr. 22, 2013; ATF–25I, 79 FR 17028, Mar. 27, 2014]

§447.22 Forgings, castings, and machined bodies.

Articles on the U.S. Munitions Import List include articles in a partially completed state (such as forgings, castings, extrusions, and machined bodies) which have reached a stage in manufacture where they are clearly identifiable as defense articles. If the end-item is an article on the U.S. Munitions Import List, (including components, accessories, attachments and parts) then the particular forging, casting, extrusion, machined body, etc., is considered a defense article subject to the controls of this part, except for such items as are in normal commercial use.

[T.D. ATF–215, 50 FR 42160, Oct. 18, 1985]

Subpart D—Registration

§ 447.31 Registration requirement.

Persons engaged in the business, in the United States, of importing articles enumerated on the U.S. Munitions Import List must register by making an application on ATF Form 4587.

[T.D. ATF–484, 67 FR 64526, Oct. 21, 2002]

§ 447.32 Application for registration and refund of fee.

(a) Application for registration must be filed on ATF Form 4587 and must be accompanied by the registration fee at the rate prescribed in this section. The appropriate ATF officer will approve the application and return the original to the applicant.

(b) Registration may be effected for periods of from 1 to 5 years at the option of the registrant by identifying on Form 4587 the period of registration desired. The registration fees are as follows:

1 year	$250
2 years	500
3 years	700
4 years	850
5 years	1,000

(c) Fees paid in advance for whole future years of a multiple year registration will be refunded upon request if the registrant ceases to engage in importing articles on the U.S. Munitions Import List. A request for a refund must be submitted to the appropriate ATF officer at the Bureau of Alcohol, Tobacco, Firearms, and Explosives, Martinsburg, WV 25405, prior to the beginning of any year for which a refund is claimed.

(Approved by the Office of Management and Budget under control number 1140–0009)

[T.D. ATF–8, 39 FR 3251, Jan. 25, 1974, as amended by T.D. ATF–215, 50 FR 42161, Oct. 18, 1985; T.D. ATF–484, 67 FR 64526, Oct. 21, 2002; ATF–11F, 73 FR 57240, Oct. 2, 2008; ATF 2013R–9F, 79 FR 46692, Aug. 11, 2014]

§ 447.33 Notification of changes in information furnished by registrants.

Registered persons shall notify the appropriate ATF officer in writing, in duplicate, of significant changes in the information set forth in their registration

(Approved by the Office of Management and Budget under control number 1140–0009)

[T.D. ATF–8, 39 FR 3251, Jan. 25, 1974, as amended by T.D. ATF–215, 50 FR 42161, Oct. 18, 1985; ATF–11F, 73 FR 57240, Oct. 2, 2008]

§ 447.34 Maintenance of records by persons required to register as importers of Import List articles.

(a) Registrants under this part engaged in the business of importing articles subject to controls under 27 CFR Parts 478 and 479 shall maintain records in accordance with the applicable provisions of those parts.

(b) Registrants under this part engaged in importing articles on the U.S. Munitions Import List subject to the permit procedures of subpart E of this part must maintain for a period of 6 years records bearing on such articles imported, including records concerning their acquisition and disposition, including Forms 6 and 6A. The appropriate ATF officer may prescribe a longer or shorter period in individual cases as such officer deems necessary. See § 478.129 of this chapter for articles subject to import control under part 478 of this chapter.

(Approved by the Office of Management and Budget under control number 1140–0032)

[T.D. ATF–8, 39 FR 3251, Jan. 25, 1974, as amended by T.D. ATF–172, 49 FR 14941, Apr. 16, 1984; T.D. ATF–215, 50 FR 42161, Oct. 18, 1985; T.D. ATF–426, 65 FR 38197, June 20, 2000; T.D. ATF–484, 67 FR 64526, Oct. 21, 2002; ATF–11F, 73 FR 57240, Oct. 2, 2008]

§ 447.35 Forms prescribed.

(a) The appropriate ATF officer is authorized to prescribe all forms required by this part. All of the information called for in each form shall be furnished as indicated by the headings on the form and the instructions on or pertaining to the form. In addition, information called for in each form shall be furnished as required by this part. The form will be filed in accordance with the instructions for the form.

(b) Forms may be requested from the ATF Distribution Center (*http://www.atf.gov*) or by calling (202) 648–6420.

[T.D. ATF–92, 46 FR 46914, Sept. 23, 1981, as amended by T.D. ATF–249, 52 FR 5961, Feb. 27, 1987; T.D. ATF–426, 65 FR 38197, June 20, 2000; T.D. ATF–484, 67 FR 64526, Oct. 21, 2002; ATF–11F, 73 FR 57240, Oct. 2, 2008; ATF 2013R–9F, 79 FR 46692, Aug. 11, 2014]

Subpart E—Permits

§447.41 Permit requirement.

(a) Articles on the U.S. Munitions Import List will not be imported into the United States except pursuant to a permit under this subpart. For articles subject to control under parts 478 or 479 of this chapter, a separate permit is not necessary.

(b) Articles on the U.S. Munitions Import List intended for the United States or any State or political subdivision thereof, or the District of Columbia, which are exempt from import controls of 27 CFR 478.115 shall not be imported into the United States, except by the United States or agency thereof, without first obtaining a permit under this subpart.

(c) A permit is not required for the importation of—

(1)(i) The U.S. Munitions Import List articles from Canada, except articles enumerated in Categories I, II, III, IV, VI(e), VIII(a), XVI, and XX; and

(ii) Nuclear weapons strategic delivery systems and all specifically designed components, parts, accessories, attachments, and associated equipment thereof (see Category XXI); or

(2) Minor components and parts for Category I(a) and I(b) firearms, except barrels, cylinders, receivers (frames) or complete breech mechanisms, when the total value does not exceed $100 wholesale in any single transaction.

[T.D. ATF–215, 50 FR 42161, Oct. 18, 1985, as amended by T.D. ATF–426, 65 FR 38197, June 20, 2000; T.D. ATF–484, 67 FR 64526, Oct. 21, 2002]

§447.42 Application for permit.

(a)(1) Persons required to obtain a permit as provided in §447.41 must file a Form 6—Part I. The application must be signed and dated and must contain the information requested on the form, including:

(i) The name, address, telephone number, license and registration number, if any (including expiration date) of the importer;

(ii) The country from which the defense article is to be imported;

(iii) The name and address of the foreign seller and foreign shipper;

(iv) A description of the defense article to be imported, including—

(A) The name and address of the manufacturer of the defense article, or "privately made firearm" (if a firearm privately made in the United States);

(B) The type (e.g., rifle, shotgun, pistol, revolver, aircraft, vessel, and in the case of ammunition only, ball, wadcutter, shot, etc.);

(C) The caliber, gauge, or size;

(D) The model;

(E) The length of barrel, if any (in inches);

(F) The overall length, if a firearm (in inches);

(G) The serial number, if known;

(H) Whether the defense article is new or used;

(I) The quantity;

(J) The unit cost of the firearm, firearm barrel, ammunition, or other defense article to be imported;

(K) The category of U.S. Munitions Import List under which the article is regulated;

(v) The specific purpose of importation, including final recipient information if different from the importer; and

(vi) Certification of origin.

(2)(i) If the appropriate ATF officer approves the application, such approved application will serve as the permit to import the defense article described therein, and importation of such defense article may continue to be made by the licensed/registered importer (if applicable) under the approved application (permit) during the period specified thereon. The appropriate ATF officer will furnish the approved application (permit) to the applicant and retain two copies thereof for administrative use.

(ii) If the Director disapproves the application, the licensed/registered importer (if applicable) will be notified of the basis for the disapproval.

(b) For additional requirements relating to the importation of plastic explosives into the United States on or after April 24, 1997, see § 555.183 of this title.

(Approved by the Office of Management and Budget under control number 1140–0005)

[T.D. ATF–215, 50 FR 42161, Oct. 18, 1985, as amended by T.D. ATF–387, 62 FR 8376, Feb. 25, 1997; T.D. ATF–426, 65 FR 38197, June 20, 2000; T.D. ATF–484, 67 FR 64526, Oct. 21, 2002; ATF–11F, 73 FR 57240, Oct. 2, 2008; ATF–2021R–05F, 87 FR 24734, Apr. 26, 2022]

§ 447.43 Terms of permit.

(a) Import permits issued under this subpart are valid for two years from their issuance date unless a different period of validity is stated thereon. They are not transferable.

(b) If shipment cannot be completed during the period of validity of the permit, another application must be submitted for permit to cover the unshipped balance. Such an application shall make reference to the previous permit and may include materials in addition to the unshipped balance.

(c) No amendments or alteration of a permit may be made, except by the appropriate ATF officer.

[T.D. ATF–8, 39 FR 3251, Jan. 25, 1974, as amended by T.D. ATF–325, 57 FR 29787, July 7, 1992; T.D. ATF–426, 65 FR 38197, June 20, 2000; ATF–26F, 79 FR 7396, Feb. 7, 2014]

§ 447.44 Permit denial, revocation or suspension.

(a) Import permits under this subpart may be denied, revoked, suspended or revised without prior notice whenever the appropriate ATF officer finds the proposed importation to be inconsistent with the purpose or in violation of section 38, Arms Export Control Act of 1976 or the regulations in this part.

(b) Whenever, after appropriate consideration, a permit application is denied or an outstanding permit is revoked, suspended, or revised, the applicant or permittee shall be promptly advised in writing of the appropriate ATF officer's decision and the reasons therefor.

(c) Upon written request made within 30 days after receipt of an adverse decision, the applicant or permittee shall be accorded an opportunity to present additional information and to have a full review of his case by the appropriate ATF officer.

(d) Unused, expired, suspended, or revoked permits must be returned immediately to the appropriate ATF officer.

[T.D. ATF–8, 39 FR 3251, Jan. 25, 1974, as amended by T.D. ATF–215, 50 FR 42161, Oct. 18, 1985]

§ 447.45 Importation.

(a) Articles subject to the import permit procedures of this subpart imported into the United States may be released from Customs custody to the person authorized to import same upon his showing that he has a permit for the importation of the article or articles to be released. For articles in Categories I and III imported by a registered importer, the importer will also submit to Customs a copy of the export license authorizing the export of the article or articles from the exporting country. If the exporting country does not require issuance of an export license, the importer must submit a certification, under penalty of perjury, to that effect.

(1) In obtaining the release from Customs custody of an article imported pursuant to a permit, the permit holder will prepare and file Form 6A according to its instructions.

(2) The ATF Form 6A must contain the information requested on the form, including:

(i) The name, address, and license number (if any) of the importer;

(ii) The name of the manufacturer of the defense article, or "privately made firearm" (if a firearm privately made in the United States);

(iii) The country of manufacture;

(iv) The type;

(v) The model;

(vi) The caliber, gauge, or size;

(vii) The serial number in the case of firearms, if known; and

(viii) The number of defense articles released.

(b) Within 15 days of the date of their release from Customs custody, the importer of the articles released will forward to the address specified on the form a copy of Form 6A on which will be reported any error or discrepancy appearing on the Form 6A certified by

Customs and serial numbers if not previously provided on ATF Form 6A.

(Approved by the Office of Management and Budget under control number 1140–0007)

[T.D. ATF–215, 50 FR 42161, Oct. 18, 1985, as amended by T.D. ATF–426, 65 FR 38197, June 20, 2000; T.D. ATF–484, 67 FR 64526, Oct. 21, 2002; ATF–11F, 73 FR 57240, Oct. 2, 2008; ATF–2021R–05F, 87 FR 24734, Apr. 26, 2022]

§447.46 Articles in transit.

Articles subject to the import permit procedures of this subpart which enter the United States for temporary deposit pending removal therefrom and such articles which are temporarily taken out of the United States for return thereto shall be regarded as in transit and will be considered neither imported nor exported under this part. Such transactions are subject to the Intransit or Temporary Export License procedures of the Department of State (see 22 CFR Part 123).

[T.D. ATF–8, 39 FR 3251, Jan. 25, 1974, as amended by T.D. ATF–215, 50 FR 42161, Oct. 18, 1985]

Subpart F—Miscellaneous Provisions

§447.51 Import certification and delivery verification.

Pursuant to agreement with the United States, certain foreign countries are entitled to request certification of legality of importation of articles on the U.S. Munitions Import List. Upon request of a foreign government, the appropriate ATF officer will certify the importation, on Form ITA–645P/ATF–4522/DSP53, for the U.S. importer. Normally, the U.S. importer will submit this form at the time he applies for an import permit. This document will serve as evidence to the government of the exporting company that the U.S. importer has complied with import regulations of the U.S. Government and is prohibited from diverting, transshipping, or reexporting the material described therein without the approval of the U.S. Government. Foreign governments may also require documentation attesting to the delivery of the material into the United States. When such delivery certification is requested by a foreign government, the U.S. importer may obtain directly from the U.S. District Director of Customs the authenticated Delivery Verification Certificate (U.S. Department of Commerce Form ITA–647P) for this purpose.

(Approved by the Office of Management and Budget under control number 0625–0064)

[T.D. ATF–215, 50 FR 42162, Oct. 18, 1985, as amended by T.D. ATF–484, 67 FR 64526, Oct. 21, 2002]

§447.52 Import restrictions applicable to certain countries.

(a) It is the policy of the United States to deny licenses and other approvals with respect to defense articles and defense services originating in certain countries or areas. This policy applies to Afghanistan, Belarus (one of the states composing the former Soviet Union), Cuba, Iran, Iraq, Libya, Mongolia, North Korea, Sudan, Syria, and Vietnam. This policy applies to countries or areas with respect to which the United States maintains an arms embargo (e.g., Burma, China, the Democratic Republic of the Congo, Haiti, Liberia, Rwanda, Somalia, Sudan, and UNITA (Angola)). It also applies when an import would not be in furtherance of world peace and the security and foreign policy of the United States.

NOTE: Changes in foreign policy may result in additions to and deletions from the above list of countries. The ATF will publish changes to this list in the FEDERAL REGISTER. Contact the Firearms and Explosives Imports Branch at (304) 616–4550 for current information.

(b) Notwithstanding paragraph (a) of this section, the appropriate ATF officer shall deny applications to import into the United States the following firearms and ammunition:

(1) Any firearm located or manufactured in Georgia, Kazakhstan, Kyrgyzstan, Moldova, Russian Federation, Turkmenistan, Ukraine, or Uzbekistan, and any firearm previously manufactured in the Soviet Union, that is not one of the models listed below:

(i) Pistols/Revolvers:

(A) German Model P08 Pistol.

(B) IZH 34M, .22 caliber Target Pistol.

(C) IZH 35M, .22 caliber Target Pistol.

(D) Mauser Model 1896 Pistol.

(E) MC–57–1 Pistol.

(F) MC–1–5 Pistol.

(G) Polish Vis Model 35 Pistol.

(H) Soviet Nagant Revolver.

(I) TOZ 35, .22 caliber Target Pistol.

(ii) Rifles:

(A) BARS–4 Bolt Action Carbine.

(B) Biathlon Target Rifle, .22LR caliber.

(C) British Enfield Rifle.

(D) CM2, .22 caliber Target Rifle (also known as SM2, 22 caliber).

(E) German Model 98K Rifle.

(F) German Model G41 Rifle.

(G) German Model G43 Rifle.

(H) IZH–94.

(I) LOS–7 Bolt Action Rifle.

(J) MC–7–07.

(K) MC–18–3.

(L) MC–19–07.

(M) MC–105–01.

(N) MC–112–02.

(O) MC–113–02.

(P) MC–115–1.

(Q) MC–125/127.

(R) MC–126.

(S) MC–128.

(T) Saiga Rifle.

(U) Soviet Model 38 Carbine.

(V) Soviet Model 44 Carbine.

(W) Soviet Model 91/30 Rifle.

(X) TOZ 18, .22 caliber Bolt Action Rifle.

(Y) TOZ 55.

(Z) TOZ 78.

(AA) Ural Target Rifle, .22LR caliber.

(BB) VEPR Rifle.

(CC) Winchester Model 1895, Russian Model Rifle;

(2) Ammunition located or manufactured in Georgia, Kazakstan, Kyrgyzstan, Moldova, Russian Federation, Turkmenistan, Ukraine, or Uzbekistan, and ammunition previously manufactured in the Soviet Union, that is 7.62 × 25mm caliber (also known as 7.63 × 25mm caliber or .30 Mauser); or

(3) A type of firearm the manufacture of which began after February 9, 1996.

(c) The provisions of paragraph (b) of this section shall not affect the fulfillment of contracts with respect to firearms or ammunition entered or withdrawn from warehouse for consumption in the United States on or before February 9, 1996.

(d) A defense article authorized for importation under this part may not be shipped on a vessel, aircraft or other means or conveyance which is owned or operated by, or leased to or from, any of the countries or areas covered by paragraph (a) of this section.

(e) Applications for permits to import articles that were manufactured in, or have been in, a country or area proscribed under this section may be approved where the articles are covered by Category I(a) of the Import List (other than those subject to the provisions of 27 CFR Part 479), are importable as curios or relics under the provisions of 27 CFR 478.118, and meet the following criteria:

(1) The articles were manufactured in a proscribed country or area prior to the date, as established by the Department of State, the country or area became proscribed, or, were manufactured in a non-proscribed country or area; and

(2) The articles have been stored for the five year period immediately prior to importation in a non-proscribed country or area.

(f) Applicants desiring to import articles claimed to meet the criteria specified in paragraph (e) of this section shall explain, and certify to, how the firearms meet the criteria. The certification statement will be prepared in letter form, executed under the penalties of perjury, and should be submitted with the application for an import permit. The certification statement must be accompanied by documentary information on the country or area of original manufacture and on the country or area of storage for the five year period immediately prior to importation. Such information may, for example, include a verifiable statement in the English language of a government official or any other person having knowledge of the date and place of manufacture and/or the place of storage; a warehouse receipt or other document which provides the required history of storage; and any other document that the applicant believes substantiates the place and date of manufacture and the place of storage. The appropriate ATF officer, however, reserves the right to determine whether documentation is acceptable. Applicants shall, when required by the appropriate ATF officer, furnish additional documentation as may be necessary to determine whether an import permit application should be approved.

[T.D. ATF–202, 50 FR 14382, Apr. 12, 1985, as amended by T.D. ATF–215, 50 FR 42162, Oct. 18, 1985; T.D. ATF–287, 54 FR 13681, Apr. 5, 1989; T.D. ATF–323, 57 FR 24189, June 8, 1992; T.D. ATF–349, 58 FR 47831, Sept. 13, 1993; T.D. ATF–367, 60 FR 47866, Sept. 15, 1995; T.D. ATF–396, 62 FR 61234, Nov. 17, 1997; T.D. ATF–484, 67 FR 64526, Oct. 21, 2002; ATF–9F, 72 FR 72938, Dec. 26, 2007]

§447.53 Exemptions.

(a) The provisions of this part are not applicable to:

(1) Importations by the United States or any agency thereof;

(2) Importation of components for items being manufactured under contract for the Department of Defense; or

(3) Importation of articles (other than those which would be "firearms" as defined in 18 U.S.C. 921(a)(3) manufactured in foreign countries for persons in the United States pursuant to Department of State approval.

(b) Any person seeking to import articles on the U.S. Munitions Import List as exempt under paragraph (a)(2) or (3) of this section may obtain release of such articles from Customs custody by submitting, to the Customs officer with authority to release, a statement claiming the exemption accompanied by satisfactory proof of eligibility. Such proof may be in the form of a letter from the Department of Defense or State, as the case may be, confirming that the conditions of the exemption are met.

[T.D. ATF–8, 39 FR 3251, Jan. 25, 1974, as amended by T.D. ATF–215, 50 FR 42162, Oct. 18, 1985]

§447.54 Administrative procedures inapplicable.

The functions conferred under section 38, Arms Export Control Act of 1976, as amended, are excluded from the operation of Chapter 5, Title 5, United States Code, with respect to Rule Making and Adjudication, 5 U.S.C. 553 and 554.

[T.D. ATF–8, 39 FR 3251, Jan. 25, 1974, as amended by T.D. ATF–215, 50 FR 42162, Oct. 18, 1985]

§447.55 Departments of State and Defense consulted.

The administration of the provisions of this part will be subject to the guidance of the Secretaries of State and Defense on matters affecting world peace and the external security and foreign policy of the United States.

§447.56 Authority of Customs officers.

(a) Officers of the U.S. Customs Service are authorized to take appropriate action to assure compliance with this part and with 27 CFR Parts 478 and 479 as to the importation or attempted importation of articles on the U.S. Munitions Import List, whether or not authorized by permit.

(b) Upon the presentation to him of a permit or written approval authorizing importation of articles on the U.S. Munitions Import List, the Customs officer who has authority to release same may require, in addition to such documents as may be required by Customs regulations, the production of other relevant documents relating to the proposed importation, including, but not limited to, invoices, orders, packing lists, shipping documents, correspondence, and instructions.

[T.D. ATF–8, 39 FR 3251, Jan. 25, 1974, as amended by T.D. ATF–215, 50 FR 42162, Oct. 18, 1985]

§447.57 U.S. military defense articles.

(a)(1) Notwithstanding any other provision of this part or of parts 478 or 479 of this chapter, no military defense article of United States manufacture may be imported into the United States if such article was furnished to a foreign government under a foreign assistance or foreign military sales program of the United States.

(2) The restrictions in paragraph (a)(1) of this section cover defense articles which are advanced in value or improved in condition in a foreign country, but do not include those which have been substantially transformed as to become, in effect, articles of foreign manufacture.

(b) Paragraph (a) of this section will not apply if:

(1) The applicant submits with the ATF Form 6—Part I application written authorization from the Department of State to import the defense article; and

(2) In the case of firearms, such firearms are curios or relics under 18 U.S.C. 925(e) and the person seeking to import such firearms provides a certification of a foreign government that the firearms were furnished to such government under a foreign assistance or foreign military sales program of the United States and that the firearms are owned by such foreign government.. (See § 478.118 of this chapter providing for the importation of certain curio or relic handguns, rifles and shotguns.)

(c) For the purpose of this section, the term "military defense article" includes all defense articles furnished to foreign governments under a foreign assistance or foreign military sales program of the United States as set forth in paragraph (a) of this section.

(Approved by the Office of Management and Budget under OMB Control No. 1140–0005)

[T.D. ATF–287, 54 FR 13681, Apr. 5, 1989, as amended by T.D. ATF–393, 62 FR 61235, Nov. 17, 1997; T.D. ATF–426, 65 FR 38198, June 20, 2000; ATF–11F, 73 FR 57240, Oct. 2, 2008]

§ 447.58 Delegations of the Director.

The regulatory authorities of the Director contained in this part are delegated to appropriate ATF officers. These ATF officers are specified in ATF O 1130.34, Delegation of the Director's Authorities in 27 CFR Part 447. ATF delegation orders, such as ATF O 1130.34, are available to any interested party by submitting a request to the ATF Distribution Center (*http:// www.atf.gov*) or by calling (202) 648–6420

[T.D. ATF–484, 67 FR 64526, Oct. 21, 2002, as amended by ATF–11F, 73 FR 57240, Oct. 2, 2008; ATF 2013R–9F, 79 FR 46692, Aug. 11, 2014]

Subpart G—Penalties, Seizures and Forfeitures

§ 447.61 Unlawful importation.

Any person who willfully:

(a) Imports articles on the U.S. Munitions Import List without a permit;

(b) Engages in the business of importing articles on the U.S. Munitions Import List without registering under this part; or

(c) Otherwise violates any provisions of this part;

Shall upon conviction be fined not more than $1,000,000 or imprisoned not more than 10 years, or both.

[T.D. ATF–8, 39 FR 3251, Jan. 25, 1974, as amended at 39 FR 4760, Feb. 7, 1974; T.D. ATF–215, 50 FR 42162, Oct. 18, 1985; T.D. ATF–287, 54 FR 13681, Apr. 5, 1989]

§ 447.62 False statements or concealment of facts.

Any person who willfully, in a registration or permit application, makes any untrue statement of a material fact or fails to state a material fact required to be stated therein or necessary to make the statements therein not misleading, shall upon conviction be fined not more than $1,000,000, or imprisoned not more than 10 years, or both.

[T.D. ATF–8, 39 FR 3251, Jan. 25, 1974, as amended by T.D. ATF–215, 50 FR 42162, Oct. 18, 1985; T.D. ATF–287, 54 FR 13681, Apr. 5, 1989]

§ 447.63 Seizure and forfeiture.

Whoever knowingly imports into the United States contrary to law any article on the U.S. Munitions Import List; or receives, conceals, buys, sells, or in any manner facilitates its transportation, concealment, or sale after importation, knowing the same to have been imported contrary to law, shall be fined not more than $10,000 or imprisoned not more than 5 years, or both; and the merchandise so imported, or the value thereof shall be forfeited to the United States.

(18 U.S.C. 545)

[T.D. ATF–8, 39 FR 3251, Jan. 25, 1974, as amended by T.D. ATF–215, 50 FR 42162, Oct. 18, 1985]

PART 478—COMMERCE IN FIREARMS AND AMMUNITION

Subpart A—Introduction

Sec.
478.1 Scope of regulations.
478.2 Relation to other provisions of law.

Subpart B—Definitions

478.11 Meaning of terms.
478.12 Definition of Frame or Receiver.

Subpart C—Administrative and Miscellaneous Provisions

478.21 Forms prescribed.
478.22 Alternate methods or procedures; emergency variations from requirements.
478.23 Right of entry and examination.
478.24 Compilation of State laws and published ordinances.
478.25 Disclosure of information.
478.25a Responses to requests for information.
478.26 Curio and relic determination.
478.27 Destructive device determination.
478.28 Transportation of destructive devices and certain firearms.
478.29 Out-of-State acquisition of firearms by nonlicensees.
478.29a Acquisition of firearms by nonresidents.
478.30 Out-of-State disposition of firearms by nonlicensees.
478.31 Delivery by common or contract carrier.
478.32 Prohibited shipment, transportation, possession, or receipt of firearms and ammunition by certain persons.
478.33 Stolen firearms and ammunition.
478.33a Theft of firearms.
478.34 Removed, obliterated, or altered serial number.
478.35 Skeet, trap, target, and similar shooting activities.
478.36 Transfer or possession of machine guns.
478.37 Manufacture, importation and sale of armor piercing ammunition.
478.38 Transportation of firearms.
478.39 Assembly of semiautomatic rifles or shotguns.
478.39a Reporting theft or loss of firearms.
478.40 [Reserved]

Subpart D—Licenses

478.41 General.
478.42 License fees.
478.43 License fee not refundable.
478.44 Original license.
478.45 Renewal of license.
478.46 Insufficient fee.
478.47 Issuance of license.
478.48 Correction of error on license.
478.49 Duration of license.
478.50 Locations covered by license.
478.51 License not transferable.
478.52 Change of address.
478.53 Change in trade name.
478.54 Change of control.
478.55 Continuing partnerships.
478.56 Right of succession by certain persons.

478.57 Discontinuance of business.
478.58 State or other law.
478.59 Abandoned application.
478.60 Certain continuances of business.

Subpart E—License Proceedings

478.71 Denial of an application for license.
478.72 Hearing after application denial.
478.73 Notice of revocation, suspension, or imposition of civil fine.
478.74 Request for hearing after notice of suspension, revocation, or imposition of civil fine.
478.75 Service on applicant or licensee.
478.76 Representation at a hearing.
478.77 Designated place of hearing.
478.78 Operations by licensee after notice.

Subpart F—Conduct of Business

478.91 Posting of license.
478.92 Identification of firearms and armor piercing ammunition by licensed manufacturers and licensed importers.
478.93 Authorized operations by a licensed collector.
478.94 Sales or deliveries between licensees.
478.95 Certified copy of license.
478.96 Out-of-State and mail order sales.
478.97 Loan or rental of firearms.
478.98 Sales or deliveries of destructive devices and certain firearms.
478.99 Certain prohibited sales or deliveries.
478.100 Conduct of business away from licensed premises.
478.101 Record of transactions.
478.102 Sales or deliveries of firearms on and after November 30, 1998.
478.103 Posting of signs and written notification to purchasers of handguns.
478.104 Secure gun storage or safety device.

Subpart G—Importation

478.111 General.
478.112 Importation by a licensed importer.
478.113 Importation by other licensees.
478.113a Importation of firearm barrels by nonlicensees.
478.114 Importation by members of the U.S. Armed Forces.
478.115 Exempt importation.
478.116 Conditional importation.
478.117 Function outside a customs territory.
478.118 Importation of certain firearms classified as curios and relics.
478.119 [Reserved]
478.120 Firearms or ammunition imported by or for a nonimmigrant alien.

Subpart H—Records

478.121 General.
478.122 Records maintained by importers.
478.123 Records maintained by manufacturers.

478.124 Firearms transaction record.
478.125 Record of receipt and disposition.
478.125a Personal firearms collection.
478.126 Furnishing transaction information.
478.126a Reporting multiple sales or other disposition of pistols and revolvers.
478.127 Discontinuance of business.
478.128 False statement or representation.
478.129 Record retention.
478.131 Firearms transactions not subject to a NICS check.
478.132 [Reserved]
478.133 Records of transactions in semiautomatic assault weapons.
478.134 Sale of firearms to law enforcement officers.

Subpart I—Exemptions, Seizures, and Forfeitures

478.141 General.
478.142 Effect of pardons and expunctions of convictions.
478.143 Relief from disabilities incurred by indictment.
478.144 Relief from disabilities under the Act.
478.145 Research organizations.
478.146 Deliveries by mail to certain persons.
478.147 Return of firearm.
478.148 Armor piercing ammunition intended for sporting or industrial purposes.
478.149 Armor piercing ammunition manufactured or imported for the purpose of testing or experimentation.
478.150 Alternative to NICS in certain geographical locations.
478.151 Semiautomatic rifles or shotguns for testing or experimentation.
478.152 Seizure and forfeiture.
478.153 [Reserved]

Subpart J [Reserved]

Subpart K—Exportation

478.171 Exportation.

AUTHORITY: 5 U.S.C. 552(a); 18 U.S.C. 847, 921–931; 44 U.S.C. 3504(h).

SOURCE: 33 FR 18555, Dec. 14, 1968, unless otherwise noted. Redesignated at 40 FR 16835, Apr. 15, 1975, and further redesignated by T.D. ATF–487, 68 FR 3750, Jan. 24, 2003.

EDITORIAL NOTE: Nomenclature changes to part 478 appear by T.D. ATF–411, 64 FR 17291, Apr. 9, 1999, T.D. ATF–487, 68 FR 3750, Jan. 24, 2003, and ATF–11F, 73 FR 57240, Oct. 2, 2008.

Subpart A—Introduction

§ 478.1   Scope of regulations.

(a) *General.* The regulations contained in this part relate to commerce in firearms and ammunition and are promulgated to implement Title I, State Firearms Control Assistance (18 U.S.C. Chapter 44), of the Gun Control Act of 1968 (82 Stat. 1213) as amended by Pub. L. 99–308 (100 Stat. 449), Pub. L. 99–360 (100 Stat. 766), Pub. L. 99–408 (100 Stat. 920), Pub. L. 103–159 (107 Stat. 1536), Pub. L. 103–322 (108 Stat. 1796), Pub. L. 104–208 (110 Stat. 3009), and Pub. L. 105–277 (112 Stat. 2681).

(b) *Procedural and substantive requirements.* This part contains the procedural and substantive requirements relative to:

(1) The interstate or foreign commerce in firearms and ammunition;

(2) The licensing of manufacturers and importers of firearms and ammunition, collectors of firearms, and dealers in firearms;

(3) The conduct of business or activity by licensees;

(4) The importation of firearms and ammunition;

(5) The records and reports required of licensees;

(6) Relief from disabilities under this part;

(7) Exempt interstate and foreign commerce in firearms and ammunition; and

(8) Restrictions on armor piercing ammunition.

[T.D. ATF–270, 53 FR 10490, Mar. 31, 1988, as amended by T.D. ATF–354, 59 FR 7112, Feb. 14, 1994; T.D. ATF–363, 60 FR 17450, Apr. 6, 1995; T.D. ATF–401, 63 FR 35522, June 30, 1998; T.D. ATF–471, 67 FR 5425, Feb. 5, 2002]

§ 478.2   Relation to other provisions of law.

The provisions in this part are in addition to, and are not in lieu of, any other provision of law, or regulations, respecting commerce in firearms or ammunition. For regulations applicable to traffic in machine guns, destructive devices, and certain other firearms, see Part 479 of this chapter. For statutes applicable to the registration and licensing of persons engaged in the business of manufacturing, importing or exporting arms, ammunition, or implements of war, see section 38 of the Arms Export Control Act (22 U.S.C. 2778) and regulations thereunder and Part 447 of this chapter. For statutes applicable to nonmailable firearms, see

18 U.S.C. 1715 and regulations thereunder.

[T.D. ATF–270, 53 FR 10490, Mar. 31, 1988]

Subpart B—Definitions

§478.11 Meaning of terms.

When used in this part and in forms prescribed under this part, where not otherwise distinctly expressed or manifestly incompatible with the intent thereof, terms shall have the meanings ascribed in this subpart. Words in the plural form shall include the singular, and vice versa, and words importing the masculine gender shall include the feminine. The terms "includes" and "including" do not exclude other things not enumerated which are in the same general class or are otherwise within the scope thereof.

Act. 18 U.S.C. Chapter 44.

Adjudicated as a mental defective. (a) A determination by a court, board, commission, or other lawful authority that a person, as a result of marked subnormal intelligence, or mental illness, incompetency, condition, or disease:

(1) Is a danger to himself or to others; or

(2) Lacks the mental capacity to contract or manage his own affairs.

(b) The term shall include—

(1) A finding of insanity by a court in a criminal case; and

(2) Those persons found incompetent to stand trial or found not guilty by reason of lack of mental responsibility pursuant to articles 50a and 72b of the Uniform Code of Military Justice, 10 U.S.C. 850a, 876b.

Admitted to the United States for lawful hunting or sporting purposes. (a) Is entering the United States to participate in a competitive target shooting event sponsored by a national, State, or local organization, devoted to the competitive use or other sporting use of firearms; or

(b) Is entering the United States to display firearms at a sports or hunting trade show sponsored by a national, State, or local firearms trade organization, devoted to the competitive use or other sporting use of firearms.

Alien. Any person not a citizen or national of the United States.

Alien illegally or unlawfully in the United States. Aliens who are unlawfully in the United States are not in valid immigrant, nonimmigrant or parole status. The term includes any alien—

(a) Who unlawfully entered the United States without inspection and authorization by an immigration officer and who has not been paroled into the United States under section 212(d)(5) of the Immigration and Nationality Act (INA);

(b) Who is a nonimmigrant and whose authorized period of stay has expired or who has violated the terms of the nonimmigrant category in which he or she was admitted;

(c) Paroled under INA section 212(d)(5) whose authorized period of parole has expired or whose parole status has been terminated; or

(d) Under an order of deportation, exclusion, or removal, or under an order to depart the United States voluntarily, whether or not he or she has left the United States.

Ammunition. Ammunition or cartridge cases, primers, bullets, or propellent powder designed for use in any firearm other than an antique firearm. The term shall not include (a) any shotgun shot or pellet not designed for use as the single, complete projectile load for one shotgun hull or casing, nor (b) any unloaded, non-metallic shotgun hull or casing not having a primer.

Antique firearm. (1) Any firearm (including any firearm with a matchlock, flintlock, percussion cap, or similar type of ignition system) manufactured in or before 1898;

(2) Any replica of any firearm described in paragraph (a) of this definition if such replica:

(i) Is not designed or redesigned for using rimfire or conventional centerfire fixed ammunition; or

(ii) Uses rimfire or conventional centerfire fixed ammunition that is no longer manufactured in the United States and that is not readily available in the ordinary channels of commercial trade; or

(3) Any muzzle loading rifle, muzzle loading shotgun, or muzzle loading pistol that is designed to use black powder, or a black powder substitute, and that cannot use fixed ammunition. For purposes of this paragraph (3), the term "antique firearm" does not include any

21

weapon that incorporates a firearm frame or receiver, any firearm that is converted into a muzzle loading weapon, or any muzzle loading weapon that can be readily converted to fire fixed ammunition by replacing the barrel, bolt, breechblock, or any combination thereof.

Armor piercing ammunition. Projectiles or projectile cores which may be used in a handgun and which are constructed entirely (excluding the presence of traces of other substances) from one or a combination of tungsten alloys, steel, iron, brass, bronze, beryllium copper, or depleted uranium; or full jacketed projectiles larger than .22 caliber designed and intended for use in a handgun and whose jacket has a weight of more than 25 percent of the total weight of the projectile. The term does not include shotgun shot required by Federal or State environmental or game regulations for hunting purposes, frangible projectiles designed for target shooting, projectiles which the Director finds are primarily intended to be used for sporting purposes, or any other projectiles or projectile cores which the Director finds are intended to be used for industrial purposes, including charges used in oil and gas well perforating devices.

ATF officer. An officer or employee of the Bureau of Alcohol, Tobacco, Firearms, and Explosives (ATF) authorized to perform any function relating to the administration or enforcement of this part.

Business premises. The property on which the manufacturing or importing of firearms or ammunition or the dealing in firearms is or will be conducted. A private dwelling, no part of which is open to the public, shall not be recognized as coming within the meaning of the term.

Chief, Federal Firearms Licensing Center (FFLC). The ATF official responsible for the issuance and renewal of licenses under this part.

Collector. Any person who acquires, holds, or disposes of firearms as curios or relics.

Collection premises. The premises described on the license of a collector as the location at which he maintains his collection of curios and relics.

Commerce. Travel, trade, traffic, commerce, transportation, or communication among the several States, or between the District of Columbia and any State, or between any foreign country or any territory or possession and any State or the District of Columbia, or between points in the same State but through any other State or the District of Columbia or a foreign country.

Committed to a mental institution. A formal commitment of a person to a mental institution by a court, board, commission, or other lawful authority. The term includes a commitment to a mental institution involuntarily. The term includes commitment for mental defectiveness or mental illness. It also includes commitments for other reasons, such as for drug use. The term does not include a person in a mental institution for observation or a voluntary admission to a mental institution.

Complete muffler or silencer device. A firearm muffler or firearm silencer that contains all component parts necessary to function, whether or not assembled or operable.

Complete weapon. A firearm other than a firearm muffler or firearm silencer that contains all component parts necessary to function, whether or not assembled or operable.

Controlled substance. A drug or other substance, or immediate precursor, as defined in section 102 of the Controlled Substances Act, 21 U.S.C. 802. The term includes, but is not limited to, marijuana, depressants, stimulants, and narcotic drugs. The term does not include distilled spirits, wine, malt beverages, or tobacco, as those terms are defined or used in Subtitle E of the Internal Revenue Code of 1986, as amended.

Crime punishable by imprisonment for a term exceeding 1 year. Any Federal, State or foreign offense for which the maximum penalty, whether or not imposed, is capital punishment or imprisonment in excess of 1 year. The term shall not include (a) any Federal or State offenses pertaining to antitrust violations, unfair trade practices, restraints of trade, or other similar offenses relating to the regulation of business practices or (b) any State offense classified by the laws of the State as a misdemeanor and punishable by a term of imprisonment of 2 years or less. What constitutes a conviction of such a crime shall be determined in accordance with the law of the jurisdiction in which the proceedings were held. Any conviction which has been expunged or set aside or for which a person has been pardoned or has had civil rights restored shall not be considered a conviction for the purposes of the Act or this part, unless such pardon, expunction, or restoration of civil rights expressly provides that the person may not ship, transport, possess, or receive firearms, or unless the person is prohibited by the law of the jurisdiction in which the proceedings were held from receiving or possessing any firearms.

Curios or relics. Firearms which are of special interest to collectors by reason of some quality other than is associated with firearms intended for sporting use or as offensive or defensive weapons. To be recognized as curios or relics, firearms must fall within one of the following categories:

(a) Firearms which were manufactured at least 50 years prior to the current date, but not including replicas thereof;

(b) Firearms which are certified by the curator of a municipal, State, or Federal museum which exhibits firearms to be curios or relics of museum interest; and

(c) Any other firearms which derive a substantial part of their monetary value from the fact that they are novel, rare, bizarre, or because of their association with some historical figure, period, or event. Proof of qualification of a particular firearm under this category may be established by evidence of present value and evidence that like firearms are not available except as collector's items, or that the value of like firearms available in ordinary commercial channels is substantially less.

Customs officer. Any officer of U.S. Customs and Border Protection, any commissioned, warrant, or petty officer of the Coast Guard, or any agent or other person authorized by law to perform the duties of a customs officer.

Dealer. Any person engaged in the business of selling firearms at whole-sale or retail; any person engaged in the business of repairing firearms or of making or fitting special barrels, stocks, or trigger mechanisms to firearms; or any person who is a pawnbroker. The term shall include any person who engages in such business or occupation on a part-time basis.

Destructive device. (a) Any explosive, incendiary, or poison gas (1) bomb, (2) grenade, (3) rocket having a propellant charge of more than 4 ounces, (4) missile having an explosive or incendiary charge of more than one-quarter ounce, (5) mine, or (6) device similar to any of the devices described in the preceding paragraphs of this definition; (b) any type of weapon (other than a shotgun or a shotgun shell which the Director finds is generally recognized as particularly suitable for sporting purposes) by whatever name known which will, or which may be readily converted to, expel a projectile by the action of an explosive or other propellant, and which has any barrel with a bore of more than one-half inch in diameter; and (c) any combination of parts either designed or intended for use in converting any device into any destructive device described in paragraph (a) or (b) of this section and from which a destructive device may be readily assembled. The term shall not include any device which is neither designed nor redesigned for use as a weapon; any device, although originally designed for use as a weapon, which is redesigned for use as a signalling, pyrotechnic, line throwing, safety, or similar device; surplus ordnance sold, loaned, or given by the Secretary of the Army pursuant to the provisions of section 4684(2), 4685, or 4686 of title 10, United States Code; or any other device which the Director finds is not likely to be used as a weapon, is an antique, or is a rifle which the owner intends to use solely for sporting, recreational, or cultural purposes.

Director. The Director, Bureau of Alcohol, Tobacco, Firearms, and Explosives, the Department of Justice, Washington, DC.

Director of Industry Operations. The principal ATF official in a Field Operations division responsible for administering regulations in this part.

Discharged under dishonorable conditions. Separation from the U.S. Armed Forces resulting from a dishonorable discharge or dismissal adjudged by a general court-martial. The term does not include any separation from the Armed Forces resulting from any other discharge, e.g., a bad conduct discharge.

Division. A Bureau of Alcohol, Tobacco, Firearms, and Explosives Division.

Engaged in the business—(a) *Manufacturer of firearms.* A person who devotes time, attention, and labor to manufacturing firearms as a regular course of trade or business with the principal objective of livelihood and profit through the sale or distribution of the firearms manufactured;

(b) *Manufacturer of ammunition.* A person who devotes time, attention, and labor to manufacturing ammunition as a regular course of trade or business with the principal objective of livelihood and profit through the sale or distribution of the ammunition manufactured;

(c) *Dealer in firearms other than a gunsmith or a pawnbroker.* A person who devotes time, attention, and labor to dealing in firearms as a regular course of trade or business with the principal objective of livelihood and profit through the repetitive purchase and resale of firearms, but such a term shall not include a person who makes occasional sales, exchanges, or purchases of firearms for the enhancement of a personal collection or for a hobby, or who sells all or part of his personal collection of firearms;

(d) *Gunsmith.* A person who, as a service performed on existing firearms not for sale or distribution, devotes time, attention, and labor to repairing or customizing firearms, making or fitting special barrels, stocks, or trigger mechanisms to firearms, or placing marks of identification on privately made firearms in accordance with this part, as a regular course of trade or business with the principal objective of livelihood and profit, but such term shall not include a person who occasionally repairs or customizes firearms (including identification), or occasionally makes or fits special barrels, stocks, or trigger mechanisms to fire-

arms. In the case of firearms for purposes of sale or distribution, such term shall include a person who performs repairs (*e.g.*, by replacing worn or broken parts) on complete weapons, or places marks of identification on privately made firearms, but shall not include a person who manufactures firearms (*i.e.*, frames or receivers or complete weapons) by completion, assembly, or applying coatings, or otherwise making them suitable for use, requiring a license as a manufacturer;

(e) *Importer of firearms.* A person who devotes time, attention, and labor to importing firearms as a regular course of trade or business with the principal objective of livelihood and profit through the sale or distribution of the firearms imported; and,

(f) *Importer of ammunition.* A person who devotes time, attention, and labor to importing ammunition as a regular course of trade or business with the principal objective of livelihood and profit through the sale or distribution of the ammunition imported.

Executed under penalties of perjury. Signed with the prescribed declaration under the penalties of perjury as provided on or with respect to the return form, or other document or, where no form of declaration is prescribed, with the declaration:

"I declare under the penalties of perjury that this—(insert type of document, such as, statement, application, request, certificate), including the documents submitted in support thereof, has been examined by me and, to the best of my knowledge and belief, is true, correct, and complete."

Federal Firearms Act. 15 U.S.C. Chapter 18.

Firearm. Any weapon, including a starter gun, which will or is designed to or may readily be converted to expel a projectile by the action of an explosive; the frame or receiver of any such weapon; any firearm muffler or firearm silencer; or any destructive device; but the term shall not include an antique firearm. In the case of a licensed collector, the term shall mean only curios and relics. The term shall include a weapon parts kit that is designed to or may readily be completed, assembled, restored, or otherwise converted to expel a projectile by the action of an explosive. The term shall not include a weapon, including a weapon parts kit, in which the frame or receiver of such weapon is destroyed as described in the definition "frame or receiver".

Firearm muffler or firearm silencer. Any device for silencing, muffling, or diminishing the report of a portable firearm, including any combination of parts, designed or redesigned, and intended for use in assembling or fabricating a firearm silencer or firearm muffler, and any part intended only for use in such assembly or fabrication.

Frame or receiver. The term "frame or receiver" shall have the same meaning as in §478.12.

Friendly foreign government. Any government with whom the United States has diplomatic relations and whom the United States has not identified as a State sponsor of terrorism.

Fugitive from justice. Any person who has fled from any State to avoid prosecution for a felony or a misdemeanor; or any person who leaves the State to avoid giving testimony in any criminal proceeding. The term also includes any person who knows that misdemeanor or felony charges are pending against such person and who leaves the State of prosecution.

Handgun. (a) Any firearm which has a short stock and is designed to be held and fired by the use of a single hand; and

(b) Any combination of parts from which a firearm described in paragraph (a) can be assembled.

Hunting license or permit lawfully issued in the United States. A license or permit issued by a State for hunting which is valid and unexpired.

Identification document. A document containing the name, residence address, date of birth, and photograph of the holder and which was made or issued by or under the authority of the United States Government, a State, political subdivision of a State, a foreign government, political subdivision of a foreign government, an international governmental or an international quasi- governmental organization which, when completed with information concerning a particular individual, is of a type intended or commonly accepted for the purpose of identification of individuals.

Importation. The bringing of a firearm or ammunition into the United States; except that the bringing of a firearm or ammunition from outside the United States into a foreign-trade zone for storage pending shipment to a foreign country or subsequent importation into this country, pursuant to this part, shall not be deemed importation.

Importer. Any person engaged in the business of importing or bringing firearms or ammunition into the United States. The term shall include any person who engages in such business on a part-time basis.

Importer's or manufacturer's serial number. The serial number placed by a licensee on a firearm, including any full or abbreviated license number, any such identification on a privately made firearm, or a serial number issued by the Director. For purposes of 18 U.S.C. 922(k) and §478.34, the term shall include any associated licensee name, or licensee city or State placed on a frame or receiver.

Indictment. Includes an indictment or information in any court, under which a crime punishable by imprisonment for a term exceeding 1 year (as defined in this section) may be prosecuted, or in military cases to any offense punishable by imprisonment for a term exceeding 1 year which has been referred to a general court-martial. An information is a formal accusation of a crime, differing from an indictment in that it is made by a prosecuting attorney and not a grand jury.

Interstate or foreign commerce. Includes commerce between any place in a State and any place outside of that State, or within any possession of the United States (not including the Canal Zone) or the District of Columbia. The term shall not include commerce between places within the same State but through any place outside of that State.

Intimate partner. With respect to a person, the spouse of the person, a former spouse of the person, an individual who is a parent of a child of the person, and an individual who cohabitates or has cohabitated with the person.

Large capacity ammunition feeding device. A magazine, belt, drum, feed strip,

25

or similar device for a firearm manufactured after September 13, 1994, that has a capacity of, or that can be readily restored or converted to accept, more than 10 rounds of ammunition. The term does not include an attached tubular device designed to accept, and capable of operating only with, .22 caliber rimfire ammunition, or a fixed device for a manually operated firearm, or a fixed device for a firearm listed in 18 U.S.C. 922, appendix A.

Licensed collector. A collector of curios and relics only and licensed under the provisions of this part.

Licensed dealer. A dealer licensed under the provisions of this part.

Licensed importer. An importer licensed under the provisions of this part.

Licensed manufacturer. A manufacturer licensed under the provisions of this part.

Machine gun. Any weapon which shoots, is designed to shoot, or can be readily restored to shoot, automatically more than one shot, without manual reloading, by a single function of the trigger. The term shall also include the frame or receiver of any such weapon, any part designed and intended solely and exclusively, or combination of parts designed and intended, for use in converting a weapon into a machine gun, and any combination of parts from which a machine gun can be assembled if such parts are in the possession or under the control of a person. For purposes of this definition, the term "automatically" as it modifies "shoots, is designed to shoot, or can be readily restored to shoot," means functioning as the result of a self-acting or self-regulating mechanism that allows the firing of multiple rounds through a single function of the trigger; and "single function of the trigger" means a single pull of the trigger and analogous motions. The term "machine gun" includes a bump-stock-type device, *i.e.*, a device that allows a semi-automatic firearm to shoot more than one shot with a single pull of the trigger by harnessing the recoil energy of the semi-automatic firearm to which it is affixed so that the trigger resets and continues firing without additional physical manipulation of the trigger by the shooter.

Manufacturer. Any person engaged in the business of manufacturing firearms or ammunition. The term shall include any person who engages in such business on a part-time basis.

Mental institution. Includes mental health facilities, mental hospitals, sanitariums, psychiatric facilities, and other facilities that provide diagnoses by licensed professionals of mental retardation or mental illness, including a psychiatric ward in a general hospital.

Misdemeanor crime of domestic violence. (a) Is a Federal, State or local offense that:

(1) Is a misdemeanor under Federal or State law or, in States which do not classify offenses as misdemeanors, is an offense punishable by imprisonment for a term of one year or less, and includes offenses that are punishable only by a fine. (This is true whether or not the State statute specifically defines the offense as a "misdemeanor" or as a "misdemeanor crime of domestic violence." The term includes all such misdemeanor convictions in Indian Courts established pursuant to 25 CFR part 11.);

(2) Has, as an element, the use or attempted use of physical force (e.g., assault and battery), or the threatened use of a deadly weapon; and

(3) Was committed by a current or former spouse, parent, or guardian of the victim, by a person with whom the victim shares a child in common, by a person who is cohabiting with or has cohabited with the victim as a spouse, parent, or guardian, (e.g., the equivalent of a "common law" marriage even if such relationship is not recognized under the law), or a person similarly situated to a spouse, parent, or guardian of the victim (e.g., two persons who are residing at the same location in an intimate relationship with the intent to make that place their home would be similarly situated to a spouse).

(b) A person shall not be considered to have been convicted of such an offense for purposes of this part unless:

(1) The person is considered to have been convicted by the jurisdiction in which the proceedings were held.

(2) The person was represented by counsel in the case, or knowingly and intelligently waived the right to counsel in the case; and

(3) In the case of a prosecution for which a person was entitled to a jury trial in the jurisdiction in which the case was tried, either

(i) The case was tried by a jury, or

(ii) The person knowingly and intelligently waived the right to have the case tried by a jury, by guilty plea or otherwise.

(c) A person shall not be considered to have been convicted of such an offense for purposes of this part if the conviction has been expunged or set aside, or is an offense for which the person has been pardoned or has had civil rights restored (if the law of the jurisdiction in which the proceedings were held provides for the loss of civil rights upon conviction for such an offense) unless the pardon, expunction, or restoration of civil rights expressly provides that the person may not ship, transport, possess, or receive firearms, and the person is not otherwise prohibited by the law of the jurisdiction in which the proceedings were held from receiving or possessing any firearms.

National Firearms Act. 26 U.S.C. Chapter 53.

NICS. The National Instant Criminal Background Check System established by the Attorney General pursuant to 18 U.S.C. 922(t).

Nonimmigrant alien. An alien in the United States in a nonimmigrant classification as defined by section 101(a)(15) of the Immigration and Nationality Act (8 U.S.C. 1101(a)(15)).

Nonimmigrant visa. A visa properly issued to an alien as an eligible nonimmigrant by a competent officer as provided in the Immigration and Nationality Act, 8 U.S.C. 1101 *et seq.*

Pawnbroker. Any person whose business or occupation includes the taking or receiving, by way of pledge or pawn, of any firearm as security for the payment or repayment of money. The term shall include any person who engages in such business on a part-time basis.

Permanently inoperable. A firearm which is incapable of discharging a shot by means of an explosive and incapable of being readily restored to a firing condition. An acceptable method of rendering most firearms permanently inoperable is to fusion weld the chamber closed and fusion weld the barrel solidly to the frame. Certain unusual firearms require other methods to render the firearm permanently inoperable. Contact ATF for instructions.

Person. Any individual, corporation, company, association, firm, partnership, society, or joint stock company.

Pistol. A weapon originally designed, made, and intended to fire a projectile (bullet) from one or more barrels when held in one hand, and having (a) a chamber(s) as an integral part(s) of, or permanently aligned with, the bore(s); and (b) a short stock designed to be gripped by one hand and at an angle to and extending below the line of the bore(s).

Principal objective of livelihood and profit. The intent underlying the sale or disposition of firearms is predominantly one of obtaining livelihood and pecuniary gain, as opposed to other intents such as improving or liquidating a personal firearms collection: *Provided,* That proof of profit shall not be required as to a person who engages in the regular and repetitive purchase and disposition of firearms for criminal purposes or terrorism. For purposes of this part, the term "terrorism" means activity, directed against United States persons, which—

(a) Is committed by an individual who is not a national or permanent resident alien of the United States;

(b) Involves violent acts or acts dangerous to human life which would be a criminal violation if committed within the jurisdiction of the United States; and

(c) Is intended—

(1) To intimidate or coerce a civilian population;

(2) To influence the policy of a government by intimidation or coercion; or

(3) To affect the conduct of a government by assassination or kidnapping.

Privately made firearm (PMF). A firearm, including a frame or receiver, completed, assembled, or otherwise produced by a person other than a licensed manufacturer, and without a serial number placed by a licensed manufacturer at the time the firearm was produced. The term shall not include a firearm identified and registered in the National Firearms Registration and Transfer Record pursuant to chapter

53, title 26, United States Code, or any firearm manufactured or made before October 22, 1968 (unless remanufactured or remade after that date).

Published ordinance. A published law of any political subdivision of a State which the Director determines to be relevant to the enforcement of this part and which is contained on a list compiled by the Director, which list is incorporated by reference in the FEDERAL REGISTER, revised annually, and furnished to licensees under this part.

Readily. A process, action, or physical state that is fairly or reasonably efficient, quick, and easy, but not necessarily the most efficient, speediest, or easiest process, action, or physical state. With respect to the classification of firearms, factors relevant in making this determination include the following:

(1) Time, *i.e.*, how long it takes to finish the process;

(2) Ease, *i.e.*, how difficult it is to do so;

(3) Expertise, *i.e.*, what knowledge and skills are required;

(4) Equipment, *i.e.*, what tools are required;

(5) Parts availability, *i.e.*, whether additional parts are required, and how easily they can be obtained;

(6) Expense, *i.e.*, how much it costs;

(7) Scope, *i.e.*, the extent to which the subject of the process must be changed to finish it; and

(8) Feasibility, *i.e.*, whether the process would damage or destroy the subject of the process, or cause it to malfunction.

Renounced U.S. citizenship. (a) A person has renounced his U.S. citizenship if the person, having been a citizen of the United States, has renounced citizenship either—

(1) Before a diplomatic or consular officer of the United States in a foreign state pursuant to 8 U.S.C. 1481(a)(5); or

(2) Before an officer designated by the Attorney General when the United States is in a state of war pursuant to 8 U.S.C. 1481(a)(6).

(b) The term shall not include any renunciation of citizenship that has been reversed as a result of administrative or judicial appeal.

Revolver. A projectile weapon, of the pistol type, having a breechloading chambered cylinder so arranged that the cocking of the hammer or movement of the trigger rotates it and brings the next cartridge in line with the barrel for firing.

Rifle. A weapon designed or redesigned, made or remade, and intended to be fired from the shoulder, and designed or redesigned and made or remade to use the energy of an explosive to fire only a single projectile through a rifled bore for each single pull of the trigger.

(1) For purposes of this definition, the term "designed or redesigned, made or remade, and intended to be fired from the shoulder" shall include a weapon that is equipped with an accessory, component, or other rearward attachment (*e.g.*, a "stabilizing brace") that provides surface area that allows the weapon to be fired from the shoulder, provided other factors, as described in paragraph (2), indicate that the weapon is designed, made, and intended to be fired from the shoulder.

(2) When a weapon provides surface area that allows the weapon to be fired from the shoulder, the following factors shall also be considered in determining whether the weapon is designed, made, and intended to be fired from the shoulder:

(i) Whether the weapon has a weight or length consistent with the weight or length of similarly designed rifles;

(ii) Whether the weapon has a length of pull, measured from the center of the trigger to the center of the shoulder stock or other rearward accessory, component or attachment (including an adjustable or telescoping attachment with the ability to lock into various positions along a buffer tube, receiver extension, or other attachment method), that is consistent with similarly designed rifles;

(iii) Whether the weapon is equipped with sights or a scope with eye relief that require the weapon to be fired from the shoulder in order to be used as designed;

(iv) Whether the surface area that allows the weapon to be fired from the shoulder is created by a buffer tube, receiver extension, or any other accessory, component, or other rearward attachment that is necessary for the cycle of operations;

(v) The manufacturer's direct and indirect marketing and promotional materials indicating the intended use of the weapon; and

(vi) Information demonstrating the likely use of the weapon in the general community.

Secure gun storage or safety device. (1) A device that, when installed on a firearm, is designed to prevent the firearm from being operated without first deactivating the device;

(2) A device incorporated into the design of the firearm that is designed to prevent the operation of the firearm by anyone not having access to the device; or

(3) A safe, gun safe, gun case, lock box, or other device that is designed to be or can be used to store a firearm and that is designed to be unlocked only by means of a key, a combination, or other similar means.

Semiautomatic assault weapon. (a) Any of the firearms, or copies or duplicates of the firearms in any caliber, known as:

(1) Norinco, Mitchell, and Poly Technologies Avtomat Kalashnikovs (all models),

(2) Action Arms Israeli Military Industries UZI and Galil,

(3) Beretta Ar70 (SC–70),

(4) Colt AR–15,

(5) Fabrique National FN/FAL, FN/LAR, and FNC,

(6) SWD M–10, M–11, M–11/9, and M–12,

(7) Steyr AUG,

(8) INTRATEC TEC–9, TEC–DC9 and TEC–22, and

(9) Revolving cylinder shotguns, such as (or similar to) the Street Sweeper and Striker 12;

(b) A semiautomatic rifle that has an ability to accept a detachable magazine and has at least 2 of—

(1) A folding or telescoping stock,

(2) A pistol grip that protrudes conspicuously beneath the action of the weapon,

(3) A bayonet mount,

(4) A flash suppressor or threaded barrel designed to accommodate a flash suppressor, and

(5) A grenade launcher;

(c) A semiautomatic pistol that has an ability to accept a detachable magazine and has at least 2 of—

(1) An ammunition magazine that attaches to the pistol outside of the pistol grip,

(2) A threaded barrel capable of accepting a barrel extender, flash suppressor, forward handgrip, or silencer,

(3) A shroud that is attached to, or partially or completely encircles, the barrel and that permits the shooter to hold the firearm with the nontrigger hand without being burned,

(4) A manufactured weight of 50 ounces or more when the pistol is unloaded, and

(5) A semiautomatic version of an automatic firearm; and

(d) A semiautomatic shotgun that has at least 2 of—

(1) A folding or telescoping stock,

(2) A pistol grip that protrudes conspicuously beneath the action of the weapon,

(3) A fixed magazine capacity in excess of 5 rounds, and

(4) An ability to accept a detachable magazine.

Semiautomatic pistol. Any repeating pistol which utilizes a portion of the energy of a firing cartridge to extract the fired cartridge case and chamber the next round, and which requires a separate pull of the trigger to fire each cartridge.

Semiautomatic rifle. Any repeating rifle which utilizes a portion of the energy of a firing cartridge to extract the fired cartridge case and chamber the next round, and which requires a separate pull of the trigger to fire each cartridge.

Semiautomatic shotgun. Any repeating shotgun which utilizes a portion of the energy of a firing cartridge to extract the fired cartridge case and chamber the next round, and which requires a separate pull of the trigger to fire each cartridge.

Short-barreled rifle. A rifle having one or more barrels less than 16 inches in length, and any weapon made from a rifle, whether by alteration, modification, or otherwise, if such weapon, as modified, has an overall length of less than 26 inches.

Short-barreled shotgun. A shotgun having one or more barrels less than 18 inches in length, and any weapon made from a shotgun, whether by alteration, modification, or otherwise, if such weapon as modified has an overall length of less than 26 inches.

Shotgun. A weapon designed or redesigned, made or remade, and intended to be fired from the shoulder, and designed or redesigned and made or remade to use the energy of an explosive to fire through a smooth bore either a number of ball shot or a single projectile for each single pull of the trigger.

State. A State of the United States. The term shall include the District of Columbia, the Commonwealth of Puerto Rico, and the possessions of the United States (not including the Canal Zone).

State of residence. The State in which an individual resides. An individual resides in a State if he or she is present in a State with the intention of making a home in that State. If an individual is on active duty as a member of the Armed Forces, the individual's State of residence is the State in which his or her permanent duty station is located, as stated in 18 U.S.C. 921(b). The following are examples that illustrate this definition:

Example 1. A maintains a home in State X. A travels to State Y on a hunting, fishing, business, or other type of trip. A does not become a resident of State Y by reason of such trip.

Example 2. A maintains a home in State X and a home in State Y. A resides in State X except for weekends or the summer months of the year and in State Y for the weekends or the summer months of the year. During the time that A actually resides in State X, A is a resident of State X, and during the time that A actually resides in State Y, A is a resident of State Y.

Example 3. A, an alien, travels to the United States on a three-week vacation to State X. A does not have a state of residence in State X because A does not have the intention of making a home in State X while on vacation. This is true regardless of the length of the vacation.

Example 4. A, an alien, travels to the United States to work for three years in State X. A rents a home in State X, moves his personal possessions into the home, and his family resides with him in the home. A intends to reside in State X during the 3-year period of his employment. A is a resident of State X.

Unlawful user of or addicted to any controlled substance. A person who uses a controlled substance and has lost the power of self-control with reference to the use of controlled substance; and

any person who is a current user of a controlled substance in a manner other than as prescribed by a licensed physician. Such use is not limited to the use of drugs on a particular day, or within a matter of days or weeks before, but rather that the unlawful use has occurred recently enough to indicate that the individual is actively engaged in such conduct. A person may be an unlawful current user of a controlled substance even though the substance is not being used at the precise time the person seeks to acquire a firearm or receives or possesses a firearm. An inference of current use may be drawn from evidence of a recent use or possession of a controlled substance or a pattern of use or possession that reasonably covers the present time, e.g., a conviction for use or possession of a controlled substance within the past year; multiple arrests for such offenses within the past 5 years if the most recent arrest occurred within the past year; or persons found through a drug test to use a controlled substance unlawfully, provided that the test was administered within the past year. For a current or former member of the Armed Forces, an inference of current use may be drawn from recent disciplinary or other administrative action based on confirmed drug use, e.g., court-martial conviction, nonjudicial punishment, or an administrative discharge based on drug use or drug rehabilitation failure.

Unserviceable firearm. A firearm which is incapable of discharging a shot by means of an explosive and is incapable of being readily restored to a firing condition.

U.S.C. The United States Code.

(5 U.S.C. 552(a), 80 Stat. 383, as amended; 18 U.S.C. 847 (84 Stat. 959); 18 U.S.C. 926 (82 Stat. 1226))

[T.D. ATF–48, 43 FR 13536, Mar. 31, 1978; 44 FR 55842, Sept. 28, 1979]

EDITORIAL NOTE: For FEDERAL REGISTER citations affecting §478.11, see the List of CFR Sections Affected, which appears in the Finding Aids section of the printed volume and at *www.govinfo.gov.*

§478.12 Definition of Frame or Receiver.

(a) Except as otherwise provided in this section, the term "frame or receiver" means the following—

(1) The term "frame" means the part of a handgun, or variants thereof, that provides housing or a structure for the component (*i.e.*, sear or equivalent) designed to hold back the hammer, striker, bolt, or similar primary energized component prior to initiation of the firing sequence, even if pins or other attachments are required to connect such component (*i.e.*, sear or equivalent) to the housing or structure.

(2) The term "receiver" means the part of a rifle, shotgun, or projectile weapon other than a handgun, or variants thereof, that provides housing or a structure for the primary component designed to block or seal the breech prior to initiation of the firing sequence (*i.e.*, bolt, breechblock, or equivalent), even if pins or other attachments are required to connect such component to the housing or structure.

(3) The terms "variant" and "variants thereof" mean a weapon utilizing a similar frame or receiver design irrespective of new or different model designations or configurations, characteristics, features, components, accessories, or attachments. For example, an AK-type firearm with a short stock (*i.e.*, pistol grip) is a pistol variant of an AK-type rifle, an AR-type firearm with a short stock (*i.e.*, pistol grip) is a pistol variant of an AR-type rifle, and a revolving cylinder shotgun is a shotgun variant of a revolver.

(4) The following are nonexclusive examples that illustrate the above definitions:

(i) *Hinged or single framed revolvers:* The frame is the part of the revolver that provides a structure designed to hold the sear.

Figure 1 to paragraph (a)(4)(i)

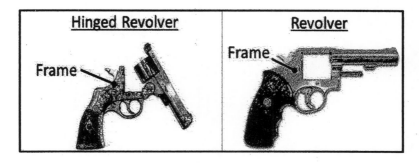

(ii) *Colt 1911, Beretta/Browning/FN Herstal/Heckler & Koch/Ruger/Sig Sauer/ Smith & Wesson/Taurus hammer-fired semiautomatic pistols:* The frame is the lower portion of the pistol, or grip, that provides housing for the sear.

Figure 2 to paragraph (a)(4)(ii)

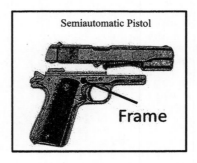

(iii) *Glock variant striker-fired semiautomatic pistols:* The frame is the lower portion of the pistol, or grip, that provides housing for the sear.

Figure 3 to paragraph (a)(4)(iii)

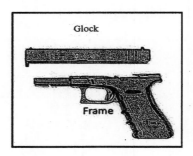

(iv) *Sig Sauer P250/P320 variant semiautomatic pistols:* The frame is the internal removable chassis of the pistol that provides housing for the sear or equivalent component.

Figure 4 to paragraph (a)(4)(iv)

(v) *Bolt action rifles:* The receiver is the part of the rifle that provides a structure for the bolt.

Figure 5 to paragraph (a)(4)(v)

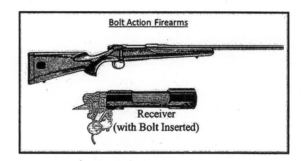

(vi) *Break action, lever action, or pump action rifles and shotguns:* The receiver is the part of the rifle or shotgun that provides housing for the bolt, breech-block, or equivalent.

Figure 6 to paragraph (a)(4)(vi)

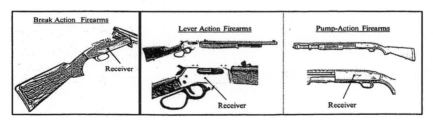

(vii) *AK variant firearms:* The receiver is the part of the weapon that provides housing for the bolt.

Figure 7 to paragraph (a)(4)(vii)

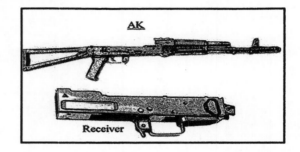

(viii) *Steyr AUG variant firearms:* The receiver is the central part of the weapon that provides housing for the bolt.

Figure 8 to paragraph (a)(4)(viii)

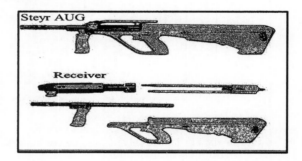

(ix) *Thompson machineguns and semiautomatic variants, and L1A1, FN FAL, FN FNC, MP38, MP40, and SIG 550 firearms, and HK machineguns and semiautomatic variants:* The receiver is the upper part of the weapon that provides housing for the bolt.

Figure 9 to paragraph (a)(4)(ix)

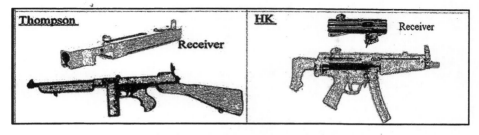

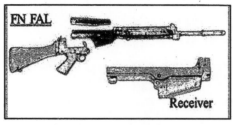

(x) *Sten, Sterling, and Kel-Tec SUB–2000 firearms:* The receiver is the central part of the weapon, or tube, that provides housing for the bolt.

Figure 10 to paragraph (a)(4)(x)

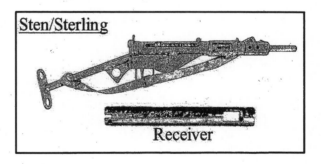

(b) *Firearm muffler or silencer frame or receiver.* The terms "frame" and "receiver" shall mean, in the case of a firearm muffler or firearm silencer, the part of the firearm, such as an outer tube or modular piece, that provides housing or a structure for the primary internal component designed to reduce the sound of a projectile (*i.e.*, baffles, baffling material, expansion chamber, or equivalent). In the case of a modular firearm muffler or firearm silencer device with more than one such part, the terms shall mean the principal housing attached to the weapon that expels a projectile, even if an adapter or other attachments are required to connect the part to the weapon. The terms shall not include a removable end cap of an outer tube or modular piece.

(c) *Partially complete, disassembled, or nonfunctional frame or receiver.* The terms "frame" and "receiver" shall include a partially complete, disassembled, or nonfunctional frame or receiver, including a frame or receiver parts kit, that is designed to or may readily be completed, assembled, restored, or otherwise converted to function as a frame or receiver, *i.e.,* to house or provide a structure for the primary energized component of a handgun, breech blocking or sealing component of a projectile weapon other than a handgun, or internal sound reduction component of a firearm muffler or firearm silencer, as the case may be. The terms shall not include a forging, casting, printing, extrusion, unmachined body, or similar article that has not yet reached a stage of manufacture where it is clearly identifiable as an unfinished component part of a weapon (*e.g.,* unformed block of metal, liquid polymer, or other raw material). When issuing a classification, the Director may consider any associated templates, jigs, molds, equipment, tools, instructions, guides, or marketing materials that are sold, distributed, or possessed with the item or kit, or otherwise made available by the seller or distributor of the item or kit to the purchaser or recipient of the item or kit. The following are non-exclusive examples that illustrate the definitions:

Example 1 to paragraph (c)—*Frame or receiver:* A frame or receiver parts kit containing a partially complete or disassembled billet or blank of a frame or receiver that is sold, distributed, or possessed with a compatible jig or template is a frame or receiver, as a person with online instructions and common hand tools may readily complete or assemble the frame or receiver parts kit to function as a frame or receiver.

Example 2 to paragraph (c)—*Frame or receiver:* A partially complete billet or blank of a frame or receiver with one or more template holes drilled or indexed in the correct location is a frame or receiver, as a person with common hand tools may readily complete the billet or blank to function as a frame or receiver.

Example 3 to paragraph (c)—*Frame or receiver:* A complete frame or receiver of a weapon that has been disassembled, damaged, split, or cut into pieces, but not destroyed in accordance with paragraph (e), is a frame or receiver.

Example 4 to paragraph (c)—*Not a receiver:* A billet or blank of an AR–15 variant receiver without critical interior areas having been indexed, machined, or formed that is not sold, distributed, or possessed with instructions, jigs, templates, equipment, or tools such that it may readily be completed is not a receiver.

Example 5 to paragraph (c)—*Not a receiver:* A flat blank of an AK variant receiver without laser cuts or indexing that is not sold, distributed, or possessed with instructions, jigs, templates, equipment, or tools is not a receiver, as a person cannot readily fold the flat to provide housing or a structure for the primary component designed to block or seal the breech prior to initiation of the firing sequence.

(d) *Multi-piece frame or receiver.* The term "multi-piece frame or receiver" shall mean a frame or receiver that may be disassembled into multiple modular subparts, *i.e.,* standardized units that may be replaced or exchanged. The term shall not include the internal frame of a pistol that is a complete removable chassis that provides housing for the sear or equivalent component, unless the chassis itself may be disassembled. The modular subpart(s) identified in accordance with § 478.92 with an importer's or manufacturer's serial number shall be presumed, absent an official determination by the Director or other reliable evidence to the contrary, to be part of the frame or receiver of a weapon or device.

(e) *Destroyed frame or receiver.* The terms "frame" and "receiver" shall not include a frame or receiver that is destroyed. For purposes of these definitions, the term "destroyed" means that the frame or receiver has been permanently altered such that it may not readily be completed, assembled, restored, or otherwise converted to function as a frame or receiver. Acceptable methods of destruction include completely melting, crushing, or shredding the frame or receiver, or other method approved by the Director.

(f)(1) *Frame or receiver classifications based on which part of the weapon was classified as such before* April 26, 2022. Except as provided in paragraph (f)(2) of this section, the terms "frame" and "receiver" shall include the specific part of a complete weapon, including variants thereof, determined (classified) by the Director to be defined as a firearm frame or receiver prior to April 26, 2022. Any such part that is identified with an importer's or manufacturer's serial number shall be presumed, absent an official determination by the Director or other reliable evidence to the contrary, to be the frame or receiver of the weapon. The following is a nonexclusive list of such weapons and the specific part determined by the Director to be the firearm frame or receiver as they existed on that date:

(i) *AR–15/M–16 variant firearms:* The receiver is the lower part of the weapon that provides housing for the trigger mechanism and hammer (*i.e.,* lower receiver).

Figure 11 to paragraph (f)(1)(i)

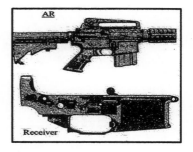

(ii) *Ruger Mark IV pistol:* The frame is the upper part of the weapon that provides housing for the bolt or breechblock.

Figure 12 to paragraph (f)(1)(ii)

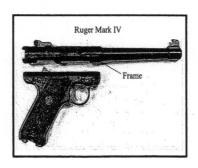

(iii) *Benelli 121 M1 Shotgun:* The receiver is the lower part of the weapon that provides housing for the trigger mechanism.

Figure 13 to paragraph (f)(1)(iii)

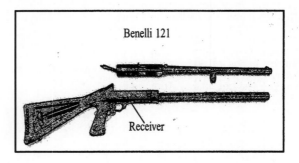

(iv) *Vickers/Maxim, Browning 1919, M2, and box-type machineguns and semiautomatic variants:* The receiver is the side plate of the weapon that is designed to hold the charging handle.

Figure 14 to paragraph (f)(1)(iv)

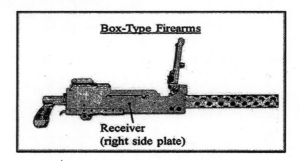

(2) *Frame or receiver classifications of partially complete, disassembled, or nonfunctional frames or receivers before* April 26, 2022. Prior determinations by the Director that a partially complete, disassembled, or nonfunctional frame or receiver, including a parts kit, was not, or did not include, a "firearm frame or receiver" under § 478.11, or "frame or receiver" under § 479.11 of this subchapter, as those terms were defined prior to April 26, 2022, shall not continue to be valid or authoritative after that date. Such determinations shall include those in which the Director determined that the item or parts kit had not yet reached a stage of manufacture to be, or include, a "firearm frame or receiver" under § 478.11, or "frame or receiver" under § 479.11 of this subchapter, as those terms were defined prior to April 26, 2022.

[ATF–2021R–05F, 87 FR 24735, Apr. 26, 2022; 87 FR 51249, 51250, Aug. 22, 2022]

Subpart C—Administrative and Miscellaneous Provisions

§ 478.21 Forms prescribed.

(a) The Director is authorized to prescribe all forms required by this part. All of the information called for in each form shall be furnished as indicated by the headings on the form and the instructions on or pertaining to the form. In addition, information called for in each form shall be furnished as required by this part.

(b) Requests for forms should be submitted to the ATF Distribution Center (*http://www.atf.gov*) or made by calling (202) 648–6420.

(5 U.S.C. 552(a); 80 Stat. 383, as amended)

[T.D. ATF–92, 46 FR 46915, Sept. 23, 1981, as amended by T.D. ATF–249, 52 FR 5962, Feb. 27, 1987; T.D. ATF–270, 53 FR 10492, Mar. 31, 1988; T.D. 372, 61 FR 20724, May 8, 1996; ATF–11F, 73 FR 57240, Oct. 2, 2008; ATF 2013R–9F, 79 FR 46692, Aug. 11, 2014]

§ 478.22 Alternate methods or procedures; emergency variations from requirements.

(a) *Alternate methods or procedures.* The licensee, on specific approval by the Director as provided in this paragraph, may use an alternate method or procedure in lieu of a method or procedure specifically prescribed in this part. The Director may approve an alternate method or procedure, subject to stated conditions, when it is found that:

(1) Good cause is shown for the use of the alternate method or procedure;

(2) The alternate method or procedure is within the purpose of, and consistent with the effect intended by, the specifically prescribed method or procedure and that the alternate method or procedure is substantially equivalent to that specifically prescribed method or procedure; and

(3) The alternate method or procedure will not be contrary to any provision of law and will not result in an increase in cost to the Government or hinder the effective administration of this part. Where the licensee desires to employ an alternate method or procedure, a written application shall be submitted to the appropriate Director of Industry Operations, for transmittal to the Director. The application shall specifically describe the proposed alternate method or procedure and shall set forth the reasons for it. Alternate methods or procedures may not be employed until the application is approved by the Director. The licensee shall, during the period of authorization of an alternate method or procedure, comply with the terms of the approved application. Authorization of

any alternate method or procedure may be withdrawn whenever, in the judgment of the Director, the effective administration of this part is hindered by the continuation of the authorization.

(b) *Emergency variations from requirements.* The Director may approve a method of operation other than as specified in this part, where it is found that an emergency exists and the proposed variation from the specified requirements are necessary and the proposed variations (1) will not hinder the effective administration of this part, and (2) will not be contrary to any provisions of law. Variations from requirements granted under this paragraph are conditioned on compliance with the procedures, conditions, and limitations set forth in the approval of the application. Failure to comply in good faith with the procedures, conditions, and limitations shall automatically terminate the authority for the variations, and the licensee shall fully comply with the prescribed requirements of regulations from which the variations were authorized. Authority for any variation may be withdrawn whenever, in the judgment of the Director, the effective administration of this part is hindered by the continuation of the variation. Where the licensee desires to employ an emergency variation, a written application shall be submitted to the appropriate Director of Industry Operations for transmittal to the Director. The application shall describe the proposed variation and set forth the reasons for it. Variations may not be employed until the application is approved.

(c) *Retention of approved variations.* The licensee shall retain, as part of the licensee's records, available for examination by ATF officers, any application approved by the Director under this section.

[T.D. ATF–270, 53 FR 10492, Mar. 31, 1988]

§ 478.23 Right of entry and examination.

(a) Except as provided in paragraph (b), any ATF officer, when there is reasonable cause to believe a violation of the Act has occurred and that evidence of the violation may be found on the premises of any licensed manufacturer, licensed importer, licensed dealer, or licensed collector, may, upon demonstrating such cause before a Federal magistrate and obtaining from the magistrate a warrant authorizing entry, enter during business hours (or, in the case of a licensed collector, the hours of operation) the premises, including places of storage, of any such licensee for the purpose of inspecting or examining:

(1) Any records or documents required to be kept by such licensee under this part and

(2) Any inventory of firearms or ammunition kept or stored by any licensed manufacturer, licensed importer, or licensed dealer at such premises or any firearms curios or relics or ammunition kept or stored by any licensed collector at such premises.

(b) Any ATF officer, without having reasonable cause to believe a violation of the Act has occurred or that evidence of the violation may be found and without demonstrating such cause before a Federal magistrate or obtaining from the magistrate a warrant authorizing entry, may enter during business hours the premises, including places of storage, of any licensed manufacturer, licensed importer, or licensed dealer for the purpose of inspecting or examining the records, documents, ammunition and firearms referred to in paragraph (a) of this section:

(1) In the course of a reasonable inquiry during the course of a criminal investigation of a person or persons other than the licensee,

(2) For insuring compliance with the recordkeeping requirements of this part:

(i) Not more than once during any 12-month period, or

(ii) At any time with respect to records relating to a firearm involved in a criminal investigation that is traced to the licensee, or

(3) When such inspection or examination may be required for determining the disposition of one or more particular firearms in the course of a bona fide criminal investigation.

(c) Any ATF officer, without having reasonable cause to believe a violation of the Act has occurred or that evidence of the violation may be found

and without demonstrating such cause before a Federal magistrate or obtaining from the magistrate a warrant authorizing entry, may enter during hours of operation the premises, including places of storage, of any licensed collector for the purpose of inspecting or examining the records, documents, firearms, and ammunition referred to in paragraph (a) of this section (1) for ensuring compliance with the recordkeeping requirements of this part not more than once during any 12-month period or (2) when such inspection or examination may be required for determining the disposition of one or more particular firearms in the course of a bona fide criminal investigation. At the election of the licensed collector, the annual inspection permitted by this paragraph shall be performed at the ATF office responsible for conducting such inspection in closest proximity to the collectors premises.

(d) The inspections and examinations provided by this section do not authorize an ATF officer to seize any records or documents other than those records or documents constituting material evidence of a violation of law. If an ATF officer seizes such records or documents, copies shall be provided the licensee within a reasonable time.

[T.D. ATF–270, 53 FR 10492, Mar. 31, 1988, as amended by T.D. ATF–363, 60 FR 17450, Apr. 6, 1995]

§ 478.24 Compilation of State laws and published ordinances.

(a) The Director shall annually revise and furnish Federal firearms licensees with a compilation of State laws and published ordinances which are relevant to the enforcement of this part. The Director annually revises the compilation and publishes it as "State Laws and Published Ordinances—Firearms" which is furnished free of charge to licensees under this part. Where the compilation has previously been furnished to licensees, the Director need only furnish amendments of the relevant laws and ordinances to such licensees.

(b) "State Laws and Published Ordinances—Firearms" is incorporated by reference in this part. It is ATF Publication 5300.5, revised yearly. The current edition is available from the Superintendent of Documents, U.S. Government Printing Office, Washington, DC 20402. It is also available for inspection at the National Archives and Records Administration (NARA). For information on the availability of this material at NARA, call 202–741–6030, or go to: *http://www.archives.gov/federal_register/code_of_federal_regulations/ibr_locations.html*. This incorporation by reference was approved by the Director of the Federal Register.

[T.D. ATF–270, 53 FR 10493, Mar. 31, 1988, as amended by 69 FR 18803, Apr. 9, 2004]

§478.25 **Disclosure of information.**

The Director of Industry Operations may make available to any Federal, State or local law enforcement agency any information which is obtained by reason of the provisions of the Act with respect to the identification of persons prohibited from purchasing or receiving firearms or ammunition who have purchased or received firearms or ammunition, together with a description of such firearms or ammunition. Upon the request of any Federal, State or local law enforcement agency, the Director of Industry Operations may provide such agency any information contained in the records required to be maintained by the Act or this part.

[T.D. ATF–270, 53 FR 10493, Mar. 31, 1988]

§478.25a **Responses to requests for information.**

Each licensee shall respond immediately to, and in no event later than 24 hours after the receipt of, a request by an ATF officer at the National Tracing Center for information contained in the records required to be kept by this part for determining the disposition of one or more firearms in the course of a bona fide criminal investigation. The requested information shall be provided orally to the ATF officer within the 24-hour period. Verification of the identity and employment of National Tracing Center personnel requesting information may be established at the time the requested information is provided by telephoning the toll-free number 1–800–

788–7132 or using the toll-free facsimile (FAX) number 1–800–788–7133.

(Approved by the Office of Management and Budget under control number 1140–0032)

[T.D. ATF–363, 60 FR 17451, Apr. 6, 1996, as amended by T.D. ATF–396, 63 FR 12646, Mar. 16, 1998; ATF–11F, 73 FR 57240, Oct. 2, 2008]

§478.26 **Curio and relic determination.**

Any person who desires to obtain a determination whether a particular firearm is a curio or relic shall submit a written request, in duplicate, for a ruling thereon to the Director. Each such request shall be executed under the penalties of perjury and shall contain a complete and accurate description of the firearm, and such photographs, diagrams, or drawings as may be necessary to enable the Director to make a determination. The Director may require the submission of the firearm for examination and evaluation. If the submission of the firearm is impractical, the person requesting the determination shall so advise the Director and designate the place where the firearm will be available for examination and evaluation.

[T.D. ATF–270, 53 FR 10493, Mar. 31, 1988]

§478.27 **Destructive device determination.**

The Director shall determine in accordance with 18 U.S.C. 921(a)(4) whether a device is excluded from the definition of a destructive device. A person who desires to obtain a determination under that provision of law for any device which he believes is not likely to be used as a weapon shall submit a written request, in triplicate, for a ruling thereon to the Director. Each such request shall be executed under the penalties of perjury and contain a complete and accurate description of the device, the name and address of the manufacturer or importer thereof, the purpose of and use for which it is intended, and such photographs, diagrams, or drawings as may be necessary to enable the Director to make his determination. The Director may require the submission to him, of a sample of such device for examination and evaluation. If the submission of such device is impracticable, the person requesting the ruling shall so advise the Director and designate the place where the device will be available for examination and evaluation.

§ 478.28 Transportation of destructive devices and certain firearms.

(a) The Director may authorize a person to transport in interstate or foreign commerce any destructive device, machine gun, short-barreled shotgun, or short-barreled rifle, if he finds that such transportation is reasonably necessary and is consistent with public safety and applicable State and local law. A person who desires to transport in interstate or foreign commerce any such device or weapon shall submit a written request so to do, in duplicate, to the Director. The request shall contain:

(1) A complete description and identification of the device or weapon to be transported;

(2) A statement whether such transportation involves a transfer of title;

(3) The need for such transportation;

(4) The approximate date such transportation is to take place;

(5) The present location of such device or weapon and the place to which it is to be transported;

(6) The mode of transportation to be used (including, if by common or contract carrier, the name and address of such carrier); and

(7) Evidence that the transportation or possession of such device or weapon is not inconsistent with the laws at the place of destination.

(b) No person shall transport any destructive device, machine gun, short-barreled shotgun, or short-barreled rifle in interstate or foreign commerce under the provisions of this section until he has received specific authorization so to do from the Director. Authorization granted under this section does not carry or import relief from any other statutory or regulatory provision relating to firearms.

(c) This section shall not be construed as requiring licensees to obtain authorization to transport destructive devices, machine guns, short-barreled shotguns, and short-barreled rifles in interstate or foreign commerce: *Provided*, That in the case of a licensed importer, licensed manufacturer, or licensed dealer, such a licensee is qualified under the National Firearms Act (see also Part 479 of this chapter) and this part to engage in the business with respect to the device or weapon to be transported, and that in the case of a licensed collector, the device or weapon to be transported is a curio or relic.

[33 FR 18555, Dec. 14, 1968. Redesignated at 40 FR 16385, Apr. 15, 1975, and amended by T.D. ATF–138, 48 FR 35399, Aug. 4, 1983]

§ 478.29 Out-of-State acquisition of firearms by nonlicensees.

No person, other than a licensed importer, licensed manufacturer, licensed dealer, or licensed collector, shall transport into or receive in the State where the person resides (or if a corporation or other business entity, where it maintains a place of business) any firearm purchased or otherwise obtained by such person outside that State: *Provided*, That the provisions of this section:

(a) Shall not preclude any person who lawfully acquires a firearm by bequest or intestate succession in a State other than his State of residence from transporting the firearm into or receiving it in that State, if it is lawful for such person to purchase or possess such firearm in that State,

(b) Shall not apply to the transportation or receipt of a rifle or shotgun obtained from a licensed manufacturer, licensed importer, licensed dealer, or licensed collector in a State other than the transferee's State of residence in an over-the-counter transaction at the licensee's premises obtained in conformity with the provisions of § 478.96(c) and

(c) Shall not apply to the transportation or receipt of a firearm obtained in conformity with the provisions of §§ 478.30 and 478.97.

[T.D. ATF–270, 53 FR 10493, Mar. 31, 1988]

§ 478.29a Acquisition of firearms by nonresidents.

No person, other than a licensed importer, licensed manufacturer, licensed dealer, or licensed collector, who does not reside in any State shall receive

42

any firearms unless such receipt is for lawful sporting purposes.

[T.D. ATF–363, 60 FR 17451, Apr. 6, 1995]

§478.30 Out-of-State disposition of firearms by nonlicensees.

No nonlicensee shall transfer, sell, trade, give, transport, or deliver any firearm to any other nonlicensee, who the transferor knows or has reasonable cause to believe does not reside in (or if the person is a corporation or other business entity, does not maintain a place of business in) the State in which the transferor resides: *Provided,* That the provisions of this section:

(a) shall not apply to the transfer, transportation, or delivery of a firearm made to carry out a bequest of a firearm to, or any acquisition by intestate succession of a firearm by, a person who is permitted to acquire or possess a firearm under the laws of the State of his residence; and

(b) shall not apply to the loan or rental of a firearm to any person for temporary use for lawful sporting purposes.

[T.D. ATF–313, 56 FR 32508, July 17, 1991; 57 FR 1205, Jan. 10, 1992]

§478.31 Delivery by common or contract carrier.

(a) No person shall knowingly deliver or cause to be delivered to any common or contract carrier for transportation or shipment in interstate or foreign commerce to any person other than a licensed importer, licensed manufacturer, licensed dealer, or licensed collector, any package or other container in which there is any firearm or ammunition without written notice to the carrier that such firearm or ammunition is being transported or shipped: *Provided,* That any passenger who owns or legally possesses a firearm or ammunition being transported aboard any common or contract carrier for movement with the passenger in interstate or foreign commerce may deliver said firearm or ammunition into the custody of the pilot, captain, conductor or operator of such common or contract carrier for the duration of that trip without violating any provision of this part.

(b) No common or contract carrier shall require or cause any label, tag, or other written notice to be placed on the outside of any package, luggage, or other container indicating that such package, luggage, or other container contains a firearm.

(c) No common or contract carrier shall transport or deliver in interstate or foreign commerce any firearm or ammunition with knowledge or reasonable cause to believe that the shipment, transportation, or receipt thereof would be in violation of any provision of this part: *Provided, however,* That the provisions of this paragraph shall not apply in respect to the transportation of firearms or ammunition in in-bond shipment under Customs laws and regulations.

(d) No common or contract carrier shall knowingly deliver in interstate or foreign commerce any firearm without obtaining written acknowledgement of receipt from the recipient of the package or other container in which there is a firearm: *Provided,* That this paragraph shall not apply with respect to the return of a firearm to a passenger who places firearms in the carrier's custody for the duration of the trip.

[33 FR 18555, Dec. 14, 1968. Redesignated at 40 FR 16385, Apr. 15, 1975, and amended by T.D. ATF–354, 59 FR 7112, Feb. 14, 1994; T.D. ATF–361, 60 FR 10786, Feb. 27, 1995]

§478.32 Prohibited shipment, transportation, possession, or receipt of firearms and ammunition by certain persons.

(a) No person may ship or transport any firearm or ammunition in interstate or foreign commerce, or receive any firearm or ammunition which has been shipped or transported in interstate or foreign commerce, or possess any firearm or ammunition in or affecting commerce, who:

(1) Has been convicted in any court of a crime punishable by imprisonment for a term exceeding 1 year,

(2) Is a fugitive from justice,

(3) Is an unlawful user of or addicted to any controlled substance (as defined in section 102 of the Controlled Substances Act, 21 U.S.C. 802),

(4) Has been adjudicated as a mental defective or has been committed to a mental institution,

(5) Being an alien—

(i) Is illegally or unlawfully in the United States; or

(ii) Except as provided in paragraph (f) of this section, has been admitted to the United States under a nonimmigrant visa: *Provided,* That the provisions of this paragraph (a)(5)(ii) do not apply to any alien who has been lawfully admitted to the United States under a nonimmigrant visa, if that alien is—

(A) Admitted to the United States for lawful hunting or sporting purposes or is in possession of a hunting license or permit lawfully issued in the United States;

(B) An official representative of a foreign government who is either accredited to the United States Government or the Government's mission to an international organization having its headquarters in the United States or is en route to or from another country to which that alien is accredited. This exception only applies if the firearm or ammunition is shipped, transported, possessed, or received in the representative's official capacity;

(C) An official of a foreign government or a distinguished foreign visitor who has been so designated by the Department of State. This exception only applies if the firearm or ammunition is shipped, transported, possessed, or received in the official's or visitor's official capacity, except if the visitor is a private individual who does not have an official capacity; or

(D) A foreign law enforcement officer of a friendly foreign government entering the United States on official law enforcement business,

(6) Has been discharged from the Armed Forces under dishonorable conditions,

(7) Having been a citizen of the United States, has renounced citizenship,

(8) Is subject to a court order that—

(i) Was issued after a hearing of which such person received actual notice, and at which such person had an opportunity to participate;

(ii) Restrains such person from harassing, stalking, or threatening an intimate partner of such person or child of such intimate partner or person, or engaging in other conduct that would place an intimate partner in reasonable fear of bodily injury to the partner or child; and

(iii)(A) Includes a finding that such person represents a credible threat to the physical safety of such intimate partner or child; or

(B) By its terms explicitly prohibits the use, attempted use, or threatened use of physical force against such intimate partner or child that would reasonably be expected to cause bodily injury, or

(9) Has been convicted of a misdemeanor crime of domestic violence.

(b) No person who is under indictment for a crime punishable by imprisonment for a term exceeding one year may ship or transport any firearm or ammunition in interstate or foreign commerce or receive any firearm or ammunition which has been shipped or transported in interstate or foreign commerce.

(c) Any individual, who to that individual's knowledge and while being employed by any person described in paragraph (a) of this section, may not in the course of such employment receive, possess, or transport any firearm or ammunition in commerce or affecting commerce or receive any firearm or ammunition which has been shipped or transported in interstate or foreign commerce.

(d) No person may sell or otherwise dispose of any firearm or ammunition to any person knowing or having reasonable cause to believe that such person:

(1) Is under indictment for, or has been convicted in any court of, a crime punishable by imprisonment for a term exceeding 1 year,

(2) Is a fugitive from justice,

(3) Is an unlawful user of or addicted to any controlled substance (as defined in section 102 of the Controlled Substances Act, 21 U.S.C. 802),

(4) Has been adjudicated as a mental defective or has been committed to a mental institution,

(5) Being an alien—

(i) Is illegally or unlawfully in the United States; or

(ii) Except as provided in paragraph (f) of this section, has been admitted to the United States under a nonimmigrant visa: *Provided,* That the provisions of this paragraph (d)(5)(ii) do not apply to any alien who has been lawfully admitted to the United States under a nonimmigrant visa, if that alien is—

(A) Admitted to the United States for lawful hunting or sporting purposes or is in possession of a hunting license or permit lawfully issued in the United States;

(B) An official representative of a foreign government who is either accredited to the United States Government or the Government's mission to an international organization having its headquarters in the United States or en route to or from another country to which that alien is accredited. This exception only applies if the firearm or ammunition is shipped, transported, possessed, or received in the representative's official capacity;

(C) An official of a foreign government or a distinguished foreign visitor who has been so designated by the Department of State. This exception only applies if the firearm or ammunition is shipped, transported, possessed, or received in the official's or visitor's official capacity, except if the visitor is a private individual who does not have an official capacity; or

(D) A foreign law enforcement officer of a friendly foreign government entering the United States on official law enforcement business,

(6) Has been discharged from the Armed Forces under dishonorable conditions,

(7) Having been a citizen of the United States, has renounced citizenship,

(8) Is subject to a court order that restrains such person from harassing, stalking, or threatening an intimate partner of such person or child of such intimate partner or person, or engaging in other conduct that would place an intimate partner in reasonable fear of bodily injury to the partner or child: *Provided,* That the provisions of this paragraph shall only apply to a court order that—

(i) Was issued after a hearing of which such person received actual notice, and at which such person had the opportunity to participate; and

(ii)(A) Includes a finding that such person represents a credible threat to the physical safety of such intimate partner or child; or

(B) By its terms explicitly prohibits the use, attempted use, or threatened use of physical force against such intimate partner or child that would reasonably be expected to cause bodily injury, or

(9) Has been convicted of a misdemeanor crime of domestic violence.

(e) The actual notice required by paragraphs (a)(8)(i) and (d)(8)(i) of this section is notice expressly and actually given, and brought home to the party directly, including service of process personally served on the party and service by mail. Actual notice also includes proof of facts and circumstances that raise the inference that the party received notice including, but not limited to, proof that notice was left at the party's dwelling house or usual place of abode with some person of suitable age and discretion residing therein; or proof that the party signed a return receipt for a hearing notice which had been mailed to the party. It does not include notice published in a newspaper.

(f) Pursuant to 18 U.S.C. 922(y)(3), any individual who has been admitted to the United States under a nonimmigrant visa may receive a waiver from the prohibition contained in paragraph (a)(5)(ii) of this section if the Attorney General approves a petition for the waiver.

[T.D. ATF–270, 53 FR 10493, Mar. 31, 1988, as amended by T.D. ATF–363, 60 FR 17451, Apr. 6, 1995; T.D. ATF–391, 62 FR 34639, June 27, 1997; T.D. ATF–401, 63 FR 35522, June 30, 1998; T.D. ATF–471, 67 FR 5425, Feb. 5, 2002; ATF–24F, 77 FR 33629, June 7, 2012]

§478.33 Stolen firearms and ammunition.

No person shall transport or ship in interstate or foreign commerce any stolen firearm or stolen ammunition knowing or having reasonable cause to believe that the firearm or ammunition was stolen, and no person shall receive, possess, conceal, store, barter, sell, or dispose of any stolen firearm or stolen ammunition, or pledge or accept as security for a loan any stolen firearm or stolen ammunition, which is moving as, which is a part of, which constitutes, or which has been shipped or transported in, interstate or foreign commerce, either before or after it was stolen, knowing or having reasonable cause to believe that the firearm or ammunition was stolen.

[T.D. ATF–363, 60 FR 17451, Apr. 6, 1995]

§ 478.33a Theft of firearms.

No person shall steal or unlawfully take or carry away from the person or the premises of a person who is licensed to engage in the business of importing, manufacturing, or dealing in firearms, any firearm in the licensee's business inventory that has been shipped or transported in interstate or foreign commerce.

[T.D. ATF–354, 59 FR 7112, Feb. 14, 1994]

§ 478.34 Removed, obliterated, or altered serial number.

No person shall knowingly transport, ship, or receive in interstate or foreign commerce any firearm which has had the importer's or manufacturer's serial number removed, obliterated, or altered, or possess or receive any firearm which has had the importer's or manufacturer's serial number removed, obliterated, or altered and has, at any time, been shipped or transported in interstate or foreign commerce.

[T.D. ATF–313, 56 FR 32508, July 17, 1991]

§ 478.35 Skeet, trap, target, and similar shooting activities.

Licensing and recordkeeping requirements, including permissible alternate records, for skeet, trap, target, and similar organized activities shall be determined by the Director of Industry Operations on a case by case basis.

§ 478.36 Transfer or possession of machine guns.

No person shall transfer or possess a machine gun except:

(a) A transfer to or by, or possession by or under the authority of, the United States, or any department or agency thereof, or a State, or a department, agency, or political subdivision thereof. (See Part 479 of this chapter); or

(b) Any lawful transfer or lawful possession of a machine gun that was lawfully possessed before May 19, 1986 (See Part 479 of this chapter).

[T.D. ATF–270, 53 FR 10494, Mar. 31, 1988]

§ 478.37 Manufacture, importation and sale of armor piercing ammunition.

No person shall manufacture or import, and no manufacturer or importer shall sell or deliver, armor piercing ammunition, except:

(a) The manufacture or importation, or the sale or delivery by any manufacturer or importer, of armor piercing ammunition for the use of the United States or any department or agency thereof or any State or any department, agency or political subdivision thereof;

(b) The manufacture, or the sale or delivery by a manufacturer or importer, of armor piercing ammunition for the purpose of exportation; or

(c) The sale or delivery by a manufacturer or importer of armor piercing ammunition for the purposes of testing or experimentation as authorized by the Director under the provisions of § 478.149.

[T.D. ATF–270, 53 FR 10494, Mar. 31, 1988]

§ 478.38 Transportation of firearms.

Notwithstanding any other provision of any law or any rule or regulation of a State or any political subdivision thereof, any person who is not otherwise prohibited by this chapter from transporting, shipping, or receiving a firearm shall be entitled to transport a firearm for any lawful purpose from any place where such person may lawfully possess and carry such firearm to any other place where such person may lawfully possess and carry such firearm if, during such transportation the firearm is unloaded, and neither the firearm nor any ammunition being transported is readily accessible or is directly accessible from the passenger compartment of such transporting vehicle: *Provided,* That in the case of a vehicle without a compartment separate from the driver's compartment the firearm or ammunition shall be contained in a locked container other than the glove compartment or console.

[T.D. ATF–270, 53 FR 10494, Mar. 31, 1988]

§478.39 Assembly of semiautomatic rifles or shotguns.

(a) No person shall assemble a semiautomatic rifle or any shotgun using more than 10 of the imported parts listed in paragraph (c) of this section if the assembled firearm is prohibited from importation under section 925(d)(3) as not being particularly suitable for or readily adaptable to sporting purposes.

(b) The provisions of this section shall not apply to:

(1) The assembly of such rifle or shotgun for sale or distribution by a licensed manufacturer to the United States or any department or agency thereof or to any State or any department, agency, or political subdivision thereof; or

(2) The assembly of such rifle or shotgun for the purposes of testing or experimentation authorized by the Director under the provisions of §478.151; or

(3) The repair of any rifle or shotgun which had been imported into or assembled in the United States prior to November 30, 1990, or the replacement of any part of such firearm.

(c) For purposes of this section, the term *imported parts* are:

(1) Frames, receivers, receiver castings, forgings or stampings

(2) Barrels

(3) Barrel extensions

(4) Mounting blocks (trunions)

(5) Muzzle attachments

(6) Bolts

(7) Bolt carriers

(8) Operating rods

(9) Gas pistons

(10) Trigger housings

(11) Triggers

(12) Hammers

(13) Sears

(14) Disconnectors

(15) Buttstocks

(16) Pistol grips

(17) Forearms, handguards

(18) Magazine bodies

(19) Followers

(20) Floorplates

[T.D. ATF–346, 58 FR 40589, July 29, 1993]

§478.39a Reporting theft or loss of firearms.

(a)(1) Each licensee shall report the theft or loss of a firearm from the licensee's inventory (including any firearm which has been transferred from the licensee's inventory to a personal collection and held as a personal firearm for at least 1 year), or from the collection of a licensed collector, within 48 hours after the theft or loss is discovered.

(2) When a firearm is stolen or lost in transit on a common or contract carrier (which for purposes of this paragraph includes the U.S. Postal Service), it is considered stolen or lost from the transferor/sender licensee's inventory for reporting purposes. Therefore, the transferor/sender of the stolen or lost firearm shall report the theft or loss of the firearm within 48 hours after the transferor/sender discovers the theft or loss.

(b) Each licensee shall report the theft or loss by telephoning ATF at 1–888–930–9275 (nationwide toll-free number), and by preparing and submitting to ATF a Federal Firearms Licensee Theft/Loss Report, ATF Form 3310.11, in accordance with the instructions on the form. The original of the report shall be retained by the licensee as part of the licensee's required records.

(c) When a licensee submits to ATF a Federal Firearms Licensee Theft/Loss Report, ATF Form 3310.11, for the theft or loss of a firearm registered under the National Firearms Act, this report also satisfies the notification requirement under §479.141 of this chapter.

(d) Theft or loss of any firearm shall also be reported to the appropriate local authorities. If the location of the theft or loss is known, the local law enforcement agency at that location would be the appropriate local authority. Otherwise, the report should be made to the local law enforcement authorities at the licensee's location or business premises.

(e) Licensees shall reflect the theft or loss of a firearm as a disposition entry in the Record of Acquisition and Disposition required by subpart H of this part not later than 7 days following discovery of the theft or loss. The disposition entry shall record whether the incident is a theft or loss, the ATF-Issued Incident Number, and the Incident Number provided by the local law enforcement agency.

(f) Licensees who report the theft or loss of a firearm and later discover its whereabouts shall advise ATF at 1–888–

47

930–9275 (nationwide toll-free number) that the firearm has been located, and shall re-enter the firearm in the Record of Acquisition and Disposition as an acquisition or disposition entry as appropriate.

[ATF 40F, 81 FR 1318, Jan. 12, 2016]

§ 478.40   [Reserved]

Subpart D—Licenses

§ 478.41   General.

(a) Each person intending to engage in business as an importer or manufacturer of firearms or ammunition, or a dealer in firearms shall, before commencing such business, obtain the license required by this subpart for the business to be operated. Each person who desires to obtain a license as a collector of curios or relics may obtain such a license under the provisions of this subpart.

(b) Each person intending to engage in business as a firearms or ammunition importer or manufacturer, or dealer in firearms shall file an application, with the required fee (see § 478.42), with ATF in accordance with the instructions on the form (see § 478.44), and, pursuant to § 478.47, receive the license required for such business from the Chief, Federal Firearms Licensing Center. Except as provided in § 478.50, a license must be obtained for each business and each place at which the applicant is to do business. A license as an importer or manufacturer of firearms or ammunition, or a dealer in firearms shall, subject to the provisions of the Act and other applicable provisions of law, entitle the licensee to transport, ship, and receive firearms and ammunition covered by such license in interstate or foreign commerce and to engage in the business specified by the license, at the location described on the license, and for the period stated on the license. However, it shall not be necessary for a licensed importer or a licensed manufacturer to also obtain a dealer's license in order to engage in business on the licensed premises as a dealer in the same type of firearms authorized by the license to be imported or manufactured. Payment of the license fee as an importer or manufacturer of destructive devices, ammuni-

tion for destructive devices or armor piercing ammunition or as a dealer in destructive devices includes the privilege of importing or manufacturing firearms other than destructive devices and ammunition for other than destructive devices or ammunition other than armor piercing ammunition, or dealing in firearms other than destructive devices, as the case may be, by such a licensee at the licensed premises.

(c) Each person seeking the privileges of a collector licensed under this part shall file an application, with the required fee (see § 478.42), with ATF in accordance with the instructions on the form (see § 478.44), and pursuant to § 478.47, receive from the Chief, Federal Firearms Licensing Center, the license covering the collection of curios and relics. A separate license may be obtained for each collection premises, and such license shall, subject to the provisions of the Act and other applicable provisions of law, entitle the licensee to transport, ship, receive, and acquire curios and relics in interstate or foreign commerce, and to make disposition of curios and relics in interstate or foreign commerce, to any other person licensed under the provisions of this part, for the period stated on the license.

(d) The collector license provided by this part shall apply only to transactions related to a collector's activity in acquiring, holding or disposing of curios and relics. A collector's license does not authorize the collector to engage in a business required to be licensed under the Act or this part. Therefore, if the acquisitions and dispositions of curios and relics by a collector bring the collector within the definition of a manufacturer, importer, or dealer under this part, he shall qualify as such. (See also § 478.93 of this part.)

(18 U.S.C. 847 (84 Stat. 959); 18 U.S.C. 926 (82 Stat. 1226))

[33 FR 18555, Dec. 14, 1968. Redesignated at 40 FR 16835, Apr. 15, 1975, and amended by T.D. ATF–270, 53 FR 10494, Mar. 31, 1988; T.D. ATF–290, 54 FR 53054, Dec. 27, 1989]

§478.42 License fees.

Each applicant shall pay a fee for obtaining a firearms license or ammunition license, a separate fee being required for each business or collecting activity at each place of such business or activity, as follows:

(a) For a manufacturer:

(1) Of destructive devices, ammunition for destructive devices or armor piercing ammunition—$1,000 per year.

(2) Of firearms other than destructive devices—$50 per year.

(3) Of ammunition for firearms other than ammunition for destructive devices or armor piercing ammunition—$10 per year.

(b) For an importer:

(1) Of destructive devices, ammunition for destructive devices or armor piercing ammunition—$1,000 per year.

(2) Of firearms other than destructive devices or ammunition for firearms other than destructive devices or ammunition other than armor piercing ammunition—$50 per year.

(c) For a dealer:

(1) In destructive devices—$1,000 per year.

(2) Who is not a dealer in destructive devices—$200 for 3 years, except that the fee for renewal of a valid license shall be $90 for 3 years.

(d) For a collector of curios and relics—$10 per year.

[T.D. ATF–270, 53 FR 10494, Mar. 31, 1988, as amended by T.D. ATF–354, 59 FR 7112, Feb. 14, 1994]

§478.43 License fee not refundable.

No refund of any part of the amount paid as a license fee shall be made where the operations of the licensee are, for any reason, discontinued during the period of an issued license. However, the license fee submitted with an application for a license shall be refunded if that application is denied or withdrawn by the applicant prior to being acted upon.

[T.D. ATF–270, 53 FR 10494, Mar. 31, 1988]

§478.44 Original license.

(a)(1) Any person who intends to engage in business as a firearms or ammunition importer or manufacturer, or firearms dealer, or who has not previously been licensed under the provisions of this part to so engage in business, or who has not timely submitted an application for renewal of the previous license issued under this part, must file an application for license, ATF Form 7 (Firearms), in duplicate, with ATF in accordance with the instructions on the form. The application must:

(i) Be executed under the penalties of perjury and the penalties imposed by 18 U.S.C. 924;

(ii) Include a photograph and fingerprints as required in the instructions on the form;

(iii) If the applicant (including, in the case of a corporation, partnership, or association, any individual possessing, directly or indirectly, the power to direct or cause the direction of the management and policies of the corporation, partnership, or association) is an alien who has been admitted to the United States under a nonimmigrant visa, applicable documentation demonstrating that the alien falls within an exception specified in 18 U.S.C. 922(y)(2) (e.g., a hunting license or permit lawfully issued in the United States) or has obtained a waiver as specified in 18 U.S.C. 922(y)(3); and

(iv) Include the appropriate fee in the form of money order or check made payable to the "Bureau of Alcohol, Tobacco, Firearms, and Explosives".

(2) ATF Form 7 may be obtained by contacting the ATF Distribution Center (See §478.21).

(b) Any person who desires to obtain a license as a collector under the Act and this part, or who has not timely submitted an application for renewal of the previous license issued under this part, shall file an application, ATF Form 7CR (Curios and Relics), with ATF in accordance with the instructions on the form. If the applicant (including, in the case of a corporation, partnership, or association, any individual possessing, directly or indirectly, the power to direct or cause the direction of the management and policies of the corporation, partnership, or association) is an alien who has been admitted to the United States under a nonimmigrant visa, the application must include applicable documentation demonstrating that the alien falls within an exception specified in 18

U.S.C. 922(y)(2) (e.g., a hunting license or permit lawfully issued in the United States) or has obtained a waiver as specified in 18 U.S.C. 922(y)(3). The application must be executed under the penalties of perjury and the penalties imposed by 18 U.S.C. 924. The application shall include the appropriate fee in the form of a money order or check made payable to the Bureau of Alcohol, Tobacco, Firearms, and Explosives. ATF Form 7CR (Curios and Relics) may be obtained by contacting the ATF Distribution Center (See § 478.21).

(Paragraphs (a) and (b) approved by the Office of Management and Budget under control number 1140–0060)

[T.D. ATF–363, 60 FR 17453, Apr. 6, 1995, as amended by T.D. ATF–471, 67 FR 5425, Feb. 5, 2002; ATF–11F, 73 FR 57240, Oct. 2, 2008; ATF–24F, 77 FR 33629, June 7, 2012]

§ 478.45   Renewal of license.

If a licensee intends to continue the business or activity described on a license issued under this part during any portion of the ensuing year, the licensee shall, unless otherwise notified in writing by the Chief, Federal Firearms Licensing Center, execute and file with ATF prior to the expiration of the license an application for a license renewal, ATF Form 8 Part II, in accordance with the instructions on the form, and the required fee. If the applicant is an alien who has been admitted to the United States under a nonimmigrant visa, the application must include applicable documentation demonstrating that the alien falls within an exception specified in 18 U.S.C. 922(y)(2) (e.g., a hunting license or permit lawfully issued in the United States) or has obtained a waiver as specified in 18 U.S.C. 922(y)(3). The Chief, Federal Firearms Licensing Center may, in writing, require the applicant for license renewal to also file completed ATF Form 7 or ATF Form 7CR in the manner required by § 478.44. In the event the licensee does not timely file an ATF Form 8 Part II, the licensee must file an ATF Form 7 or ATF Form 7CR as required by § 478.44, and obtain the required license before continuing business or collecting activity. If an ATF Form 8 Part II is not timely received through the mails, the licensee should so notify the Chief, Federal Firearms Licensing Center.

(Approved by the Office of Management and Budget under control number 1140–0060)

[ATF–11F, 73 FR 57241, Oct. 2, 2008, as amended by ATF–24F, 77 FR 33629, June 7, 2012]

§ 478.46   Insufficient fee.

If an application is filed with an insufficient fee, the application and any fee submitted will be returned to the applicant.

(18 U.S.C. 847 (84 Stat. 959); 18 U.S.C. 926 (82 Stat. 1226))

[T.D. ATF–200, 50 FR 10498, Mar. 15, 1985]

§ 478.47   Issuance of license.

(a) Upon receipt of a properly executed application for a license on ATF Form 7, ATF Form 7CR, or ATF Form 8 Part II, the Chief, Federal Firearms Licensing Center, shall, upon finding through further inquiry or investigation, or otherwise, that the applicant is qualified, issue the appropriate license. Each license shall bear a unique license number and such number may be assigned to the licensee to whom issued for so long as the licensee maintains continuity of renewal in the same location (State).

(b) The Chief, Federal Firearms Licensing Center, shall approve a properly executed application for license on ATF Form 7, ATF Form 7CR, or ATF Form 8 Part II, if:

(1) The applicant is 21 years of age or over;

(2) The applicant (including, in the case of a corporation, partnership, or association, any individual possessing, directly or indirectly, the power to direct or cause the direction of the management and policies of the corporation, partnership, or association) is not prohibited under the provisions of the Act from shipping or transporting in interstate or foreign commerce, or possessing in or affecting commerce, any firearm or ammunition, or from receiving any firearm or ammunition which has been shipped or transported in interstate or foreign commerce;

(3) The applicant has not willfully violated any of the provisions of the Act or this part;

(4) The applicant has not willfully failed to disclose any material information required, or has not made any false statement as to any material fact, in connection with his application; and

(5) The applicant has in a State (i) premises from which he conducts business subject to license under the Act or from which he intends to conduct such business within a reasonable period of time, or (ii) in the case of a collector, premises from which he conducts his collecting subject to license under the Act or from which he intends to conduct such collecting within a reasonable period of time.

(c) The Chief, Federal Firearms Licensing Center, shall approve or the Director of Industry Operations shall deny an application for a license within the 60-day period beginning on the date the properly executed application was received: *Provided,* That when an applicant for license renewal is a person who is, pursuant to the provisions of §478.78, §478.143, or §478.144, conducting business or collecting activity under a previously issued license, action regarding the application will be held in abeyance pending the completion of the proceedings against the applicant's existing license or license application, final determination of the applicant's criminal case, or final action by the Director on an application for relief submitted pursuant to §478.144, as the case may be.

(d) When the Director of Industry Operations or the Chief, Federal Firearms Licensing Center fails to act on an application for a license within the 60-day period prescribed by paragraph (c) of this section, the applicant may file an action under section 1361 of title 28, United States Code, to compel ATF to act upon the application.

(18 U.S.C. 847 (84 Stat. 959); 18 U.S.C. 926 (82 Stat. 1226))

[33 FR 18555, Dec. 14, 1968. Redesignated at 40 FR 16835, Apr. 15, 1975, and amended by T.D. ATF–135, 48 FR 24068, May 31, 1983; T.D. ATF–241, 51 FR 39619, Oct. 29, 1986; T.D. ATF–270, 53 FR 10495, Mar. 31, 1988; T.D. ATF–290, 54 FR 53054, Dec. 27, 1989; T.D. ATF–363, 60 FR 17453, Apr. 6, 1995; ATF–11F, 73 FR 57241, Oct. 2, 2008; ATF–2021R–05F; 87 FR 24741, Apr. 26, 2022]

§478.48 Correction of error on license.

(a) Upon receipt of a license issued under the provisions of this part, each licensee shall examine same to ensure that the information contained thereon is accurate. If the license is incorrect, the licensee shall return the license to the Chief, Federal Firearms Licensing Center, with a statement showing the nature of the error. The Chief, Federal Firearms Licensing Center, shall correct the error, if the error was made in his office, and return the license. However, if the error resulted from information contained in the licensee's application for the license, the Chief, Federal Firearms Licensing Center, shall require the licensee to file an amended application setting forth the correct information and a statement explaining the error contained in the application. Upon receipt of the amended application and a satisfactory explanation of the error, the Chief, Federal Firearms Licensing Center, shall make the correction on the license and return same to the licensee.

(b) When the Chief, Federal Firearms Licensing Center, finds through any means other than notice from the licensee that an incorrect license has been issued, the Chief, Federal Firearms Licensing Center, may require the holder of the incorrect license to (1) return the license for correction, and (2) if the error resulted from information contained in the licensee's application for the license, the Chief, Federal Firearms Licensing Center, shall require the licensee to file an amended application setting forth the correct information, and a statement explaining the error contained in the application. The Chief, Federal Firearms Licensing Center, then shall make the correction on the license and return same to the licensee.

[33 FR 18555, Dec. 14, 1968. Redesignated at 40 FR 16835, Apr. 15, 1975, and amended by T.D. ATF–290, 54 FR 53054, Dec. 27, 1989]

§478.49 Duration of license.

The license entitles the person to whom issued to engage in the business or activity specified on the license, within the limitations of the Act and the regulations contained in this part,

§ 478.50

for a three year period, unless terminated sooner.

[T.D. ATF–270, 53 FR 10495, Mar. 31, 1988]

§ 478.50   Locations covered by license.

The license covers the class of business or the activity specified in the license at the address specified therein. A separate license must be obtained for each location at which a firearms or ammunition business or activity requiring a license under this part is conducted except:

(a) No license is required to cover a separate warehouse used by the licensee solely for storage of firearms or ammunition if the records required by this part are maintained at the licensed premises served by such warehouse, or if such warehouse is used by the licensee for the storage of records as provided in § 478.129;

(b) A licensed collector may acquire curios and relics at any location, and dispose of curios or relics to any licensee or to other persons who are residents of the State where the collector's license is held and the disposition is made;

(c) A licensee may conduct business at a gun show pursuant to the provision of § 478.100; or

(d) A licensed importer, manufacturer, or dealer may engage in the business of dealing in curio or relic firearms with another licensee at any location pursuant to the provisions of § 478.100.

[T.D. ATF–191, 49 FR 46890, Nov. 29, 1984, as amended by T.D. ATF–401, 63 FR 35523, June 30, 1998; ATF–2021R–05F; 87 FR 24741, Apr. 26, 2022]

§ 478.51   License not transferable.

Licenses issued under this part are not transferable. In the event of the lease, sale, or other transfer of the operations authorized by the license, the successor must obtain the license required by this part prior to commencing such operations. However, for rules on right of succession, see § 478.56.

§ 478.52   Change of address.

(a) Licensees may during the term of their current license remove their business or activity to a new location at which they intend regularly to carry on such business or activity by filing an Application for an Amended Federal Firearms License, ATF Form 5300.38, in duplicate, not less than 30 days prior to such removal with the Chief, Federal Firearms Licensing Center. The ATF Form 5300.38 shall be completed in accordance with the instructions on the form. The application must be executed under the penalties of perjury and penalties imposed by 18 U.S.C. 924. The application shall be accompanied by the licensee's original license. The Chief, Federal Firearms Licensing Center, may, in writing, require the applicant for an amended license to also file completed ATF Form 7 or ATF Form 7CR, or portions thereof, in the manner required by § 478.44.

(b) Upon receipt of a properly executed application for an amended license, the Chief, Federal Firearms Licensing Center, shall, upon finding through further inquiry or investigation, or otherwise, that the applicant is qualified at the new location, issue the amended license, and return it to the applicant. The license shall be valid for the remainder of the term of the original license. The Chief, Federal Firearms Licensing Center, shall, if the applicant is not qualified, refer the application for amended license to the Director of Industry Operations for denial in accordance with § 478.71.

(Approved by the Office of Management and Budget under control number 1140–0040)

[T.D. ATF–363, 60 FR 17453, Apr. 6, 1995, as amended by ATF–11F, 73 FR 57241, Oct. 2, 2008]

§ 478.53   Change in trade name.

A licensee continuing to conduct business at the location shown on his license is not required to obtain a new license by reason of a mere change in trade name under which he conducts his business: *Provided,* That such licensee furnishes his license for endorsement of such change to the Chief, Federal Firearms Licensing Center within 30 days from the date the licensee begins his business under the new trade name.

[33 FR 18555, Dec. 14, 1968. Redesignated at 40 FR 16835, Apr. 15, 1975, and amended by T.D. ATF–48, 44 FR 55842, Sept. 28, 1979; T.D. ATF–290, 54 FR 53055, Dec. 27, 1989]

§478.54 Change of control.

In the case of a corporation or association holding a license under this part, if actual or legal control of the corporation or association changes, directly or indirectly, whether by reason of change in stock ownership or control (in the licensed corporation or in any other corporation), by operations of law, or in any other manner, the licensee shall, within 30 days of such change, give written notification thereof, executed under the penalties of perjury, to the Chief, Federal Firearms Licensing Center. Upon expiration of the license, the corporation or association must file a Form 7 (Firearms) as required by §478.44.

[33 FR 18555, Dec. 14, 1968. Redesignated at 40 FR 16835, Apr. 15, 1975, and amended by T.D. ATF–290, 54 FR 53054, Dec. 27, 1989]

§478.55 Continuing partnerships.

Where, under the laws of the particular State, the partnership is not terminated on death or insolvency of a partner, but continues until the winding up of the partnership affairs is completed, and the surviving partner has the exclusive right to the control and possession of the partnership assets for the purpose of liquidation and settlement, such surviving partner may continue to operate the business under the license of the partnership. If such surviving partner acquires the business on completion of the settlement of the partnership, he shall obtain a license in his own name from the date of acquisition, as provided in §478.44. The rule set forth in this section shall also apply where there is more than one surviving partner.

§478.56 Right of succession by certain persons.

(a) Certain persons other than the licensee may secure the right to carry on the same firearms or ammunition business at the same address shown on, and for the remainder of the term of, a current license. Such persons are:

(1) The surviving spouse or child, or executor, administrator, or other legal representative of a deceased licensee; and

(2) A receiver or trustee in bankruptcy, or an assignee for benefit of creditors.

(b) In order to secure the right provided by this section, the person or persons continuing the business shall furnish the license for that business for endorsement of such succession to the Chief, Federal Firearms Licensing Center, within 30 days from the date on which the successor begins to carry on the business.

[33 FR 18555, Dec. 14, 1968. Redesignated at 40 FR 16835, Apr. 15, 1975, and amended by T.D. ATF–48, 44 FR 55842, Sept. 28, 1979; T.D. ATF–290, 54 FR 53055, Dec. 27, 1989; ATF 2013R–9F, 79 FR 46692, Aug. 11, 2014]

§478.57 Discontinuance of business.

Where a firearm or ammunition business is either discontinued or succeeded by a new owner, the owner of the business discontinued or succeeded shall within 30 days thereof furnish to the Chief, Federal Firearms Licensing Center notification of the discontinuance or succession. (See also §478.127.)

[33 FR 18555, Dec. 14, 1968. Redesignated at 40 FR 16835, Apr. 15, 1975, and amended by T.D. ATF–48, 44 FR 55842, Sept. 28, 1979; T.D. ATF–290, 54 FR 53055, Dec. 27, 1989; T.D. ATF–363, 60 FR 17453, Apr. 6, 1995; T.D. ATF–383, 61 FR 39321, July 29, 1996; ATF 2014R–42, 84 FR 12094, Apr. 1, 2019]

§478.58 State or other law.

A license issued under this part confers no right or privilege to conduct business or activity contrary to State or other law. The holder of such a license is not by reason of the rights and privileges granted by that license immune from punishment for operating a firearm or ammunition business or activity in violation of the provisions of any State or other law. Similarly, compliance with the provisions of any State or other law affords no immunity under Federal law or regulations.

§478.59 Abandoned application.

Upon receipt of an incomplete or improperly executed application on ATF form 7 (5310.12), or ATF Form 8 (5310.11) Part II, the applicant shall be notified of the deficiency in the application. If the application is not corrected and returned within 30 days following the date of notification, the application shall be considered as having been abandoned and the license fee returned.

[T.D. ATF–135, 48 FR 24068, May 31, 1983]

§ 478.60 Certain continuances of business.

A licensee who furnishes his license to the Chief, Federal Firearms Licensing Center for correction or endorsement in compliance with the provisions contained in this subpart may continue his operations while awaiting its return.

[33 FR 18555, Dec. 14, 1968. Redesignated at 40 FR 16835, Apr. 15, 1975, and amended by T.D. ATF–290, 54 FR 53054, Dec. 27, 1989]

Subpart E—License Proceedings

§ 478.71 Denial of an application for license.

Whenever the Director has reason to believe that an applicant is not qualified to receive a license under the provisions of § 478.47, he may issue a notice of denial, on Form 4498, to the applicant. The notice shall set forth the matters of fact and law relied upon in determining that the application should be denied, and shall afford the applicant 15 days from the date of receipt of the notice in which to request a hearing to review the denial. If no request for a hearing is filed within such time, the application shall be disapproved and a copy, so marked, shall be returned to the applicant.

[33 FR 18555, Dec. 14, 1968. Redesignated at 40 FR 16835, Apr. 15, 1975, and amended by T.D. ATF–270, 53 FR 10495, Mar. 31, 1988; ATF–27P, 74 FR 1878, Jan. 14, 2009]

§ 478.72 Hearing after application denial.

If the applicant for an original or renewal license desires a hearing to review the denial of his application, he shall file a request therefor, in duplicate, with the Director of Industry Operations within 15 days after receipt of the notice of denial. The request should include a statement of the reasons therefor. On receipt of the request, the Director of Industry Operations shall, as expeditiously as possible, make the necessary arrangements for the hearing and advise the applicant of the date, time, location, and the name of the officer before whom the hearing will be held. Such notification shall be made not less than 10 days in advance of the date set for the hearing. During the hearing the applicant will have the opportunity to submit facts and arguments for review and consideration; offers of settlement will not be entertained at the hearing but may be made before or after the hearing. On conclusion of the hearing and consideration of all relevant facts and circumstances presented by the applicant or his representative, the Director shall render his decision confirming or reversing the denial of the application. A copy of the application, marked "Disapproved," will be returned to the applicant. If the decision is that the license applied for should be issued, the applicant shall be so notified, in writing, and the license shall be issued as provided by § 478.47.

[33 FR 18555, Dec. 14, 1968, as amended by ATF–27P, 74 FR 1878, Jan. 14, 2009; ATF 2013R–9F, 79 FR 46692, Aug. 11, 2014; ATF 2008R–15P; 81 FR 32235, May 23, 2016]

§ 478.73 Notice of revocation, suspension, or imposition of civil fine.

(a) *Basis for action.* Whenever the Director has reason to believe that a licensee has willfully violated any provision of the Act or this part, a notice of revocation of the license, ATF Form 4500, may be issued. In addition, a notice of revocation of the license, on ATF Form 4500, may be issued whenever the Director has reason to believe that a licensee fails to have secure gun storage or safety devices available at any place in which firearms are sold under the license to persons who are not licensees (except in any case in which a secure gun storage or safety device is temporarily unavailable because of theft, casualty loss, consumer sales, backorders from a manufacturer, or any other similar reason beyond the control of the licensee). In addition, pursuant to 18 U.S.C. 922(t)(5) and 18 U.S.C. 924(p), a notice of revocation, suspension, or imposition of a civil fine may be issued on ATF Form 4500 whenever the Director has reason to believe that a licensee has knowingly transferred a firearm to an unlicensed person and knowingly failed to comply with the requirements of 18 U.S.C.

922(t)(1) with respect to the transfer and, at the time that the transferee most recently proposed the transfer, the national instant criminal background check system was operating and information was available to the system demonstrating that the transferee's receipt of a firearm would violate 18 U.S.C. 922(g) or 922(n) or State law; or that a licensee has violated 18 U.S.C. 922(z)(1) by selling, delivering, or transferring any handgun to any person other than a licensee, unless the transferee was provided with a secure gun storage or safety device for that handgun.

(b) *Issuance of notice.* The notice shall set forth the matters of fact constituting the violations specified, dates, places, and the sections of law and regulations violated. The Director shall afford the licensee 15 days from the date of receipt of the notice in which to request a hearing prior to suspension or revocation of the license, or imposition of a civil fine. If the licensee does not file a timely request for a hearing, the Director shall issue a final notice of suspension or revocation and/or imposition of a civil fine on ATF Form 5300.13, as provided in §478.74.

[T.D. ATF–415, 63 FR 58278, Oct. 29, 1998, as amended by ATF–27P, 74 FR 1878, Jan. 14, 2009; ATF 2013R–9F, 79 FR 46692, Aug. 11, 2014; ATF 2008R–15P, 81 FR 32235, May 23, 2016; ATF 24P, 87 FR 193, Jan. 4, 2022]

§478.74 Request for hearing after notice of suspension, revocation, or imposition of civil fine.

If a licensee desires a hearing after receipt of a notice of suspension or revocation of a license, or imposition of a civil fine, the licensee shall file a request, in duplicate, with the Director of Industry Operations within 15 days after receipt of the notice of suspension or revocation of a license, or imposition of a civil fine. On receipt of such request, the Director of Industry Operations shall, as expeditiously as possible, make necessary arrangements for the hearing and advise the licensee of the date, time, location and the name of the officer before whom the hearing will be held. Such notification shall be made no less than 10 days in advance of the date set for the hearing. On conclusion of the hearing and consideration of all the relevant presentations made by the licensee or the licensee's representative, the Director shall render a decision and shall prepare a brief summary of the findings and conclusions on which the decision is based. If the decision is that the license should be revoked, or, in actions under 18 U.S.C. 922(t)(5) or 924(p), that the license should be revoked or suspended, or that a civil fine should be imposed, a certified copy of the summary shall be furnished to the licensee with the final notice of revocation, suspension, or imposition of a civil fine on ATF Form 5300.13. If the decision is that the license should not be revoked, or in actions under 18 U.S.C. 922(t)(5) or 924(p), that the license should not be revoked or suspended, and a civil fine should not be imposed, the licensee shall be notified in writing. During the hearing the licensee will have the opportunity to submit facts and arguments for review and consideration; offers of settlement will not be entertained at the hearing but may be made before or after the hearing.

[T.D. ATF–415, 63 FR 58278, Oct. 29, 1998, as amended by ATF–27P, 74 FR 1878, Jan. 14, 2009; ATF 2013R–9F, 79 FR 46692, Aug. 11, 2014; ATF 2008R–15P, 81 FR 32235, May 23, 2016]

§478.75 Service on applicant or licensee.

All notices and other documents required to be served on an applicant or licensee under this subpart shall be served by certified mail or by personal delivery. Where service is by certified mail, a signed duplicate original copy of the formal document shall be mailed, with return receipt requested, to the applicant or licensee at the address stated in his application or license, or at his last known address. Where service is by personal delivery, a signed duplicate original copy of the formal document shall be delivered to the applicant or licensee, or, in the case of a corporation, partnership, or association, by delivering it to an officer, manager, or general agent thereof, or to its attorney of record.

[33 FR 18555, Dec. 14, 1968. Redesignated at 40 FR 16835, Apr. 15, 1975, and further redesignated by T.D. ATF–241, 51 FR 39619, Oct. 29, 1986; T.D. ATF–270, 53 FR 10496, Mar. 31, 1988]

§ 478.76 Representation at a hearing.

Applicants or licensees may represent themselves or be represented by an attorney, a certified public accountant, or any other person, specifically designated in a duly executed power of attorney that shall be filed in the proceeding by the applicant or licensee. The applicant or licensee shall file waivers, if applicable, under the Privacy Act of 1974 and 26 U.S.C. 6103(c) (confidentiality and disclosure of returns and return information). The Director of Industry Operations may be represented in proceedings under §§ 478.72 and 478.74 by an attorney in the Office of Chief Counsel who is authorized to execute and file motions, briefs, and other papers in the proceeding, on behalf of the Director of Industry Operations, in the attorney's own name as "Attorney for the Government."

[ATF 33F, 84 FR 64743, Nov. 25, 2019]

§ 478.77 Designated place of hearing.

The designated place of the hearing shall be a location convenient to the aggrieved party.

[T.D. ATF–270, 53 FR 10496, Mar. 31, 1988]

§ 478.78 Operations by licensee after notice.

In any case where denial, suspension, or revocation proceedings are pending before the Bureau of Alcohol, Tobacco, Firearms, and Explosives, or notice of denial, suspension, or revocation has been served on the licensee and he has filed timely request for a hearing, the license in the possession of the licensee shall remain in effect even though such license has expired, or the suspension or revocation date specified in the notice of revocation on Form 4500 served on the licensee has passed: *Provided,* That with respect to a license that has expired, the licensee has timely filed an application for the renewal of his license. If a licensee is dissatisfied with a posthearing decision revoking or suspending the license or denying the application or imposing a civil fine, as the case may be, he may, pursuant to 18 U.S.C. 923(f)(3), within 60 days after receipt of the final notice denying the application or revoking or suspending the license or imposing a civil fine, file a petition for judicial review of such action. Such petition should be filed with the U.S. district court for the district in which the applicant or licensee resides or has his principal place of business. In such case, when the Director finds that justice so requires, he may postpone the effective date of suspension or revocation of a license or authorize continued operations under the expired license, as applicable, pending judicial review.

[T.D. ATF–415, 63 FR 58278, Oct. 29, 1998, as amended by ATF–27P, 74 FR 1878, Jan. 14, 2009; ATF 2013R–9F, 79 FR 46692, Aug. 11, 2014]

Subpart F—Conduct of Business

§ 478.91 Posting of license.

Any license issued under this part shall be kept posted and kept available for inspection on the premises covered by the license.

§ 478.92 Identification of firearms and armor piercing ammunition by licensed manufacturers and licensed importers.

(a)(1) *Firearms manufactured or imported by licensees.* Except as otherwise provided in this section, licensed manufacturers and licensed importers of firearms must legibly identify each firearm they manufacture or import as follows:

(i) *Serial number, name, place of business.* By engraving, casting, stamping (impressing), or otherwise conspicuously placing or causing to be engraved, cast, stamped (impressed) or otherwise placed on the frame or receiver thereof, an individual serial number, in a manner not susceptible of being readily obliterated, altered, or removed. The serial number must not duplicate any serial number placed by the licensee on any other firearm. The frame or receiver must also be marked with either: their name (or recognized abbreviation), and city and State (or recognized abbreviation) where they maintain their place of business; or their name (or recognized abbreviation) and the serial number beginning with their abbreviated Federal firearms license number, which is the first three and last five digits, as a prefix to the unique identification number, followed by a hyphen, *e.g.,* "12345678-[unique identification number]"; and

(ii) *Model, caliber or gauge, foreign manufacturer, country of manufacture.* By engraving, casting, stamping (impressing), or otherwise conspicuously placing or causing to be engraved, cast, stamped (impressed) or placed on the frame or receiver, or barrel or pistol slide (if applicable) thereof, certain additional information. This information must be placed in a manner not susceptible of being readily obliterated, altered, or removed. The additional information shall include:

(A) The model, if such designation has been made;

(B) The caliber or gauge;

(C) When applicable, the name of the foreign manufacturer; and

(D) In the case of an imported firearm, the name of the country in which it was manufactured. For additional requirements relating to imported firearms, see Customs regulations at 19 CFR part 134.

(iii) *Multi-piece frame or receiver.* In the case of a multi-piece frame or receiver, the modular subpart that is the outermost housing or structure designed to house, hold, or contain either the sear or equivalent component of a handgun, breech blocking or sealing component of a projectile weapon other than a handgun, or internal sound reduction component of a firearm muffler or firearm silencer, as the case may be, shall be the subpart of the multi-piece frame or receiver identified in accordance with this section. If more than one subpart is similarly designed to house, hold, or contain such primary component (*e.g.*, left and right halves), each of those subparts must be identified with the same serial number and associated licensee information not duplicated on any other frame or receiver. The identified subpart(s) of a complete (assembled or unassembled) multi-piece frame or receiver shall not be removed and replaced (*see* § 478.34, 18 U.S.C. 922(k), and 26 U.S.C. 5861(g) and (h)), unless—

(A) The subpart replacement is not a firearm under 26 U.S.C. 5845;

(B) The subpart replacement is identified by the licensed manufacturer of the original subpart with the same serial number and associated licensee information in the manner prescribed by this section; and

(C) The original subpart is destroyed under the licensed manufacturer's control or direct supervision prior to such placement.

(iv) *Frame or receiver, machinegun conversion part, or muffler or silencer part disposed of separately.* Each part defined as a frame or receiver or modular subpart thereof described in paragraph (a)(1)(iii) of this section, machinegun, or firearm muffler or firearm silencer that is not a component part of a complete weapon or complete muffler or silencer device at the time it is sold, shipped, or otherwise disposed of by the licensee must be identified as required by this section with an individual serial number not duplicated on any other firearm and all additional identifying information, except that the model designation and caliber or gauge may be omitted if that information is unknown at the time the part is identified.

(v) *Size and depth of markings.* The engraving, casting, or stamping (impressing) of the serial number and additional information must be to a minimum depth of .003 inch, and the serial number and any associated license number in a print size no smaller than $\frac{1}{16}$ inch. The size of the serial and license number is measured as the distance between the latitudinal ends of the character impression bottoms (bases). The depth of all markings required by this section is measured from the flat surface of the metal and not the peaks or ridges.

(vi) *Period of time to identify firearms.* Licensed manufacturers shall identify firearms they manufacture within the period of time set forth in the following subparagraphs (A) and (B), and licensed importers must identify firearms they import within the period prescribed in § 478.112. For purposes of these subparagraphs, firearms awaiting materials, parts, or equipment repair to be completed are presumed, absent reliable evidence to the contrary, to be in the manufacturing process.

(A) *Complete non-National Firearms Act weapons, and frames or receivers of such weapons.* Complete weapons not defined as firearms under 26 U.S.C. 5845 shall be identified not later than the seventh day following the date the entire manufacturing process has ended for the weapon, or prior to disposition, whichever is sooner. Each part, including a replacement part, defined as a frame or receiver or modular subpart thereof described in paragraph (a)(1)(iii) of this section (other than a machinegun or firearm muffler or firearm silencer) that is not a component part of a complete weapon at the time it is sold, shipped, or otherwise disposed of shall be identified not later than the seventh day following the date the entire manufacturing process has ended for the frame or receiver or modular subpart, or prior to disposition, whichever is sooner.

(B) *Complete National Firearms Act weapons and devices, and machinegun and muffler or silencer parts.* Complete weapons defined as firearms under 26 U.S.C. 5845, and complete muffler or silencer devices, shall be identified not later than close of the next business day following the date the entire manufacturing process has ended for the weapon or device, or prior to disposition, whichever is sooner. Each part or modular subpart defined as a machinegun (*i.e.,* frame or receiver or conversion part), or firearm muffler or firearm silencer, that is not a component part of a complete weapon or complete firearm muffler or silencer device at the time it is sold, shipped, or otherwise disposed of shall be identified not later than close of the next business day following the date the entire manufacturing process has ended for the part, or prior to disposition, whichever is sooner.

(2) *Privately made firearms (PMFs).* Unless previously identified by another licensee in accordance with, and except as otherwise provided by, this section, licensees must legibly and conspicuously identify each privately made firearm or "PMF" received or otherwise acquired (including from a personal collection) not later than the seventh day following the date of receipt or other acquisition, or before the date of disposition (including to a personal collection), whichever is sooner. PMFs must be identified by placing, or causing to be placed under the licensee's direct supervision, an individual serial number on the frame or receiver, which must not duplicate any serial number placed by the licensee on any

other firearm. The serial number must begin with the licensee's abbreviated Federal firearms license number, which is the first three and last five digits, as a prefix to a unique identification number, followed by a hyphen, *e.g.,* "12345678-[unique identification number]". The serial number must be placed in a manner otherwise in accordance with this section, including the requirements that the serial number be at the minimum size and depth, and not susceptible of being readily obliterated, altered, or removed. An acceptable method of identifying a PMF is by placing the serial number on a metal plate that is permanently embedded into a polymer frame or receiver, or other method approved by the Director.

(3) *Meaning of marking terms.* For purposes of this section, the term "identify" means placing marks of identification, the terms "legible" and "legibly" mean that the identification markings (including a unique identification number) use exclusively Roman letters (*e.g.,* A, a, B, b, C, c) and Arabic numerals (*e.g.,* 1, 2, 3), or solely Arabic numerals, and may include a hyphen, and the terms "conspicuous" and "conspicuously" mean that the identification markings are capable of being easily seen with the naked eye during normal handling of the firearm, and are unobstructed by other markings when the complete weapon or device is assembled.

(4) *Exceptions*—(i) *Alternate means of identification.* The Director may authorize other means of identification to identify firearms upon receipt of a letter application or prescribed form from the licensee showing that such other identification is reasonable and will not hinder the effective administration of this part.

(ii) *Destructive devices.* In the case of a destructive device, the Director may authorize other means of identification to identify that weapon upon receipt of a letter application or prescribed form from the licensee. The application shall show that engraving, casting, or stamping (impressing) such a weapon as required by this section would be dangerous or impractical and that the alternate means of identification proposed will not hinder the effective administration of this part.

(iii) *Adoption of identifying markings.* Licensees may adopt existing markings previously placed on a firearm and are not required to mark a serial number or other identifying markings in accordance with this section, as follows:

(A) *Newly manufactured firearms.* Licensed manufacturers may adopt the serial number and other identifying markings previously placed on a firearm by another licensed manufacturer provided the firearm has not been sold, shipped, or otherwise disposed of to a person other than a licensee, and the serial number adopted is not duplicated on any other firearm.

(B) *Remanufactured or imported firearms.* Licensed manufacturers and licensed importers may adopt the serial number or other identifying markings previously placed on a firearm that otherwise meets the requirements of this section that has been sold, shipped, or otherwise disposed of to a person other than a licensee provided that, within the period and in the manner herein prescribed, the licensee legibly and conspicuously places, or causes to be placed, on the frame or receiver either: Their name (or recognized abbreviation), and city and State (or recognized abbreviation) where they maintain their place of business; or their name (or recognized abbreviation) and abbreviated Federal firearms license number, which is the first three and last five digits, individually (*i.e.,* not as a prefix to the serial number adopted) after the letters "FFL", in the following format: "FFL12345678". The serial number adopted must not duplicate any serial number adopted or placed on any other firearm, except that if a licensed importer receives two or more firearms with the same foreign manufacturer's serial number, the importer may adopt the serial number by adding letters or numbers to that serial number, and may include a hyphen.

(C) *Manufacturers performing gunsmithing services.* Licensed manufacturers may adopt the serial number or other identifying markings previously placed on a firearm by another licensee provided the manufacturer is performing services for a nonlicensee as a gunsmith (as defined in §478.11) on existing firearms not for sale or distribution.

(D) *Privately made firearms marked by nonlicensees.* Unless previously identified by another licensee in accordance with this section, licensees may adopt a unique identification number previously placed on a privately made firearm by an unlicensed person, but not duplicated on any other firearm of the licensee, that otherwise meets the identification requirements of this section provided that, within the period and in the manner herein prescribed, the licensee legibly and conspicuously places, or causes to be placed, on the frame or receiver thereof a serial number beginning with their abbreviated Federal firearms license number, which is the first three and last five digits, followed by a hyphen, before the existing unique identification number, *e.g.,* "12345678-[unique identification number]".

(iv)(A) *Firearm muffler or silencer parts transferred between qualified manufacturers for further manufacture or to complete new devices.* Licensed manufacturers qualified under 27 CFR part 479 may transfer a part defined as a firearm muffler or firearm silencer to another qualified manufacturer without immediately identifying or registering such part provided that it is for further manufacture (*i.e.,* machining, coating, *etc.*) or manufacturing a complete muffler or silencer device. Once the new device with such part is completed, the manufacturer who completes the device shall identify, record, and register it in the manner and within the period specified in this part for a complete muffler or silencer device.

(B) *Firearm muffler or silencer replacement parts transferred to qualified manufacturers or dealers to repair existing devices.* Licensed manufacturers qualified under part 479 may transfer a replacement part defined as a firearm muffler or firearm silencer other than a frame or receiver to a qualified manufacturer or dealer without identifying or registering such part provided that it is for repairing a complete muffler or silencer device that was previously identified, recorded, and registered in accordance with this part and part 479.

(v) *Frames or receivers designed before August 24, 2022.* Licensed manufacturers and licensed importers may continue to identify the same component of a firearm (other than a PMF) defined as a frame or receiver as it existed before August 24, 2022 with the same information required to be marked by paragraphs (a)(1)(i) and (a)(1)(ii) of this section that were in effect prior to that date, and any rules necessary to ensure such identification shall remain effective for that purpose. Any frame or receiver with a new design manufactured after August 24, 2022 must be marked with the identifying information and within the period prescribed by this section. For purposes of this paragraph, the term "new design" means that the design of the existing frame or receiver has been functionally modified or altered, as distinguished from performing a cosmetic process that adds to or changes the decoration of the frame or receiver (*e.g.,* painting or engraving), or by adding or replacing stocks, barrels, or accessories to the frame or receiver.

(vi) *Privately made firearms acquired before August 24, 2022.* Licensees shall identify in the manner prescribed by this section, or cause another person to so identify, each privately made firearm received or otherwise acquired (including from a personal collection) by the licensee before August 24, 2022within sixty (60) days from that date, or prior to the date of final disposition (including to a personal collection), whichever is sooner.

(b) *Armor piercing ammunition*—(1) *Marking of ammunition.* Each licensed manufacturer or licensed importer of armor piercing ammunition shall identify such ammunition by means of painting, staining or dying the exterior of the projectile with an opaque black coloring. This coloring must completely cover the point of the projectile and at least 50 percent of that portion of the projectile which is visible when the projectile is loaded into a cartridge case.

(2) *Labeling of packages.* Each licensed manufacturer or licensed importer of armor piercing ammunition shall clearly and conspicuously label each package in which armor piercing ammunition is contained, e.g., each box,

carton, case, or other container. The label shall include the words "ARMOR PIERCING" in block letters at least ¼ inch in height. The lettering shall be located on the exterior surface of the package which contains information concerning the caliber or gauge of the ammunition. There shall also be placed on the same surface of the package in block lettering at least ⅛ inch in height the words "FOR GOVERN-MENTAL ENTITIES OR EXPOR-TATION ONLY." The statements required by this subparagraph shall be on a contrasting background.

(c) *Voluntary classification of firearms and armor piercing ammunition.* The Director may issue a determination (classification) to a person whether an item, including a kit, is a firearm or armor piercing ammunition as defined in this part upon receipt of a written request or form prescribed by the Director. Each such voluntary request or form submitted shall be executed under the penalties of perjury with a complete and accurate description of the item or kit, the name and address of the manufacturer or importer thereof, and a sample of such item or kit for examination. A firearm sample must include all accessories and attachments relevant to such classification as each classification is limited to the firearm in the configuration submitted. Each request for classification of a partially complete, disassembled, or nonfunctional item or kit must contain any associated templates, jigs, molds, equipment, or tools that are made available by the seller or distributor of the item or kit to the purchaser or recipient of the item or kit, and any instructions, guides, or marketing materials if they will be made available by the seller or distributor with the item or kit. Upon completion of the examination, the Director may return the sample to the person who made the request unless a determination is made that return of the sample would be or place the person in violation of law. Submissions of armor piercing ammunition with a projectile or projectile core constructed entirely from one or a combination of tungsten steel alloys, steel, iron, brass, bronze, beryllium copper, or depleted uranium must include a list of known handguns in which the ammunition may be used. Except for the classification of a specific component as the frame or receiver of a particular weapon, a determination made by the Director under this paragraph shall not be deemed by any person to be applicable to or authoritative with respect to any other sample, design, model, or configuration.

(Approved by the Office of Management and Budget under control number 1140–0050)

[T.D. ATF–270, 53 FR 10496, Mar. 31, 1988, as amended by T.D. ATF–363, 60 FR 17454, Apr. 6, 1995; T.D. ATF–383, 61 FR 39321, July 29, 1996; T.D. ATF–396, 63 FR 12646, Mar. 16, 1998; T.D. ATF–461, 66 FR 40600, Aug. 3, 2001; ATF–11F, 73 FR 57241, Oct. 2, 2008; ATF 2014R–42, 84 FR 12094, Apr. 1, 2019; ATF–2021R–05F; 87 FR 24741, Apr. 26, 2022; 87 FR 51250, Aug. 22, 2022]

§ 478.93 Authorized operations by a licensed collector.

The license issued to a collector of curios or relics under the provisions of this part shall cover only transactions by the licensed collector in curios and relics. The collector's license is of no force or effect and a licensed collector is of the same status under the Act and this part as a nonlicensee with respect to (a) any acquisition or disposition of firearms other than curios or relics, or any transportation, shipment, or receipt of firearms other than curios or relics in interstate or foreign commerce, and (b) any transaction with a nonlicensee involving any firearm other than a curio or relic. (See also § 478.50.) A collectors license is not necessary to receive or dispose of ammunition, and a licensed collector is not precluded by law from receiving or disposing of armor piercing ammunition. However, a licensed collector may not dispose of any ammunition to a person prohibited from receiving or possessing ammunition (see § 478.99(c)). Any licensed collector who disposes of armor piercing ammunition must record the disposition as required by § 478.125 (a) and (b).

[T.D. ATF–270, 53 FR 10496, Mar. 31, 1988]

§ 478.94 Sales or deliveries between licensees.

A licensed importer, licensed manufacturer, or licensed dealer selling or otherwise disposing of firearms, and a licensed collector selling or otherwise disposing of curios or relics, to another licensee shall verify the identity and licensed status of the transferee prior to making the transaction. Verification shall be established by the transferee furnishing to the transferor a certified copy of the transferee's license and by such other means as the transferor deems necessary: *Provided,* That it shall not be required (a) for a transferee who has furnished a certified copy of its license to a transferor to again furnish such certified copy to that transferor during the term of the transferee's current license, (b) for a licensee to furnish a certified copy of its license to another licensee if a firearm is being returned either directly or through another licensee to such licensee and (c) for licensees of multi-licensed business organizations to furnish certified copies of their licenses to other licensed locations operated by such organization: *Provided further,* That a multilicensed business organization may furnish to a transferor, in lieu of a certified copy of each license, a list, certified to be true, correct and complete, containing the name, address, license number, and the date of license expiration of each licensed location operated by such organization, and the transferor may sell or otherwise dispose of firearms as provided by this section to any licensee appearing on such list without requiring a certified copy of a license therefrom. A transferor licensee who has the certified information required by this section may sell or dispose of firearms to a licensee for not more than 45 days following the expiration date of the transferee's license.

(Approved by the Office of Management and Budget under control number 1140–0032)

[T.D. ATF–270, 53 FR 10496, Mar. 31, 1988, as amended by ATF–11F, 73 FR 57241, Oct. 2, 2008]

§ 478.95 Certified copy of license.

The license furnished to each person licensed under the provisions of this part contains a purchasing certification statement. This original license may be reproduced and the reproduction then certified by the licensee for use pursuant to § 478.94. If the licensee desires an additional copy of the license for certification (instead of making a reproduction of the original license), the licensee may submit a request, in writing, for a certified copy or copies of the license to the Chief, Federal Firearms Licensing Center. The request must set forth the name, trade name (if any) and address of the licensee, and the number of license copies desired. There is a charge of $1 for each copy. The fee paid for copies of the license must accompany the request for copies. The fee may be paid by cash, or money order or check made payable to the Bureau of Alcohol, Tobacco, Firearms, and Explosives.

(Approved by the Office of Management and Budget under control number 1140–0032)

[T.D. ATF–270, 53 FR 10497, Mar. 31, 1988, as amended by T.D. ATF–290, 54 FR 53055, Dec. 27, 1989; ATF–11F, 73 FR 57241, Oct. 2, 2008; ATF 2014R–42, 84 FR 12094, Apr. 1, 2019]

§ 478.96 Out-of-State and mail order sales.

(a) The provisions of this section shall apply when a firearm is purchased by or delivered to a person not otherwise prohibited by the Act from purchasing or receiving it.

(b) A licensed importer, licensed manufacturer, or licensed dealer may sell a firearm that is not subject to the provisions of § 478.102(a) to a nonlicensee who does not appear in person at the licensee's business premises if the nonlicensee is a resident of the same State in which the licensee's business premises are located, and the nonlicensee furnishes to the licensee the firearms transaction record, Form 4473, required by § 478.124. The nonlicensee shall attach to such record a true copy of any permit or other information required pursuant to any statute of the State and published ordinance applicable to the locality in which he resides. The licensee shall prior to shipment or delivery of the firearm, forward by registered or certified mail (return receipt requested) a copy of the record, Form 4473, to the chief law enforcement officer named on such record, and delay shipment or delivery of the firearm for a period of at least 7 days following receipt by the licensee of the return receipt evidencing delivery of the copy of the record to

such chief law enforcement officer, or the return of the copy of the record to him due to the refusal of such chief law enforcement officer to accept same in accordance with U.S. Postal Service regulations. The original Form 4473, and evidence of receipt or rejection of delivery of the copy of the Form 4473 sent to the chief law enforcement officer shall be retained by the licensee as a part of the records required of him to be kept under the provisions of subpart H of this part.

(c)(1) A licensed importer, licensed manufacturer, or licensed dealer may sell or deliver a rifle or shotgun, and a licensed collector may sell or deliver a rifle or shotgun that is a curio or relic to a nonlicensed resident of a State other than the State in which the licensee's place of business is located if—

(i) The purchaser meets with the licensee in person at the licensee's premises to accomplish the transfer, sale, and delivery of the rifle or shotgun;

(ii) The licensed importer, licensed manufacturer, or licensed dealer complies with the provisions of § 478.102;

(iii) The purchaser furnishes to the licensed importer, licensed manufacturer, or licensed dealer the firearms transaction record, Form 4473, required by § 478.124; and

(iv) The sale, delivery, and receipt of the rifle or shotgun fully comply with the legal conditions of sale in both such States.

(2) For purposes of paragraph (c) of this section, any licensed manufacturer, licensed importer, or licensed dealer is presumed, in the absence of evidence to the contrary, to have had actual knowledge of the State laws and published ordinances of both such States.

(Approved by the Office of Management and Budget under control number 1140–0021)

[33 FR 18555, Dec. 14, 1968. Redesignated at 40 FR 16835, Apr. 15, 1975, and amended by T.D. ATF–48, 44 FR 55842, Sept. 28, 1979; T.D. ATF–241, 51 FR 39620, Oct. 29, 1986; T.D. ATF–270, 53 FR 10497, Mar. 31, 1988; T.D. ATF–354, 59 FR 7112, Feb. 14, 1994; T.D. ATF–415, 63 FR 58278, Oct. 29, 1998; ATF–11F, 73 FR 57241, Oct. 2, 2008]

§ 478.97 Loan or rental of firearms.

(a) A licensee may lend or rent a firearm to any person for temporary use off the premises of the licensee for lawful sporting purposes: *Provided,* That the delivery of the firearm to such person is not prohibited by §478.99(b) or §478.99(c), the licensee complies with the requirements of §478.102, and the licensee records such loan or rental in the records required to be kept by him under Subpart H of this part.

(b) A club, association, or similar organization temporarily furnishing firearms (whether by loan, rental, or otherwise) to participants in a skeet, trap, target, or similar shooting activity for use at the time and place such activity is held does not, unattended by other circumstances, cause such club, association, or similar organization to be engaged in the business of a dealer in firearms or as engaging in firearms transactions. Therefore, licensing and recordkeeping requirements contained in this part pertaining to firearms transactions would not apply to this temporary furnishing of firearms for use on premises on which such an activity is conducted.

[T.D. ATF–415, 63 FR 58278, Oct. 29, 1998]

§478.98 Sales or deliveries of destructive devices and certain firearms.

The sale or delivery by a licensee of any destructive device, machine gun, short-barreled shotgun, or short-barreled rifle, to any person other than another licensee who is licensed under this part to deal in such device or firearm, is prohibited unless the person to receive such device or firearm furnishes to the licensee a sworn statement setting forth

(a) The reasons why there is a reasonable necessity for such person to purchase or otherwise acquire the device or weapon; and

(b) That such person's receipt or possession of the device or weapon would be consistent with public safety. Such sworn statement shall be made on the application to transfer and register the firearm required by Part 479 of this chapter. The sale or delivery of the device or weapon shall not be made until the application for transfer is approved by the Director and returned to the licensee (transferor) as provided in Part 479 of this chapter.

[T.D. ATF–270, 53 FR 10497, Mar. 31, 1988]

§478.99 Certain prohibited sales or deliveries.

(a) *Interstate sales or deliveries.* A licensed importer, licensed manufacturer, licensed dealer, or licensed collector shall not sell or deliver any firearm to any person not licensed under this part and who the licensee knows or has reasonable cause to believe does not reside in (or if a corporation or other business entity, does not maintain a place of business in) the State in which the licensee's place of business or activity is located: *Provided,* That the foregoing provisions of this paragraph (1) shall not apply to the sale or delivery of a rifle or shotgun (curio or relic, in the case of a licensed collector) to a resident of a State other than the State in which the licensee's place of business or collection premises is located if the requirements of §478.96(c) are fully met, and (2) shall not apply to the loan or rental of a firearm to any person for temporary use for lawful sporting purposes (see §478.97).

(b) *Sales or deliveries to underaged persons.* A licensed importer, licensed manufacturer, licensed dealer, or licensed collector shall not sell or deliver (1) any firearm or ammunition to any individual who the importer, manufacturer, dealer, or collector knows or has reasonable cause to believe is less than 18 years of age, and, if the firearm, or ammunition, is other than a shotgun or rifle, or ammunition for a shotgun or rifle, to any individual who the importer, manufacturer, dealer, or collector knows or has reasonable cause to believe is less than 21 years of age, or (2) any firearm to any person in any State where the purchase or possession by such person of such firearm would be in violation of any State law or any published ordinance applicable at the place of sale, delivery, or other disposition, unless the importer, manufacturer, dealer, or collector knows or has reasonable cause to believe that the purchase or possession would not be in violation of such State law or such published ordinance.

(c) *Sales or deliveries to prohibited categories of persons.* A licensed manufacturer, licensed importer, licensed dealer, or licensed collector shall not sell or otherwise dispose of any firearm or ammunition to any person knowing or having reasonable cause to believe that such person:

(1) Is, except as provided by § 478.143, under indictment for, or, except as provided by § 478.144, has been convicted in any court of a crime punishable by imprisonment for a term exceeding 1 year;

(2) Is a fugitive from justice;

(3) Is an unlawful user of or addicted to any controlled substance (as defined in section 102 of the Controlled Substance Act, 21 U.S.C. 802);

(4) Has been adjudicated as a mental defective or has been committed to any mental institution;

(5) Is an alien illegally or unlawfully in the United States or, except as provided in § 478.32(f), is an alien who has been admitted to the United States under a nonimmigrant visa: *Provided,* That the provisions of this paragraph (c)(5) do not apply to any alien who has been lawfully admitted to the United States under a nonimmigrant visa if that alien is—

(i) Admitted to the United States for lawful hunting or sporting purposes or is in possession of a hunting license or permit lawfully issued in the United States;

(ii) An official representative of a foreign government who is either accredited to the United States Government or the Government's mission to an international organization having its headquarters in the United States or en route to or from another country to which that alien is accredited. This exception only applies if the firearm or ammunition is shipped, transported, possessed, or received in the representative's official capacity;

(iii) An official of a foreign government or a distinguished foreign visitor who has been so designated by the Department of State. This exception only applies if the firearm or ammunition is shipped, transported, possessed, or received in the official's or visitor's official capacity, except if the visitor is a private individual who does not have an official capacity; or

(iv) A foreign law enforcement officer of a friendly foreign government entering the United States on official law enforcement business;

(6) Has been discharged from the Armed Forces under dishonorable conditions;

(7) Who, having been a citizen of the United States, has renounced citizenship;

(8) Is subject to a court order that restrains such person from harassing, stalking, or threatening an intimate partner of such person or child of such intimate partner or person, or engaging in other conduct that would place an intimate partner in reasonable fear of bodily injury to the partner or child, except that this paragraph shall only apply to a court order that—

(i) Was issued after a hearing of which such person received actual notice, and at which such person had the opportunity to participate; and

(ii)(A) Includes a finding that such person represents a credible threat to the physical safety of such intimate partner or child; or

(B) By its terms explicitly prohibits the use, attempted use, or threatened use of physical force against such intimate partner or child that would reasonably be expected to cause bodily injury, or

(9) Has been convicted of a misdemeanor crime of domestic violence.

(d) *Manufacture, importation, and sale of armor piercing ammunition by licensed importers and licensed manufacturers.* A licensed importer or licensed manufacturer shall not import or manufacture armor piercing ammunition or sell or deliver such ammunition, except:

(1) For use of the United States or any department or agency thereof or any State or any department, agency, or political subdivision thereof;

(2) For the purpose of exportation; or

(3) For the purpose of testing or experimentation authorized by the Director under the provisions of § 478.149.

(e) *Transfer of armor piercing ammunition by licensed dealers.* A licensed dealer shall not willfully transfer armor piercing ammunition: *Provided,* That armor piercing ammunition received and maintained by the licensed dealer as business inventory prior to August 28, 1986, may be transferred to any department or agency of the United States or any State or political subdivision thereof if a record of such ammunition is maintained in the form and manner prescribed by §478.125(c). Any licensed dealer who violates this paragraph is subject to license revocation. See subpart E of this part. For purposes of this paragraph, the Director shall furnish each licensed dealer information defining which projectiles are considered armor piercing. Such information may not be all-inclusive for purposes of the prohibition on manufacture, importation, or sale or delivery by a manufacturer or importer of such ammunition or 18 U.S.C. 929 relating to criminal misuse of such ammunition.

[T.D. ATF–270, 53 FR 10497, Mar. 31, 1988, as amended by T.D. ATF–363, 60 FR 17454, Apr. 6, 1995; T.D. ATF–401, 63 FR 35523, June 30, 1998; T.D. ATF–471, 67 FR 5426, Feb. 5, 2002; ATF–24F, 77 FR 33629, June 7, 2012]

§478.100 Conduct of business away from licensed premises.

(a)(1) A licensee may conduct business temporarily at a gun show or event as defined in paragraph (b) if the gun show or event is located in the same State specified on the license: *Provided,* That such business shall not be conducted from any motorized or towed vehicle. The premises of the gun show or event at which the licensee conducts business shall be considered part of the licensed premises. Accordingly, no separate fee or license is required for the gun show or event locations. However, licensees shall comply with the provisions of §478.91 relating to posting of licenses (or a copy thereof) while conducting business at the gun show or event.

(2) A licensed importer, manufacturer, or dealer may engage in the business of dealing in curio or relic firearms with another licensee at any location.

(b) A gun show or an event is a function sponsored by any national, State, or local organization, devoted to the collection, competitive use, or other sporting use of firearms, or an organization or association that sponsors functions devoted to the collection, competitive use, or other sporting use of firearms in the community.

(c) Licensees conducting business at locations other than the premises specified on their license under the provisions of paragraph (a) of this section

shall maintain firearms records in the form and manner prescribed by subpart H of this part. In addition, records of firearms transactions conducted at such locations shall include the location of the sale or other disposition, be entered in the acquisition and disposition records of the licensee, and retained on the premises specified on the license.

[T.D. ATF–270, 53 FR 10498, Mar. 31, 1988, as amended by T.D. ATF–401, 63 FR 35523, June 30, 1998]

§478.101 Record of transactions.

Every licensee shall maintain firearms and armor piercing ammunition records in such form and manner as is prescribed by subpart H of this part.

[T.D. ATF–270, 53 FR 10498, Mar. 31, 1988]

§478.102 Sales or deliveries of firearms on and after November 30, 1998.

(a) *Background check.* Except as provided in paragraph (d) of this section, a licensed importer, licensed manufacturer, or licensed dealer (the licensee) shall not sell, deliver, or transfer a firearm to any other person who is not licensed under this part unless the licensee meets the following requirements:

(1) Before the completion of the transfer, the licensee has contacted NICS;

(2)(i) NICS informs the licensee that it has no information that receipt of the firearm by the transferee would be in violation of Federal or State law and provides the licensee with a unique identification number; or

(ii) Three business days (meaning days on which State offices are open) have elapsed from the date the licensee contacted NICS and NICS has not notified the licensee that receipt of the firearm by the transferee would be in violation of law; and

(3) The licensee verifies the identity of the transferee by examining the identification document presented in accordance with the provisions of §478.124(c).

Example for paragraph (a). A licensee contacts NICS on Thursday, and gets a "delayed" response. The licensee does not get a further response from NICS. If State offices are not open on Saturday and Sunday, 3 business days would have elapsed on the following Tuesday. The licensee may transfer the firearm on the next day, Wednesday.

(b) *Transaction number.* In any transaction for which a licensee receives a transaction number from NICS (which shall include either a NICS transaction number or, in States where the State is recognized as a point of contact for NICS checks, a State transaction number), such number shall be recorded on a firearms transaction record, Form 4473, which shall be retained in the records of the licensee in accordance with the provisions of § 478.129. This applies regardless of whether the transaction is approved or denied by NICS, and regardless of whether the firearm is actually transferred.

(c) *Time limitation on NICS checks.* A NICS check conducted in accordance with paragraph (a) of this section may be relied upon by the licensee only for use in a single transaction, and for a period not to exceed 30 calendar days from the date that NICS was initially contacted. If the transaction is not completed within the 30-day period, the licensee shall initiate a new NICS check prior to completion of the transfer.

Example 1 for paragraph (c). A purchaser completes the Form 4473 on December 15, 1998, and a NICS check is initiated by the licensee on that date. The licensee is informed by NICS that the information available to the system does not indicate that receipt of the firearm by the transferee would be in violation of law, and a unique identification number is provided. However, the State imposes a 7-day waiting period on all firearms transactions, and the purchaser does not return to pick up the firearm until January 22, 1999. The licensee must conduct another NICS check before transferring the firearm to the purchaser.

Example 2 for paragraph (c). A purchaser completes the Form 4473 on January 25, 1999, and arranges for the purchase of a single firearm. A NICS check is initiated by the licensee on that date. The licensee is informed by NICS that the information available to the system does not indicate that receipt of the firearm by the transferee would be in violation of law, and a unique identification number is provided. The State imposes a 7-day waiting period on all firearms transactions, and the purchaser returns to pick up the firearm on February 15, 1999. Before the licensee executes the Form 4473, and the firearm is transferred, the purchaser decides to purchase an additional firearm. The transfer of these two firearms is considered a single transaction; accordingly, the licensee may add the second firearm to the Form 4473, and transfer that firearm without conducting another NICS check.

Example 3 for paragraph (c). A purchaser completes a Form 4473 on February 15, 1999. The licensee receives a unique identification number from NICS on that date, the Form 4473 is executed by the licensee, and the firearm is transferred. On February 20, 1999, the purchaser returns to the licensee's premises and wishes to purchase a second firearm. The purchase of the second firearm is a separate transaction; thus, a new NICS check must be initiated by the licensee.

(d) *Exceptions to NICS check.* The provisions of paragraph (a) of this section shall not apply if—

(1) The transferee has presented to the licensee a valid permit or license that—

(i) Allows the transferee to possess, acquire, or carry a firearm;

(ii) Was issued not more than 5 years earlier by the State in which the transfer is to take place; and

(iii) The law of the State provides that such a permit or license is to be issued only after an authorized government official has verified that the information available to such official does not indicate that possession of a firearm by the transferee would be in violation of Federal, State, or local law: *Provided,* That on and after November 30, 1998, the information available to such official includes the NICS;

(2) The firearm is subject to the provisions of the National Firearms Act and has been approved for transfer under 27 CFR part 479; or

(3) On application of the licensee, in accordance with the provisions of § 478.150, the Director has certified that compliance with paragraph (a)(1) of this section is impracticable.

(e) The document referred to in paragraph (d)(1) of this section (or a copy thereof) shall be retained or the required information from the document shall be recorded on the firearms transaction record in accordance with the provisions of § 478.131.

(Approved by the Office of Management and Budget under control number 1140–0045)

[T.D. ATF–415, 63 FR 58279, Oct. 29, 1998, as amended by ATF–11F, 73 FR 57241, Oct. 2, 2008]

§478.103 Posting of signs and written notification to purchasers of handguns.

(a) Each licensed importer, manufacturer, dealer, or collector who delivers a handgun to a nonlicensee shall provide such nonlicensee with written notification as described in paragraph (b) of this section.

(b) The written notification (ATF I 5300.2) required by paragraph (a) of this section shall state as follows:

(1) The misuse of handguns is a leading contributor to juvenile violence and fatalities.

(2) Safely storing and securing firearms away from children will help prevent the unlawful possession of handguns by juveniles, stop accidents, and save lives.

(3) Federal law prohibits, except in certain limited circumstances, anyone under 18 years of age from knowingly possessing a handgun, or any person from transferring a handgun to a person under 18.

(4) A knowing violation of the prohibition against selling, delivering, or otherwise transferring a handgun to a person under the age of 18 is, under certain circumstances, punishable by up to 10 years in prison.

FEDERAL LAW

The Gun Control Act of 1968, 18 U.S.C. Chapter 44, provides in pertinent part as follows:

18 U.S.C. 922(x)

(x)(1) It shall be unlawful for a person to sell, deliver, or otherwise transfer to a person who the transferor knows or has reasonable cause to believe is a juvenile—

(A) a handgun; or

(B) ammunition that is suitable for use only in a handgun.

(2) It shall be unlawful for any person who is a juvenile to knowingly possess—

(A) a handgun; or

(B) ammunition that is suitable for use only in a handgun.

(3) This subsection does not apply to—

(A) a temporary transfer of a handgun or ammunition to a juvenile or to the possession or use of a handgun or ammunition by a juvenile if the handgun and ammunition are possessed and used by the juvenile—

(i) in the course of employment, in the course of ranching or farming related to activities at the residence of the juvenile (or on property used for ranching or farming at which the juvenile, with the permission of the property owner or lessee, is performing activities related to the operation of the farm or ranch), target practice, hunting, or a course of instruction in the safe and lawful use of a handgun;

(ii) with the prior written consent of the juvenile's parent or guardian who is not prohibited by Federal, State, or local law from possessing a firearm, except—

(I) during transportation by the juvenile of an unloaded handgun in a locked container directly from the place of transfer to a place at which an activity described in clause (i) is to take place and transportation by the juvenile of that handgun, unloaded and in a locked container, directly from the place at which such an activity took place to the transferor; or

(II) with respect to ranching or farming activities as described in clause (i) a juvenile may possess and use a handgun or ammunition with the prior written approval of the juvenile's parent or legal guardian and at the direction of an adult who is not prohibited by Federal, State, or local law from possessing a firearm;

(iii) the juvenile has the prior written consent in the juvenile's possession at all times when a handgun is in the possession of the juvenile; and

(iv) in accordance with State and local law;

(B) a juvenile who is a member of the Armed Forces of the United States or the National Guard who possesses or is armed with a handgun in the line of duty;

(C) a transfer by inheritance of title (but not possession) of a handgun or ammunition to a juvenile; or

(D) the possession of a handgun or ammunition by a juvenile taken in defense of the juvenile or other persons against an intruder into the residence of the juvenile or a residence in which the juvenile is an invited guest.

(4) A handgun or ammunition, the possession of which is transferred to a juvenile in circumstances in which the transferor is not in violation of this subsection shall not be subject to permanent confiscation by the Government if its possession by the juvenile subsequently becomes unlawful because of the conduct of the juvenile, but shall be returned to the lawful owner when such handgun or ammunition is no longer required by the Government for the purposes of investigation or prosecution.

(5) For purposes of this subsection, the term "juvenile" means a person who is less than 18 years of age.

(6)(A) In a prosecution of a violation of this subsection, the court shall require the presence of a juvenile defendant's parent or legal guardian at all proceedings.

(B) The court may use the contempt power to enforce subparagraph (A).

(C) The court may excuse attendance of a parent or legal guardian of a juvenile defendant at a proceeding in a prosecution of a violation of this subsection for good cause shown.

18 U.S.C. 924(a)(6)

(6)(A)(i) A juvenile who violates section 922(x) shall be fined under this title, imprisoned not more than 1 year, or both, except that a juvenile described in clause (ii) shall be sentenced to probation on appropriate conditions and shall not be incarcerated unless the juvenile fails to comply with a condition of probation.

(ii) A juvenile is described in this clause if—

(I) the offense of which the juvenile is charged is possession of a handgun or ammunition in violation of section 922(x)(2); and

(II) the juvenile has not been convicted in any court of an offense (including an offense under section 922(x) or a similar State law, but not including any other offense consisting of conduct that if engaged in by an adult would not constitute an offense) or adjudicated as a juvenile delinquent for conduct that if engaged in by an adult would constitute an offense.

(B) A person other than a juvenile who knowingly violates section 922(x)—

(i) shall be fined under this title, imprisoned not more than 1 year, or both; and

(ii) if the person sold, delivered, or otherwise transferred a handgun or ammunition to a juvenile knowing or having reasonable cause to know that the juvenile intended to carry or otherwise possess or discharge or otherwise use the handgun or ammunition in the commission of a crime of violence, shall be fined under this title, imprisoned not more than 10 years, or both.

(c) This written notification shall be delivered to the nonlicensee on ATF I 5300.2, or in the alternative, the same written notification may be delivered to the nonlicensee on another type of written notification, such as a manufacturer's or importer's brochure accompanying the handgun; a manufacturer's or importer's operational manual accompanying the handgun; or a sales receipt or invoice applied to the handgun package or container delivered to a nonlicensee. Any written notification delivered to a nonlicensee other than on ATF I 5300.2 shall include the language set forth in paragraph (b) of this section in its entirety. Any written notification other than ATF I 5300.2 shall be legible, clear, and conspicuous, and the required language

shall appear in type size no smaller than 10-point type.

(d) Except as provided in paragraph (f) of this section, each licensed importer, manufacturer, or dealer who delivers a handgun to a nonlicensee shall display at its licensed premises (including temporary business locations at gun shows) a sign as described in paragraph (e) of this section. The sign shall be displayed where customers can readily see it. Licensed importers, manufacturers, and dealers will be provided with such signs by ATF. Replacement signs may be requested from the ATF Distribution Center.

(e) The sign (ATF I 5300.1) required by paragraph (d) of this section shall state as follows:

(1) The misuse of handguns is a leading contributor to juvenile violence and fatalities.

(2) Safely storing and securing firearms away from children will help prevent the unlawful possession of handguns by juveniles, stop accidents, and save lives.

(3) Federal law prohibits, except in certain limited circumstances, anyone under 18 years of age from knowingly possessing a handgun, or any person from transferring a handgun to a person under 18.

(4) A knowing violation of the prohibition against selling, delivering, or otherwise transferring a handgun to a person under the age of 18 is, under certain circumstances, punishable by up to 10 years in prison.

NOTE: ATF I 5300.2 provides the complete language of the statutory prohibitions and exceptions provided in 18 U.S.C. 922(x) and the penalty provisions of 18 U.S.C. 924(a)(6). The Federal firearms licensee posting this sign will provide you with a copy of this publication upon request. Requests for additional copies of ATF I 5300.2 should be submitted to the ATF Distribution Center (*http://www.atf.gov*) or made by calling (202) 648–6420.

(f) The sign required by paragraph (d) of this section need not be posted on the premises of any licensed importer, manufacturer, or dealer whose only dispositions of handguns to nonlicensees are to nonlicensees who do not appear at the licensed premises and the dispositions otherwise comply with the provisions of this part.

[T.D. ATF–402, 63 FR 37742, July 13, 1998, as amended by ATF 2013R–9F, 79 FR 46692, Aug. 11, 2014]

§478.104 Secure gun storage or safety device.

(a) Any person who applies to be a licensed firearms dealer must certify on ATF Form 7 (5310.12), Application for Federal Firearms License, that compatible secure gun storage or safety devices will be available at any place where firearms are sold under the license to nonlicensed individuals (subject to the exception that in any case in which a secure gun storage or safety device is temporarily unavailable because of theft, casualty, loss, consumer sales, backorders from a manufacturer, or any other similar reason beyond the control of the licensee, the dealer shall not be considered in violation of the requirement to make available such a device).

(b) Any person who applies to be a licensed firearms importer or a licensed manufacturer and will be engaged in business on the licensed premises as a dealer in the same type of firearms authorized by the license to be imported or manufactured must make the certification required under paragraph (a) of this section.

(c) Each licensee described in this section must have compatible secure gun storage or safety devices available at any place in which firearms are sold under the license to persons who are not licensees. However, such licensee shall not be considered to be in violation of this requirement if a secure gun storage or safety device is temporarily unavailable because of theft, casualty loss, consumer sales, backorders from a manufacturer, or any other similar reason beyond the control of the licensee.

[ATF 24P, 87 FR 193, Jan. 4, 2022]

Subpart G—Importation

§478.111 General.

(a) Section 922(a)(3) of the Act makes it unlawful, with certain exceptions not pertinent here, for any person other than a licensee to transport into or receive in the State where the person resides any firearm purchased or otherwise obtained by the person outside of that State. However, section 925(a)(4) provides a limited exception for the transportation, shipment, receipt or importation of certain firearms and ammunition by certain members of the United States Armed Forces. Section 922(1) of the Act makes it unlawful for any person knowingly to import or bring into the United States or any possession thereof any firearm or ammunition except as provided by section 925(d) of the Act, which section provides standards for importing or bringing firearms or ammunition into the United States. Section 925(d) also provides standards for importing or bringing firearm barrels into the United States. Accordingly, no firearm, firearm barrel, or ammunition may be imported or brought into the United States except as provided by this part.

(b) Where a firearm, firearm barrel, or ammunition is imported and the authorization for importation required by this subpart has not been obtained by the person importing same, such person shall:

(1) Store, at the person's expense, such firearm, firearm barrel, or ammunition at a facility designated by U.S Customs or the Director of Industry Operations to await the issuance of the required authorization or other disposition; or

(2) Abandon such firearm, firearm barrel, or ammunition to the U.S. Government; or

(3) Export such firearm, firearm barrel, or ammunition.

(c) Any inquiry relative to the provisions or procedures under this subpart, other than that pertaining to the payment of customs duties or the release from Customs custody of firearms, firearm barrels, or ammunition authorized by the Director to be imported, shall be directed to the Director of Industry Operations for reply.

[T.D. ATF–270, 53 FR 10498, Mar. 31, 1988]

§478.112 Importation by a licensed importer.

(a) No firearm, firearm barrel, or ammunition shall be imported or brought into the United States by a licensed importer (as defined in §478.11) unless the Director has authorized the importation of the firearm, firearm barrel, or ammunition.

(b)(1) An application for a permit, ATF Form 6—Part I, to import or bring a firearm, firearm barrel, or ammunition into the United States or a possession thereof under this section must be filed, in triplicate, with the Director. The application must be signed and dated and must contain the information requested on the form, including:

(i) The name, address, telephone number, and license number (including expiration date) of the importer;

(ii) The country from which the firearm, firearm barrel, or ammunition is to be imported;

(iii) The name and address of the foreign seller and foreign shipper;

(iv) A description of the firearm, firearm barrel, or ammunition to be imported, including:

(A) The name and address of the manufacturer;

(B) The type (*e.g.*, rifle, shotgun, pistol, revolver and, in the case of ammunition only, ball, wadcutter, shot, etc.);

(C) The caliber, gauge, or size;

(D) The model;

(E) The barrel length, if a firearm or firearm barrel (in inches);

(F) The overall length, if a firearm (in inches);

(G) The serial number, if known;

(H) Whether the firearm is new or used;

(I) The quantity;

(J) The unit cost of the firearm, firearm barrel, or ammunition to be imported;

(v) The specific purpose of importation, including final recipient information if different from the importer;

(vi) Verification that if a firearm, it will be identified as required by this part; and

(vii)(A) If a firearm or ammunition imported or brought in for scientific or research purposes, a statement describing such purpose; or

(B) If a firearm or ammunition for use in connection with competition or training pursuant to Chapter 401 of Title 10, U.S.C., a statement describing such intended use; or

(C) If an unserviceable firearm (other than a machine gun) being imported as a curio or museum piece, a description of how it was rendered unserviceable and an explanation of why it is a curio or museum piece; or

(D) If a firearm other than a surplus military firearm, of a type that does not fall within the definition of a firearm under section 5845(a) of the Internal Revenue Code of 1986, and is for sporting purposes, an explanation of why the firearm is generally recognized as particularly suitable for or readily adaptable to sporting purposes; or

(E) If ammunition being imported for sporting purposes, a statement why the ammunition is particularly suitable for or readily adaptable to sporting purposes; or

(F) If a firearm barrel for a handgun, an explanation why the handgun is generally recognized as particularly suitable for or readily adaptable to sporting purposes.

(2)(i) If the Director approves the application, such approved application will serve as the permit to import the firearm, firearm barrel, or ammunition described therein, and importation of such firearms, firearm barrels, or ammunition may continue to be made by the licensed importer under the approved application (permit) during the period specified thereon. The Director will furnish the approved application (permit) to the applicant and retain two copies thereof for administrative use.

(ii) If the Director disapproves the application, the licensed importer will be notified of the basis for the disapproval.

(c) A firearm, firearm barrel, or ammunition imported or brought into the United States or a possession thereof under the provisions of this section by a licensed importer may be released from Customs custody to the licensed importer upon showing that the importer has obtained a permit from the Director for the importation of the firearm, firearm barrel, or ammunition to be released. The importer will also submit to Customs a copy of the export license authorizing the export of the firearm, firearm barrel, or ammunition from the exporting country. If the exporting country does not require issuance of an export license, the importer must submit a certification, under penalty of perjury, to that effect.

(1) In obtaining the release from Customs custody of a firearm, firearm barrel, or ammunition authorized by this section to be imported through the use of a permit, the licensed importer will

prepare ATF Form 6A, in duplicate, and furnish the original ATF Form 6A to the Customs officer releasing the firearm, firearm barrel, or ammunition. The Customs officer will, after certification, forward the ATF Form 6A to the address specified on the form.

(2) The ATF Form 6A must contain the information requested on the form, including:

(i) The name, address, and license number of the importer;

(ii) The name of the manufacturer of the firearm, firearm barrel, or ammunition;

(iii) The country of manufacture;

(iv) The type;

(v) The model;

(vi) The caliber, gauge, or size;

(vii) The serial number in the case of firearms, if known; and

(viii) The number of firearms, firearm barrels, or rounds of ammunition released.

(d) Within 15 days of the date of release from Customs custody, the licensed importer must:

(1) Forward to the address specified on the form a copy of ATF Form 6A on which must be reported any error or discrepancy appearing on the ATF Form 6A certified by Customs and serial numbers if not previously provided on ATF Form 6A;

(2) Pursuant to §478.92, place all required identification data on each imported firearm if same did not bear such identification data at the time of its release from Customs custody; and

(3) Post in the records required to be maintained by the importer under subpart H of this part all required information regarding the importation.

(Paragraph (b) approved by the Office of Management and Budget under control number 1140–0005; paragraphs (c) and (d) approved by the Office of Management and Budget under control number 1140–0007)

[T.D. ATF–270, 53 FR 10498, Mar. 31, 1988, as amended by T.D. ATF–426, 65 FR 38198, June 20, 2000; ATF–11F, 73 FR 57241, Oct. 2, 2008]

§478.113 Importation by other licensees.

(a) No person other than a licensed importer (as defined in §478.11) shall engage in the business of importing firearms or ammunition. Therefore, no firearm or ammunition shall be imported or brought into the United States or a possession thereof by any licensee other than a licensed importer unless the Director issues a permit authorizing the importation of the firearm or ammunition. No barrel for a handgun not generally recognized as particularly suitable for or readily adaptable to sporting purposes shall be imported or brought into the United States or a possession thereof by any person. Therefore, no firearm barrel shall be imported or brought into the United States or possession thereof by any licensee other than a licensed importer unless the Director issues a permit authorizing the importation of the firearm barrel.

(b)(1) An application for a permit, ATF Form 6—Part I, to import or bring a firearm, firearm barrel, or ammunition into the United States or a possession thereof by a licensee, other than a licensed importer, must be filed, in triplicate, with the Director. The application must be signed and dated and must contain the information requested on the form, including:

(i) The name, address, telephone number, and license number (including expiration date) of the applicant;

(ii) The country from which the firearm, firearm barrel, or ammunition is to be imported;

(iii) The name and address of the foreign seller and foreign shipper;

(iv) A description of the firearm, firearm barrel, or ammunition to be imported, including:

(A) The name and address of the manufacturer;

(B) The type (e.g., rifle, shotgun, pistol, revolver and, in the case of ammunition only, ball, wadcutter, shot, etc.);

(C) The caliber, gauge, or size;

(D) The model;

(E) The barrel length, if a firearm or firearm barrel (in inches);

(F) The overall length, if a firearm (in inches);

(G) The serial number, if known;

(H) Whether the firearm is new or used;

(I) The quantity;

(J) The unit cost of the firearm, firearm barrel, or ammunition to be imported;

(v) The specific purpose of importation, including final recipient information if different from the applicant; and

(vi)(A) If a firearm or ammunition imported or brought in for scientific or research purposes, a statement describing such purpose; or

(B) If a firearm or ammunition for use in connection with competition or training pursuant to Chapter 401 of Title 10, U.S.C., a statement describing such intended use; or

(C) If an unserviceable firearm (other than a machine gun) being imported as a curio or museum piece, a description of how it was rendered unserviceable and an explanation of why it is a curio or museum piece; or

(D) If a firearm other than a surplus military firearm, of a type that does not fall within the definition of a firearm under section 5845(a) of the Internal Revenue Code of 1986, and is for sporting purposes, an explanation of why the firearm is generally recognized as particularly suitable for or readily adaptable to sporting purposes; or

(E) If ammunition being imported for sporting purposes, a statement why the ammunition is particularly suitable for or readily adaptable to sporting purposes; or

(F) If a firearm barrel for a handgun, an explanation why the handgun is generally recognized as particularly suitable for or readily adaptable to sporting purposes.

(2)(i) If the Director approves the application, such approved application will serve as the permit to import the firearm, firearm barrel, or ammunition described therein, and importation of such firearms, firearm barrels, or ammunition may continue to be made by the applicant under the approved application (permit) during the period specified thereon. The Director will furnish the approved application (permit) to the applicant and retain two copies thereof for administrative use.

(ii) If the Director disapproves the application, the applicant will be notified of the basis for the disapproval.

(c) A firearm, firearm barrel, or ammunition imported or brought into the United States or a possession thereof under the provisions of this section may be released from Customs custody

to the licensee upon showing that the licensee has obtained a permit from the Director for the importation of the firearm, firearm barrel, or ammunition to be released.

(1) In obtaining the release from Customs custody of a firearm, firearm barrel, or ammunition authorized by this section to be imported through the use of a permit, the licensee will prepare ATF Form 6A, in duplicate, and furnish the original ATF Form 6A to the Customs officer releasing the firearm, firearm barrel, or ammunition. The Customs officer will, after certification, forward the ATF Form 6A to the address specified on the form.

(2) The ATF Form 6A must contain the information requested on the form, including:

(i) The name, address, and license number of the licensee;

(ii) The name of the manufacturer of the firearm, firearm barrel, or ammunition;

(iii) The country of manufacture;

(iv) The type;

(v) The model;

(vi) The caliber, gauge, or size;

(vii) The serial number in the case of firearms; and

(viii) The number of firearms, firearm barrels, or rounds of ammunition released.

(Paragraph (b) approved by the Office of Management and Budget under control number 1140–0005; paragraph (c) approved by the Office of Management and Budget under control number 1140–0007)

[T.D. ATF–270, 53 FR 10499, Mar. 31, 1988, as amended by T.D. ATF–426, 65 FR 38199, June 20, 2000; ATF–11F, 73 FR 57241, Oct. 2, 2008]

§ 478.113a Importation of firearm barrels by nonlicensees.

(a) A permit will not be issued for a firearm barrel for a handgun not generally recognized as particularly suitable for or readily adaptable to sporting purposes. No firearm barrel shall be imported or brought into the United States or possession thereof by any nonlicensee unless the Director issues a permit authorizing the importation of the firearm barrel.

(b)(1) An application for a permit, ATF Form 6—Part I, to import or bring a firearm barrel into the United States or a possession thereof under this section must be filed, in triplicate, with the Director. The application must be signed and dated and must contain the information requested on the form, including:

(i) The name, address, and telephone number of the applicant;

(ii) The country from which the firearm barrel is to be imported;

(iii) The name and address of the foreign seller and foreign shipper;

(iv) A description of the firearm barrel to be imported, including:

(A) The name and address of the manufacturer;

(B) The type (e.g., rifle, shotgun, pistol, revolver);

(C) The caliber, gauge, or size;

(D) The model;

(E) The barrel length (in inches);

(F) The quantity;

(G) The unit cost of the firearm barrel;

(v) The specific purpose of importation, including final recipient information if different from the importer; and

(vi) If a handgun barrel, an explanation of why the barrel is for a handgun that is generally recognized as particularly suitable for or readily adaptable to sporting purposes.

(2)(i) If the Director approves the application, such approved application will serve as the permit to import the firearm barrel, and importation of such firearm barrels may continue to be made by the applicant under the approved application (permit) during the period specified thereon. The Director will furnish the approved application (permit) to the applicant and retain two copies thereof for administrative use.

(ii) If the Director disapproves the application, the applicant will be notified of the basis for the disapproval.

(c) A firearm barrel imported or brought into the United States or a possession thereof under the provisions of this section may be released from Customs custody to the person importing the firearm barrel upon showing that the person has obtained a permit from the Director for the importation of the firearm barrel to be released.

(1) In obtaining the release from Customs custody of a firearm barrel authorized by this section to be imported

through the use of a permit, the person importing the firearm barrel will prepare ATF Form 6A, in duplicate, and furnish the original ATF Form 6A to the Customs officer releasing the firearm barrel. The Customs officer will, after certification, forward the ATF Form 6A to the address specified on the form.

(2) The ATF Form 6A must contain the information requested on the form, including:

(i) The name and address of the person importing the firearm barrel;

(ii) The name of the manufacturer of the firearm barrel;

(iii) The country of manufacture;

(iv) The type;

(v) The model;

(vi) The caliber or gauge of the firearm barrel so released; and

(vii) The number of firearm barrels released.

(Paragraph (b) approved by the Office of Management and Budget under control number 1140–0005; paragraph (c) approved by the Office of Management and Budget under control number 1140–0007)

[T.D. ATF–270, 53 FR 10499, Mar. 31, 1988, as amended by T.D. ATF–426, 65 FR 38200, June 20, 2000; ATF–11F, 73 FR 57241, Oct. 2, 2008]

§478.114 Importation by members of the U.S. Armed Forces.

(a) The Director may issue a permit authorizing the importation of a firearm or ammunition into the United States to the place of residence of any military member of the U.S. Armed Forces who is on active duty outside the United States, or who has been on active duty outside the United States within the 60-day period immediately preceding the intended importation: *Provided,* That such firearm or ammunition is generally recognized as particularly suitable for or readily adaptable to sporting purposes and is intended for the personal use of such member.

(1) An application for a permit, ATF Form 6—Part II, to import a firearm or ammunition into the United States under this section must be filed, in triplicate, with the Director. The application must be signed and dated and must contain the information requested on the form, including:

(i) The name, current address, and telephone number of the applicant;

(ii) Certification that the transportation, receipt, or possession of the firearm or ammunition to be imported would not constitute a violation of any provision of the Act or of any State law or local ordinance at the place of the applicant's residence;

(iii) The country from which the firearm or ammunition is to be imported;

(iv) The name and address of the foreign seller and foreign shipper;

(v) A description of the firearm or ammunition to be imported, including:

(A) The name and address of the manufacturer;

(B) The type (e.g., rifle, shotgun, pistol, revolver and, in the case of ammunition only, ball, wadcutter, shot, etc.);

(C) The caliber, gauge, or size;

(D) The model;

(E) The barrel length, if a firearm (in inches);

(F) The overall length, if a firearm (in inches);

(G) The serial number;

(H) Whether the firearm is new or used;

(I) The quantity;

(J) The unit cost of the firearm or ammunition to imported;

(vi) The specific purpose of importation, that is—

(A) That the firearm or ammunition being imported is for the personal use of the applicant; and

(B) If a firearm, a statement that it is not a surplus military firearm, that it does not fall within the definition of a firearm under section 5845(a) of the Internal Revenue Code of 1986, and an explanation of why the firearm is generally recognized as particularly suitable for or readily adaptable to sporting purposes; or

(C) If ammunition, a statement why it is generally recognized as particularly suitable for or readily adaptable to sporting purposes; and

(vii) The applicant's date of birth;

(viii) The applicant's rank or grade;

(ix) The applicant's place of residence;

(x) The applicant's present foreign duty station or last foreign duty station, as the case may be;

(xi) The date of the applicant's reassignment to a duty station within the United States, if applicable; and

(xii) The military branch of which the applicant is a member.

(2)(i) If the Director approves the application, such approved application will serve as the permit to import the firearm or ammunition described therein. The Director will furnish the approved application (permit) to the applicant and retain two copies thereof for administrative use.

(ii) If the Director disapproves the application, the applicant will be notified of the basis for the disapproval.

(b) Except as provided in paragraph (b)(3) of this section, a firearm or ammunition imported into the United States under the provisions of this section by the applicant may be released from Customs custody to the applicant upon showing that the applicant has obtained a permit from the Director for the importation of the firearm or ammunition to be released.

(1) In obtaining the release from Customs custody of a firearm or ammunition authorized by this section to be imported through the use of a permit, the military member of the U.S. Armed Forces will prepare ATF Form 6A and furnish the completed form to the Customs officer releasing the firearm or ammunition. The Customs officer will, after certification, forward the ATF Form 6A to the address specified on the form.

(2) The ATF Form 6A must contain the information requested on the form, including:

(i) The name and address of the military member;

(ii) The name of the manufacturer of the firearm or ammunition;

(iii) The country of manufacture;

(iv) The type;

(v) The model;

(vi) The caliber, gauge, or size;

(vii) The serial number in the case of firearms; and

(viii) If applicable, the number of firearms or rounds of ammunition released.

(3) When such military member is on active duty outside the United States, the military member may appoint, in writing, an agent to obtain the release of the firearm or ammunition from

Customs custody for such member. Such agent will present sufficient identification of the agent and the written authorization to act on behalf of such military member to the Customs officer who is to release the firearm or ammunition.

(c) Firearms determined by the Department of Defense to be war souvenirs may be imported into the United States by the military members of the U.S. Armed Forces under such provisions and procedures as the Department of Defense may issue.

(Paragraph (a) approved by the Office of Management and Budget under control number 1140–0006; paragraph (b) approved by the Office of Management and Budget under control number 1140–0007)

[T.D. ATF–270, 53 FR 10500, Mar. 31, 1988, as amended by T.D. ATF–426, 65 FR 38200, June 20, 2000; ATF–11F, 73 FR 57241, Oct. 2, 2008]

§478.115 Exempt importation.

(a) Firearms and ammunition may be brought into the United States or any possession thereof by any person who can establish to the satisfaction of Customs that such firearm or ammunition was previously taken out of the United States or any possession thereof by such person. Registration on Customs Form 4457 or on any other registration document available for this purpose may be completed before departure from the United States at any U.S. customhouse or any office of an Director of Industry Operations. A bill of sale or other commercial document showing transfer of the firearm or ammunition in the United States to such person also may be used to establish proof that the firearm or ammunition was taken out of the United States by such person. Firearms and ammunition furnished under the provisions of section 925(a)(3) of the Act to military members of the U.S. Armed Forces on active duty outside of the United States also may be imported into the United States or any possession thereof by such military members upon establishing to the satisfaction of Customs that such firearms and ammunition were so obtained.

(b) Firearms, firearm barrels, and ammunition may be imported or brought into the United States by or for the United States or any department or agency thereof, or any State or any department, agency, or political subdivision thereof. A firearm, firearm barrel or ammunition imported or brought into the United States under this paragraph may be released from Customs custody upon a showing that the firearm, firearm barrel or ammunition is being imported or brought into the United States by or for such a governmental entity.

(c) The provisions of this subpart shall not apply with respect to the importation into the United States of any antique firearm.

(d) Firearms and ammunition are not imported into the United States, and the provisions of this subpart shall not apply, when such firearms and ammunition are brought into the United States by:

(1) A nonresident of the United States for legitimate hunting or lawful sporting purposes, and such firearms and such ammunition as remains following such shooting activity are to be taken back out of the territorial limits of the United States by such person upon conclusion of the shooting activity;

(2) Foreign military personnel on official assignment to the United States who bring such firearms or ammunition into the United States for their exclusive use while on official duty in the United States, and such firearms and unexpended ammunition are taken back out of the territorial limits of the United States by such foreign military personnel when they leave the United States;

(3) Official representatives of foreign governments who are accredited to the U.S. Government or are en route to or from other countries to which accredited, and such firearms and unexpended ammunition are taken back out of the territorial limits of the United States by such official representatives of foreign governments when they leave the United States;

(4) Officials of foreign governments and distinguished foreign visitors who have been so designated by the Department of State, and such firearms and unexpended ammunition are taken back out of the territorial limits of the United States by such officials of foreign governments and distinguished

foreign visitors when they leave the United States; and

(5) Foreign law enforcement officers of friendly foreign governments entering the United States on official law enforcement business, and such firearms and unexpended ammunition are taken back out of the territorial limits of the United States by such foreign law enforcement officers when they leave the United States.

(e) Notwithstanding the provisions of paragraphs (d) (1), (2), (3), (4) and (5) of this section, the Secretary of the Treasury or his delegate may in the interest of public safety and necessity require a permit for the importation or bringing into the United States of any firearms or ammunition.

[33 FR 18555, Dec. 14, 1968. Redesignated at 40 FR 16835, Apr. 15, 1975, and amended by T.D. ATF–58, 44 FR 32367, June 6, 1979; T.D. ATF– 270, 53 FR 10500, Mar. 31, 1988; T.D. ATF–471, 67 FR 5426, Feb. 5, 2002]

§ 478.116 Conditional importation.

The Director shall permit the conditional importation or bringing into the United States or any possession thereof of any firearm, firearm barrel, or ammunition for the purpose of examining and testing the firearm, firearm barrel, or ammunition in connection with making a determination as to whether the importation or bringing in of such firearm, firearm barrel, or ammunition will be authorized under this part. An application on ATF Form 6 for such conditional importation shall be filed, in duplicate, with the Director. The Director may impose conditions upon any importation under this section including a requirement that the firearm, firearm barrel, or ammunition be shipped directly from Customs custody to the Director and that the person importing or bringing in the firearm, firearm barrel, or ammunition must agree to either export the firearm, firearm barrel, or ammunition or destroy same if a determination is made that the firearm, firearm barrel, or ammunition may not be imported or brought in under this part. A firearm, firearm barrel, or ammunition imported or brought into the United States or any possession thereof under the provisions of this section shall be released from Customs custody upon the payment of customs duties, if applicable, and in the manner prescribed in the conditional authorization issued by the Director.

[T.D. ATF–383, 61 FR 39321, July 29, 1996, as amended by ATF 2014R–42, 84 FR 12094, Apr. 1, 2019]

§ 478.117 Function outside a customs territory.

In the insular possessions of the United States outside customs territory, the functions performed by U.S. Customs officers under this subpart within a customs territory may be performed by the appropriate authorities of a territorial government or other officers of the United States who have been designated to perform such functions. For the purpose of this subpart, the term customs territory means the United States, the District of Columbia, and the Commonwealth of Puerto Rico.

§ 478.118 Importation of certain firearms classified as curios or relics.

Notwithstanding any other provision of this part, a licensed importer may import all rifles and shotguns classified by the Director as curios or relics, and all handguns classified by the Director as curios or relics that are determined to be generally recognized as particularly suitable for or readily adaptable to sporting purposes. The importation of such curio or relic firearms must be in accordance with the applicable importation provisions of this part and the importation provisions of 27 CFR part 447. Curios or relics which fall within the definition of "firearm" under 26 U.S.C. 5845(a) must also meet the importation provisions of 27 CFR part 479 before they may be imported.

[T.D. ATF–202, 50 FR 14383, Apr. 12, 1985]

§ 478.119 [Reserved]

§ 478.120 Firearms or ammunition imported by or for a nonimmigrant alien.

(a) *General.* A nonimmigrant alien temporarily importing or bringing firearms or ammunition into the United States for lawful hunting or sporting purposes must first obtain an approved ATF Form 6NIA (5330.3D).

(b) *Aliens admitted to the United States under a nonimmigrant visa.* (1) Any alien lawfully admitted to the United States under a nonimmigrant visa who completes an ATF Form 6NIA to import firearms or ammunition into the United States, or any licensee who completes an ATF Form 6 to import firearms or ammunition for such nonimmigrant alien, must attach applicable documentation to the Form 6NIA or Form 6 establishing the nonimmigrant alien falls within an exception specified in 18 U.S.C. 922(y)(2) (e.g., a hunting license or permit lawfully issued in the United States) or has obtained a waiver as specified in 18 U.S.C. 922(y)(3).

(2) Aliens admitted to the United States under a nonimmigrant visa importing or bringing firearms or ammunition into the United States must provide the United States Customs and Border Protection with applicable documentation (e.g., a hunting license or permit lawfully issued in the United States) establishing the nonimmigrant alien falls within an exception specified in 18 U.S.C. 922(y)(2) or has obtained a waiver as specified in 18 U.S.C. 922(y)(3) before the firearm or ammunition may be imported. This provision applies in all cases, whether or not a Form 6 is needed to bring the firearms or ammunition into the United States.

(Approved by the Office of Management and Budget under control number 1140–0060)

[ATF–24F, 77 FR 33629, June 7, 2012]

Subpart H—Records

§478.121 General.

(a) The records pertaining to firearms transactions prescribed by this part shall be retained on the licensed premises in the manner prescribed by this subpart and for the length of time prescribed by §478.129. The records pertaining to ammunition prescribed by this part shall be retained on the licensed premises in the manner prescribed by §478.125.

(b) ATF officers may, for the purposes and under the conditions prescribed in §478.23, enter the premises of any licensed importer, licensed manufacturer, licensed dealer, or licensed collector for the purpose of examining or inspecting any record or document required by or obtained under this part. Section 923(g) of the Act requires licensed importers, licensed manufacturers, licensed dealers, and licensed collectors to make such records available for such examination or inspection during business hours or, in the case of licensed collectors, hours of operation, as provided in §478.23.

(c) Each licensed importer, licensed manufacturer, licensed dealer, and licensed collector shall maintain such records of importation, production, shipment, receipt, sale, or other disposition, whether temporary or permanent, of firearms and such records of the disposition of ammunition as the regulations contained in this part prescribe. Section 922(m) of the Act makes it unlawful for any licensed importer, licensed manufacturer, licensed dealer, or licensed collector knowingly to make any false entry in, to fail to make appropriate entry in, or to fail to properly maintain any such record.

(d) For recordkeeping requirements for sales by licensees at gun shows see §478.100(c).

(Information collection requirements in paragraph (a) approved by the Office of Management and Budget under control number 1140–0020; information collection requirements in paragraphs (b) and (c) approved by the Office of Management and Budget under control number 1140–0032)

[33 FR 18555, Dec. 14, 1968. Redesignated at 40 FR 16835, Apr. 15, 1975, and amended by T.D. ATF–191, 49 FR 46891, Nov. 29, 1984; T.D. ATF–208, 50 FR 26703, June 28, 1985; T.D. ATF–270, 53 FR 10501, Mar. 31, 1988; ATF–11F, 73 FR 57241, Oct. 2, 2008]

§478.122 Records maintained by importers.

(a) Except for adjustment or repair of a firearm that is returned to the person from whom it was received on the same day, each licensed importer shall record the name of the importer and manufacturer, type, model, caliber or gauge, country or countries of manufacture (if imported), and serial number (including any associated license number either as a prefix, or if remanufactured or imported, separated by a semicolon) of each firearm imported or otherwise acquired (including a frame or receiver to be disposed of separately), the date of such importation or other acquisition, and if otherwise acquired, the name and address, or the name and license number of the person from whom it was received. Privately made firearms shall be recorded in accordance with § 478.125(i). The information required by this paragraph shall be recorded not later than 15 days following the date of importation or other acquisition in a format containing the applicable columns set forth in paragraph (b) of this section.

(b) A record of each firearm disposed of by an importer and a separate record of armor piercing ammunition dispositions to governmental entities, for exportation, or for testing or experimentation authorized under the provisions of § 478.149 shall be maintained by the licensed importer on the licensed premises. The record shall show the date of such sale or other disposition, and the name and license number of the licensee to whom the firearm was transferred, or if disposed of to a non-licensee, the name and address of the person, or the transaction number of the Firearms Transaction Record, Form 4473, if the licensee transferring the firearm sequentially numbers the Forms 4473 and files them numerically. In the event the licensee records a duplicate entry with the same firearm and acquisition information, whether to close out an old record book or for any other reason, the licensee shall record a reference to the date and location of the subsequent entry (*e.g.,* date of new entry, book name/number, page number, and line number) as the disposition. The information required by this paragraph (b) shall be entered in the proper record book not later than the seventh day following the date of the transaction. Such information shall be recorded in formats containing the applicable columns below, except that for armor piercing ammunition, the information and format shall also include the quantity of projectiles:

TABLE 1 TO PARAGRAPH (b)—FIREARMS IMPORTER OR MANUFACTURER ACQUISITION AND DISPOSITION RECORD

Description of firearm						Import/manufacture/acquisition		Disposition		
Importer, manufacturer, and/or "privately made firearm" (PMF) (if privately made in the U.S.)	Type	Model	Caliber or gauge	Country or countries of manufacture (if imported)	Serial No.	Date of import, manufacture, or acquisition	Name and address of nonlicensee; or if licensee, name and license No. (if acquired)	Date of disposition	Name	Address of nonlicensee; license No. of licensee; or Form 4473 transaction No. if such forms filed numerically

TABLE 2 TO PARAGRAPH (b)—ARMOR PIERCING AMMUNITION IMPORTER OR MANUFACTURER DISPOSITION RECORD

Date of disposition	Manufacturer	Caliber or gauge	Quantity of projectiles	Transferee—name and address

(c) The Director may authorize alternate records to be maintained by a licensed importer to record the acquisition and disposition of firearms and armor piercing ammunition when it is shown by the licensed importer that such alternate records will accurately and readily disclose the information required by this section. A licensed importer who proposes to use alternate records shall submit a letter application to the Director and shall describe the proposed alternate records and the need therefor. Such alternate records shall not be employed by the licensed importer until approval in such regard is received from the Director.

[ATF–2021R–05F, 87 FR 24743, Apr. 26, 2022]

§478.123 Records maintained by manufacturers.

(a) Except for adjustment or repair of a firearm that is returned to the person from whom it was received on the same day, each licensed manufacturer shall record the name of the manufacturer and importer (if any), type, model, caliber or gauge, and serial number (including any associated license number either as a prefix, or if remanufactured or imported, separated by a semicolon) of each firearm manufactured or otherwise acquired (including a frame or receiver to be disposed of separately), the date of such manufacture or other acquisition, and if otherwise acquired, the name and address or the name and license number of the person from whom it was received. Privately made firearms shall be recorded in accordance with §478.125(i). The information required by this paragraph shall, in the case of a firearm other than a firearm defined in 26 U.S.C. 5845, be recorded not later than the seventh day following the date of such manufacture or other acquisition. In the case of a firearm defined in 26 U.S.C. 5845, such information shall be recorded by close of the next business day following the

date of such manufacture or other acquisition, except that, when a commercial record is held by the licensed manufacturer separately from other commercial documents and readily available for inspection, containing all acquisition information required for the record, the period for making the required entry into the record may be delayed not to exceed the seventh day following the date of receipt. The information required by this paragraph shall be recorded in a format containing the applicable columns prescribed by §478.122.

(b) A record of each firearm disposed of by a manufacturer and a separate record of armor piercing ammunition dispositions to governmental entities, for exportation, or for testing or experimentation authorized under the provisions of §478.149 shall be maintained by the licensed manufacturer on the licensed premises. The record shall show the date of such sale or other disposition, and the name and license number of the licensee to whom the firearms were transferred, or if disposed of to a nonlicensee, the name and address of the person, or the transaction number of the Firearms Transaction Record, Form 4473, if the licensee transferring the firearm sequentially numbers the Forms 4473 and files them numerically. In the event the licensee records a duplicate entry with the same firearm and acquisition information, whether to close out an old record book or for any other reason, the licensee shall record a reference to the date and location of the subsequent entry (e.g., date of new entry, book name/number, page number, and line number) as the disposition. The information required by this paragraph shall be entered in the proper record book not later than the seventh day following the date of the transaction. Such information shall be recorded in a format containing the applicable columns prescribed by §478.122, except that for armor piercing ammunition, the information and format shall also include the quantity of projectiles.

(c) The Director may authorize alternate records to be maintained by a licensed manufacturer to record the acquisition or disposition of firearms and armor piercing ammunition when it is shown by the licensed manufacturer that such alternate records will accurately and readily disclose the information required by this section. A licensed manufacturer who proposes to use alternate records shall submit a letter application to the Director and shall describe the proposed alternate record and the need therefor. Such alternate records shall not be employed by the licensed manufacturer until approval in such regard is received from the Director.

[ATF–2021R–05F, 87 FR 24744, Apr. 26, 2022]

§478.124 Firearms transaction record.

(a) A licensed importer, licensed manufacturer, or licensed dealer shall not sell or otherwise dispose, temporarily or permanently, of any firearm to any person, other than another licensee, unless the licensee records the transaction on a firearms transaction record, Form 4473: *Provided,* That a firearms transaction record, Form 4473, shall not be required to record the disposition made of a firearm delivered to a licensee for the sole purpose of repair or customizing when such firearm or a replacement firearm is returned to the person from whom received.

(b) A licensed manufacturer, licensed importer, or licensed dealer shall retain in alphabetical (by name of purchaser), chronological (by date of disposition), or numerical (by transaction number) order, and as a part of the required records, each Form 4473 obtained in the course of transferring custody of the firearms.

(c)(1) Prior to making an over-the-counter transfer of a firearm to a non-licensee who is a resident of the State in which the licensee's business premises is located, the licensed importer, licensed manufacturer, or licensed dealer so transferring the firearm shall obtain a Form 4473 from the transferee showing the transferee's name, sex,

residence address (including county or similar political subdivision), date and place of birth; height, weight and race of the transferee; the transferee's country of citizenship; the transferee's INS-issued alien number or admission number; the transferee's State of residence; and certification by the transferee that the transferee is not prohibited by the Act from transporting or shipping a firearm in interstate or foreign commerce or receiving a firearm which has been shipped or transported in interstate or foreign commerce or possessing a firearm in or affecting commerce.

(2) In order to facilitate the transfer of a firearm and enable NICS to verify the identity of the person acquiring the firearm, ATF Form 4473 also requests certain optional information. This information includes the transferee's social security number. Such information may help avoid the possibility of the transferee being misidentified as a felon or other prohibited person.

(3) After the transferee has executed the Form 4473, the licensee:

(i) Shall verify the identity of the transferee by examining the identification document (as defined in §478.11) presented, and shall note on the Form 4473 the type of identification used;

(ii) [Reserved]

(iii) Must, in the case of a transferee who is an alien admitted to the United States under a nonimmigrant visa who states that he or she falls within an exception to, or has a waiver from, the prohibition in section 922(g)(5)(B) of the Act, have the transferee present applicable documentation establishing the exception or waiver, note on the Form 4473 the type of documentation provided, and attach a copy of the documentation to the Form 4473; and

(iv) Shall comply with the requirements of §478.102 and record on the form the date on which the licensee contacted the NICS, as well as any response provided by the system, including any identification number provided by the system.

(4) The licensee shall identify the firearm to be transferred by listing on the Form 4473 the name of the manufacturer, the name of the importer (if any), the type, model, caliber or gauge, and the serial number (including any

associated license number either as a prefix, or if remanufactured or imported, separated by a semicolon) of the firearm. Where no manufacturer name has been identified on a privately made firearm, the words "privately made firearm" (or abbreviation "PMF") shall be recorded as the name of the manufacturer.

(5) The licensee shall sign and date the form if the licensee does not know or have reasonable cause to believe that the transferee is disqualified by law from receiving the firearm and transfer the firearm described on the Form 4473.

(d) Prior to making an over-the-counter transfer of a shotgun or rifle under the provisions contained in §478.96(c) to a nonlicensee who is not a resident of the State in which the licensee's business premises is located, the licensee so transferring the shotgun or rifle, and such transferee, shall comply with the requirements of paragraph (c) of this section.

(e) Prior to making a transfer of a firearm to any nonlicensee who is not a resident of the State in which the licensee's business premises is located, and such nonlicensee is acquiring the firearm by loan or rental from the licensee for temporary use for lawful sporting purposes, the licensed importer, licensed manufacturer, or licensed dealer so furnishing the firearm, and such transferee, shall comply with the provisions of paragraph (c) of this section.

(f) Form 4473 shall be submitted, in duplicate, to a licensed importer, licensed manufacturer, or licensed dealer by a transferee who is purchasing or otherwise acquiring a firearm by other than an over-the-counter transaction, who is not subject to the provisions of §478.102(a), and who is a resident of the State in which the licensee's business premises are located. The Form 4473 shall show the name, address, date and place of birth, height, weight, and race of the transferee; and the title, name, and address of the principal law enforcement officer of the locality to which the firearm will be delivered. The transferee also must date and execute the sworn statement contained on the form showing, in case the firearm to be transferred is a firearm other than a shotgun or rifle, the transferee is 21 years or more of age; in case the firearm to be transferred is a shotgun or rifle, the transferee is 18 years or more of age; whether the transferee is a citizen of the United States; the transferee's State of residence; the transferee is not prohibited by the provisions of the Act from shipping or transporting a firearm in interstate or foreign commerce or receiving a firearm which has been shipped or transported in interstate or foreign commerce or possessing a firearm in or affecting commerce; and the transferee's receipt of the firearm would not be in violation of any statute of the State or published ordinance applicable to the locality in which the transferee resides. The licensee shall identify the firearm to be transferred by listing in the Forms 4473 the name of the manufacturer, the name of the importer (if any), the type, model, caliber or gauge, and the serial number of the firearm to be transferred. Where no manufacturer name has been identified on a privately made firearm, the words "privately made firearm" (or abbreviation "PMF") shall be recorded as the name of the manufacturer. The licensee shall prior to shipment or delivery of the firearm to such transferee, forward by registered or certified mail (return receipt requested) a copy of the Form 4473 to the principal law enforcement officer named in the Form 4473 by the transferee, and shall delay shipment or delivery of the firearm to the transferee for a period of at least 7 days following receipt by the licensee of the return receipt evidencing delivery of the copy of the Form 4473 to such principal law enforcement officer, or the return of the copy of the Form 4473 to the licensee due to the refusal of such principal law enforcement officer to accept same in accordance with U.S. Postal Service regulations. The original Form 4473, and evidence of receipt or rejection of delivery of the copy of the Form 4473 sent to the principal law enforcement officer, shall be retained by the licensee as a part of the records required to be kept under this subpart.

(g) A licensee who sells or otherwise disposes of a firearm to a nonlicensee who is other than an individual, shall obtain from the transferee the information required by this section from an individual authorized to act on behalf of the transferee. In addition, the licensee shall obtain from the individual acting on behalf of the transferee a written statement, executed under the penalties of perjury, that the firearm is being acquired for the use of and will be the property of the transferee, and showing the name and address of that transferee.

(h) The requirements of this section shall be in addition to any other recordkeeping requirement contained in this part.

(i) A licensee may obtain, upon request, an emergency supply of Forms 4473 from any Director of Industry Operations. For normal usage, a licensee should request a year's supply from the ATF Distribution Center (See §478.21).

(Paragraph (c) approved by the Office of Management and Budget under control numbers 1140–0045, 1140–0020, and 1140–0060; paragraph (f) approved by the Office of Management and Budget under control number 1140–0021; all other recordkeeping approved by the Office of Management and Budget under control number 1140–0020)

[33 FR 18555, Dec. 14, 1968, as amended by T.D. ATF–172, 49 FR 14942, Apr. 16, 1984; T.D. ATF–241, 51 FR 39625, Oct. 29, 1986; T.D. ATF–270, 53 FR 10502, Mar. 31, 1988; T.D. ATF–389, 62 FR 19444, Apr. 21, 1997; T.D. ATF–415, 63 FR 58279, Oct. 29, 1998; T.D. ATF–471, 67 FR 5426, Feb. 5, 2002; ATF–11F, 73 FR 57241, Oct. 2, 2008; ATF–24F and 22I, 77 FR 33630, 33634, June 7, 2012; ATF–2021R–05F, 87 FR 24744, Apr. 26, 2022]

§478.125 Record of receipt and disposition.

(a) *Armor piercing ammunition sales by licensed collectors to nonlicensees.* The sale or other disposition of armor piercing ammunition by licensed collectors shall be recorded in a bound record at the time a transaction is made. The bound record shall be maintained in chronological order by date of sale or disposition of the armor piercing ammunition, and shall be retained on the licensed premises of the licensee for a period not less than two years following the date of the recorded sale or disposition of the armor piercing ammunition. The bound record entry shall show:

(1) The date of the transaction;

(2) The name of the manufacturer;

(3) The caliber or gauge;

(4) The quantity of projectiles;

(5) The name, address, and date of birth of the nonlicensee; and

(6) The method used to establish the identity of the armor piercing ammunition purchaser.

The format required for the bound record is as follows:

DISPOSITION RECORD OF ARMOR PIERCING AMMUNITION

| | | | | Purchaser | | Enter a (x) in the "known" column if purchaser is personally known to you. Otherwise, establish the purchaser's identification | | |
Date	Manufacturer	Caliber or gauge	Quantity of projectiles	Name and address	Date of birth	Known	Driver's license	Other type (specify)

However, when a commercial record is made at the time a transaction is made, a licensee may delay making an entry into the bound record if the provisions of paragraph (d) of this section are complied with.

(b) *Armor piercing ammunition sales by licensed collectors to licensees.* Sales or other dispositions of armor piercing ammunition from a licensed collector to another licensee shall be recorded and maintained in the manner prescribed in §478.122(b) for importers: *Provided,* That the license number of the transferee may be recorded in lieu of the transferee's address.

(c) *Armor piercing ammunition sales by licensed dealers to governmental entities.* A record of armor piercing ammunition disposed of by a licensed dealer to a governmental entity pursuant to § 478.99(e) shall be maintained by the licensed dealer on the licensed premises and shall show the name of the manufacturer, the caliber or gauge, the quantity, the name and address of the entity to which the armor piercing ammunition was transferred, and the date of the transaction. Such information shall be recorded under the format prescribed by § 478.122(b). Each licensed dealer disposing of armor piercing ammunition pursuant to § 478.99(e) shall also maintain a record showing the date of acquisition of such ammunition which shall be filed in an orderly manner separate from other commercial records maintained and be readily available for inspection. The records required by this paragraph shall be retained on the licensed premises of the licensee for a period not less than two years following the date of the recorded sale or disposition of the armor piercing ammunition.

(d) *Commercial records of armor piercing ammunition transactions.* When a commercial record is made at the time of sale or other disposition of armor piercing ammunition, and such record contains all information required by the bound record prescribed by paragraph (a) of this section, the licensed collector transferring the armor piercing ammunition may, for a period not exceeding 7 days following the date of such transfer, delay making the required entry into such bound record: *Provided,* That the commercial record pertaining to the transfer is:

(1) Maintained by the licensed collector separate from other commercial documents maintained by such licensee, and

(2) Is readily available for inspection on the licensed premises until such time as the required entry into the bound record is made.

(e) *Firearms receipt and disposition by dealers.* Except for adjustment or repair of a firearm that is returned to the person from whom it was received on the same day, each licensed dealer shall enter into a record each receipt and disposition of firearms. In addition, before commencing or continuing a firearms business, each licensed dealer shall inventory the firearms possessed for such business and shall record the

same in the record required by this paragraph. The record required by this paragraph shall be maintained in bound form in the format prescribed below. The purchase or other acquisition of a firearm shall, except as provided in paragraphs (g) and (i) of this section, be recorded not later than the close of the next business day following the date of such purchase or acquisition. The record shall show the date of receipt, the name and address or the name and license number of the person from whom received, the name of the manufacturer and importer (if any), the model, serial number (including any associated license number either as a prefix, or if remanufactured or imported, separated by a semicolon), type, and the caliber or gauge of the firearm. In the event the licensee records a duplicate entry with the same firearm and acquisition information, whether to close out an old record book or for any other reason, the licensee shall record a reference to the date and location of the subsequent entry (*e.g.,* date of new entry, book name/number, page number, and line number) as the disposition. The sale or other disposition of a firearm shall be recorded by the licensed dealer not later than seven days following the date of such transaction. When such disposition is made to a nonlicensee, the firearms transaction record, Form 4473, obtained by the licensed dealer shall be retained, until the transaction is recorded, separate from the licensee's Form 4473 file and be readily available for inspection. When such disposition is made to a licensee, the commercial record of the transaction shall be retained, until the transaction is recorded, separate from other commercial documents maintained by the licensed dealer, and be readily available for inspection. The record shall show the date of the sale or other disposition of each firearm, the name and address of the person to whom the firearm is transferred, or the name and license number of the person to whom transferred if such person is a licensee, or the firearms transaction record, Form 4473, transaction number if the licensed dealer transferring the firearm sequentially numbers the Forms 4473 and files them numerically. The format required for the record of receipt and disposition of firearms is as follows:

TABLE 2 TO PARAGRAPH (e)—FIREARMS DEALER ACQUISITION AND DISPOSITION RECORD

Description of firearm				Receipt		Disposition		
Manufacturer, importer (if any), or "privately made firearm" (PMF)	Model	Serial No.	Type	Caliber or gauge	Date	Name and address of nonlicensee; or if licensee, name and license No.	Date	Name	Address of nonlicensee; license No. of licensee; or Form 4473 transaction No. if such forms filed numerically

(f) *Firearms receipt and disposition by licensed collectors.* (1) Each licensed collector shall enter into a record each receipt and disposition of firearms curios or relics. The record required by this paragraph shall be maintained in bound form under the format prescribed below. The purchase or other acquisition of a curio or relic shall, except as provided in paragraphs (g) and (i) of this section, be recorded not later than the close of the next business day following the date of such purchase or other acquisition. The record shall show the date of receipt, the name and address or the name and license number of the person from whom received, the name of the manufacturer and importer (if any), the model, serial number (including any associated license number either as a prefix, or if remanufactured or imported, separated by a semicolon), type, and the caliber or gauge of the firearm curio or relic. In the event the licensee records a duplicate entry with the same firearm and acquisition information, whether to close out an old record book or for any other reason, the licensee shall record a reference to the date and location of the subsequent entry (*e.g.*, date of new entry, book name/number, page number, and line number) as the disposition. The sale or other disposition of a curio or relic shall be recorded by the licensed collector not later than seven days following the date of such transaction. When such disposition is made to a licensee, the commercial record of the transaction shall be retained, until the transaction is recorded, separate from other commercial documents maintained by the licensee, and be readily available for inspection. The record shall show the date of the sale or other disposition of each firearm curio or relic, the name and address of the person to whom the firearm curio or relic is transferred, or the name and license number of the person to whom transferred if such person is a licensee, and the date of birth of the transferee if other than a licensee. In addition, the licensee shall cause the transferee, if other than a licensee, to be identified in any manner customarily used in commercial transactions (*e.g.*, a driver's license), and note on the record the method used.

(2) The format required for the record of receipt and disposition of firearms by collectors is as follows:

Table 3 to Paragraph (f)(2)—Firearms Collector Acquisition and Disposition Record

Description of firearm				Receipt		Disposition		
Manufacturer, importer (if any), or "privately made firearm" (PMF)	Model	Serial No.	Type	Caliber or gauge	Date	Name and address of nonlicensee; or if licensee, name and license No.	Date	Name and address of nonlicensee; or if licensee, name and license No.	Date of birth if nonlicensee	Driver's license No. or other identification if nonlicensee

(g) *Commercial records of firearms received.* When a commercial record is held by a licensed dealer or licensed collector showing the acquisition of a firearm or firearm curio or relic, and such record contains all acquisition information required by the bound record prescribed by paragraphs (e) and (f) of this section, the licensed dealer or licensed collector acquiring such firearm or curio or relic, may, for a period not exceeding 7 days following the date of such acquisition, delay making the required entry into such bound record: *Provided,* That the commercial record is, until such time as the required entry into the bound record is made, (1) maintained by the licensed dealer or licensed collector separate from other commercial documents maintained by such licensee, and (2) readily available for inspection on the licensed premises: *Provided further,* That when disposition is made of a firearm or firearm curio or relic not entered in the bound record under the provisions of this paragraph, the licensed dealer or licensed collector making such disposition shall enter all required acquisition information regarding the firearm or firearm curio or relic in the bound record at the time such transfer or disposition is made.

(h) *Alternate records.* Notwithstanding the provisions of paragraphs (a), (e), and (f) of this section, the Director of Industry Operations may authorize alternate records to be maintained by a licensed dealer or licensed collector to record the acquisition and disposition of firearms or curios or relics and the disposition of armor piercing ammunition when it is shown by the licensed dealer or the licensed collector that such alternate records will accurately and readily disclose the required information. A licensed dealer or licensed collector who proposes to use alternate records shall submit a letter application, in duplicate, to the Director of Industry Operations and shall describe the proposed alternate records and the need therefor. Such alternate records shall not be employed by the licensed dealer or licensed collector until approval in such regard is received from the Director of Industry Operations.

(i) *Privately made firearms.* Except for adjustment or repair of a firearm that is returned to the person from whom it was received on the same day, licensees must record each receipt or other acquisition (including from a personal collection) and disposition (including to a personal collection) of a privately made firearm within the timeframe required by paragraph (e) of this section for firearms. For purposes of this paragraph, the terms "receipt" and "acquisition" shall include same-day or on-the-spot placement of identifying markings unless another licensee is placing the markings for, and under the direct supervision of, the licensee who recorded the acquisition. In that case, the licensee placing the markings need not record an acquisition from the supervising licensee or disposition upon return. The serial number need not be immediately recorded if the firearm is being identified by the licensee, or under the licensee's direct supervision with the licensee's serial number, in accordance with § 478.92(a)(2). Once the privately made firearm is so identified, the licensee shall update the record of acquisition entry with the serial number, including the license number prefix, and shall record its disposition in accordance with this section. In this part and part 447, where no manufacturer name has been identified on a privately made firearm (if privately made in the United States), the words "privately made firearm" (or abbreviation "PMF") shall be recorded as the name of the manufacturer.

(Approved by the Office of Management and Budget under control number 1140–0032)

[T.D. ATF–270, 53 FR 10503, Mar. 31, 1988, as amended by T.D. ATF–273, 53 FR 24687, June 30, 1988; T.D. ATF–313, 56 FR 32508, July 17, 1991; T.D. ATF–389, 62 FR 19445, Apr. 21, 1997; ATF–11F, 73 FR 57241, Oct. 2, 2008; ATF–22I, 77 FR 33634, June 7, 2012; ATF–19 F, 79 FR 45092, Aug. 4, 2014; ATF 2015R–26, 81 FR 38071, June 13, 2016; ATF–2021R–05F, 87 FR 24745, Apr. 26, 2022; 87 FR 51250, Aug. 22, 2022]

§ 478.125a Personal firearms collection.

(a) Notwithstanding any other provision of this subpart, a licensed manufacturer, licensed importer, or licensed dealer is not required to comply with the provisions of § 478.102 or record on a firearms transaction record, Form 4473, the sale or other disposition of a firearm maintained as part of the licensee's personal firearms collection: *Provided,* That

(1) The licensee has maintained the firearm as part of such collection for 1 year from the date the firearm was transferred from the business inventory into the personal collection or otherwise acquired as a personal firearm,

(2) The licensee recorded in the bound record prescribed by §478.125(e) the receipt of the firearm into the business inventory or other acquisition,

(3) The licensee recorded the firearm as a disposition in the bound record prescribed by §478.125(e) when the firearm was transferred from the business inventory into the personal firearms collection or otherwise acquired as a personal firearm, and

(4) The licensee enters the sale or other disposition of the firearm from the personal firearms collection into a bound record, under the format prescribed below, identifying the firearm transferred by recording the name of the manufacturer and importer (if any), the model, serial number (including any associated license number either as a prefix, or if remanufactured or imported, separated by a semicolon), type, and the caliber or gauge, and showing the date of the sale or other disposition, the name and address of the transferee, or the name and business address of the transferee if such person is a licensee, and the date of birth of the transferee if other than a licensee. In addition, the licensee shall cause the transferee, if other than a licensee, to be identified in any manner customarily used in commercial transactions (e.g., a drivers license). Where no manufacturer name has been identified on a privately made firearm, the words "privately made firearm" (or abbreviation "PMF") shall be recorded as the name of the manufacturer. The format required for the disposition record of personal firearms is as follows:

TABLE 1 TO PARAGRAPH (a)(4)—DISPOSITION RECORD OF PERSONAL FIREARMS

Description of firearm				Disposition		
Manufacturer, importer (if any), or "privately made firearm" (PMF)	Model	Serial No.	Type	Caliber or gauge	Date	Name and address (business address if licensee)	Date of birth if nonlicensee

(b) Any licensed manufacturer, licensed importer, or licensed dealer selling or otherwise disposing of a firearm from the licensee's personal firearms collection under this section shall be subject to the restrictions imposed by the Act and this part on the dispositions of firearms by persons other than licensed manufacturers, licensed importers, and licensed dealers.

(Approved by the Office of Management and Budget under control number 1140–0032)

[T.D. ATF–270, 53 FR 10504, Mar. 31, 1988, as amended by T.D. ATF–313, 56 FR 32509, July 17, 1991; T.D. ATF–415, 63 FR 58280, Oct. 29, 1998; ATF–11F, 73 FR 57242, Oct. 2, 2008; ATF 2015R–26, 81 FR 38071, June 13, 2016; ATF–2021R–05F, 87 FR 24746, Apr. 26, 2022]

§ 478.126   Furnishing transaction information.

(a) Each licensee shall, when required by letter issued by the Director of Industry Operations, and until notified to the contrary in writing by such officer, submit on Form 5300.5, Report of Firearms Transactions, for the periods and at the times specified in the letter issued by the Director of Industry Operations, all record information required by this subpart, or such lesser record information as the Director of Industry Operations in his letter may specify.

(b) The Director of Industry Operations may authorize the information to be submitted in a manner other than that prescribed in paragraph (a) of this section when it is shown by a licensee that an alternate method of reporting is reasonably necessary and will not unduly hinder the effective administration of this part. A licensee who proposes to use an alternate method of reporting shall submit a letter application, in duplicate, to the Director of Industry Operations and shall describe the proposed alternate method of reporting and the need therefor. An alternate method of reporting shall not be employed by the licensee until approval in such regard is received from the Director of Industry Operations.

(Approved by the Office of Management and Budget under control number 1140–0032)

[33 FR 18555, Dec. 14, 1968. Redesignated at 40 FR 16835, Apr. 15, 1975, and amended by T.D. ATF–172, 49 FR 14942, Apr. 16, 1984; ATF–11F, 73 FR 57242, Oct. 2, 2008; ATF 2013R–9F, 79 FR 46692, Aug. 11, 2014]

§ 478.126a   Reporting multiple sales or other disposition of pistols and revolvers.

Each licensee shall prepare a report of multiple sales or other disposition whenever the licensee sells or otherwise disposes of, at one time or during any five consecutive business days, two or more pistols, or revolvers, or any combination of pistols and revolvers totaling two or more, to an unlicensed person: *Provided,* That a report need not be made where pistols or revolvers, or any combination thereof, are returned to the same person from whom they were received. The report shall be prepared on Form 3310.4, Report of Multiple Sale or Other Disposition of Pistols and Revolvers. Not later than the close of business on the day that the multiple sale or other disposition occurs, the licensee shall forward two copies of Form 3310.4 to the ATF office specified thereon and one copy to the State police or to the local law enforcement agency in which the sale or other disposition took place. Where the State or local law enforcement officials have notified the licensee that a particular official has been designated to receive Forms 3310.4, the licensee shall forward such forms to that designated official. The licensee shall retain one copy of Form 3310.4 and attach it to the firearms transaction record, Form 4473, executed upon delivery of the pistols or revolvers.

Example. 1. A licensee sells a pistol and revolver in a single transaction to an unlicensed person. This is a multiple sale and must be reported not later than the close of business on the date of the transaction.

Example. 2. A licensee sells a pistol on Monday and sells a revolver on the following Friday to the same unlicensed person. This is a multiple sale and must be reported not later than the close of business on Friday. If the licensee sells the same unlicensed person another pistol or revolver on the following

Monday, this would constitute an additional multiple sale and must also be reported.

Example 3. A licensee maintaining business hours on Monday through Saturday sells a revolver to an unlicensed person on Monday and sells another revolver to the same person on the following Saturday. This does not constitute a multiple sale and need not be reported since the sales did not occur during five consecutive business days.

(Approved by the Office of Management and Budget under control number 1140–0003)

[T.D. ATF–16, 40 FR 19202, May 2, 1975, as amended by T.D. ATF–172, 49 FR 14942, Apr. 16, 1984; T.D. ATF–270, 53 FR 10505, Mar. 31, 1988; T.D. ATF–354, 59 FR 7113, Feb. 14, 1994; T.D. ATF–361, 60 FR 10787, Feb. 27, 1995; ATF–11F, 73 FR 57242, Oct. 2, 2008]

§478.127 Discontinuance of business.

Where a licensed business is discontinued and succeeded by a new licensee, the records prescribed by this subpart shall appropriately reflect such facts and shall be delivered to the successor. Where discontinuance of the business is absolute, the records shall be delivered within 30 days following the business discontinuance to the ATF Out-of-Business Records Center, 244 Needy Road, Martinsburg, West Virginia 25405, or to any ATF office in the division in which the business was located: *Provided, however,* Where State law or local ordinance requires the delivery of records to other responsible authority, the Chief, Federal Firearms Licensing Center may arrange for the delivery of the records required by this subpart to such authority: *Provided further,* That where a licensed business is discontinued and succeeded by a new licensee, the records may be delivered within 30 days following the business discontinuance to the ATF Out-of-Business Records Center or to any ATF office in the division in which the business was located.

[T.D. ATF–290, 54 FR 53055, Dec. 27, 1989, as amended by T.D. ATF–363, 60 FR 17455, Apr. 6, 1995; ATF–11F, 73 FR 57242, Oct. 2, 2008]

§478.128 False statement or representation.

(a) Any person who knowingly makes any false statement or representation in applying for any license or exemption or relief from disability, under the provisions of the Act, shall be fined not more than $5,000 or imprisoned not more than 5 years, or both.

(b) Any person other than a licensed manufacturer, licensed importer, licensed dealer, or licensed collector who knowingly makes any false statement or representation with respect to any information required by the provisions of the Act or this part to be kept in the records of a person licensed under the Act or this part shall be fined not more than $5,000 or imprisoned not more than 5 years, or both.

(c) Any licensed manufacturer, licensed importer, licensed dealer, or licensed collector who knowingly makes any false statement or representation with respect to any information required by the provisions of the Act or this part to be kept in the records of a person licensed under the Act or this part shall be fined not more than $1,000 or imprisoned not more than 1 year, or both.

[T.D. ATF–270, 53 FR 10505, Mar. 31, 1988]

§478.129 Record retention.

(a) *Records prior to Act.* Licensed importers and licensed manufacturers may dispose of records of sale or other disposition of firearms prior to December 16, 1968. Licensed dealers and licensed collectors may dispose of all records of firearms transactions that occurred prior to December 16, 1968.

(b) *Firearms Transaction Record.* Licensees shall retain each Form 4473 until business or licensed activity is discontinued, either on paper, or in an electronic alternate method approved by the Director, at the business premises readily accessible for inspection under this part. Paper forms over 20 years of age may be stored at a separate warehouse, which shall be considered part of the business premises for this purpose and subject to inspection under this part. Forms 4473 shall be retained in the licensee's records as provided in §478.124(b), provided that Forms 4473 with respect to which a sale, delivery, or transfer did not take place shall be separately retained in alphabetical (by name of transferee) or chronological (by date of transferee's certification) order.

(c) *Statement of intent to obtain a handgun, reports of multiple sales or other disposition of pistols and revolvers, and reports of theft or loss of firearms.* Licensees shall retain each Form 5300.35 (Statement of Intent to Obtain a Handgun(s)) for a period of not less than 5 years after notice of the intent to obtain the handgun was forwarded to the chief law enforcement officer, as defined in § 478.150(c). Licensees shall retain each copy of Form 3310.4 (Report of Multiple Sale or Other Disposition of Pistols and Revolvers) for a period of not less than 5 years after the date of sale or other disposition. Licensees shall retain each copy of Form 3310.11 (Federal Firearms Licensee Theft/Loss Report) for a period of not less than 5 years after the date the theft or loss was reported to ATF.

(d) *Records of importation and manufacture.* Licensees shall maintain records of the importation, manufacture, or other acquisition of firearms, including ATF Forms 6 and 6A as required by subpart G of this part, until business or licensed activity is discontinued. Licensed importers' records and licensed manufacturers' records of the sale or other disposition of firearms after December 15, 1968, shall be retained until business is discontinued, either on paper or in an electronic alternate method approved by the Director, at the business premises readily accessible for inspection under this part. Paper records that do not contain any open disposition entries and with no dispositions recorded within 20 years may be stored at a separate warehouse, which shall be considered part of the business premises for this purpose and subject to inspection under this part.

(e) *Records of dealers and collectors.* The records prepared by licensed dealers and licensed collectors of the sale or other disposition of firearms and the corresponding record of receipt of such firearms shall be retained until business or licensed activity is discontinued, either on paper, or in an electronic alternate method approved by the Director, at the business or collection premises readily accessible for inspection under this part. Paper records that do not contain any open disposition entries and with no dispositions recorded within 20 years may be stored at a separate warehouse, which shall be considered part of the business or collection premises for this purpose and subject to inspection under this part.

(f) *Retention of records of transactions in semiautomatic assault weapons.* The documentation required by §§ 478.40(c) and 478.132 shall be retained in the licensee's permanent records for a period of not less than 5 years after the date of sale or other disposition.

(Paragraph (b) approved by the Office of Management and Budget under control number 1512–0544; Paragraph (c) approved by the Office of Management and Budget under control numbers 1512–0520, 1512–0006, and 1512–0524; Paragraph (f) approved by the Office of Management and Budget under control number 1512–0526; all other recordkeeping approved by the Office of Management and Budget under control number 1512–0129)

[T.D. ATF–208, 50 FR 26704, June 28, 1985 and correctly designated at 50 FR 35081, Aug. 29, 1985, as amended by T.D. ATF–273, 53 FR 24687, June 30, 1988; T.D. ATF–361, 60 FR 10787, Feb. 27, 1995; T.D. ATF–363, 60 FR 17455, Apr. 6, 1995; T.D. ATF–415, 63 FR 58280, Oct. 29, 1998; T.D. ATF–426, 65 FR 38201, June 20, 2000; ATF–2021R–05F, 87 FR 24746, Apr. 26, 2022]

§ 478.131 Firearms transactions not subject to a NICS check.

(a)(1) A licensed importer, licensed manufacturer, or licensed dealer whose sale, delivery, or transfer of a firearm is made pursuant to the alternative provisions of § 478.102(d) and is not subject to the NICS check prescribed by § 478.102(a) shall maintain the records required by paragraph (a) of this section.

(2) If the transfer is pursuant to a permit or license in accordance with § 478.102(d)(1), the licensee shall either retain a copy of the purchaser's permit or license and attach it to the firearms transaction record, Form 4473, or record on the firearms transaction record, Form 4473, any identifying number, the date of issuance, and the expiration date (if provided) from the permit or license.

(3) If the transfer is pursuant to a certification by ATF in accordance with §§ 478.102(d)(3) and 478.150, the licensee shall maintain the certification as part of the records required to be kept under this subpart and for the period prescribed for the retention of Form 5300.35 in § 478.129(c).

(b) The requirements of this section shall be in addition to any other recordkeeping requirements contained in this part.

(Approved by the Office of Management and Budget under control number 1140–0045)

[T.D. ATF–415, 63 FR 58280, Oct. 29, 1998, as amended by ATF–11F, 73 FR 57242, Oct. 2, 2008]

§ 478.132 [Reserved]

§ 478.133 Records of transactions in semiautomatic assault weapons.

The evidence specified in § 478.40(c), relating to transactions in semiautomatic assault weapons, shall be retained in the permanent records of the manufacturer or dealer and in the records of the licensee to whom the weapons are transferred.

(Approved by the Office of Management and Budget under control number 1140–0041)

[T.D. ATF–363, 60 FR 17455, Apr. 6, 1995, as amended by ATF–11F, 73 FR 57242, Oct. 2, 2008]

§ 478.134 Sale of firearms to law enforcement officers.

(a) Law enforcement officers purchasing firearms for official use who provide the licensee with a certification on agency letterhead, signed by a person in authority within the agency (other than the officer purchasing the firearm), stating that the officer will use the firearm in official duties and that a records check reveals that the purchasing officer has no convictions for misdemeanor crimes of domestic violence are not required to complete Form 4473 or Form 5300.35. The law enforcement officer purchasing the firearm may purchase a firearm from a licensee in another State, regardless of where the officer resides or where the agency is located.

(b)(1) The following individuals are considered to have sufficient authority to certify that law enforcement officers purchasing firearms will use the firearms in the performance of official duties:

(i) In a city or county police department, the director of public safety or the chief or commissioner of police.

(ii) In a sheriff's office, the sheriff.

(iii) In a State police or highway patrol department, the superintendent or the supervisor in charge of the office to which the State officer or employee is assigned.

(iv) In Federal law enforcement offices, the supervisor in charge of the office to which the Federal officer or employee is assigned.

(2) An individual signing on behalf of the person in authority is acceptable, provided there is a proper delegation of authority.

(c) Licensees are not required to prepare a Form 4473 or Form 5300.35 covering sales of firearm made in accordance with paragraph (a) of this section to law enforcement officers for official use. However, disposition to the officer must be entered into the licensee's permanent records, and the certification letter must be retained in the licensee's files.

[T.D. ATF–401, 63 FR 35523, June 30, 1998]

Subpart I—Exemptions, Seizures, and Forfeitures

§ 478.141 General.

With the exception of §§ 478.32(a)(9) and (d)(9) and 478.99(c)(9), the provisions of this part shall not apply with respect to:

(a) The transportation, shipment, receipt, possession, or importation of any firearm or ammunition imported for, sold or shipped to, or issued for the use of, the United States or any department or agency thereof or any State or any department, agency, or political subdivision thereof.

(b) The shipment or receipt of firearms or ammunition when sold or issued by the Secretary of the Army pursuant to section 4308 of Title 10, U.S.C., and the transportation of any such firearm or ammunition carried out to enable a person, who lawfully received such firearm or ammunition from the Secretary of the Army, to engage in military training or in competitions.

(c) The shipment, unless otherwise prohibited by the Act or any other Federal law, by a licensed importer, licensed manufacturer, or licensed dealer to a member of the U.S. Armed Forces on active duty outside the United States or to clubs, recognized by the Department of Defense, whose entire membership is composed of such members of the U.S. Armed Forces, and such members or clubs may receive a firearm or ammunition determined by the Director to be generally recognized as particularly suitable for sporting purposes and intended for the personal use of such member or club. Before making a shipment of firearms or ammunition under the provisions of this paragraph, a licensed importer, licensed manufacturer, or licensed dealer may submit a written request, in duplicate, to the Director for a determination by the Director whether such shipment would constitute a violation of the Act or any other Federal law, or whether the firearm or ammunition is considered by the Director to be generally recognized as particularly suitable for sporting purposes.

(d) The transportation, shipment, receipt, possession, or importation of any antique firearm.

[33 FR 18555, Dec. 14, 1968. Redesignated at 40 FR 10835, Apr. 15, 1975, and amended by T.D. ATF–241, 51 FR 39628, Oct. 29, 1986; T.D. ATF–270, 53 FR 10505, Mar. 31, 1988; T.D. ATF–313, 56 FR 32509, July 17, 1991; T.D. ATF–401, 63 FR 35523, June 30, 1998]

§ 478.142 Effect of pardons and expunctions of convictions.

(a) A pardon granted by the President of the United States regarding a Federal conviction for a crime punishable by imprisonment for a term exceeding 1 year shall remove any disability which otherwise would be imposed by the provisions of this part with respect to that conviction.

(b) A pardon granted by the Governor of a State or other State pardoning authority or by the pardoning authority of a foreign jurisdiction with respect to a conviction, or any expunction, reversal, setting aside of a conviction, or other proceeding rendering a conviction nugatory, or a restoration of civil rights shall remove any disability which otherwise would be imposed by the provisions of this part with respect to the conviction, unless:

(1) The pardon, expunction, setting aside, or other proceeding rendering a conviction nugatory, or restoration of civil rights expressly provides that the person may not ship, transport, possess or receive firearms; or

(2) The pardon, expunction, setting aside, or other proceeding rendering a conviction nugatory, or restoration of civil rights did not fully restore the rights of the person to possess or receive firearms under the law of the jurisdiction where the conviction occurred.

[T.D. ATF–270, 53 FR 10505, Mar. 31, 1988]

§ 478.143 Relief from disabilities incurred by indictment.

A licensed importer, licensed manufacturer, licensed dealer, or licensed collector who is indicted for a crime punishable by imprisonment for a term exceeding 1 year may, notwithstanding any other provision of the Act, continue operations pursuant to his existing license during the term of such indictment and until any conviction pursuant to the indictment becomes final: *Provided,* That if the term of the license expires during the period between the date of the indictment and the date the conviction thereunder becomes final, such importer, manufacturer, dealer, or collector must file a timely application for the renewal of his license in order to continue operations. Such application shall show that the applicant is under indictment for a crime punishable by imprisonment for a term exceeding 1 year.

§ 478.144 Relief from disabilities under the Act.

(a) Any person may make application for relief from the disabilities under section 922 (g) and (n) of the Act (see § 478.32).

(b) An application for such relief shall be filed, in triplicate, with the Director. It shall include the information required by this section and such other supporting data as the Director and the applicant deem appropriate.

(c) Any record or document of a court or other government entity or official required by this paragraph to be furnished by an applicant in support of an application for relief shall be certified by the court or other government entity or official as a true copy. An application shall include:

(1) In the case of an applicant who is an individual, a written statement from each of 3 references, who are not related to the applicant by blood or

marriage and have known the applicant for at least 3 years, recommending the granting of relief;

(2) Written consent to examine and obtain copies of records and to receive statements and information regarding the applicant's background, including records, statements and other information concerning employment, medical history, military service, and criminal record;

(3) In the case of an applicant under indictment, a copy of the indictment or information;

(4) In the case of an applicant having been convicted of a crime punishable by imprisonment for a term exceeding 1 year, a copy of the indictment or information on which the applicant was convicted, the judgment of conviction or record of any plea of nolo contendere or plea of guilty or finding of guilt by the court, and any pardon, expunction, setting aside or other record purporting to show that the conviction was rendered nugatory or that civil rights were restored;

(5) In the case of an applicant who has been adjudicated a mental defective or committed to a mental institution, a copy of the order of a court, board, commission, or other lawful authority that made the adjudication or ordered the commitment, any petition that sought to have the applicant so adjudicated or committed, any medical records reflecting the reasons for commitment and diagnoses of the applicant, and any court order or finding of a court, board, commission, or other lawful authority showing the applicant's discharge from commitment, restoration of mental competency and the restoration of rights;

(6) In the case of an applicant who has been discharged from the Armed Forces under dishonorable conditions, a copy of the applicant's summary of service record (Department of Defense Form 214), charge sheet (Department of Defense Form 458), and final court martial order;

(7) In the case of an applicant who, having been a citizen of the United States, has renounced his or her citizenship, a copy of the formal renunciation of nationality before a diplomatic or consular officer of the United States in a foreign state or before an officer designated by the Attorney General when the United States was in a state of war (see 8 U.S.C. 1481(a) (5) and (6)); and

(8) In the case of an applicant who has been convicted of a misdemeanor crime of domestic violence, a copy of the indictment or information on which the applicant was convicted, the judgment of conviction or record of any plea of nolo contendere or plea of guilty or finding of guilt by the court, and any pardon, expunction, setting aside or other record purporting to show that the conviction was rendered nugatory or that civil rights were restored.

(d) The Director may grant relief to an applicant if it is established to the satisfaction of the Director that the circumstances regarding the disability, and the applicant's record and reputation, are such that the applicant will not be likely to act in a manner dangerous to public safety, and that the granting of the relief would not be contrary to the public interest. The Director will not ordinarily grant relief if the applicant has not been discharged from parole or probation for a period of at least 2 years. Relief will not be granted to an applicant who is prohibited from possessing all types of firearms by the law of the State where such applicant resides.

(e) In addition to meeting the requirements of paragraph (d) of this section, an applicant who has been adjudicated a mental defective or committed to a mental institution will not be granted relief unless the applicant was subsequently determined by a court, board, commission, or other lawful authority to have been restored to mental competency, to be no longer suffering from a mental disorder, and to have had all rights restored.

(f) Upon receipt of an incomplete or improperly executed application for relief, the applicant shall be notified of the deficiency in the application. If the application is not corrected and returned within 30 days following the date of notification, the application shall be considered as having been abandoned.

(g) Whenever the Director grants relief to any person pursuant to this section, a notice of such action shall be promptly published in the FEDERAL REGISTER, together with the reasons therefor.

(h) A person who has been granted relief under this section shall be relieved of any disabilities imposed by the Act with respect to the acquisition, receipt, transfer, shipment, transportation, or possession of firearms or ammunition and incurred by reason of such disability.

(i)(1) A licensee who incurs disabilities under the Act (see § 478.32(a)) during the term of a current license or while the licensee has pending a license renewal application, and who files an application for removal of such disabilities, shall not be barred from licensed operations for 30 days following the date on which the applicant was first subject to such disabilities (or 30 days after the date upon which the conviction for a crime punishable by imprisonment for a term exceeding 1 year becomes final), and if the licensee files the application for relief as provided by this section within such 30-day period, the licensee may further continue licensed operations during the pendency of the application. A licensee who does not file such application within such 30-day period shall not continue licensed operations beyond 30 days following the date on which the licensee was first subject to such disabilities (or 30 days from the date the conviction for a crime punishable by imprisonment for a term exceeding 1 year becomes final).

(2) In the event the term of a license of a person expires during the 30-day period specified in paragraph (i)(1) of this section, or during the pendency of the application for relief, a timely application for renewal of the license must be filed in order to continue licensed operations. Such license application shall show that the applicant is subject to Federal firearms disabilities, shall describe the event giving rise to such disabilities, and shall state when the disabilities were incurred.

(3) A licensee shall not continue licensed operations beyond 30 days following the date the Director issues notification that the licensee's applications for removal of disabilities has been denied.

(4) When as provided in this paragraph a licensee may no longer continue licensed operations, any application for renewal of license filed by the licensee during the pendency of the application for removal of disabilities shall be denied by the Director of Industry Operations.

[T.D. ATF-270, 53 FR 10506, Mar. 31, 1988, as amended by T.D. ATF-313, 56 FR 32509, July 17, 1991; 56 FR 43649, Sept. 3, 1991; T.D. ATF-401, 63 FR 35523, June 30, 1998]

§ 478.145   Research organizations.

The provisions of § 478.98 with respect to the sale or delivery of destructive devices, machine guns, short-barreled shotguns, and short-barreled rifles shall not apply to the sale or delivery of such devices and weapons to any research organization designated by the Director to receive same. A research organization desiring such designation shall submit a letter application, in duplicate, to the Director. Such application shall contain the name and address of the research organization, the names and addresses of the persons directing or controlling, directly or indirectly, the policies and management of such organization, the nature and purpose of the research being conducted, a description of the devices and weapons to be received, and the identity of the person or persons from whom such devices and weapons are to be received.

[T.D. ATF-270, 53 FR 10507, Mar. 31, 1988]

§ 478.146   Deliveries by mail to certain persons.

The provisions of this part shall not be construed as prohibiting a licensed importer, licensed manufacturer, or licensed dealer from depositing a firearm for conveyance in the mails to any officer, employee, agent, or watchman who, pursuant to the provisions of section 1715 of title 18, U.S.C., is eligible to receive through the mails pistols, revolvers, and other firearms capable of being concealed on the person, for use in connection with his official duties.

§ 478.147   Return of firearm.

A person not otherwise prohibited by Federal, State or local law may ship a firearm to a licensed importer, licensed manufacturer, or licensed dealer for any lawful purpose, and, notwithstanding any other provision of this part, the licensed manufacturer, licensed importer, or licensed dealer may return in interstate or foreign commerce to that person the firearm or a replacement firearm of the same kind and type. See §478.124(a) for requirements of a Form 4473 prior to return. A person not otherwise prohibited by Federal, State or local law may ship a firearm curio or relic to a licensed collector for any lawful purpose, and, notwithstanding any other provision of this part, the licensed collector may return in interstate or foreign commerce to that person the firearm curio or relic.

[T.D. ATF–270, 53 FR 10507, Mar. 31, 1988]

§478.148 Armor piercing ammunition intended for sporting or industrial purposes.

The Director may exempt certain armor piercing ammunition from the requirements of this part. A person who desires to obtain an exemption under this section for any such ammunition which is primarily intended for sporting purposes or intended for industrial purposes, including charges used in oil and gas well perforating devices, shall submit a written request to the Director. Each request shall be executed under the penalties of perjury and contain a complete and accurate description of the ammunition, the name and address of the manufacturer or importer, the purpose of and use for which it is designed and intended, and any photographs, diagrams, or drawings as may be necessary to enable the Director to make a determination. The Director may require that a sample of the ammunition be submitted for examination and evaluation.

[T.D. ATF–270, 53 FR 10507, Mar. 31, 1988]

§478.149 Armor piercing ammunition manufactured or imported for the purpose of testing or experimentation.

The provisions of §§478.37 and 478.99(d) with respect to the manufacture or importation of armor piercing ammunition and the sale or delivery of armor piercing ammunition by manufacturers and importers shall not apply to the manufacture, importation, sale or delivery of armor piercing ammunition for the purpose of testing or experimentation as authorized by the Director. A person desiring such authorization to receive armor piercing ammunition shall submit a letter application, in duplicate, to the Director. Such application shall contain the name and addresses of the persons directing or controlling, directly or indirectly, the policies and management of the applicant, the nature or purpose of the testing or experimentation, a description of the armor piercing ammunition to be received, and the identity of the manufacturer or importer from whom such ammunition is to be received. The approved application shall be submitted to the manufacturer or importer who shall retain a copy as part of the records required by subpart H of this part.

[T.D. ATF–270, 53 FR 10507, Mar. 31, 1988]

§478.150 Alternative to NICS in certain geographical locations.

(a) The provisions of §478.102(d)(3) shall be applicable when the Director has certified that compliance with the provisions of §478.102(a)(1) is impracticable because:

(1) The ratio of the number of law enforcement officers of the State in which the transfer is to occur to the number of square miles of land area of the State does not exceed 0.0025;

(2) The business premises of the licensee at which the transfer is to occur are extremely remote in relation to the chief law enforcement officer; and

(3) There is an absence of telecommunications facilities in the geographical area in which the business premises are located.

(b) A licensee who desires to obtain a certification under this section shall submit a written request to the Director. Each request shall be executed under the penalties of perjury and contain information sufficient for the Director to make such certification. Such information shall include statistical data, official reports, or other statements of government agencies pertaining to the ratio of law enforcement officers to the number of square miles of land area of a State and statements of government agencies and private

99

utility companies regarding the absence of telecommunications facilities in the geographical area in which the licensee's business premises are located.

(c) For purposes of this section and § 478.129(c), the "chief law enforcement officer" means the chief of police, the sheriff, or an equivalent officer or the designee of any such individual.

(Approved by the Office of Management and Budget under control number 1140–0045)

[T.D. ATF–415, 63 FR 58280, Oct. 29, 1998, as amended by ATF–11F, 73 FR 57242, Oct. 2, 2008]

§ 478.151 Semiautomatic rifles or shotguns for testing or experimentation.

(a) The provisions of § 478.39 shall not apply to the assembly of semiautomatic rifles or shotguns for the purpose of testing or experimentation as authorized by the Director.

(b) A person desiring authorization to assemble nonsporting semiautomatic rifles or shotguns shall submit a written request, in duplicate, to the Director. Each such request shall be executed under the penalties of perjury and shall contain a complete and accurate description of the firearm to be assembled, and such diagrams or drawings as may be necessary to enable the Director to make a determination. The Director may require the submission of the firearm parts for examination and evaluation. If the submission of the firearm parts is impractical, the person requesting the authorization shall so advise the Director and designate the place where the firearm parts will be available for examination and evaluation.

(Paragraph (b) approved by the Office of Management and Budget under control number 1140–0037)

[T.D. ATF–346, 58 FR 40590, July 29, 1993, as amended by ATF–11F, 73 FR 57242, Oct. 2, 2008]

§ 478.152 Seizure and forfeiture.

(a) Any firearm or ammunition involved in or used in any knowing violation of subsections (a)(4), (a)(6), (f), (g), (h), (i), (j), or (k) of section 922 of the Act, or knowing importation or bringing into the United States or any possession thereof any firearm or ammuni-

tion in violation of section 922(l) of the Act, or knowing violation of section 924 of the Act, or willful violation of any other provision of the Act or of this part, or any violation of any other criminal law of the United States, or any firearm or ammunition intended to be used in any offense referred to in paragraph (c) of this section, where such intent is demonstrated by clear and convincing evidence, shall be subject to seizure and forfeiture, and all provisions of the Internal Revenue Code of 1986 relating to the seizure, forfeiture, and disposition of firearms, as defined in section 5845(a) of that Code, shall, so far as applicable, extend to seizures and forfeitures under the provisions of the Act: *Provided,* That upon acquittal of the owner or possessor, or dismissal of the charges against such person other than upon motion of the Government prior to trial, or lapse of or court termination of the restraining order to which he is subject, the seized or relinquished firearms or ammunition shall be returned forthwith to the owner or possessor or to a person delegated by the owner or possessor unless the return of the firearms or ammunition would place the owner or possessor or the delegate of the owner or possessor in violation of law. Any action or proceeding for the forfeiture of firearms or ammunition shall be commenced within 120 days of such seizure.

(b) Only those firearms or quantities of ammunition particularly named and individually identified as involved in or used in any violation of the provisions of the Act or this part, or any other criminal law of the United States or as intended to be used in any offense referred to in paragraph (c) of this section, where such intent is demonstrated by clear and convincing evidence, shall be subject to seizure, forfeiture and disposition.

(c) The offenses referred to in paragraphs (a) and (b) of this section for which firearms and ammunition intended to be used in such offenses are subject to seizure and forfeiture are:

(1) Any crime of violence, as that term is defined in section 924(c)(3) of the Act;

(2) Any offense punishable under the Controlled Substances Act (21 U.S.C. 801 *et seq.*) or the Controlled Substances

Import and Export Act (21 U.S.C. 951 *et seq.*);

(3) Any offense described in section 922(a)(1), 922(a)(3), 922(a)(5), or 922(b)(3) of the Act, where the firearm or ammunition intended to be used in such offense is involved in a pattern of activities which includes a violation of any offense described in section 922(a)(1), 922(a)(3), 922(a)(5), or 922(b)(3) of the Act;

(4) Any offense described in section 922(d) of the Act where the firearm or ammunition is intended to be used in such offense by the transferor of such firearm or ammunition;

(5) Any offense described in section 922(i), 922(j), 922(l), 922(n), or 924(b) of the Act; and

(6) Any offense which may be prosecuted in a court of the United States which involves the exportation of firearms or ammunition.

[T.D. ATF–270, 53 FR 10507, Mar. 31, 1988; Redesignated by T.D. ATF–354, 59 FR 7114, Feb. 14, 1994, and further redesignated by T.D. ATF–361, 60 FR 10788, Feb. 27, 1995; T.D. ATF–363, 60 FR 17455, Apr. 6, 1995]

§ 478.153 [Reserved]

Subpart J [Reserved]

Subpart K—Exportation

§ 478.171 Exportation.

Firearms and ammunition shall be exported in accordance with the applicable provisions of section 38 of the Arms Export Control Act (22 U.S.C. 2778) and regulations thereunder. However, licensed manufacturers, licensed importers, and licensed dealers exporting firearms shall maintain records showing the manufacture or acquisition of the firearms as required by this part and records showing the name and address of the foreign consignee of the firearms and the date the firearms were exported. Licensed manufacturers and licensed importers exporting armor piercing ammunition shall maintain records showing the name and address of the foreign consignee and the date

the armor piercing ammunition was exported.

[T.D. ATF–270, 53 FR 10507, Mar. 31, 1988; T.D. ATF–363, 60 FR 17456, Apr. 6, 1995; ATF 2014R–42, 84 FR 12094, Apr. 1, 2019; ATF 2019R–03, 84 FR 60334, Nov. 8, 2019]

PART 479—MACHINE GUNS, DESTRUCTIVE DEVICES, AND CERTAIN OTHER FIREARMS

Subpart A—Scope of Regulations

Sec.
479.1 General.

Subpart B—Definitions

479.11 Meaning of terms.

Subpart C—Administrative and Miscellaneous Provisions

479.21 Forms prescribed.
479.22 Right of entry and examination.
479.23 Restrictive use of required information.
479.24 Destructive device determination.
479.25 Collector's items.
479.26 Alternate methods or procedures; emergency variations from requirements.

Subpart D—Special (Occupational) Taxes

479.31 Liability for tax.
479.32 Special (occupational) tax rates.
479.32a Reduced rate of tax for small importers and manufacturers.
479.33 Special exemption.
479.34 Special tax registration and return.
479.35 Employer identification number.
479.36 The special tax stamp, receipt for special (occupational) taxes.
479.37 Certificates in lieu of stamps lost or destroyed.
479.38 Engaging in business at more than one location.
479.39 Engaging in more than one business at the same location.
479.40 Partnership liability.
479.41 Single sale.

CHANGE OF OWNERSHIP

479.42 Changes through death of owner.
479.43 Changes through bankruptcy of owner.
479.44 Change in partnership or unincorporated association.
479.45 Changes in corporation.

CHANGE OF BUSINESS LOCATION

479.46 Notice by taxpayer.

CHANGE OF TRADE NAME

479.47   Notice by taxpayer.

PENALTIES AND INTEREST

479.48   Failure to pay special (occupational) tax.
479.49   Failure to register change or removal.
479.50   Delinquency.
479.51   Fraudulent return.

APPLICATION OF STATE LAWS

479.52   State regulations.

Subpart E—Tax on Making Firearms

479.61   Rate of tax.

APPLICATION TO MAKE A FIREARM

479.62   Application to make.
479.63   Identification of applicant.
479.64   Procedure for approval of application.
479.65   Denial of application.
479.66   Subsequent transfer of firearms.
479.67   Cancellation of stamp.

EXCEPTIONS TO TAX ON MAKING FIREARMS

479.68   Qualified manufacturer.
479.69   Making a firearm for the United States.
479.70   Certain government entities.

REGISTRATION

479.71   Proof of registration.

Subpart F—Transfer Tax

479.81   Scope of tax.
479.82   Rate of tax.
479.83   Transfer tax in addition to import duty.

APPLICATION AND ORDER FOR TRANSFER OF FIREARM

479.84   Application to transfer.
479.85   Identification of transferee.
479.86   Action on application.
479.87   Cancellation of stamp.

EXEMPTIONS RELATING TO TRANSFERS OF FIREARMS

479.88   Special (occupational) taxpayers.
479.89   Transfers to the United States.
479.90   Certain government entities.
479.90a Estates.
479.91   Unserviceable firearms.
479.92   Transportation of firearms to effect transfer.

OTHER PROVISIONS

479.93   Transfers of firearms to certain persons.

Subpart G—Registration and Identification of Firearms

479.101   Registration of firearms.
479.102   Identification of firearms.
479.103   Registration of firearms manufactured.
479.104   Registration of firearms by certain governmental entities.

MACHINE GUNS

479.105   Transfer and possession of machine guns.

Subpart H—Importation and Exportation

IMPORTATION

479.111   Procedure.
479.112   Registration of imported firearms.
479.113   Conditional importation.

EXPORTATION

479.114   Application and permit for exportation of firearms.
479.115   Action by Director.
479.116   Procedure by exporter.
479.117   Action by Customs.
479.118   Proof of exportation.
479.119   Transportation of firearms to effect exportation.
479.120   Refunds.
479.121   Insular possessions.

ARMS EXPORT CONTROL ACT

479.122   Requirements.

Subpart I—Records and Returns

479.131   Records.

Subpart J—Stolen or Lost Firearms or Documents

479.141   Stolen or lost firearms.
479.142   Stolen or lost documents.

Subpart K—Examination of Books and Records

479.151   Failure to make returns: Substitute returns.
479.152   Penalties (records and returns).

Subpart L—Distribution and Sale of Stamps

479.161   National Firearms Act stamps.
479.162   Stamps authorized.
479.163   Reuse of stamps prohibited.

Subpart M—Redemption of or Allowance for Stamps or Refunds

479.171   Redemption of or allowance for stamps.
479.172   Refunds.

Subpart N—Penalties and Forfeitures

479.181 Penalties.
479.182 Forfeitures.

Subpart O—Other Laws Applicable

479.191 Applicability of other provisions of internal revenue laws.
479.192 Commerce in firearms and ammunition.
479.193 Arms Export Control Act.

AUTHORITY: 26 U.S.C. 5812; 26 U.S.C. 5822; 26 U.S.C. 7801; 26 U.S.C. 7805.

SOURCE: 36 FR 14256, Aug. 3, 1971, unless otherwise noted. Redesignated at 40 FR 16835, Apr. 15, 1975, and further redesignated by T.D. ATF–487, 68 FR 3752, Jan. 24, 2003.

EDITORIAL NOTE: Nomenclature changes to part 479 appear by T.D. ATF–487, 68 FR 3752, Jan. 24, 2003.

Subpart A—Scope of Regulations

§ 479.1 General.

This part contains the procedural and substantive requirements relative to the importation, manufacture, making, exportation, identification and registration of, and the dealing in, machine guns, destructive devices and certain other firearms under the provisions of the National Firearms Act (26 U.S.C. Chapter 53).

[36 FR 14256, Aug. 3, 1971. Redesignated at 40 FR 16835, Apr. 15, 1975, and amended by T.D. ATF–48, 44 FR 55842, Sept. 28, 1979]

Subpart B—Definitions

§ 479.11 Meaning of terms.

When used in this part and in forms prescribed under this part, where not otherwise distinctly expressed or manifestly incompatible with the intent thereof, terms shall have the meanings ascribed in this section. Words in the plural form shall include the singular, and vice versa, and words importing the masculine gender shall include the feminine. The terms "includes" and "including" do not exclude other things not enumerated which are in the same general class or are otherwise within the scope thereof.

Antique firearm. Any firearm not designed or redesigned for using rim fire or conventional center fire ignition with fixed ammunition and manufactured in or before 1898 (including any matchlock, flintlock, percussion cap, or similar type of ignition system or replica thereof, whether actually manufactured before or after the year 1898) and also any firearm using fixed ammunition manufactured in or before 1898, for which ammunition is no longer manufactured in the United States and is not readily available in the ordinary channels of commercial trade.

Any other weapon. Any weapon or device capable of being concealed on the person from which a shot can be discharged through the energy of an explosive, a pistol or revolver having a barrel with a smooth bore designed or redesigned to fire a fixed shotgun shell, weapons with combination shotgun and rifle barrels 12 inches or more, less than 18 inches in length, from which only a single discharge can be made from either barrel without manual reloading, and shall include any such weapon which may be readily restored to fire. Such term shall not include a pistol or a revolver having a rifled bore, or rifled bores, or weapons designed, made, or intended to be fired from the shoulder and not capable of firing fixed ammunition.

ATF officer. An officer or employee of the Bureau of Alcohol, Tobacco, Firearms, and Explosives (ATF) authorized to perform any function relating to the administration or enforcement of this part.

Complete muffler or silencer device. A muffler or silencer that contains all component parts necessary to function, whether or not assembled or operable.

Complete weapon. A firearm other than a muffler or silencer that contains all component parts necessary to function, whether or not assembled or operable.

Customs officer. Any officer of U.S. Customs and Border Protection, any commissioned, warrant, or petty officer of the Coast Guard, or any agent or other person authorized by law to perform the duties of a customs officer.

Dealer. Any person, not a manufacturer or importer, engaged in the business of selling, renting, leasing, or loaning firearms and shall include pawnbrokers who accept firearms as collateral for loans.

Destructive device. (a) Any explosive, incendiary, or poison gas (1) bomb, (2) grenade, (3) rocket having a propellent charge of more than 4 ounces, (4) missile having an explosive or incendiary charge of more than one-quarter ounce, (5) mine, or (6) similar device; (b) any type of weapon by whatever name known which will, or which may be readily converted to, expel a projectile by the action of an explosive or other propellant, the barrel or barrels of which have a bore of more than one-half inch in diameter, except a shotgun or shotgun shell which the Director finds is generally recognized as particularly suitable for sporting purposes; and (c) any combination of parts either designed or intended for use in converting any device into a destructive device as described in paragraphs (a) and (b) of this definition and from which a destructive device may be readily assembled. The term shall not include any device which is neither designed or redesigned for use as a weapon; any device, although originally designed for use as a weapon, which is redesigned for use as a signaling, pyrotechnic, line throwing, safety, or similar device; surplus ordnance sold, loaned, or given by the Secretary of the Army under 10 U.S.C. 4684(2), 4685, or 4686, or any device which the Director finds is not likely to be used as a weapon, or is an antique or is a rifle which the owner intends to use solely for sporting purposes.

Director. The Director, Bureau of Alcohol, Tobacco, Firearms, and Explosives, the Department of Justice, Washington, DC.

Director, Industry Operations. The principal regional official responsible for administering regulations in this part.

Director of the Service Center. A director of an Internal Revenue Service Center in an internal revenue region.

District director. A district director of the Internal Revenue Service in an internal revenue district.

Executed under penalties of perjury. Signed with the prescribed declaration under the penalties of perjury as provided on or with respect to the return, form, or other document or, where no form of declaration is prescribed, with the declaration:

"I declare under the penalties of perjury that this—(insert type of document, such as, statement, application, request, certificate), including the documents submitted in support thereof, has been examined by me and, to the best of my knowledge and belief, is true, correct, and complete."

Exportation. The severance of goods from the mass of things belonging to this country with the intention of uniting them to the mass of things belonging to some foreign country.

Exporter. Any person who exports firearms from the United States.

Firearm. (a) A shotgun having a barrel or barrels of less than 18 inches in length; (b) a weapon made from a shotgun if such weapon as modified has an overall length of less than 26 inches or a barrel or barrels of less than 18 inches in length; (c) a rifle having a barrel or barrels of less than 16 inches in length; (d) a weapon made from a rifle if such weapon as modified has an overall length of less than 26 inches or a barrel or barrels of less than 16 inches in length; (e) any other weapon, as defined in this subpart; (f) a machine gun; (g) a muffler or a silencer for any firearm whether or not such firearm is included within this definition; and (h) a destructive device. The term shall not include an antique firearm or any device (other than a machine gun or destructive device) which, although designed as a weapon, the Director finds by reason of the date of its manufacture, value, design, and other characteristics is primarily a collector's item and is not likely to be used as a weapon. For purposes of this definition, the length of the barrel having an integral chamber(s) on a shotgun or rifle shall be determined by measuring the distance between the muzzle and the face of the bolt, breech, or breech block when closed and when the shotgun or rifle is cocked. The overall length of a weapon made from a shotgun or rifle is the distance between the extreme ends of the weapon measured along a line parallel to the center line of the bore.

Fixed ammunition. That self-contained unit consisting of the case, primer, propellant charge, and projectile or projectiles.

Frame or receiver. The term "frame or receiver" shall have the same meaning as in § 478.12 of this subchapter.

Importation. The bringing of a firearm within the limits of the United States or any territory under its control or jurisdiction, from a place outside thereof (whether such place be a foreign country or territory subject to the jurisdiction of the United States), with intent to unlade. Except that, bringing a firearm from a foreign country or a territory subject to the jurisdiction of the United States into a foreign trade zone for storage pending shipment to a foreign country or subsequent importation into this country, under Title 26 of the United States Code, and this part, shall not be deemed importation.

Importer. Any person who is engaged in the business of importing or bringing firearms into the United States.

Machine gun. Any weapon which shoots, is designed to shoot, or can be readily restored to shoot, automatically more than one shot, without manual reloading, by a single function of the trigger. The term shall also include the frame or receiver of any such weapon, any part designed and intended solely and exclusively, or combination of parts designed and intended, for use in converting a weapon into a machine gun, and any combination of parts from which a machine gun can be assembled if such parts are in the possession or under the control of a person. For purposes of this definition, the term "automatically" as it modifies "shoots, is designed to shoot, or can be readily restored to shoot," means functioning as the result of a self-acting or self-regulating mechanism that allows the firing of multiple rounds through a single function of the trigger; and "single function of the trigger" means a single pull of the trigger and analogous motions. The term "machine gun" includes a bump-stock-type device, *i.e.*, a device that allows a semi-automatic firearm to shoot more than one shot with a single pull of the trigger by harnessing the recoil energy of the semi-automatic firearm to which it is affixed so that the trigger resets and continues firing without additional physical manipulation of the trigger by the shooter.

Make. This term and the various derivatives thereof shall include manufacturing (other than by one qualified to engage in such business under this part), putting together, altering, any combination of these, or otherwise producing a firearm.

Manual reloading. The inserting of a cartridge or shell into the chamber of a firearm either with the hands or by means of a mechanical device controlled and energized by the hands.

Manufacturer. Any person who is engaged in the business of manufacturing firearms.

Muffler or silencer. Any device for silencing, muffling, or diminishing the report of a portable firearm, including any combination of parts, designed or redesigned, and intended for the use in assembling or fabricating a firearm silencer or firearm muffler, and any part intended only for use in such assembly or fabrication.

Person. A partnership, company, association, trust, corporation, including each responsible person associated with such an entity; an estate; or an individual.

Pistol. A weapon originally designed, made, and intended to fire a projectile (bullet) from one or more barrels when held in one hand, and having (a) a chamber(s) as an integral part(s) of, or permanently aligned with, the bore(s); and (b) a short stock designed to be gripped by one hand and at an angle to and extending below the line of the bore(s).

Privately made firearm (PMF). The term "privately made firearm (PMF)" shall have the same meaning as in §478.11 of this subchapter.

Readily. A process, action, or physical state that is fairly or reasonably efficient, quick, and easy, but not necessarily the most efficient, speediest, or easiest process, action, or physical state. With respect to the classification of firearms, factors relevant in making this determination include the following:

(1) Time, *i.e.*, how long it takes to finish the process;

(2) Ease, *i.e.*, how difficult it is to do so;

(3) Expertise, *i.e.*, what knowledge and skills are required;

(4) Equipment, *i.e.*, what tools are required;

(5) Parts availability, *i.e.*, whether additional parts are required, and how easily they can be obtained;

(6) Expense, *i.e.*, how much it costs;

(7) Scope, *i.e.*, the extent to which the subject of the process must be changed to finish it; and

(8) Feasibility, *i.e.*, whether the process would damage or destroy the subject of the process, or cause it to malfunction.

Responsible person. In the case of an unlicensed entity, including any trust, partnership, association, company (including any Limited Liability Company (LLC)), or corporation, any individual who possesses, directly or indirectly, the power or authority to direct the management and policies of the trust or entity to receive, possess, ship, transport, deliver, transfer, or otherwise dispose of a firearm for, or on behalf of, the trust or legal entity. In the case of a trust, those persons with the power or authority to direct the management and policies of the trust include any person who has the capability to exercise such power and possesses, directly or indirectly, the power or authority under any trust instrument, or under State law, to receive, possess, ship, transport, deliver, transfer, or otherwise dispose of a firearm for, or on behalf of, the trust. Examples of who may be considered a responsible person include settlors/grantors, trustees, partners, members, officers, directors, board members, or owners. An example of who may be excluded from this definition of responsible person is the beneficiary of a trust, if the beneficiary does not have the capability to exercise the powers or authorities enumerated in this section.

Revolver. A projectile weapon, of the pistol type, having a breechloading chambered cylinder so arranged that the cocking of the hammer or movement of the trigger rotates it and brings the next cartridge in line with the barrel for firing.

Rifle. A weapon designed or redesigned, made or remade, and intended to be fired from the shoulder and designed or redesigned and made or remade to use the energy of the explosive in a fixed cartridge to fire only a single projectile through a rifled bore for each single pull of the trigger, and shall include any such weapon which may be readily restored to fire a fixed cartridge.

(1) For purposes of this definition, the term "designed or redesigned, made or remade, and intended to be fired from the shoulder" shall include a weapon that is equipped with an accessory, component, or other rearward attachment (*e.g.*, a "stabilizing brace") that provides surface area that allows the weapon to be fired from the shoulder, provided other factors, as described in paragraph (2), indicate that the weapon is designed, made, and intended to be fired from the shoulder.

(2) When a weapon provides surface area that allows the weapon to be fired from the shoulder, the following factors shall also be considered in determining whether the weapon is designed, made, and intended to be fired from the shoulder:

(i) Whether the weapon has a weight or length consistent with the weight or length of similarly designed rifles;

(ii) Whether the weapon has a length of pull, measured from the center of the trigger to the center of the shoulder stock or other rearward accessory, component or attachment (including an adjustable or telescoping attachment with the ability to lock into various positions along a buffer tube, receiver extension, or other attachment method), that is consistent with similarly designed rifles;

(iii) Whether the weapon is equipped with sights or a scope with eye relief that require the weapon to be fired from the shoulder in order to be used as designed;

(iv) Whether the surface area that allows the weapon to be fired from the shoulder is created by a buffer tube, receiver extension, or any other accessory, component, or other rearward attachment that is necessary for the cycle of operations;

(v) The manufacturer's direct and indirect marketing and promotional materials indicating the intended use of the weapon; and

(vi) Information demonstrating the likely use of the weapon in the general community.

Shotgun. A weapon designed or redesigned, made or remade, and intended to be fired from the shoulder and designed or redesigned and made or remade to use the energy of the explosive in a fixed shotgun shell to fire through a smooth bore either a number of projectiles (ball shot) or a single projectile for each pull of the trigger, and shall include any such weapon which may be readily restored to fire a fixed shotgun shell.

Transfer. This term and the various derivatives thereof shall include selling, assigning, pledging, leasing, loaning, giving away, or otherwise disposing of. For purposes of this part, the term shall not include the temporary conveyance of a lawfully possessed firearm to a manufacturer or dealer qualified under this part for the sole purpose of repair, identification, evaluation, research, testing, or calibration and return to the same lawful possessor.

United States. The States and the District of Columbia.

U.S.C. The United States Code.

Unserviceable firearm. A firearm which is incapable of discharging a shot by means of an explosive and incapable of being readily restored to a firing condition.

(26 U.S.C. 7805 (68A Stat. 917), 27 U.S.C. 205 (49 Stat. 981 as amended), 18 U.S.C. 926 (82 Stat. 959), and sec. 38, Arms Export Control Act (22 U.S.C. 2778, 90 Stat. 744))

[T.D. ATF–48, 43 FR 13538, Mar. 31, 1978; 44 FR 55842, Sept. 28, 1979; T.D. ATF–241, 51 FR 39630, Oct. 29, 1986; T.D. ATF–270, 53 FR 10492, Mar. 31, 1988; T.D. ATF–396, 63 FR 12647, Mar. 16, 1998; ATF 2013R–9F, 79 FR 46692, Aug. 11, 2014; ATF–41F, 81 FR 2721, Jan. 15, 2016; ATF 2018R–22F, 83 FR 66554, Dec. 26, 2018; ATF–2021R–05F, 87 FR 24747, Apr. 26, 2022; 87 FR 51250, Aug. 22, 2022; ATF–2021R–08F, 88 FR 6575, Jan. 31, 2023]

Subpart C—Administrative and Miscellaneous Provisions

§479.21 Forms prescribed.

(a) The Director is authorized to prescribe all forms required by this part. All of the information called for in each form shall be furnished as indicated by the headings on the form and the instructions on or pertaining to the form. In addition, information called for in each form shall be furnished as required by this part. Each form requiring that it be executed under penalties of perjury shall be executed under penalties of perjury.

(b) Requests for forms should be submitted to the ATF Distribution Center

(*http://www.atf.gov*) or made by calling (202) 648–6420.

(5 U.S.C. 552(a); 80 Stat. 383, as amended)

[T.D. ATF–92, 46 FR 46916, Sept. 23, 1981, as amended by T.D. ATF–241, 51 FR 39630, Oct. 29, 1986; T.D. ATF–270, 53 FR 10508, Mar. 31, 1988; T.D. 372, 61 FR 20725, May 8, 1996; ATF–11F, 73 FR 57242, Oct. 2, 2008; ATF 2013R–9F, 79 FR 46693, Aug. 11, 2014]

§479.22 Right of entry and examination.

Any ATF officer or employee of the Bureau of Alcohol, Tobacco, Firearms, and Explosives duly authorized to perform any function relating to the administration or enforcement of this part may enter during business hours the premises (including places of storage) of any importer or manufacturer of or dealer in firearms, to examine any books, papers, or records required to be kept pursuant to this part, and any firearms kept by such importer, manufacturer or dealer on such premises, and may require the production of any books, papers, or records necessary to determine any liability for tax under 26 U.S.C. Chapter 53, or the observance of 26 U.S.C. Chapter 53, and this part.

[36 FR 14256, Aug. 3, 1971. Redesignated at 40 FR 16835, Apr. 15, 1975, and amended by T.D. ATF–48, 44 FR 55842, Sept. 28, 1979; ATF 2013R–9F, 79 FR 46693, Aug. 11, 2014]

§479.23 Restrictive use of required information.

No information or evidence obtained from an application, registration, or record required to be submitted or retained by a natural person in order to comply with any provision of 26 U.S.C. Chapter 53, or this part or section 207 of the Gun Control Act of 1968 shall be used, directly or indirectly, as evidence against that person in a criminal proceeding with respect to a violation of law occurring prior to or concurrently with the filing of the application or registration, or the compiling of the record containing the information or evidence: *Provided, however,* That the provisions of this section shall not preclude the use of any such information or evidence in a prosecution or other action under any applicable provision of law with respect to the furnishing of false information.

[36 FR 14256, Aug. 3, 1971. Redesignated at 40 FR 16835, Apr. 15, 1975, and amended by T.D. ATF–48, 44 FR 55842, Sept. 28, 1979]

§ 479.24 Destructive device determination.

The Director shall determine in accordance with 26 U.S.C. 5845(f), whether a device is excluded from the definition of a destructive device. A person who desires to obtain a determination under that provision of law for any device which he believes is not likely to be used as a weapon shall submit a written request, in triplicate, for a ruling thereon to the Director. Each such request shall be executed under the penalties of perjury and contain a complete and accurate description of the device, the name and address of the manufacturer or importer thereof, the purpose of and use for which it is intended, and such photographs, diagrams, or drawings as may be necessary to enable the Director to make his determination. The Director may require the submission to him, of a sample of such device for examination and evaluation. If the submission of such device is impracticable, the person requesting the ruling shall so advise the Director and designate the place where the device will be available for examination and evaluation.

[36 FR 14256, Aug. 3, 1971. Redesignated at 40 FR 16835, Apr. 15, 1975, and amended by T.D. ATF–48, 44 FR 55842, Sept. 28, 1979]

§ 479.25 Collector's items.

The Director shall determine in accordance with 26 U.S.C. 5845(a), whether a firearm or device, which although originally designed as a weapon, is by reason of the date of its manufacture, value, design, and other characteristics primarily a collector's item and is not likely to be used as a weapon. A person who desires to obtain a determination under that provision of law shall follow the procedures prescribed in § 479.24 relating to destructive device determinations, and shall include information as to date of manufacture, value, design and other characteristics which would sustain a finding that the firearm or device is primarily a collector's item

and is not likely to be used as a weapon.

[36 FR 14256, Aug. 3, 1971. Redesignated at 40 FR 16835, Apr. 15, 1975, and amended by T.D. ATF–48, 44 FR 55842, Sept. 28, 1979]

§ 479.26 Alternate methods or procedures; emergency variations from requirements.

(a) *Alternate methods or procedures.* Any person subject to the provisions of this part, on specific approval by the Director as provided in this paragraph, may use an alternate method or procedure in lieu of a method or procedure specifically prescribed in this part. The Director may approve an alternate method or procedure, subject to stated conditions, when it is found that:

(1) Good cause is shown for the use of the alternate method or procedure;

(2) The alternate method or procedure is within the purpose of, and consistent with the effect intended by, the specifically prescribed method or procedure and that the alternate method or procedure is substantially equivalent to that specifically prescribed method or procedure; and

(3) The alternate method or procedure will not be contrary to any provision of law and will not result in an increase in cost to the Government or hinder the effective administration of this part. Where such person desires to employ an alternate method or procedure, a written application shall be submitted to the appropriate Director, Industry Operations, for transmittal to the Director. The application shall specifically describe the proposed alternate method or procedure and shall set forth the reasons for it. Alternate methods or procedures may not be employed until the application is approved by the Director. Such person shall, during the period of authorization of an alternate method or procedure, comply with the terms of the approved application. Authorization of any alternate method or procedure may be withdrawn whenever, in the judgment of the Director, the effective administration of this part is hindered by the continuation of the authorization.

(b) *Emergency variations from requirements.* The Director may approve a method of operation other than as specified in this part, where it is found that an emergency exists and the proposed variation from the specified requirements are necessary and the proposed variations (1) will not hinder the effective administration of this part, and (2) will not be contrary to any provisions of law. Variations from requirements granted under this paragraph are conditioned on compliance with the procedures, conditions, and limitations set forth in the approval of the application. Failure to comply in good faith with the procedures, conditions, and limitations shall automatically terminate the authority for the variations, and the person granted the variance shall fully comply with the prescribed requirements of regulations from which the variations were authorized. Authority for any variation may be withdrawn whenever, in the judgment of the Director, the effective administration of this part is hindered by the continuation of the variation. Where a person desires to employ an emergency variation, a written application shall be submitted to the appropriate Director, Industry Operations for transmittal to the Director. The application shall describe the proposed variation and set forth the reasons for it. Variations may not be employed until the application is approved.

(c) *Retention of approved variations.* The person granted the variance shall retain and make available for examination by ATF officers any application approved by the Director under this section.

[T.D. ATF–270, 53 FR 10508 Mar. 31, 1988, as amended by ATF 2013R–9F, 79 FR 46693, Aug. 11, 2014]

Subpart D—Special (Occupational) Taxes

§479.31 Liability for tax.

(a) *General.* Every person who engages in the business of importing, manufacturing, or dealing in (including pawnbrokers) firearms in the United States shall pay a special (occupational) tax at a rate specified by §479.32. The tax shall be paid on or before the date of commencing the taxable business, and thereafter every year on or before July 1. Special (occupational) tax shall not be prorated. The tax shall be computed for the entire tax year (July 1 through June 30), regardless of the portion of the year during which the taxpayer engages in business. Persons commencing business at any time after July 1 in any year are liable for the special (occupational) tax for the entire tax year.

(b) *Each place of business taxable.* An importer, manufacturer, or dealer in firearms incurs special tax liability at each place of business where an occupation subject to special tax is conducted. A place of business means the entire office, plant or area of the business in any one location under the same proprietorship. Passageways, streets, highways, rail crossings, waterways, or partitions dividing the premises are not sufficient separation to require additional special tax, if the divisions of the premises are otherwise contiguous. See also §§479.38–479.39.

(26 U.S.C. 5143, 5801, 5846)

[T.D. ATF–271, 53 FR 17550, May 17, 1988]

§479.32 Special (occupational) tax rates.

Except as provided in §479.32a, the special (occupational) tax rates effective January 1, 1988, are as follows:

	Per year or fraction thereof
Class 1—Importer of firearms (including an importer only of weapons classified as "any other weapon")	$1,000
Class 2—Manufacturer of firearms (including a manufacturer only of weapons classified as "any other weapon")	1,000
Class 3—Dealer in firearms (including a dealer only of weapons classified as "any other weapon")	500

[T.D. ATF–271, 53 FR 17550, May 17, 1988; ATF 2014R–42, 84 FR 12094, Apr. 1, 2019]

§479.32a Reduced rate of tax for small importers and manufacturers.

(a) *General.* Effective January 1, 1988, 26 U.S.C. 5801(b) provides for a reduced rate of special tax with respect to any importer or manufacturer whose gross receipts (for the most recent taxable year ending before the first day of the taxable period to which the special tax imposed by §479.32 relates) are less than $500,000. The rate of tax for such an importer or manufacturer is $500 per year or fraction thereof. The "taxable year" to be used for determining gross receipts is the taxpayer's income tax year. All gross receipts of the taxpayer shall be included, not just the gross receipts of the business subject to special tax. Proprietors of new businesses that have not yet begun a taxable year, as well as proprietors of existing businesses that have not yet ended a taxable year, who commence a new activity subject to special tax, quality for the reduced special (occupational) tax rate, unless the business is a member of a "controlled group"; in that case, the rules of paragraph (b) of this section shall apply.

(b) *Controlled group.* All persons treated as one taxpayer under 26 U.S.C. 5061(e)(3) shall be treated as one taxpayer for the purpose of determining gross receipts under paragraph (a) of this section. "Controlled group" means a controlled group of corporations, as defined in 26 U.S.C. 1563 and implementing regulations in 26 CFR 1.1563–1 through 1.1563–4, except that the words "at least 80 percent" shall be replaced by the words "more than 50 percent" in each place they appear in subsection (a) of 26 U.S.C. 1563, as well as in the implementing regulations. Also, the rules for a "controlled group of corporations" apply in a similar fashion to groups which include partnerships and/or sole proprietorships. If one entity maintains more than 50% control over a group consisting of corporations and one, or more, partnerships and/or sole proprietorships, all of the members of the controlled group are one taxpayer for the purpose of this section.

(c) *Short taxable year.* Gross receipts for any taxable year of less than 12 months shall be annualized by multiplying the gross receipts for the short period by 12 and dividing the result by the number of months in the short period, as required by 26 U.S.C. 448(c)(3).

(d) *Returns and allowances.* Gross receipts for any taxable year shall be reduced by returns and allowances made during that year under 26 U.S.C. 448(c)(3).

(26 U.S.C. 448, 5061, 5801)

[T.D. ATF–271, 53 FR 17550, May 17, 1988]

§ 479.33 Special exemption.

(a) Any person required to pay special (occupational) tax under this part shall be relieved from payment of that tax if he establishes to the satisfaction of the Director that his business is conducted exclusively with, or on behalf of, the United States or any department, independent establishment, or agency thereof. The Director may relieve any person manufacturing firearms for or on behalf of the United States from compliance with any provision of this part in the conduct of the business with respect to such firearms.

(b) The exemption in this section may be obtained by filing with the Director an application, in letter form, setting out the manner in which the applicant conducts his business, the type of firearm to be manufactured, and proof satisfactory to the Director of the existence of the contract with the United States, department, independent establishment, or agency thereof, under which the applicant intends to operate.

§ 479.34 Special tax registration and return.

(a) *General.* Special tax shall be paid by return. The prescribed return is ATF Form 5630.7, Special Tax Registration and Return. Special tax returns, with payment of tax, shall be filed with ATF in accordance with instructions on the form. Properly completing, signing, and timely filing of a return (Form 5630.7) constitutes compliance with 26 U.S.C. 5802.

(b) *Preparation of ATF Form 5630.7.* All of the information called for on Form 5630.7 shall be provided, including:

(1) The true name of the taxpayer.

(2) The trade name(s) (if any) of the business(es) subject to special tax.

(3) The employer identification number (see § 479.35).

(4) The exact location of the place of business, by name and number of building or street, or if these do not exist, by some description in addition to the post office address. In the case of one return for two or more locations, the address to be shown shall be the taxpayer's principal place of business (or principal office, in the case of a corporate taxpayer).

(5) The class(es) of special tax to which the taxpayer is subject.

(6) Ownership and control information: That is, the name, position, and residence address of every owner of the business and of every person having power to control its management and policies with respect to the activity subject to special tax. "Owner of the business" shall include every partner, if the taxpayer is a partnership, and every person owning 10% or more of its stock, if the taxpayer is a corporation. However, the ownership and control information required by this paragraph need not be stated if the same information has been previously provided to ATF in connection with a license application under Part 478 of this chapter, and if the information previously provided is still current.

(c) *Multiple locations and/or classes of tax.* A taxpayer subject to special tax for the same period at more than one location or for more than one class of tax shall—

(1) File one special tax return, ATF Form 5630.7, with payment of tax, to cover all such locations and classes of tax; and

(2) Prepare, in duplicate, a list identified with the taxpayer's name, address (as shown on ATF Form 5630.7), employer identification number, and period covered by the return. The list shall show, by States, the name, address, and tax class of each location for which special tax is being paid. The original of the list shall be filed with ATF in accordance with instructions on the return, and the copy shall be retained at the taxpayer's principal place of business (or principal office, in the case of a corporate taxpayer) for not less than 3 years.

(d) *Signing of ATF Forms 5630.7*—(1) *Ordinary returns.* The return of an individual proprietor shall be signed by the individual. The return of a partnership shall be signed by a general partner. The return of a corporation shall be signed by any officer. In each case, the person signing the return shall designate his or her capacity as "individual owner," "member of firm," or, in the case of a corporation, the title of the officer.

(2) *Fiduciaries.* Receivers, trustees, assignees, executors, administrators, and other legal representatives who continue the business of a bankrupt, insolvent, deceased person, etc., shall indicate the fiduciary capacity in which they act.

(3) *Agent or attorney in fact.* If a return is signed by an agent or attorney in fact, the signature shall be preceded by the name of the principal and followed by the title of the agent or attorney in fact. A return signed by a person as agent will not be accepted unless there is filed, with the ATF office with which the return is required to be filed, a power of attorney authorizing the agent to perform the act.

(4) *Perjury statement.* ATF Forms 5630.7 shall contain or be verified by a written declaration that the return has been executed under the penalties of perjury.

(e) *Identification of taxpayer.* If the taxpayer is an individual, with the initial return such person shall securely attach to Form 5630.7 a photograph of the individual 2 × 2 inches in size, clearly showing a full front view of the features of the individual with head bare, with the distance from the top of the head to the point of the chin approximately 1¼ inches, and which shall have been taken within 6 months prior to the date of completion of the return. The individual shall also attach to the return a properly completed FBI Form FD–258 (Fingerprint Card). The fingerprints must be clear for accurate classification and should be taken by someone properly equipped to take them: *Provided,* That the provisions of this paragraph shall not apply to individuals who have filed with ATF a properly executed Application for License under 18 U.S.C. Chapter 44, Firearms, ATF Form 7 (5310.12), as specified in § 478.44(a).

(26 U.S.C. 5142, 5802, 5846, 6061, 6065, 6151)

[T.D. ATF–271, 53 FR 17551, May 17, 1988, as amended by T.D. ATF–363, 60 FR 17456, Apr. 6, 1995; ATF 2013R–9F, 79 FR 46693, Aug. 11, 2014]

§ 479.35 Employer identification number.

(a) *Requirement.* The employer identification number (defined in 26 CFR 301.7701–12) of the taxpayer who has been assigned such a number shall be shown on each special tax return, including amended returns, filed under this subpart. Failure of the taxpayer to include the employer identification number may result in the imposition of the penalty specified in § 70.113 of this chapter.

(b) *Application for employer identification number.* Each taxpayer who files a special tax return, who has not already been assigned an employer identification number, shall file IRS Form SS–4 to apply for one. The taxpayer shall apply for and be assigned only one employer identification number, regardless of the number of places of business for which the taxpayer is required to file a special tax return. The employer identification number shall be applied for no later than 7 days after the filing of the taxpayer's first special tax return. IRS Form SS–4 may be obtained from the director of an IRS service center or from any IRS district director.

(c) *Preparation and filing of IRS Form SS–4.* The taxpayer shall prepare and file IRS Form SS–4, together with any supplementary statement, in accordance with the instructions on the form or issued in respect to it.

(26 U.S.C. 6109)

[T.D. ATF–271, 53 FR 17551, May 17, 1988, as amended by T.D. ATF–301, 55 FR 47657, Nov. 14, 1990]

§ 479.36 The special tax stamp, receipt for special (occupational) taxes.

Upon filing a properly completed and executed return (Form 5630.7) accompanied by remittance of the full amount due, the taxpayer will be issued a special tax stamp as evidence of payment of the special (occupational) tax.

[36 FR 14256, Aug. 3, 1971. Redesignated at 40 FR 16835, Apr. 15, 1975, and amended by T.D. ATF–251, 52 FR 19334, May 22, 1987; T.D. ATF–363, 60 FR 17456, Apr. 6, 1995]

§ 479.37 Certificates in lieu of stamps lost or destroyed.

When a special tax stamp has been lost or destroyed, such fact should be reported immediately to the Chief, National Firearms Act Branch who issued the stamp. A certificate in lieu of the lost or destroyed stamp will be issued to the taxpayer upon the submission of an affidavit showing to the satisfaction

of the Chief, National Firearms Act Branch that the stamp was lost or destroyed.

[36 FR 14256, Aug. 3, 1971. Redesignated at 40 FR 16835, Apr. 15, 1975, and amended by T.D. ATF–251, 52 FR 19334, May 22, 1987; ATF 2013R–9F, 79 FR 46693, Aug. 11, 2014]

§ 479.38 Engaging in business at more than one location.

A person shall pay the special (occupational) tax for each location where he engages in any business taxable under 26 U.S.C. 5801. However, a person paying a special (occupational) tax covering his principal place of business may utilize other locations solely for storage of firearms without incurring special (occupational) tax liability at such locations. A manufacturer, upon the single payment of the appropriate special (occupational) tax, may sell firearms, if such firearms are of his own manufacture, at the place of manufacture and at his principal office or place of business if no such firearms, except samples, are kept at such office or place of business. When a person changes the location of a business for which he has paid the special (occupational) tax, he will be liable for another such tax unless the change is properly registered with the Chief, National Firearms Act Branch for the region in which the special tax stamp was issued, as provided in § 479.46.

[36 FR 14256, Aug. 3, 1971. Redesignated at 40 FR 16835, Apr. 15, 1975, and amended by T.D. ATF–48, 44 FR 55842, Sept. 28, 1979; T.D. ATF–251, 52 FR 19334, May 22, 1987; T.D. ATF–271, 53 FR 17551, May 17, 1988; ATF 2013R–9F, 79 FR 46693, Aug. 11, 2014]

§ 479.39 Engaging in more than one business at the same location.

If more than one business taxable under 26 U.S.C. 5801, is carried on at the same location during a taxable year, the special (occupational) tax imposed on each such business must be paid. This section does not require a qualified manufacturer or importer to qualify as a dealer if such manufacturer or importer also engages in business on his qualified premises as a dealer. However, a qualified manufacturer who engages in business as an importer must also qualify as an importer. Further, a qualified dealer is not entitled to engage in business as a manufacturer or importer.

[36 FR 14256, Aug. 3, 1971. Redesignated at 40 FR 16835, Apr. 15, 1975, and amended by T.D. ATF–48, 44 FR 55842, Sept. 28, 1979; T.D. ATF–271, 53 FR 17551, May 17, 1988]

§479.40 Partnership liability.

Any number of persons doing business in partnership at any one location shall be required to pay but one special (occupational) tax.

§479.41 Single sale.

A single sale, unattended by circumstances showing the one making the sale to be engaged in business, does not create special (occupational) tax liability.

CHANGE OF OWNERSHIP

§479.42 Changes through death of owner.

Whenever any person who has paid special (occupational) tax dies, the surviving spouse or child, or executors or administrators, or other legal representatives, may carry on this business for the remainder of the term for which tax has been paid and at the place (or places) for which the tax was paid, without any additional payment, subject to the following conditions. If the surviving spouse or child, or executor or administrator, or other legal representative of the deceased taxpayer continues the business, such person shall, within 30 days after the date on which the successor begins to carry on the business, file a new return, Form 5630.7, with ATF in accordance with the instructions on the form. The return thus executed shall show the name of the original taxpayer, together with the basis of the succession. (As to liability in case of failure to register, see §479.49.)

[T.D. ATF–70, 45 FR 33979, May 21, 1980, as amended by T.D. ATF–251, 52 FR 19334, May 22, 1987; T.D. ATF–363, 60 FR 17456, Apr. 6, 1995]

§479.43 Changes through bankruptcy of owner.

A receiver or referee in bankruptcy may continue the business under the stamp issued to the taxpayer at the place and for the period for which the tax was paid. An assignee for the benefit of creditors may continue business under his assignor's special tax stamp without incurring additional special (occupational) tax liability. In such cases, the change shall be registered with ATF in a manner similar to that required by §479.42.

[36 FR 14256, Aug. 3, 1971. Redesignated at 40 FR 16835, Apr. 15, 1975, and amended by T.D. ATF–251, 52 FR 19334, May 22, 1987]

§479.44 Change in partnership or unincorporated association.

When one or more members withdraw from a partnership or an unincorporated association, the remaining member, or members, may, without incurring additional special (occupational) tax liability, carry on the same business at the same location for the balance of the taxable period for which special (occupational) tax was paid, provided any such change shall be registered in the same manner as required by §479.42. Where new member(s) are taken into a partnership or an unincorporated association, the new firm so constituted may not carry on business under the special tax stamp of the old firm. The new firm must file a return, pay the special (occupational) tax and register in the same manner as a person who first engages in business is required to do under §479.34 even though the name of the new firm may be the same as that of the old. Where the members of a partnership or an unincorporated association, which has paid special (occupational) tax, form a corporation to continue the business, a new special tax stamp must be taken out in the name of the corporation.

§479.45 Changes in corporation.

Additional special (occupational) tax is not required by reason of a mere change of name or increase in the capital stock of a corporation if the laws of the State of incorporation provide for such change or increase without the formation of a new corporation. A stockholder in a corporation who after its dissolution continues the business, incurs new special (occupational) tax liability.

CHANGE OF BUSINESS LOCATION

§ 479.46 Notice by taxpayer.

Whenever during the taxable year a taxpayer intends to remove his business to a location other than specified in his last special (occupational) tax return (see § 479.34), he shall file with ATF (a) a return, Form 5630.7, bearing the notation "Removal Registry," and showing the new address intended to be used, (b) his current special tax stamp, and (c) a letter application requesting the amendment of his registration. The Chief, National Firearms Act Branch, upon approval of the application, shall return the special tax stamp, amended to show the new business location. Firearms operations shall not be commenced at the new business location by the taxpayer prior to the required approval of his application to so change his business location.

[36 FR 14256, Aug. 3, 1971. Redesignated at 40 FR 16835, Apr. 15, 1975, and amended by T.D. ATF–251, 52 FR 19334, May 22, 1987; T.D. ATF–363, 60 FR 17456, Apr. 6, 1995; ATF 2013R–9F, 79 FR 46693, Aug 11, 2014]

CHANGE OF TRADE NAME

§ 479.47 Notice by taxpayer.

Whenever during the taxable year a taxpayer intends to change the name of his business, he shall file with ATF (a) a return, Form 5630.7, bearing the notation "Amended," and showing the trade name intended to be used, (b) his current special tax stamp, and (c) a letter application requesting the amendment of his registration. The Chief, National Firearms Act Branch, upon approval of the application, shall return the special tax stamp, amended to show the new trade name. Firearms operations shall not be commenced under the new trade name by the taxpayer prior to the required approval of his application to so change the trade name.

[36 FR 14256, Aug. 3, 1971. Redesignated at 40 FR 16835, Apr. 15, 1975, and amended by T.D. ATF–251, 52 FR 19334, May 22, 1987; T.D. ATF–363, 60 FR 17456, Apr. 6, 1995; ATF 2013R–9F, 79 FR 46693, Aug. 11, 2014]

PENALTIES AND INTEREST

§ 479.48 Failure to pay special (occupational) tax.

Any person who engages in a business taxable under 26 U.S.C. 5801, without timely payment of the tax imposed with respect to such business (see § 479.34) shall be liable for such tax, plus the interest and penalties thereon (see 26 U.S.C. 6601 and 6651). In addition, such person may be liable for criminal penalties under 26 U.S.C. 5871.

[36 FR 14256, Aug. 3, 1971. Redesignated at 40 FR 16835, Apr. 15, 1975, and amended by T.D. ATF–48, 44 FR 55842, Sept. 28, 1979]

§ 479.49 Failure to register change or removal.

Any person succeeding to and carrying on a business for which special (occupational) tax has been paid without registering such change within 30 days thereafter, and any taxpayer removing his business with respect to which special (occupational) tax has been paid to a place other than that for which tax was paid without obtaining approval therefor (see § 479.46), will incur liability to an additional payment of the tax, addition to tax and interest, as provided in sections 5801, 6651, and 6601, respectively, I.R.C., for failure to make return (see § 479.50) or pay tax, as well as criminal penalties for carrying on business without payment of special (occupational) tax (see section 5871 I.R.C.).

§ 479.50 Delinquency.

Any person liable for special (occupational) tax under section 5801, I.R.C., who fails to file a return (Form 5630.7), as prescribed, will be liable for a delinquency penalty computed on the amount of tax due unless a return (Form 5630.7) is later filed and failure to file the return timely is shown to the satisfaction of the Chief, National Firearms Act Branch, to be due to reasonable cause. The delinquency penalty to be added to the tax is 5 percent if the failure is for not more than 1 month, with an additional 5 percent for each additional month or fraction thereof during which failure continues, not to exceed 25 percent in the aggregate (section 6651, I.R.C.). However, no delinquency penalty is assessed where the 50 percent addition to tax is assessed for fraud (see §479.51).

[36 FR 14256, Aug. 3, 1971. Redesignated at 40 FR 16835, Apr. 15, 1975, and amended by T.D. ATF–251, 52 FR 19334, May 22, 1987; T.D. ATF–363, 60 FR 17453, Apr. 6, 1996; ATF 2013R–9F, 79 FR 46693, Aug. 11, 2014]

§479.51   Fraudulent return.

If any part of any underpayment of tax required to be shown on a return is due to fraud, there shall be added to the tax an amount equal to 50 percent of the underpayment, but no delinquency penalty shall be assessed with respect to the same underpayment (section 6653, I.R.C.).

APPLICATION OF STATE LAWS

§479.52   State regulations.

Special tax stamps are merely receipts for the tax. Payment of tax under Federal law confers no privilege to act contrary to State law. One to whom a special tax stamp has been issued may still be punishable under a State law prohibiting or controlling the manufacture, possession or transfer of firearms. On the other hand, compliance with State law confers no immunity under Federal law. Persons who engage in the business of importing, manufacturing or dealing in firearms, in violation of the law of a State, are nevertheless required to pay special (occupational) tax as imposed under the internal revenue laws of the United States. For provisions relating to restrictive use of information furnished to comply with the provisions of this part see §479.23.

Subpart E—Tax on Making Firearms

§479.61   Rate of tax.

Except as provided in this subpart, there shall be levied, collected, and paid upon the making of a firearm a tax at the rate of $200 for each firearm made. This tax shall be paid by the person making the firearm. Payment of the tax on the making of a firearm shall be represented by a $200 adhesive stamp bearing the words "National Firearms Act." The stamps are maintained by the Director.

[T.D. ATF–270, 53 FR 10508, Mar. 31, 1988]

APPLICATION TO MAKE A FIREARM

§479.62   Application to make.

(a) *General.* No person shall make a firearm unless the person has filed with the Director a completed application on ATF Form 1 (5320.1), Application to Make and Register a Firearm, in duplicate, executed under the penalties of perjury, to make and register the firearm and has received the approval of the Director to make the firearm, which approval shall effectuate registration of the firearm to the applicant. If the applicant is not a licensed manufacturer, importer, or dealer qualified under this part and is a partnership, company (including a Limited Liability Company (LLC)), association, trust, or corporation, all information on the Form 1 application shall be furnished for each responsible person of the applicant

(b) *Preparation of ATF Form 1.* All of the information called for on Form 1 shall be provided, including:

(1) The type of application, *i.e.*, tax paid or tax exempt. If the making of the firearm is taxable, the applicant shall submit a remittance in the amount of $200 with the application in accordance with the instructions on the form;

(2) The identity of the applicant. If an individual, the applicant shall provide the applicant's name, address, and date of birth, and also comply with the identification requirements prescribed in §479.63(a). If other than an individual, the applicant shall provide its name, address, and employer identification number, if any, as well as the name and address of each responsible person. Each responsible person of the applicant also shall comply with the identification requirements prescribed in §479.63(b);

(3) A description of the firearm to be made by type; caliber, gauge, or size; model; length of barrel; serial number; other marks of identification; and the name and address of the original manufacturer (if the applicant is not the original manufacturer);

(4) The applicant's Federal firearms license number (if any);

(5) The applicant's special (occupational) tax stamp (if applicable); and

(6) If the applicant (including, if other than an individual, any responsible person) is an alien admitted under a nonimmigrant visa, applicable documentation demonstrating that the nonimmigrant alien falls within an exception to 18 U.S.C. 922(g)(5)(B) under 18 U.S.C. 922(y)(2), or has obtained a waiver of that provision under 18 U.S.C. 922(y)(3).

(c) *Notification of chief law enforcement officer.* Prior to the submission of the application to the Director, all applicants and responsible persons shall forward a completed copy of Form 1 or a completed copy of Form 5320.23, respectively, to the chief law enforcement officer of the locality in which the applicant or responsible person is located. The chief law enforcement officer is the local chief of police, county sheriff, head of the State police, or State or local district attorney or prosecutor. If the applicant is not a licensed manufacturer, importer, or dealer qualified under this part and is a partnership, company, association, or corporation, for purposes of this section, it is considered located at its principal office or principal place of business; if a trust, for purposes of this section, it is considered located at the primary location at which the firearm will be maintained.

(d) *Approval of Form 1.* If the application is approved, the Director will affix a National Firearms Act stamp to the original application in the space provided therefor and properly cancel the stamp (*see* §479.67). The approved application will then be returned to the applicant.

[ATF–41F, 81 FR 2721, Jan. 15, 2016]

§479.63 Identification of applicant.

(a) If the applicant is an individual, the applicant shall:

(1) Securely attach to each copy of the Form 1, in the space provided on the form, a 2 x 2-inch photograph of the applicant, clearly showing a full front view of the features of the applicant with head bare, with the distance from the top of the head to the point of the chin approximately 1¼ inches, and

which shall have been taken within 1 year prior to the date of the application; and

(2) Attach to the application two properly completed FBI Forms FD–258 (Fingerprint Card). The fingerprints must be clear for accurate classification and should be taken by someone properly equipped to take them.

(b) If the applicant is not a licensed manufacturer, importer, or dealer qualified under this part and is a partnership, company (including a Limited Liability Company (LLC)), association, trust, or corporation, the applicant shall:

(1) Be identified on the Form 1 by the name and exact location of the place of business, including the name and number of the building and street, and the name of the county in which the business is located or, in the case of a trust, the primary location at which the firearm will be maintained. In the case of two or more locations, the address shown shall be the principal place of business (or principal office, in the case of a corporation) or, in the case of a trust, the primary location at which the firearm will be maintained;

(2) Except as provided in paragraph (c) of this section, attach to the application—

(i) Documentation evidencing the existence and validity of the entity, which includes complete and unredacted copies of partnership agreements, articles of incorporation, corporate registration, and declarations of trust, with any trust schedules, attachments, exhibits, and enclosures;

(ii) A completed ATF Form 5320.23 for each responsible person. Form 5320.23 requires certain identifying information, including each responsible person's full name, position, home address, date of birth, and country of citizenship if other than the United States;

(iii) In the space provided on Form 5320.23, a 2 x 2-inch photograph of each responsible person, clearly showing a full front view of the features of the responsible person with head bare, with the distance from the top of the head to the point of the chin approximately 1¼ inches, and which shall have been taken within 1 year prior to the date of the application;

116

(iv) Two properly completed FBI Forms FD–258 (Fingerprint Card) for each responsible person. The fingerprints must be clear for accurate classification and should be taken by someone properly equipped to take them.

(c) If the applicant entity has had an application approved as a maker or transferee within the preceding 24 months, and there has been no change to the documentation previously provided, the entity may provide a certification that the information has not been changed since the prior approval and shall identify the application for which the documentation had been submitted by form number, serial number, and date approved.

[ATF–41F, 81 FR 2721, Jan. 15, 2016]

§479.64 Procedure for approval of application.

The application to make a firearm, Form 1 (Firearms), must be forwarded directly, in duplicate, by the maker of the firearm to the Director in accordance with the instructions on the form. The Director will consider the application for approval or disapproval. If the application is approved, the Director will return the original thereof to the maker of the firearm and retain the duplicate. Upon receipt of the approved application, the maker is authorized to make the firearm described therein. The maker of the firearm shall not, under any circumstances, make the firearm until the application, satisfactorily executed, has been forwarded to the Director and has been approved and returned by the Director with the National Firearms Act stamp affixed. If the application is disapproved, the original Form 1 (Firearms) and the remittance submitted by the applicant for the purchase of the stamp will be returned to the applicant with the reason for disapproval stated on the form.

[T.D. ATF–270, 53 FR 10509, Mar. 31, 1988]

§479.65 Denial of application.

An application to make a firearm shall not be approved by the Director if the making or possession of the firearm would place the person making the firearm in violation of law.

§479.66 Subsequent transfer of firearms.

Where a firearm which has been made in compliance with 26 U.S.C. 5821, and the regulations contained in this part, is to be transferred subsequently, the transfer provisions of the firearms laws and regulations must be complied with. (See subpart F of this part).

[36 FR 14256, Aug. 3, 1971. Redesignated at 40 FR 16835, Apr. 15, 1975, and amended by T.D. ATF–48, 44 FR 55842, Sept. 28, 1979]

§479.67 Cancellation of stamp.

The person affixing to a Form 1 (Firearms) a "National Firearms Act" stamp shall cancel it by writing or stamping thereon, in ink, his initials, and the day, month and year, in such manner as to render it unfit for reuse. The cancellation shall not so deface the stamp as to prevent its denomination and genuineness from being readily determined.

EXCEPTIONS TO TAX ON MAKING FIREARMS

§479.68 Qualified manufacturer.

A manufacturer qualified under this part to engage in such business may make firearms without payment of the making tax. However, such manufacturer shall report and register each firearm made in the manner prescribed by this part.

[36 FR 14256, Aug. 3, 1971. Redesignated at 40 FR 16835, Apr. 15, 1975, and amended by T.D. ATF–271, 53 FR 17551, May 17, 1988]

§479.69 Making a firearm for the United States.

A firearm may be made by, or on behalf of, the United States or any department, independent establishment, or agency thereof without payment of the making tax. However, if a firearm is to be made on behalf of the United States, the maker must file an application, in duplicate, on Form 1 (Firearms) and obtain the approval of the Director in the manner prescribed in §479.62.

§479.70 Certain government entities.

A firearm may be made without payment of the making tax by, or on behalf of, any State, or possession of the

United States, any political subdivision thereof, or any official police organization of such a government entity engaged in criminal investigations. Any person making a firearm under this exemption shall first file an application, in duplicate, on Form 1 (Firearms) and obtain the approval of the Director as prescribed in § 479.62.

REGISTRATION

§ 479.71 Proof of registration.

The approval by the Director of an application, Form 1 (Firearms), to make a firearm under this subpart shall effectuate registration of the firearm described in the Form 1 (Firearms) to the person making the firearm. The original Form 1 (Firearms) showing approval by the Director shall be retained by the maker to establish proof of his registration of the firearm described therein, and shall be made available to any ATF officer on request.

Subpart F—Transfer Tax

§ 479.81 Scope of tax.

Except as otherwise provided in this part, each transfer of a firearm in the United States is subject to a tax to be represented by an adhesive stamp of the proper denomination bearing the words "National Firearms Act" to be affixed to the Form 4 (Firearms), Application for Transfer and Registration of Firearm, as provided in this subpart.

§ 479.82 Rate of tax.

The transfer tax imposed with respect to firearms transferred within the United States is at the rate of $200 for each firearm transferred, except that the transfer tax on any firearm classified as "any other weapon" shall be at the rate of $5 for each such firearm transferred. The tax imposed on the transfer of the firearm shall be paid by the transferor.

§ 479.83 Transfer tax in addition to import duty.

The transfer tax imposed by section 5811, I.R.C., is in addition to any import duty.

APPLICATION AND ORDER FOR TRANSFER OF FIREARM

§ 479.84 Application to transfer.

(a) *General.* Except as otherwise provided in this subpart, no firearm may be transferred in the United States unless an application, Form 4 (5320.4), Application for Tax Paid Transfer and Registration of Firearm, in duplicate, executed under the penalties of perjury, to transfer the firearm and register it to the transferee has been filed with and approved by the Director. The application shall be filed by the transferor. If the transferee is not a licensed manufacturer, importer, or dealer qualified under this part and is a partnership, company (including a Limited Liability Company (LLC)), association, trust, or corporation, all information on the Form 4 application shall be furnished for each responsible person of the transferee.

(b) *Preparation of ATF Form 4.* All of the information called for on Form 4 shall be provided, including:

(1) The type of firearm being transferred. If the firearm is other than one classified as "any other weapon," the applicant shall submit a remittance in the amount of $200 with the application in accordance with the instructions on the form. If the firearm is classified as "any other weapon," the applicant shall submit a remittance in the amount of $5;

(2) The identity of the transferor by name and address and, if the transferor is other than a natural person, the title or legal status of the person executing the application in relation to the transferor;

(3) The transferor's Federal firearms license number (if any);

(4) The transferor's special (occupational) tax stamp (if any);

(5) The identity of the transferee by name and address and, if the transferee is a person not qualified as a manufacturer, importer, or dealer under this part, the transferee shall be further identified in the manner prescribed in § 479.85;

(6) The transferee's Federal firearms license number (if any);

(7) The transferee's special (occupational) tax stamp (if applicable); and

(8) A description of the firearm to be transferred by name and address of the manufacturer or importer (if known); caliber, gauge, or size; model; serial number; in the case of a short-barreled shotgun or a short-barreled rifle, the length of the barrel; in the case of a weapon made from a rifle or shotgun, the overall length of the weapon and the length of the barrel; and any other identifying marks on the firearm. In the event the firearm does not bear a serial number, the applicant shall obtain a serial number from ATF and shall stamp (impress) or otherwise conspicuously place such serial number on the firearm in a manner not susceptible of being readily obliterated, altered, or removed.

(9) If the transferee (including, if other than an individual, any responsible person) is an alien admitted under a nonimmigrant visa, applicable documentation demonstrating that the nonimmigrant alien falls within an exception to 18 U.S.C. 922(g)(5)(B) under 18 U.S.C. 922(y)(2), or has obtained a waiver of that provision under 18 U.S.C. 922(y)(3).

(c) *Notification of chief law enforcement officer.* Prior to the submission of the application to the Director, all transferees and responsible persons shall forward a completed copy of Form 4 or a completed copy of Form 5320.23, respectively, to the chief law enforcement officer of the locality in which the transferee or responsible person is located. The chief law enforcement officer is the local chief of police, county sheriff, head of the State police, State or local district attorney or prosecutor. If the transferee is not a licensed manufacturer, importer, or dealer qualified under this part and is a partnership, company, association, or corporation, for purposes of this section, it is considered located at its principal office or principal place of business; if the transferee is not a licensed manufacturer, importer, or dealer qualified under this part and is a trust, for purposes of this section, it is considered located at the primary location at which the firearm will be maintained.

(d) *Approval of Form 4.* If the application is approved, the Director will affix a National Firearms Act stamp to the original application in the space provided therefor and properly cancel the stamp (*see* § 479.87). The approved application will then be returned to the transferor.

[ATF–41F, 81 FR 2722, Jan. 15, 2016]

§ 479.85 Identification of transferee.

(a) If the transferee is an individual, such person shall:

(1) Securely attach to each copy of the Form 4, in the space provided on the form, a 2 x 2-inch photograph of the applicant, clearly showing a full front view of the features of the applicant with head bare, with the distance from the top of the head to the point of the chin approximately 1¼ inches, and which shall have been taken within 1 year prior to the date of the application; and

(2) Attach to the application two properly completed FBI Forms FD–258 (Fingerprint Card). The fingerprints must be clear for accurate classification and should be taken by someone properly equipped to take them.

(b) If the transferee is not a licensed manufacturer, importer, or dealer qualified under this part and is a partnership, company, association, trust, or corporation, such person shall:

(1) Be identified on the Form 4 by the name and exact location of the place of business, including the name and number of the building and street, and the name of the county in which the business is located or, in the case of a trust, the primary location at which the firearm will be maintained. In the case of two or more locations, the address shown shall be the principal place of business (or principal office, in the case of a corporation) or, in the case of a trust, the primary location at which the firearm will be maintained;

(2) Except as provided in paragraph (c) of this section, attach to the application—

(i) Documentation evidencing the existence and validity of the entity, which includes complete and unredacted copies of partnership agreements, articles of incorporation, corporate registration, and declarations of trust, with any trust schedules, attachments, exhibits, and enclosures;

(ii) A completed ATF Form 5320.23 for each responsible person. Form 5320.23

requires certain identifying information, including the responsible person's full name, position, home address, date of birth, and country of citizenship if other than the United States;

(iii) In the space provided on Form 5320.23, a 2 x 2-inch photograph of each responsible person, clearly showing a full front view of the features of the responsible person with head bare, with the distance from the top of the head to the point of the chin approximately 1¼ inches, and which shall have been taken within 1 year prior to the date of the application; and

(iv) Two properly completed FBI Forms FD–258 (Fingerprint Card) for each responsible person. The fingerprints must be clear for accurate classification and should be taken by someone properly equipped to take them.

(c) If the applicant entity has had an application approved as a maker or transferee within the preceding 24 months, and there has been no change to the documentation previously provided, the entity may provide a certification that the information has not been changed since the prior approval and shall identify the application for which the documentation had been submitted by form number, serial number, and date approved.

[ATF–41F, 81 FR 2722, Jan. 15, 2016]

§ 479.86 Action on application.

The Director will consider a completed and properly executed application, Form 4 (Firearms), to transfer a firearm. If the application is approved, the Director will affix the appropriate National Firearms Act stamp, cancel it, and return the original application showing approval to the transferor who may then transfer the firearm to the transferee along with the approved application. The approval of an application, Form 4 (Firearms), by the Director will effectuate registration of the firearm to the transferee. The transferee shall not take possession of a firearm until the application, Form 4 (Firearms), for the transfer filed by the transferor has been approved by the Director and registration of the firearm is effectuated to the transferee. The transferee shall retain the approved application as proof that the firearm described therein is registered to the

transferee, and shall make the approved Form 4 (Firearms) available to any ATF officer on request. If the application, Form 4 (Firearms), to transfer a firearm is disapproved by the Director, the original application and the remittance for purchase of the stamp will be returned to the transferor with reasons for the disapproval stated on the application. An application, Form 4 (Firearms), to transfer a firearm shall be denied if the transfer, receipt, or possession of a firearm would place the transferee in violation of law. In addition to any other records checks that may be conducted to determine whether the transfer, receipt, or possession of a firearm would place the transferee in violation of law, the Director shall contact the National Instant Criminal Background Check System.

[T.D. ATF–270, 53 FR 10509, Mar. 31, 1988, as amended by T.D. ATF–415, 63 FR 58281, Oct. 29, 1998]

§ 479.87 Cancellation of stamp.

The method of cancellation of the stamp required by this subpart as prescribed in § 479.67 shall be used.

EXEMPTIONS RELATING TO TRANSFERS OF FIREARMS

§ 479.88 Special (occupational) taxpayers.

(a) A firearm registered to a person qualified under this part to engage in business as an importer, manufacturer, or dealer may be transferred by that person without payment of the transfer tax to any other person qualified under this part to manufacture, import, or deal in firearms.

(b) The exemption provided in paragraph (a) of this section shall be obtained by the transferor of the firearm filing with the Director an application, Form 3 (Firearms), Application for Tax-exempt Transfer of Firearm and Registration to Special (Occupational) Taxpayer, in duplicate, executed under the penalties of perjury. The application, Form 3 (Firearms), shall (1) show the name and address of the transferor and of the transferee, (2) identify the Federal firearms license and special (occupational) tax stamp of the transferor and of the transferee, (3) show the name and address of the manufacturer and the importer of the firearm, if known, (4) show the type, model, overall length (if applicable), length of barrel, caliber, gauge or size, serial number, and other marks of identification of the firearm, and (5) contain a statement by the transferor that he is entitled to the exemption because the transferee is a person qualified under this part to manufacture, import, or deal in firearms. If the Director approves an application, Form 3 (Firearms), he shall return the original Form 3 (Firearms) to the transferor with the approval noted thereon. Approval of an application, Form 3 (Firearms), by the Director shall remove registration of the firearm reported thereon from the transferor and shall effectuate the registration of that firearm to the transferee. Upon receipt of the approved Form 3 (Firearms), the transferor shall deliver same with the firearm to the transferee. The transferor shall not transfer the firearm to the transferee until his application, Form 3 (Firearms), has been approved by the Director and the original thereof has been returned to the transferor. If the Director disapproves the application, Form 3 (Firearms), he shall return the original Form 3 (Firearms) to the transferor with the reasons for the disapproval stated thereon.

(c) The transferor shall be responsible for establishing the exempt status of the transferee before making a transfer under the provisions of this section. Therefore, before engaging in transfer negotiations with the transferee, the transferor should satisfy himself as to the claimed exempt status of the transferee and the bona fides of the transaction. If not fully satisfied, the transferor should communicate with the Director, report all circumstances regarding the proposed transfer, and await the Director's advice before making application for the transfer. An unapproved transfer or a transfer to an unauthorized person may subject the transferor to civil and criminal liabilities. (See 26 U.S.C. 5852, 5861, and 5871.)

[36 FR 14256, Aug. 3, 1971. Redesignated at 40 FR 16835, Apr. 15, 1975, and amended by T.D. ATF–48, 44 FR 55842, Sept. 28, 1979; T.D. ATF–271, 53 FR 17551, May 17, 1988]

§ 479.89 Transfers to the United States.

A firearm may be transferred to the United States or any department, independent establishment or agency thereof without payment of the transfer tax. However, the procedures for the transfer of a firearm as provided in §479.90 shall be followed in a tax-exempt transfer of a firearm under this section, unless the transferor is relieved of such requirement under other provisions of this part.

§ 479.90 Certain government entities.

(a) A firearm may be transferred without payment of the transfer tax to or from any State, possession of the United States, any political subdivision thereof, or any official police organization of such a governmental entity engaged in criminal investigations.

(b) The exemption provided in paragraph (a) of this section shall be obtained by the transferor of the firearm filing with the Director an application, Form 5 (Firearms), Application for Tax-exempt Transfer and Registration of Firearm, in duplicate, executed under the penalties of perjury. The application shall (1) show the name and address of the transferor and of the transferee, (2) identify the Federal firearms license and special (occupational) tax stamp, if any, of the transferor and of the transferee, (3) show the name and address of the manufacturer and the importer of the firearm, if known, (4) show the type, model, overall length (if applicable), length of barrel, caliber, gauge or size, serial number, and other marks of identification of the firearm, and (5) contain a statement by the transferor that the transferor is entitled to the exemption because either the transferor or the transferee is a governmental entity coming within the purview of paragraph (a) of this section. In the case of a transfer of a firearm by a governmental entity to a transferee who is a person not qualified as a manufacturer, importer, or dealer under this part, the transferee shall be further identified in the manner prescribed in §479.85. If the Director approves an application, Form 5 (Firearms), the original Form 5 (Firearms) shall be returned to the transferor with the approval noted thereon. Approval of an application, Form 5 (Firearms), by the Director shall effectuate the registration of that firearm to the transferee. Upon receipt of the approved Form 5 (Firearms), the transferor shall deliver same with the firearm to the transferee. The transferor shall not transfer the firearm to the transferee until the application, Form 5 (Firearms), has been approved by the Director and the original thereof has been returned to the transferor. If the Director disapproves the application, Form 5 (Firearms), the original Form 5 (Firearms) shall be returned to the transferor with the reasons for the disapproval stated thereon. An application by a governmental entity to transfer a firearm shall be denied if the transfer, receipt, or possession of a firearm would place the transferee in violation of law.

(c) The transferor shall be responsible for establishing the exempt status of the transferee before making a transfer under the provisions of this section. Therefore, before engaging in transfer negotiations with the transferee, the transferor should satisfy himself of the claimed exempt status of the transferee and the bona fides of the transaction. If not fully satisfied, the transferor should communicate with the Director, report all circumstances regarding the proposed transfer, and await the Director's advice before making application for transfer. An unapproved transfer or a transfer to an unauthorized person may subject the transferor to civil and criminal liabilities. (See 26 U.S.C. 5852, 5861, and 5871.)

[36 FR 14256, Aug. 3, 1971. Redesignated at 40 FR 16835, Apr. 15, 1975, and amended by T.D. ATF–48, 44 FR 55842, Sept. 28, 1979; T.D. ATF–241, 51 FR 39632, Oct. 29, 1986; T.D. ATF–270, 53 FR 10510, Mar. 31, 1988; ATF–41F, 81 FR 2723, Jan. 15, 2016]

§ 479.90a Estates.

(a) The executor, administrator, personal representative, or other person authorized under State law to dispose of property in an estate (collectively "executor") may possess a firearm registered to a decedent during the term of probate without such possession being treated as a "transfer" as defined in § 479.11. No later than the close of probate, the executor must submit an application to transfer the firearm to beneficiaries or other transferees in accordance with this section. If the transfer is to a beneficiary, the executor shall file an ATF Form 5 (5320.5), Application for Tax Exempt Transfer and Registration of Firearm, to register a firearm to any beneficiary of an estate in accordance with § 479.90. The executor will identify the estate as the transferor, and will sign the form on behalf of the decedent, showing the executor's title (*e.g.*, executor, administrator, personal representative, etc.) and the date of filing. The executor must also provide the documentation prescribed in paragraph (c) of this section.

(b) If there are no beneficiaries of the estate or the beneficiaries do not wish to possess the registered firearm, the executor will dispose of the property outside the estate (*i.e.*, to a non-beneficiary). The executor shall file an ATF Form 4 (5320.4), Application for Tax Paid Transfer and Registration of Firearm, in accordance with § 479.84. The executor, administrator, personal representative, or other authorized person must also provide documentation prescribed in paragraph (c) of this section.

(c) The executor, administrator, personal representative, or other person authorized under State law to dispose of property in an estate shall submit with the transfer application documentation of the person's appointment as executor, administrator, personal representative, or as an authorized person, a copy of the decedent's death certificate, a copy of the will (if any), any other evidence of the person's authority to dispose of property, and any other document relating to, or affecting the disposition of firearms from the estate.

[ATF–41F, 81 FR 2723, Jan. 15, 2016]

§ 479.91 Unserviceable firearms.

An unserviceable firearm may be transferred as a curio or ornament without payment of the transfer tax. However, the procedures for the transfer of a firearm as provided in § 479.90 shall be followed in a tax-exempt transfer of a firearm under this section, except a statement shall be entered on the transfer application, Form 5 (Firearms), by the transferor that he is entitled to the exemption because the firearm to be transferred is unservicable and is being transferred as a curio or ornament. An unapproved transfer, the transfer of a firearm under the provisions of this section which is in fact not an unserviceable firearm, or the transfer of an unserviceable firearm as something other than a curio or ornament, may subject the transferor to civil and criminal liabilities. (See 26 U.S.C. 5811, 5852, 5861, and 5871.)

[36 FR 14256, Aug. 3, 1971. Redesignated at 40 FR 16835, Apr. 15, 1975, and amended by T.D. ATF–48, 44 FR 55843, Sept. 28, 1979]

§ 479.92 Transportation of firearms to effect transfer.

Notwithstanding any provision of § 478.28 of this chapter, it shall not be required that authorization be obtained from the Director for the transportation in interstate or foreign commerce of a firearm in order to effect the transfer of a firearm authorized under the provisions of this subpart.

[T.D. ATF–270, 53 FR 10510, Mar. 31, 1988]

OTHER PROVISIONS

§ 479.93 Transfers of firearms to certain persons.

Where the transfer of a destructive device, machine gun, short-barreled shotgun, or short-barreled rifle is to be made by a person licensed under the provisions of Title I of the Gun Control Act of 1968 (82 Stat. 1213) to a person not so licensed, the sworn statement required by § 478.98 of this chapter shall be attached to and accompany the transfer application required by this subpart.

Subpart G—Registration and Identification of Firearms

§ 479.101 Registration of firearms.

(a) The Director shall maintain a central registry of all firearms in the United States which are not in the possession of or under the control of the United States. This registry shall be known as the National Firearms Registration and Transfer Record and shall include:

(1) Identification of the firearm as required by this part;

(2) Date of registration; and

(3) Identification and address of person entitled to possession of the firearm as required by this part.

(b) Each manufacturer, importer, and maker shall register each firearm he manufactures, imports, or makes in the manner prescribed by this part. Each firearm transferred shall be registered to the transferee by the transferor in the manner prescribed by this part. No firearm may be registered by a person unlawfully in possession of the firearm except during an amnesty period established under section 207 of the Gun Control Act of 1968 (82 Stat. 1235).

(c) A person shown as possessing firearms by the records maintained by the Director pursuant to the National Firearms Act (26 U.S.C. Chapter 53) in force on October 31, 1968, shall be considered to have registered the firearms in his possession which are disclosed by that record as being in his possession on October 31, 1968.

(d) The National Firearms Registration and Transfer Record shall include firearms registered to the possessors thereof under the provisions of section 207 of the Gun Control Act of 1968.

(e) A person possessing a firearm registered to him shall retain proof of registration which shall be made available to any ATF officer upon request.

(f) A firearm not identified as required by this part shall not be registered.

[36 FR 14256, Aug. 3, 1971. Redesignated at 40 FR 16835, Apr. 15, 1975, and amended by T.D. ATF–48, 44 FR 55843, Sept. 28, 1979]

§ 479.102 Identification of firearms.

(a) *Identification required.* Except as otherwise provided in this section, you, as a manufacturer, importer, or maker of a firearm, must legibly identify the firearm as follows:

(1) *Serial number, name, place of business.* By engraving, casting, stamping (impressing), or otherwise conspicuously placing or causing to be engraved, cast, stamped (impressed) or otherwise placed on the frame or receiver thereof, an individual serial number, in a manner not susceptible of being readily obliterated, altered, or

removed. The serial number must not duplicate any serial number placed by you on any other firearm. The frame or receiver must also be marked with either: Your name (or recognized abbreviation) and city and State (or recognized abbreviation) where you as a manufacturer or importer maintain your place of business, or in the case of a maker, where you made the firearm; or if a manufacturer or importer, your name (or recognized abbreviation) and the serial number that begins with your abbreviated Federal firearms license number, which is the first three and last five digits, as a prefix to a unique identification number, followed by a hyphen, *e.g.*, "12345678-[unique identification number]"; and

(2) *Model, caliber or gauge, foreign manufacturer, country of manufacture.* By engraving, casting, stamping (impressing), or otherwise conspicuously placing or causing to be engraved, cast, stamped (impressed) or placed on the frame or receiver, or barrel or pistol slide (if applicable) thereof certain additional information. This information must be placed in a manner not susceptible of being readily obliterated, altered, or removed. The additional information shall include:

(i) The model, if such designation has been made;

(ii) The caliber or gauge;

(iii) When applicable, the name of the foreign manufacturer or maker; and

(iv) In the case of an imported firearm, the name of the country in which it was manufactured. For additional requirements relating to imported firearms, see Customs regulations at 19 CFR part 134.

(3) *Multi-piece frame or receiver.* In the case of a multi-piece frame or receiver, the modular subpart that is the outermost housing or structure designed to house, hold, or contain either the primary energized component of a handgun, breech blocking or sealing component of a projectile weapon other than a handgun, or internal sound reduction component of a firearm muffler or firearm silencer, as the case may be, shall be the subpart of a multi-piece frame or receiver identified in accordance with this section. If more than one subpart is similarly designed to house, hold, or contain such primary compo-

nent (*e.g.*, left and right halves), each of those subparts must be identified with the same serial number and associated licensee information not duplicated on any other frame or receiver. The identified subpart(s) of a complete (assembled or unassembled) multi-piece frame or receiver shall not be removed and replaced (*see* § 478.34 of this subchapter, 18 U.S.C. 922(k), and 26 U.S.C. 5861(g) and (h)), unless—

(i) The subpart replacement is not a firearm under 26 U.S.C. 5845;

(ii) The subpart replacement is identified by the qualified manufacturer of the original subpart with the same serial number and associated licensee information in the manner prescribed by this section; and

(iii) The original subpart is destroyed under the manufacturer's control or direct supervision prior to such placement.

(4) *Frame or receiver, machine gun conversion part, or silencer part disposed of separately.* Each part defined as a frame or receiver or modular subpart thereof described in paragraph (a)(3) of this section, machinegun, or firearm muffler or firearm silencer that is not a component part of a complete weapon or complete muffler or silencer device at the time it is sold, shipped, or otherwise disposed of by you must be identified as required by this section with an individual serial number not duplicated on any other firearm and all additional identifying information, except that the model designation and caliber or gauge may be omitted if that information is unknown at the time the part is identified.

(5) *Size and depth of markings.* The engraving, casting, or stamping (impressing) of the serial number and additional information must be to a minimum depth of .003 inch, and the serial number and any associated license number in a print size no smaller than $\frac{1}{16}$ inch. The size of the serial and license number is measured as the distance between the latitudinal ends of the character impression bottoms (bases). The depth of all markings required by this section is measured from the flat surface of the metal and not the peaks or ridges.

(6) *Period of time to identify firearms.* You, as a manufacturer, shall identify

a complete weapon or complete muffler or silencer device no later than close of the next business day following the date the entire manufacturing process has ended for the weapon or device, or prior to disposition, whichever is sooner. You must identify each part or modular subpart defined as a machine gun (frame or receiver, or conversion part) or muffler or silencer that is not a component part of a complete weapon or complete muffler or silencer device at the time it is sold, shipped, or otherwise disposed of no later than close of the next business day following the date the entire manufacturing process has ended for the part, or prior to disposition, whichever is sooner. For purposes of this paragraph, firearms awaiting materials, parts, or equipment repair to be completed are presumed, absent reliable evidence to the contrary, to be in the manufacturing process. Importers must identify imported firearms within the period prescribed in §478.112 of this subchapter.

(7) *Meaning of marking terms.* For purposes of this section, the term "identify" means placing marks of identification, the terms "legible" and "legibly" mean that the identification markings (including any unique identification number) use exclusively Roman letters (*e.g.*, A, a, B, b, C, c) and Arabic numerals (*e.g.*, 1, 2, 3), or solely Arabic numerals, and may include a hyphen, and the terms "conspicuous" and "conspicuously" mean that the identification markings are capable of being easily seen with the naked eye during normal handling of the firearm and are unobstructed by other markings when the complete weapon or device is assembled.

(b) *Exceptions—*(1) *Alternate means of identification.* The Director may authorize other means of identification to identify firearms upon receipt of a letter application or prescribed form from you showing that such other identification is reasonable and will not hinder the effective administration of this part.

(2) *Destructive devices.* In the case of a destructive device, the Director may authorize other means of identification to identify that weapon upon receipt of a letter application or prescribed form from you. The application shall show that engraving, casting, or stamping (impressing) such a weapon as required by this section would be dangerous or impracticable and that the alternate means of identification proposed will not hinder the effective administration of this part.

(3) *Adoption of identifying markings.* You may adopt existing markings and are not required to mark a serial number or other identifying markings previously placed on a firearm in accordance with this section, as follows:

(i) *Newly manufactured firearms.* Manufacturers may adopt the serial number and other identifying markings previously placed on a firearm by another manufacturer provided the firearm has not been sold, shipped, or otherwise disposed of to a person other than a qualified manufacturer, importer, or dealer, and the serial number adopted is not duplicated on any other firearm.

(ii) *Remanufactured or imported firearms.* Manufacturers and importers may adopt the serial number or other identifying markings previously placed on a firearm that otherwise meets the requirements of this section that has been sold, shipped, or otherwise disposed of to a person other than a licensee provided that, within the period and in the manner herein prescribed, the manufacturer or importer legibly and conspicuously places, or causes to be placed, on the frame or receiver either: Their name (or recognized abbreviation), and city and State (or recognized abbreviation) where they maintain their place of business; or their name (or recognized abbreviation) and abbreviated Federal firearms license number, which is the first three and last five digits, individually (*i.e.*, not as a prefix to the serial number adopted) after the letters "FFL", in the following format: "FFL12345678". The serial number adopted must not duplicate any serial number adopted or placed on any other firearm, except that if an importer receives two or more firearms with the same foreign manufacturer's serial number, the importer may adopt the serial number by adding letters or numbers to that serial number, and may include a hyphen.

(iii) *Manufacturers performing gunsmithing services.* Manufacturers may adopt the serial number or other identifying markings previously placed on a firearm by a qualified manufacturer, importer, or dealer, provided the manufacturer is performing services as a gunsmith (as defined in § 478.11 of this subchapter) on existing firearms not for sale or distribution.

(4)(i) *Firearm muffler or silencer parts transferred between qualified manufacturers for further manufacture or to complete new devices.* Manufacturers qualified under this part may transfer a part defined as a muffler or silencer to another qualified manufacturer without immediately identifying or registering such part provided that it is for further manufacture (*i.e.,* machining, coating, *etc.*) or manufacturing a complete muffler or silencer device. Once the new device with such part is completed, the manufacturer who completes the device shall identify and register it in the manner and within the period specified in this part for a complete muffler or silencer device.

(ii) *Firearm muffler or silencer replacement parts transferred to qualified manufacturers or dealers to repair existing devices.* Manufacturers qualified under this part may transfer a replacement part defined as a muffler or silencer other than a frame or receiver to a qualified manufacturer or dealer without identifying or registering such part provided that it is for repairing a complete muffler or silencer device that was previously identified and registered in accordance with this part and part 478.

(5) *Frames or receivers designed before August 24, 2022.* Manufacturers and importers may continue to identify the same component of a firearm defined as a frame or receiver as it existed before August 24, 2022 with the same information required to be marked by paragraphs (a)(1) and (a)(2) of this section that were in effect prior to that date, and any rules necessary to ensure such identification shall remain effective for that purpose. Any frame or receiver with a new design manufactured after August 24, 2022 must be marked with the identifying information and within the period prescribed by this section. For purposes of this paragraph, the term "new design" means that the design of the existing frame or receiver has been functionally modified or altered, as distinguished from performing a cosmetic process that adds to or changes the decoration of the frame or receiver (*e.g.,* painting or engraving), or by adding or replacing stocks, barrels, or accessories to the frame or receiver.

(c) *Voluntary classification of firearms.* The Director may issue a determination (classification) to a person whether an item, including a kit, is a firearm as defined in this part upon receipt of a written request or form prescribed by the Director. Each such voluntary request or form submitted shall be executed under the penalties of perjury with a complete and accurate description of the item or kit, the name and address of the manufacturer or importer thereof, and a sample of such item or kit for examination. A firearm sample must include all accessories and attachments relevant to such classification as each classification is limited to the firearm in the configuration submitted. Each request for classification of a partially complete, disassembled, or nonfunctional item or kit must contain any associated templates, jigs, molds, equipment, or tools that are made available by the seller or distributor of the item or kit to the purchaser or recipient of the item or kit, and any instructions, guides, or marketing materials if they will be made available by the seller or distributor with the item or kit. Upon completion of the examination, the Director may return the sample to the person who made the request unless a determination is made that return of the sample would be or place the person in violation of law. Except for the classification of a specific component as the frame or receiver of a particular weapon, a determination made by the Director under this paragraph shall not be deemed by any person to be applicable to or authoritative with respect to any other sample, design, model, or configuration.

[ATF–2021R–05F, 87 FR 24747, Apr. 26, 2022; 87 FR 51250, Aug. 22, 2022]

§479.103 Registration of firearms manufactured.

Each manufacturer qualified under this part shall file with the Director an accurate notice on Form 2 (Firearms), Notice of Firearms Manufactured or Imported, executed under the penalties of perjury, to show his manufacture of firearms. The notice shall set forth the name and address of the manufacturer, identify his special (occupational) tax stamp and Federal firearms license, and show the date of manufacture, the type, model, length of barrel, overall length, caliber, gauge or size, serial numbers, and other marks of identification of the firearms he manufactures, and the place where the manufactured firearms will be kept. Except as provided in §479.102(b)(4), all firearms manufactured by him during a single day shall be included on one notice, Form 2 (Firearms), filed by the manufacturer no later than the close of the next business day. The manufacturer shall prepare the notice, Form 2 (Firearms), in duplicate, file the original notice as prescribed herein and keep the copy with the records required by subpart I of this part at the premises covered by his special (occupational) tax stamp. Receipt of the notice, Form 2 (Firearms), by the Director shall effectuate the registration of the firearms listed on that notice. The requirements of this part relating to the transfer of a firearm are applicable to transfers by qualified manufacturers.

[36 FR 14256, Aug. 3, 1971. Redesignated at 40 FR 16835, Apr. 15, 1975, and further redesignated by T.D. ATF–487, 68 FR 3752, Jan. 24, 2003, as amended by ATF–2021R–05F, 87 FR 24747, Apr. 26, 2022]

§479.104 Registration of firearms by certain governmental entities.

Any State, any political subdivision thereof, or any official police organization of such a government entity engaged in criminal investigations, which acquires for official use a firearm not registered to it, such as by abandonment or by forfeiture, will register such firearm with the Director by filing Form 10 (Firearms), Registration of Firearms Acquired by Certain Governmental Entities, and such registration shall become a part of the National Firearms Registration and Transfer Record. The application shall identify the applicant, describe each firearm covered by the application, show the location where each firearm usually will be kept, and, if the firearm is unserviceable, the application shall show how the firearm was made unserviceable. This section shall not apply to a firearm merely being held for use as evidence in a criminal proceeding. The Form 10 (Firearms) shall be executed in duplicate in accordance with the instructions thereon. Upon registering the firearm, the Director shall return the original Form 10 (Firearms) to the registrant with notification thereon that registration of the firearm has been made. The registration of any firearm under this section is for official use only and a subsequent transfer will be approved only to other governmental entities for official use.

[36 FR 14256, Aug. 3, 1971. Redesignated at 40 FR 16835, Apr. 15, 1975, and amended by T.D. ATF–241, 51 FR 39633, Oct. 29, 1986; T.D. ATF–270, 53 FR 10510, Mar. 31, 1988]

MACHINE GUNS

§479.105 Transfer and possession of machine guns.

(a) *General.* As provided by 26 U.S.C. 5812 and 26 U.S.C. 5822, an application to make or transfer a firearm shall be denied if the making, transfer, receipt, or possession of the firearm would place the maker or transferee in violation of law. Section 922(o), Title 18, U.S.C., makes it unlawful for any person to transfer or possess a machine gun, except a transfer to or by, or possession by or under the authority of, the United States or any department or agency thereof or a State, or a department, agency, or political subdivision thereof; or any lawful transfer or lawful possession of a machine gun that was lawfully possessed before May 19, 1986. Therefore, notwithstanding any other provision of this part, no application to make, transfer, or import a machine gun will be approved except as provided by this section.

(b) *Machine guns lawfully possessed prior to May 19, 1986.* A machine gun possessed in compliance with the provisions of this part prior to May 19, 1986, may continue to be lawfully possessed by the person to whom the machine gun is registered and may, upon compliance with the provisions of this part, be lawfully transferred to and possessed by the transferee.

(c) *Importation and manufacture.* Subject to compliance with the provisions of this part, importers and manufacturers qualified under this part may import and manufacture machine guns on or after May 19, 1986, for sale or distribution to any department or agency of the United States or any State or political subdivision thereof, or for use by dealers qualified under this part as sales samples as provided in paragraph (d) of this section. The registration of such machine guns under this part and their subsequent transfer shall be conditioned upon and restricted to the sale or distribution of such weapons for the official use of Federal, State or local governmental entities. Subject to compliance with the provisions of this part, manufacturers qualified under this part may manufacture machine guns on or after May 19, 1986, for exportation in compliance with the Arms Export Control Act (22 U.S.C. 2778) and regulations prescribed thereunder by the Department of State.

(d) *Dealer sales samples.* Subject to compliance with the provisions of this part, applications to transfer and register a machine gun manufactured or imported on or after May 19, 1986, to dealers qualified under this part will be approved if it is established by specific information the expected governmental customers who would require a demonstration of the weapon, information as to the availability of the machine gun to fill subsequent orders, and letters from governmental entities expressing a need for a particular model or interest in seeing a demonstration of a particular weapon. Applications to transfer more than one machine gun of a particular model to a dealer must also establish the dealer's need for the quantity of samples sought to be transferred.

(e) *The making of machine guns on or after May 19, 1986.* Subject to compliance with the provisions of this part, applications to make and register machine guns on or after May 19, 1986, for the benefit of a Federal, State or local governmental entity (e.g., an invention

for possible future use of a governmental entity or the making of a weapon in connection with research and development on behalf of such an entity) will be approved if it is established by specific information that the machine gun is particularly suitable for use by Federal, State or local governmental entities and that the making of the weapon is at the request and on behalf of such an entity.

(f) *Discontinuance of business.* Since section 922(o), Title 18, U.S.C., makes it unlawful to transfer or possess a machine gun except as provided in the law, any qualified manufacturer, importer, or dealer intending to discontinue business shall, prior to going out of business, transfer in compliance with the provisions of this part any machine gun manufactured or imported after May 19, 1986, to a Federal, State or local governmental entity, qualified manufacturer, qualified importer, or, subject to the provisions of paragraph (d) of this section, dealer qualified to possess such, machine gun.

[T.D. ATF–270, 53 FR 10510, Mar. 31, 1988]

Subpart H—Importation and Exportation

IMPORTATION

§ 479.111 Procedure.

(a) No firearm shall be imported or brought into the United States or any territory under its control or jurisdiction unless the person importing or bringing in the firearm establishes to the satisfaction of the Director that the firearm to be imported or brought in is being imported or brought in for:

(1) The use of the United States or any department, independent establishment, or agency thereof or any State or possession or any political subdivision thereof; or

(2) Scientific or research purposes; or

(3) Testing or use as a model by a registered manufacturer or solely for use as a sample by a registered importer or registered dealer.

The burden of proof is affirmatively on any person importing or bringing the firearm into the United States or any territory under its control or jurisdiction to show that the firearm is being imported or brought in under one of the above paragraphs. Any person desiring to import or bring a firearm into the United States under this paragraph shall file with the Director an application on Form 6 (Firearms), Application and Permit for Importation of Firearms, Ammunition and Implements of War, in triplicate, executed under the penalties of perjury. The application shall show the information required by subpart G of Part 478 of this chapter. A detailed explanation of why the importation of the firearm falls within the standards set out in this paragraph shall be attached to the application. The person seeking to import or bring in the firearm will be notified of the approval or disapproval of his application. If the application is approved, the original Form 6 (Firearms) will be returned to the applicant showing such approval and he will present the approved application, Form 6 (Firearms), to the Customs officer at the port of importation. The approval of an application to import a firearm shall be automatically terminated at the expiration of two years from the date of approval unless, upon request, it is further extended by the Director. If the firearm described in the approved application is not imported prior to the expiration of the approval, the Director shall be so notified. Customs officers will not permit release of a firearm from Customs custody, except for exportation, unless covered by an application which has been approved by the Director and which is currently effective. The importation or bringing in of a firearm not covered by an approved application may subject the person responsible to civil and criminal liabilities. (26 U.S.C. 5861, 5871, and 5872.)

(b) Part 478 of this chapter also contains requirements and procedures for the importation of firearms into the United States. A firearm may not be imported into the United States under this part unless those requirements and procedures are also complied with by the person importing the firearm.

(c) The provisions of this subpart shall not be construed as prohibiting the return to the United States or any territory under its control or jurisdiction of a firearm by a person who can establish to the satisfaction of Customs that (1) the firearm was taken out of the United States or any territory under its control or jurisdiction by such person, (2) the firearm is registered to that person, and (3) if appropriate, the authorization required by Part 478 of this chapter for the transportation of such a firearm in interstate or foreign commerce has been obtained by such person.

[36 FR 14256, Aug. 3, 1971. Redesignated at 40 FR 16835, Apr. 15, 1975, and amended by T.D. ATF–48, 44 FR 55843, Sept. 28, 1979; ATF–325, 57 FR 29787, July 7, 1992; ATF–26F, 79 FR 7396, Feb. 7, 2014]

§479.112 Registration of imported firearms.

(a) Each importer shall file with the Director an accurate notice on Form 2 (Firearms), Notice of Firearms Manufactured or Imported, executed under the penalties of perjury, showing the importation of a firearm. The notice shall set forth the name and address of the importer, identify the importer's special (occupational) tax stamp and Federal firearms license, and show the import permit number, the date of release from Customs custody, the type, model, length of barrel, overall length, caliber, gauge or size, serial number, and other marks of identification of the firearm imported, and the place where the imported firearm will be kept. The Form 2 (Firearms) covering an imported firearm shall be filed by the importer no later than fifteen (15) days from the date the firearm was released from Customs custody. The importer shall prepare the notice, Form 2 (Firearms), in duplicate, file the original return as prescribed herein, and keep the copy with the records required by subpart I of this part at the premises covered by the special (occupational) tax stamp. The timely receipt by the Director of the notice, Form 2 (Firearms), and the timely receipt by the Director of the copy of Form 6A (Firearms), Release and Receipt of Imported Firearms, Ammunition and Implements of War, required by §478.112 of this chapter, covering the weapon reported on the Form 2 (Firearms) by the qualified importer, shall effectuate the registration of the firearm to the importer.

(b) The requirements of this part relating to the transfer of a firearm are applicable to the transfer of imported firearms by a qualified importer or any other person.

(c) Subject to compliance with the provisions of this part, an application, Form 6 (Firearms), to import a firearm by an importer or dealer qualified under this part, for use as a sample in connection with sales of such firearms to Federal, State or local governmental entities, will be approved if it is established by specific information attached to the application that the firearm is suitable or potentially suitable for use by such entities. Such information must show why a sales sample of a particular firearm is suitable for such use and the expected governmental customers who would require a demonstration of the firearm. Information as to the availability of the firearm to fill subsequent orders and letters from governmental entities expressing a need for a particular model or interest in seeing a demonstration of a particular firearm would establish suitability for governmental use. Applications to import more than one firearm of a particular model for use as a sample by an importer or dealer must also establish the importer's or dealer's need for the quantity of samples sought to be imported.

(d) Subject to compliance with the provisions of this part, an application, Form 6 (Firearms), to import a firearm by an importer or dealer qualified under this part, for use as a sample in connection with sales of such firearms to Federal, State or local governmental entities, will be approved if it is established by specific information attached to the application that the firearm is particularly suitable for use by such entities. Such information must show why a sales sample of a particular firearm is suitable for such use and the expected governmental customers who would require a demonstration of the firearm. Information as to the availability of the firearm to fill subsequent orders and letters from governmental entities expressing a need for a particular model or interest in seeing a demonstration of a particular firearm would establish suitability for governmental use. Applications to im-

port more than one firearm of a particular model for use as a sample by an importer or dealer must also establish the importer's or dealer's need for the quantity of samples sought to be imported.

[36 FR 14256, Aug. 3, 1971. Redesignated at 40 FR 16835, Apr. 15, 1975, and amended by T.D. ATF–241, 51 FR 39633, Oct. 29, 1986; T.D. ATF–270, 53 FR 10511, Mar. 31, 1988]

§ 479.113   Conditional importation.

The Director shall permit the conditional importation or bringing into the United States of any firearm for the purpose of examining and testing the firearm in connection with making a determination as to whether the importation or bringing in of such firearm will be authorized under this subpart. An application under this section shall be filed on Form 6 (Firearms), in triplicate, with the Director. The Director may impose conditions upon any importation under this section including a requirement that the firearm be shipped directly from Customs custody to the Director and that the person importing or bringing in the firearm must agree to either export the weapon or destroy it if a final determination is made that it may not be imported or brought in under this subpart. A firearm so imported or brought into the United States may be released from Customs custody in the manner prescribed by the conditional authorization of the Director.

[T.D. ATF–270, 53 FR 10511, Mar. 31, 1988]

EXPORTATION

§ 479.114   Application and permit for exportation of firearms.

Any person desiring to export a firearm without payment of the transfer tax must file with the Director an application on Form 9 (Firearms), Application and Permit for Exportation of Firearms, in quadruplicate, for a permit providing for deferment of tax liability. Part 1 of the application shall show the name and address of the foreign consignee, number of firearms covered by the application, the intended port of exportation, a complete description of each firearm to be exported, the name, address, State Department license number (or date of application if not issued), and identification of the special (occupational) tax stamp of the transferor. Part 1 of the application shall be executed under the penalties of perjury by the transferor and shall be supported by a certified copy of a written order or contract of sale or other evidence showing that the firearm is to be shipped to a foreign designation. Where it is desired to make a transfer free of tax to another person who in turn will export the firearm, the transferor shall likewise file an application supported by evidence that the transfer will start the firearm in course of exportation, except, however, that where such transferor and exporter are registered special-taxpayers the transferor will not be required to file an application on Form 9 (Firearms).

§479.115 Action by Director.

If the application is acceptable, the Director will execute the permit, Part 2 of Form 9 (Firearms), to export the firearm described on the form and return three copies thereof to the applicant. Issuance of the permit by the Director will suspend assertion of tax liability for a period of six (6) months from the date of issuance. If the application is disapproved, the Director will indicate thereon the reason for such action and return the forms to the applicant.

§479.116 Procedure by exporter.

Shipment may not be made until the permit, Form 9 (Firearms), is received from the Director. If exportation is to be made by means other than by parcel post, two copies of the form must be addressed to the District Director of Customs at the port of exportation, and must precede or accompany the shipment in order to permit appropriate inspection prior to lading. If exportation is to be made by parcel post, one copy of the form must be presented to the postmaster at the office receiving the parcel who will execute Part 4 of such form and return the form to the exporter for transmittal to the Director. In the event exportation is not effected, all copies of the form must be immediately returned to the Director for cancellation.

§479.117 Action by Customs.

Upon receipt of a permit, Form 9 (Firearms), in duplicate, authorizing the exportation of firearms, the District Director of Customs may order such inspection as deemed necessary prior to lading of the merchandise. If satisfied that the shipment is proper and the information contained in the permit to export is in agreement with information shown in the shipper's export declaration, the District Director of Customs will, after the merchandise has been duly exported, execute the certificate of exportation (Part 3 of Form 9 (Firearms)). One copy of the form will be retained with the shipper's export declaration and the remaining copy thereof will be transmitted to the Director.

§479.118 Proof of exportation.

Within a six-month's period from date of issuance of the permit to export firearms, the exporter shall furnish or cause to be furnished to the Director (a) the certificate of exportation (Part 3 of Form 9 (Firearms)) executed by the District Director of Customs as provided in §479.117, or (b) the certificate of mailing by parcel post (Part 4 of Form 9 (Firearms)) executed by the postmaster of the post office receiving the parcel containing the firearm, or (c) a certificate of landing executed by a Customs officer of the foreign country to which the firearm is exported, or (d) a sworn statement of the foreign consignee covering the receipt of the firearm, or (e) the return receipt, or a reproduced copy thereof, signed by the addressee or his agent, where the shipment of a firearm was made by insured or registered parcel post. Issuance of a permit to export a firearm and furnishing of evidence establishing such exportation under this section will relieve the actual exporter and the person selling to the exporter for exportation from transfer tax liability. Where satisfactory evidence of exportation of a firearm is not furnished within the stated period, the transfer tax will be assessed.

§479.119 Transportation of firearms to effect exportation.

Notwithstanding any provision of §478.28 of this chapter, it shall not be required that authorization be obtained from the Director for the transportation in interstate or foreign commerce of a firearm in order to effect the exportation of a firearm authorized under the provisions of this subpart.

[T.D. ATF–270, 53 FR 10511, Mar. 31, 1988]

§ 479.120 Refunds.

Where, after payment of tax by the manufacturer, a firearm is exported, and satisfactory proof of exportation (see § 479.118) is furnished, a claim for refund may be submitted on Form 843 (see § 479.172). If the manufacturer waives all claim for the amount to be refunded, the refund shall be made to the exporter. A claim for refund by an exporter of tax paid by a manufacturer should be accompanied by waiver of the manufacturer and proof of tax payment by the latter.

§ 479.121 Insular possessions.

Transfers of firearms to persons in the insular possessions of the United States are exempt from transfer tax, provided title in cases involving change of title (and custody or control, in cases not involving change of title), does not pass to the transferee or his agent in the United States. However, such exempt transactions must be covered by approved permits and supporting documents corresponding to those required in the case of firearms exported to foreign countries (see §§ 479.114 and 479.115), except that the Director may vary the requirements herein set forth in accordance with the requirements of the governing authority of the insular possession. Shipments to the insular possessions will not be authorized without compliance with the requirements of the governing authorities thereof. In the case of a nontaxable transfer to a person in such insular possession, the exemption extends only to such transfer and not to prior transfers.

ARMS EXPORT CONTROL ACT

§ 479.122 Requirements.

(a) Persons engaged in the business of importing firearms are required by the Arms Export Control Act (22 U.S.C. 2778) to register with the Director. (See Part 447 of this chapter.)

(b) Persons engaged in the business of exporting firearms caliber .22 or larger are subject to the requirements of a license issued by the Secretary of State. Application for such license should be made to the Office of Munitions Control, Department of State, Washington, DC 20502, prior to exporting firearms.

[36 FR 14256, Aug. 3, 1971. Redesignated at 40 FR 16835, Apr. 15, 1975, and amended by T.D. ATF–241, 51 FR 39634, Oct. 29, 1986; T.D. ATF–270, 53 FR 10511, Mar. 31, 1988]

Subpart I—Records and Returns

§ 479.131 Records.

For the purposes of this part, each manufacturer, importer, and dealer in firearms shall keep and maintain such records regarding the manufacture, importation, acquisition (whether by making, transfer, or otherwise), receipt, and disposition of firearms as are prescribed, and in the manner and place required, by part 478 of this chapter. In addition, each manufacturer, importer, and dealer shall maintain, in chronological order, at his place of business a separate record consisting of the documents required by this part showing the registration of any firearm to him. If firearms owned or possessed by a manufacturer, importer, or dealer are stored or kept on premises other than the place of business shown on his special (occupational) tax stamp, the record establishing registration shall show where such firearms are stored or kept. The records required by this part shall be readily accessible for inspection at all reasonable times by ATF officers.

(Approved by the Office of Management and Budget under control number 1140–0032)

[36 FR 14256, Aug. 3, 1971. Redesignated by 40 FR 16835, Apr. 15, 1975, and amended by T.D. ATF–172, 49 FR 14942, Apr. 16, 1984; ATF–11F, 73 FR 57242, Oct. 2, 2008]

Subpart J—Stolen or Lost Firearms or Documents

§ 479.141 Stolen or lost firearms.

Whenever any registered firearm is stolen or lost, the person losing possession thereof will, immediately upon discovery of such theft or loss, make a report to the Director showing the following:

(a) Name and address of the person in whose name the firearm is registered, (b) kind of firearm, (c) serial number, (d) model, (e) caliber, (f) manufacturer of the firearm, (g) date and place of theft or loss, and (h) complete statement of facts and circumstances surrounding such theft or loss.

§ 479.142   Stolen or lost documents.

When any Forms 1, 2, 3, 4, 5, 6A, or 10 (Firearms) evidencing possession of a firearm is stolen, lost, or destroyed, the person losing possession will immediately upon discovery of the theft, loss, or destruction report the matter to the Director. The report will show in detail the circumstances of the theft, loss, or destruction and will include all known facts which may serve to identify the document. Upon receipt of the report, the Director will make such investigation as appears appropriate and may issue a duplicate document upon such conditions as the circumstances warrant.

Subpart K—Examination of Books and Records

§ 479.151   Failure to make returns: Substitute returns.

If any person required by this part to make returns shall fail or refuse to make any such return within the time prescribed by this part or designated by the Director, then the return shall be made by an ATF officer upon inspection of the books, but the making of such return by an ATF officer shall not relieve the person from any default or penalty incurred by reason of failure to make such return.

(53 Stat. 437; 26 U.S.C. 6020)

§ 479.152   Penalties (records and returns).

Any person failing to keep records or make returns, or making, or causing the making of, a false entry on any application, return or record, knowing such entry to be false, is liable to fine and imprisonment as provided in section 5871, I.R.C.

Subpart L—Distribution and Sale of Stamps

§ 479.161   National Firearms Act stamps.

"National Firearms Act" stamps evidencing payment of the transfer tax or tax on the making of a firearm are maintained by the Director. The remittance for purchase of the appropriate tax stamp shall be submitted with the application. Upon approval of the application, the Director will cause the appropriate tax to be paid by affixing the appropriate stamp to the application.

[T.D. ATF–270, 53 FR 10511, Mar. 31, 1988]

§ 479.162   Stamps authorized.

Adhesive stamps of the $5 and $200 denomination, bearing the words "National Firearms Act," have been prepared and only such stamps shall be used for the payment of the transfer tax and for the tax on the making of a firearm.

[T.D. ATF–270, 53 FR 10511, Mar. 31, 1988]

§ 479.163   Reuse of stamps prohibited.

A stamp once affixed to one document cannot lawfully be removed and affixed to another. Any person willfully reusing such a stamp shall be subject to the penalty prescribed by 26 U.S.C. 7208.

[36 FR 14256, Aug. 3, 1971. Redesignated by 40 FR 16835, Apr. 15, 1975, and amended by T.D. ATF–48, 44 FR 55843, Sept. 28, 1979]

Subpart M—Redemption of or Allowance for Stamps or Refunds

§ 479.171   Redemption of or allowance for stamps.

Where a National Firearms Act stamp is destroyed, mutilated or rendered useless after purchase, and before liability has been incurred, such stamp may be redeemed by giving another stamp in lieu thereof. Claim for redemption of the stamp should be filed on ATF Form 2635 (5620.8) with the Director. Such claim shall be accompanied by the stamp or by a satisfactory explanation of the reasons why the stamp cannot be returned, and shall be filed within 3 years after the purchase of the stamp.

(68A Stat. 830; 26 U.S.C. 6805)

[T.D. ATF–270, 53 FR 10511, Mar. 31, 1988]

§ 479.172　Refunds.

As indicated in this part, the transfer tax or tax on the making of a firearm is ordinarily paid by the purchase and affixing of stamps, while special tax stamps are issued in payment of special (occupational) taxes. However, in exceptional cases, transfer tax, tax on the making of firearms, and/or special (occupational) tax may be paid pursuant to assessment. Claims for refunds of such taxes, paid pursuant to assessment, shall be filed on ATF Form 2635 (5620.8) within 3 years next after payment of the taxes. Such claims shall be filed with the Chief, National Firearms Act Branch serving the region in which the tax was paid. (For provisions relating to hand-carried documents and manner of filing, see 26 CFR 301.6091–1(b) and 301.6402–2(a).) When an applicant to make or transfer a firearm wishes a refund of the tax paid on an approved application where the firearm was not made pursuant to an approved Form 1 (Firearms) or transfer of the firearm did not take place pursuant to an approved Form 4 (Firearms), the applicant shall file a claim for refund of the tax on ATF Form 2635 (5620.8) with the Director. The claim shall be accompanied by the approved application bearing the stamp and an explanation why the tax liability was not incurred. Such claim shall be filed within 3 years next after payment of the tax.

(68A Stat. 808, 830; 26 U.S.C. 6511, 6805)

[T.D. ATF–270, 53 FR 10512, Mar. 31, 1988, as amended by ATF 2013R–9F, 79 FR 46693, Aug. 11, 2014]

Subpart N—Penalties and Forfeitures

§ 479.181　Penalties.

Any person who violates or fails to comply with the requirements of 26 U.S.C. Chapter 53 shall, upon conviction, be subject to the penalties imposed under 26 U.S.C. 5871.

[T.D. ATF–48, 44 FR 55843, Sept. 28, 1979]

§ 479.182　Forfeitures.

Any firearm involved in any violation of the provisions of 26 U.S.C. Chapter 53, shall be subject to seizure, and forfeiture under the internal revenue laws: *Provided, however,* That the disposition of forfeited firearms shall be in conformance with the requirements of 26 U.S.C. 5872. In addition, any vessel, vehicle or aircraft used to transport, carry, convey or conceal or possess any firearm with respect to which there has been committed any violation of any provision of 26 U.S.C. Chapter 53, or the regulations in this part issued pursuant thereto, shall be subject to seizure and forfeiture under the Customs laws, as provided by the act of August 9, 1939 (49 U.S.C. App., Chapter 11).

[T.D. ATF–270, 53 FR 10512, Mar. 31, 1988]

Subpart O—Other Laws Applicable

§ 479.191　Applicability of other provisions of internal revenue laws.

All of the provisions of the internal revenue laws not inconsistent with the provisions of 26 U.S.C. Chapter 53 shall be applicable with respect to the taxes imposed by 26 U.S.C. 5801, 5811, and 5821 (see 26 U.S.C. 5846).

[T.D. ATF–48, 44 FR 55843, Sept. 28, 1979]

§ 479.192　Commerce in firearms and ammunition.

For provisions relating to commerce in firearms and ammunition, including the movement of destructive devices, machine guns, short-barreled shotguns, or short-barreled rifles, see 18 U.S.C. Chapter 44, and Part 478 of this chapter issued pursuant thereto.

[36 FR 14256, Aug. 3, 1971. Redesignated by 40 FR 16835, Apr. 15, 1975, and amended by T.D. ATF–48, 44 FR 55843, Sept. 28, 1979]

§ 479.193　Arms Export Control Act.

For provisions relating to the registration and licensing of persons engaged in the business of manufacturing, importing or exporting arms, ammunition, or implements of war, see the Arms Export Control Act (22 U.S.C.

2778), and the regulations issued pursu- ant thereto. (See also Part 447 of this chapter.)

[T.D. ATF–270, 53 FR 10512, Mar. 31, 1988]

SUBCHAPTER C—EXPLOSIVES

PART 555—COMMERCE IN EXPLOSIVES

Subpart A—Introduction

Sec.
555.1 Scope of regulations.
555.2 Relation to other provisions of law.

Subpart B—Definitions

555.11 Meaning of terms.

Subpart C—Administrative and Miscellaneous Provisions

555.21 Forms prescribed.
555.22 Alternate methods or procedures; emergency variations from requirements.
555.23 List of explosive materials.
555.24 Right of entry and examination.
555.25 Disclosure of information.
555.26 Prohibited shipment, transportation, receipt, possession, or distribution of explosive materials.
555.27 [Reserved]
555.28 Stolen explosive materials.
555.29 Unlawful storage.
555.30 Reporting theft or loss of explosive materials.
555.31 Inspection of site of accidents or fires; right of entry.
555.32 Special explosive devices.
555.33 Background checks and clearances.
555.34 Replacement of stolen or lost ATF Form 5400.30 (Intrastate Purchase of Explosives Coupon (IPEC)).

Subpart D—Licenses and Permits

555.41 General.
555.42 License fees.
555.43 Permit fees.
555.44 License or permit fee not refundable.
555.45 Original license or permit.
555.46 Renewal of license or permit.
555.47 Insufficient fee.
555.48 Abandoned application.
555.49 Issuance of license or permit.
555.50 Correction of error on license or permit.
555.51 Duration of license or permit.
555.52 Limitations on license or permit.
555.53 License and permit not transferable.
555.54 Change of address.
555.56 Change in trade name.
555.57 Change of control, change in responsible persons, and change of employees.
555.58 Continuing partnerships.
555.59 Right of succession by certain persons.

555.60 Certain continuances of business or operations.
555.61 Discontinuance of business or operations.
555.62 State or other law.
555.63 Explosives magazine changes.

Subpart E—License and Permit Proceedings

555.71 Opportunity for compliance.
555.72 Denial of initial application.
555.73 Hearing after initial application is denied.
555.74 Denial of renewal application or revocation of license or permit.
555.75 Hearing after denial of renewal application or revocation of license or permit.
555.76 Action by Director, Industry Operations.
555.77 Designated place of hearing.
555.78 Representation at a hearing.
555.79 Appeal on petition to the Director.
555.80 Court review.
555.81 Service on applicant, licensee, or permittee.
555.82 Rules of practice in license and permit proceedings.
555.83 Operations by licensees or permittees after notice of denial or revocation.

Subpart F—Conduct of Business or Operations

555.101 Posting of license or user permit.
555.102 Authorized operations by permittees.
555.103 Transactions among licensees/permittees and transactions among licensees and holders of user permits.
555.104 Certified copy of license or permit.
555.105 Distributions to limited permittees.
555.106 Certain prohibited distributions.
555.107 Record of transactions.
555.108 Importation.
555.109 Identification of explosive materials.
555.110 Furnishing of samples (Effective on and after January 24, 2003).

Subpart G—Records and Reports

555.121 General.
555.122 Records maintained by licensed importers.
555.123 Records maintained by licensed manufacturers.
555.124 Records maintained by licensed dealers.
555.125 Records maintained by permittees.
555.126 Limited Permittee Transaction Report for distribution of explosive materials.
555.127 Daily summary of magazine transactions.

555.128 Discontinuance of business.
555.129 Exportation.
555.130 [Reserved]

Subpart H—Exemptions

555.141 Exemptions.
555.142 Relief from disabilities.

Subpart I—Unlawful Acts, Penalties, Seizures, and Forfeitures

555.161 Engaging in business without a license.
555.162 False statement or representation.
555.163 False entry in record.
555.164 Unlawful storage.
555.165 Failure to report theft or loss.
555.166 Seizure or forfeiture.

Subpart J—Marking of Plastic Explosives

555.180 Prohibitions relating to unmarked plastic explosives.
555.181 Reporting of plastic explosives.
555.182 Exceptions.
555.183 Importations of plastic explosives on or after April 24, 1997.
555.184 Statements of process and samples.
555.185 Criminal sanctions.
555.186 Seizure or forfeiture.

Subpart K—Storage

555.201 General.
555.202 Classes of explosive materials.
555.203 Types of magazines.
555.204 Inspection of magazines.
555.205 Movement of explosive materials.
555.206 Location of magazines.
555.207 Construction of type 1 magazines.
555.208 Construction of type 2 magazines.
555.209 Construction of type 3 magazines.
555.210 Construction of type 4 magazines.
555.211 Construction of type 5 magazines.
555.212 Smoking and open flames.
555.213 Quantity and storage restrictions.
555.214 Storage within types 1, 2, 3, and 4 magazines.
555.215 Housekeeping.
555.216 Repair of magazines.
555.217 Lighting.
555.218 Table of distances for storage of explosive materials.
555.219 Table of distances for storage of low explosives.
555.220 Table of separation distances of ammonium nitrate and blasting agents from explosives or blasting agents.
555.221 Requirements for display fireworks, pyrotechnic compositions, and explosive materials used in assembling fireworks or articles pyrotechnic.
555.222 Table of distances between fireworks process buildings and between fireworks process and fireworks nonprocess buildings.
555.223 Table of distances between fireworks process buildings and other specified areas.
555.224 Table of distances for the storage of display fireworks (except bulk salutes).

AUTHORITY: 18 U.S.C. 847.

SOURCE: T.D. ATF–87, 46 FR 40384, Aug. 7, 1981, unless otherwise noted. Redesignated by T.D. ATF–487, 68 FR 3748, Jan. 24, 2003.

EDITORIAL NOTE: Nomenclature changes to part 555 appear by T.D. ATF–487, 68 FR 3748, Jan. 24, 2003.

Subpart A—Introduction

§555.1 Scope of regulations.

(a) *In general.* The regulations contained in this part relate to commerce in explosives and implement Title XI, Regulation of Explosives (18 U.S.C. Chapter 40; 84 Stat. 952), of the Organized Crime Control Act of 1970 (84 Stat. 922), Pub. L. 103–322 (108 Stat. 1796), Pub. L. 104–132 (110 Stat. 1214), and Pub. L. 107–296 (116 Stat. 2135).

(b) *Procedural and substantive requirements.* This part contains the procedural and substantive requirements relative to:

(1) The interstate or foreign commerce in explosive materials;

(2) The licensing of manufacturers and importers of, and dealers in, explosive materials;

(3) The issuance of permits;

(4) The conduct of business by licensees and operations by permittees;

(5) The storage of explosive materials;

(6) The records and reports required of licensees and permittees;

(7) Relief from disabilities under this part;

(8) Exemptions, unlawful acts, penalties, seizures, and forfeitures; and

(9) The marking of plastic explosives.

[T.D. ATF–87, 46 FR 40384, Aug. 7, 1981, as amended by T.D. ATF–363, 60 FR 17449, Apr. 6, 1995; T.D. ATF–387, 62 FR 8376, Feb. 25, 1997; ATF No. 1, 68 FR 13780, Mar. 20, 2003]

§555.2 Relation to other provisions of law.

The provisions in this part are in addition to, and are not in lieu of, any other provision of law, or regulations, respecting commerce in explosive materials. For regulations applicable to commerce in firearms and ammunition, see Part 478 of this chapter. For regulations applicable to traffic in machine guns, destructive devices, and certain other firearms, see Part 479 of this chapter. For statutes applicable to the registration and licensing of persons engaged in the business of manufacturing, importing or exporting arms, ammunition, or implements of war, see section 38 of the Arms Export Control Act (22 U.S.C. 2778), and regulations of Part 447 of this chapter and in Parts 121 through 128 of Title 22, Code of Federal Regulations. For statutes applicable to nonmailable materials, see 18 U.S.C. 1716 and implementing regulations. For statutes applicable to water quality standards, see 33 U.S.C. 1341.

Subpart B—Definitions

§ 555.11 Meaning of terms.

When used in this part, terms are defined as follows in this section. Words in the plural form include the singular, and vice versa, and words indicating the masculine gender include the feminine. The terms "includes" and "including" do not exclude other things not named which are in the same general class or are otherwise within the scope of the term defined.

Act. 18 U.S.C. Chapter 40.

Adjudicated as a mental defective. (a) A determination by a court, board, commission, or other lawful authority that a person, as a result of marked subnormal intelligence, or mental illness, incompetency, condition, or disease:

(1) Is a danger to himself or to others; or

(2) Lacks the mental capacity to contract or manage his own affairs.

(b) The term will include—

(1) A finding of insanity by a court in a criminal case; and

(2) Those persons found incompetent to stand trial or found not guilty by reason of lack of mental responsibility by any court or pursuant to articles 50a and 76b of the Uniform Code of Military Justice, 10 U.S.C. 850a, 876b.

Alien. Any person who is not a citizen or national of the United States.

Ammunition. Small arms ammunition or cartridge cases, primers, bullets, or smokeless propellants designed for use in small arms, including percussion caps, and ³⁄₃₂ inch and other external burning pyrotechnic hobby fuses. The term does not include black powder.

Appropriate identifying information. The term means, in relation to an individual:

(a) The full name, date of birth, place of birth, sex, race, street address, State of residence, telephone numbers (home and work), country or countries of citizenship, and position at the employer's business or operations of responsible persons and employees authorized to possess explosive materials;

(b) The business name, address, and license or permit number with which the responsible person or employee is affiliated;

(c) If an alien, INS-issued alien number or admission number; and

(d) Social security number, as optional information (this information is not required but is helpful in avoiding misidentification when a background check is conducted).

Approved storage facility. A place where explosive materials are stored, consisting of one or more approved magazines, conforming to the requirements of this part and covered by a license or permit issued under this part.

Articles pyrotechnic. Pyrotechnic devices for professional use similar to consumer fireworks in chemical composition and construction but not intended for consumer use. Such articles meeting the weight limits for consumer fireworks but not labeled as such and classified by U.S. Department of Transportation regulations in 49 CFR 172.101 as UN0431 or UN0432.

Artificial barricade. An artificial mound or revetted wall of earth of a minimum thickness of three feet, or any other approved barricade that offers equivalent protection.

ATF. The Bureau of Alcohol, Tobacco, Firearms and Explosives, Department of Justice.

ATF officer. An officer or employee of the Bureau of Alcohol, Tobacco, Firearms and Explosives (ATF), Department of Justice authorized to perform any function relating to the administration or enforcement of this part.

Authority having jurisdiction for fire safety. The fire department having jurisdiction over sites where explosives are manufactured or stored.

Barricaded. The effective screening of a magazine containing explosive materials from another magazine, a building, a railway, or a highway, either by a natural barricade or by an artificial barricade. To be properly barricaded, a straight line from the top of any sidewall of the magazine containing explosive materials to the eave line of any other magazine or building, or to a point 12 feet above the center of a railway or highway, will pass through the natural or artificial barricade.

Blasting agent. Any material or mixture, consisting of fuel and oxidizer, that is intended for blasting and not otherwise defined as an explosive; if the finished product, as mixed for use or shipment, cannot be detonated by means of a number 8 test blasting cap when unconfined. A number 8 test blasting cap is one containing 2 grams of a mixture of 80 percent mercury fulminate and 20 percent potassium chlorate, or a blasting cap of equivalent strength. An equivalent strength cap comprises 0.40–0.45 grams of PETN base charge pressed in an aluminum shell with bottom thickness not to exceed to 0.03 of an inch, to a specific gravity of not less than 1.4 g/cc., and primed with standard weights of primer depending on the manufacturer.

Bulk salutes. Salute components prior to final assembly into aerial shells, and finished salute shells held separately prior to being packed with other types of display fireworks.

Bullet-sensitive explosive materials. Explosive materials that can be exploded by 150-grain M2 ball ammunition having a nominal muzzle velocity of 2700 fps (824 mps) when fired from a .30 caliber rifle at a distance of 100 ft (30.5 m), measured perpendicular. The test material is at a temperature of 70 to 75 degrees F (21 to 24 degrees C) and is placed against a ½ inch (12.4 mm) steel backing plate.

Bureau. The Bureau of Alcohol, Tobacco, Firearms and Explosives, Department of Justice.

Business premises. When used with respect to a manufacturer, importer, or dealer, the property on which explosive materials are manufactured, imported, stored or distributed. The premises include the property where the records of a manufacturer, importer, or dealer are kept if different than the premises where explosive materials are manufactured, imported, stored or distributed. When used with respect to a user of explosive materials, the property on which the explosive materials are received or stored. The premises includes the property where the records of the users are kept if different than the premises where explosive materials are received or stored.

Chief, Firearms and Explosives Licensing Center. The ATF official responsible for the issuance and renewal of licenses and permits under this part.

Committed to a mental institution. A formal commitment of a person to a mental institution by a court, board, commission, or other lawful authority. The term includes a commitment to a mental institution involuntarily. The term includes commitment for mental defectiveness or mental illness. It also includes commitments for other reasons, such as for drug use. The term does not include a person in a mental institution for observation or a voluntary admission to a mental institution.

Common or contract carrier. Any individual or organization engaged in the business of transporting passengers or goods.

Consumer fireworks. Any small firework device designed to produce visible effects by combustion and which must comply with the construction, chemical composition, and labeling regulations of the U.S. Consumer Product Safety Commission, as set forth in title 16, Code of Federal Regulations, parts 1500 and 1507. Some small devices designed to produce audible effects are included, such as whistling devices, ground devices containing 50 mg or less of explosive materials, and aerial devices containing 130 mg or less of explosive materials. Consumer fireworks are classified as fireworks UN0336, and UN0337 by the U.S. Department of Transportation at 49 CFR 172.101. This term does not include fused setpieces containing components which together exceed 50 mg of salute powder.

Controlled substance. A drug or other substance, or immediate precursor, as defined in section 102 of the Controlled Substances Act, 21 U.S.C. 802. The term includes, but is not limited to, marijuana, depressants, stimulants, and narcotic drugs. The term does not include distilled spirits, wine, malt beverages, or tobacco, as those terms are defined or used in Subtitle E of the Internal Revenue Code of 1986, as amended.

Crime punishable by imprisonment for a term exceeding one year. Any offense for which the maximum penalty, whether or not imposed, is capital punishment or imprisonment in excess of one year. The term does not include (a) any Federal or State offenses pertaining to antitrust violations, unfair trade practices, restraints of trade, or (b) any State offense (other than one involving a firearm or explosive) classified by the laws of the State as a misdemeanor and punishable by a term of imprisonment of two years or less.

Customs officer. Any officer of U.S. Customs and Border Protection, any commissioned, warrant, or petty officer of the Coast Guard, or any agent or other person authorized by law to perform the duties of a customs officer.

Dealer. Any person engaged in the business of distributing explosive materials at wholesale or retail.

Detonator. Any device containing a detonating charge that is used for initiating detonation in an explosive. The term includes, but is not limited to, electric blasting caps of instantaneous and delay types, blasting caps for use with safety fuses, detonating-cord delay connectors, and nonelectric instantaneous and delay blasting caps.

Director. The Director, Bureau of Alcohol, Tobacco, Firearms and Explosives, Department of Justice.

Director, Industry Operations. The principal field division official responsible for administering regulations in this part.

Discharged under dishonorable conditions. Separation from the U.S. Armed Forces resulting from a dishonorable discharge or dismissal adjudged by general court-martial. The term does not include any separation from the Armed Forces resulting from any other discharge, *e.g.*, a bad conduct discharge.

Display fireworks. Large fireworks designed primarily to produce visible or audible effects by combustion, deflagration, or detonation. This term includes, but is not limited to, salutes containing more than 2 grains (130 mg) of explosive materials, aerial shells containing more than 40 grams of pyrotechnic compositions, and other display pieces which exceed the limits of explosive materials for classification as "consumer fireworks." Display fireworks are classified as fireworks UN0333, UN0334 or UN0335 by the U.S. Department of Transportation at 49 CFR 172.101. This term also includes fused setpieces containing components which together exceed 50 mg of salute powder.

Distribute. To sell, issue, give, transfer, or otherwise dispose of. The term does not include a mere change of possession from a person to his agent or employee in connection with the agency or employment.

Executed under penalties of perjury. Signed with the required declaration under the penalties of perjury as provided on or with respect to the return, form, or other document or, where no form of declaration is required, with the declaration:

"I declare under the penalties of perjury that this—(insert type of document, such as, statement, application, request, certificate), including the documents submitted in support thereof, has been examined by me and, to the best of my knowledge and belief, is true, correct, and complete".

Explosive actuated device. Any tool or special mechanized device which is actuated by explosives, but not a propellent actuated device.

Explosive materials. Explosives, blasting agents, water gels and detonators. Explosive materials include, but are not limited to, all items in the "List of Explosive Materials" provided for in § 555.23.

Explosives. Any chemical compound, mixture, or device, the primary or common purpose of which is to function by explosion. The term includes, but is not limited to, dynamite and other high explosives, black powder, pellet powder, initiating explosives, detonators, safety fuses, squibs, detonating cord, igniter cord, and igniters.

Fireworks. Any composition or device designed to produce a visible or an audible effect by combustion, deflagration, or detonation, and which meets the definition of "consumer fireworks" or "display fireworks" as defined by this section.

Fireworks mixing building. Any building or area used for mixing and blending pyrotechnic compositions except wet sparkler mix.

Fireworks nonprocess building. Any office building or other building or area in a fireworks plant where no fireworks, pyrotechnic compositions or explosive materials are processed or stored.

Fireworks plant. All land and buildings thereon used for or in connection with the assembly or processing of fireworks, including warehouses used with or in connection with fireworks plant operations.

Fireworks plant warehouse. Any building or structure used exclusively for the storage of materials which are neither explosive materials nor pyrotechnic compositions used to manufacture or assemble fireworks.

Fireworks process building. Any mixing building; any building in which pyrotechnic compositions or explosive materials is pressed or otherwise prepared for finished and assembly; or any finishing or assembly building.

Fireworks shipping building. A building used for the packing of assorted display fireworks into shipping cartons for individual public displays and for the loading of packaged displays for shipment to purchasers.

Flash powder. An explosive material intended to produce an audible report and a flash of light when ignited which includes but is not limited to oxidizers such as potassium chlorate or potassium perchlorate, and fuels such as sulfur or aluminum powder.

Fugitive from justice. Any person who has fled from the jurisdiction of any court of record to avoid prosecution for any crime or to avoid giving testimony in any criminal proceeding. The term also includes any person who has been convicted of any crime and has fled to avoid imprisonment.

Hardwood. Oak, maple, ash, hickory, or other hard wood, free from loose knots, spaces, or similar defects.

Highway. Any public street, public alley, or public road, including a privately financed, constructed, or maintained road that is regularly and openly traveled by the general public.

Identification document. A document containing the name, residence address, date of birth, and photograph of the holder and which was made or issued by or under the authority of the United States Government, a State, political subdivision of a State, a foreign government, a political subdivision of a foreign government, an international governmental or an international quasi-governmental organization which, when completed with information concerning a particular individual, is of a type intended or commonly accepted for the purpose of identification of individuals.

Importer. Any person engaged in the business of importing or bringing explosive materials into the United States for purposes of sale or distribution.

Indictment. Includes an indictment or information in any court under which a crime punishable by imprisonment for a term exceeding one year may be prosecuted.

Inhabited building. Any building regularly occupied in whole or in part as a habitation for human beings, or any church, schoolhouse, railroad station, store, or other structure where people are accustomed to assemble, except any building occupied in connection with the manufacture, transportation, storage, or use of explosive materials.

Interstate or foreign commerce. Commerce between any place in a State and any place outside of that State, or within any possession of the United States or the District of Columbia, and commerce between places within the same State but through any place outside of that State.

Licensed dealer. A dealer licensed under this part.

Licensed importer. An importer licensed under this part.

Licensed manufacturer. A manufacturer licensed under this part to engage in the business of manufacturing explosive materials for purposes of sale or distribution or for his own use.

141

Licensee. Any importer, manufacturer, or dealer licensed under this part.

Limited permit. A permit issued to a person authorizing him to receive for his use explosive materials from a licensee or permittee in his state of residence on no more than 6 occasions during the 12-month period in which the permit is valid. A limited permit does not authorize the receipt or transportation of explosive materials in interstate or foreign commerce.

Magazine. Any building or structure, other than an explosives manufacturing building, used for storage of explosive materials.

Manufacturer. Any person engaged in the business of manufacturing explosive materials for purposes of sale or distribution or for his own use.

Mass detonation (mass explosion). Explosive materials mass detonate (mass explode) when a unit or any part of a larger quantity of explosive material explodes and causes all or a substantial part of the remaining material to detonate or explode.

Mental institution. Includes mental health facilities, mental hospitals, sanitariums, psychiatric facilities, and other facilities that provide diagnoses by licensed professionals of mental retardation or mental illness, including a psychiatric ward in a general hospital.

Natural barricade. Natural features of the ground, such as hills, or timber of sufficient density that the surrounding exposures which require protection cannot be seen from the magazine when the trees are bare of leaves.

Number 8 test blasting cap. (See definition of "blasting agent.")

Permittee. Any user of explosives for a lawful purpose who has obtained either a user permit or a limited permit under this part.

Person. Any individual, corporation, company, association, firm, partnership, society, or joint stock company.

Plywood. Exterior, construction grade (laminated wood) plywood.

Propellant actuated device. (a) Any tool or special mechanized device or gas generator system that is actuated by a propellant or which releases and directs work through a propellant charge.

(b) The term does not include—

(1) Hobby rocket motors consisting of ammonium perchlorate composite propellant, black powder, or other similar low explosives, regardless of amount; and

(2) Rocket-motor reload kits that can be used to assemble hobby rocket motors containing ammonium perchlorate composite propellant, black powder, or other similar low explosives, regardless of amount.

Pyrotechnic compositions. A chemical mixture which, upon burning and without explosion, produces visible, brilliant displays, bright lights, or sounds.

Railway. Any steam, electric, or other railroad or railway which carries passengers for hire.

Region. A geographical region of the Bureau of Alcohol, Tobacco, Firearms, and Explosives, Department of Justice.

Renounced U.S. citizenship. (a) A person has renounced his U.S. citizenship if the person, having been a citizen of the United States, has renounced citizenship either—

(1) Before a diplomatic or consular officer of the United States in a foreign state pursuant to 8 U.S.C. 1481(a)(5); or

(2) Before an officer designated by the Attorney General when the United States is in a state of war pursuant to 8 U.S.C. 1481(a)(6).

(b) The term will not include any renunciation of citizenship that has been reversed as a result of administrative or judicial appeal.

Responsible person. An individual who has the power to direct the management and policies of the applicant pertaining to explosive materials. Generally, the term includes partners, sole proprietors, site managers, corporate officers and directors, and majority shareholders.

Salute. An aerial shell, classified as a display firework, that contains a charge of flash powder and is designed to produce a flash of light and a loud report as the pyrotechnic effect.

Screen barricade. Any barrier that will contain the embers and debris from a fire or deflagration in a process building, thus preventing propagation of fire to other buildings or areas. Such barriers shall be constructed of metal roofing, ¼ to ½ inch (6 to 13 mm) mesh screen, or equivalent material. The barrier extends from floor level to a height such that a straight line from the top of any side wall of the donor building to the eave line of any exposed building intercepts the screen at a point not less than 5 feet (1.5 m) from the top of the screen. The top 5 feet (1.5 m) of the screen is inclined towards the donor building at an angle of 30 to 45 degrees.

Softwood. Fir, pine, or other soft wood, free from loose knots, spaces, or similar defects.

State. A State of the United States. The term includes the District of Columbia, the Commonwealth of Puerto Rico, and the possessions of the United States.

State of residence. The State in which an individual regularly resides or maintains his home. Temporary stay in a State does not make the State of temporary stay the State of residence.

Theatrical flash powder. Flash powder commercially manufactured in premeasured kits not exceeding 1 ounce and mixed immediately prior to use and intended for use in theatrical shows, stage plays, band concerts, magic acts, thrill shows, and clown acts in circuses.

Unlawful user of or addicted to any controlled substance. A person who uses a controlled substance and has lost the power of self-control with reference to the use of a controlled substance; and any person who is a current user of a controlled substance in a manner other than as prescribed by a licensed physician. Such use is not limited to the use of drugs on a particular day, or within a matter of days or weeks before possession of the explosive materials, but rather that the unlawful use has occurred recently enough to indicate that the individual is actively engaged in such conduct. A person may be an unlawful current user of a controlled substance even though the substance is not being used at the precise time the person seeks to acquire explosive materials or receives or possesses explosive materials. An inference of current use may be drawn from evidence of a recent use or possession of a controlled substance or a pattern of use or possession that reasonably covers the present time, e.g., a conviction for use or possession of a controlled substance within the past year; multiple arrests for

such offenses within the past 5 years if the most recent arrest occurred within the past year; or persons found through a drug test to use a controlled substance unlawfully, provided that the test was administered within the past year. For a current or former member of the Armed Forces, an inference of current use may be drawn from recent disciplinary or other administrative action based on confirmed drug use, e.g., court-martial conviction, nonjudicial punishment, or an administrative discharge based on drug use or drug rehabilitation failure.

U.S.C. The United States Code.

User-limited permit. A user permit valid only for a single purchase transaction, a new permit being required for a subsequent purchase transaction.

User permit. A permit issued to a person authorizing him (a) to acquire for his own use explosive materials from a licensee in a State other than the State in which he resides or from a foreign country, and (b) to transport explosive materials in interstate or foreign commerce.

Water gels. Explosives or blasting agents that contain a substantial proportion of water.

(18 U.S.C. 847 (84 Stat. 959); 18 U.S.C. 926 (82 Stat. 1226)

[T.D. ATF–87, 46 FR 40384, Aug. 7, 1981]

EDITORIAL NOTE: For FEDERAL REGISTER citations affecting §555.11, see the List of CFR Sections Affected, which appears in the Finding Aids section of the printed volume and at *www.govinfo.gov*.

Subpart C—Administrative and Miscellaneous Provisions

§555.21 Forms prescribed.

(a) The Director is authorized to prescribe all forms required by this part. All of the information called for in each form shall be furnished as indicated by the headings on the form and the instructions on or pertaining to the form. In addition, information called for in each form shall be furnished as required by this part.

(b) Requests for forms should be submitted to the ATF Distribution Center (*http://www.atf.gov*) or made by calling (202) 648–6420.

[T.D. ATF–92, 46 FR 46916, Sept. 23, 1981, as amended by T.D. ATF–249, 52 FR 5961, Feb. 27, 1987; T.D. 372, 61 FR 20724, May 8, 1996; ATF–11F, 73 FR 57242, Oct. 2, 2008; ATF 2013R–9F, 79 FR 46693, Aug. 11, 2014]

§ 555.22 Alternate methods or procedures; emergency variations from requirements.

(a) *Alternate methods or procedures.* The permittee or licensee, on specific approval by the Director as provided by this paragraph, may use an alternate method or procedure in lieu of a method or procedure specifically prescribed in this part. The Director may approve an alternate method or procedure, subject to stated conditions, when he finds that:

(1) Good cause is shown for the use of the alternate method or procedure;

(2) The alternate method or procedure is within the purpose of, and consistent with the effect intended by, the specifically prescribed method or procedure and that the alternate method or procedure is substantially equivalent to that specifically prescribed method or procedure; and

(3) The alternate method or procedure will not be contrary to any provision of law and will not result in an increase in cost to the Government or hinder the effective administration of this part.

Where the permittee or licensee desires to employ an alternate method or procedure, he shall submit a written application to the Director, Industry Operations, for transmittal to the Director. The application shall specifically describe the proposed alternate method or procedure and shall set forth the reasons for it. Alternate methods or procedures may not be employed until the application is approved by the Director. The permittee or licensee shall, during the period of authorization of an alternate method or procedure, comply with the terms of the approved application. Authorization of any alternate method or procedure may be withdrawn whenever, in the judgment of the Director, the effective administration of this part is hindered by the continuation of the authorization. As used in this paragraph, alternate methods or procedures include alternate construction or equipment.

(b) *Emergency variations from requirements.* The Director may approve construction, equipment, and methods of operation other than as specified in this part, where he finds that an emergency exists and the proposed variations from the specified requirements are necessary and the proposed variations:

(1) Will afford security and protection that are substantially equivalent to those prescribed in this part;

(2) Will not hinder the effective administration of this part; and

(3) Will not be contrary to any provisions of law.

Variations from requirements granted under this paragraph are conditioned on compliance with the procedures, conditions, and limitations set forth in the approval of the application. Failure to comply in good faith with the procedures, conditions, and limitations shall automatically terminate the authority for the variations and the licensee or permittee shall fully comply with the prescribed requirements of regulations from which the variations were authorized. Authority for any variation may be withdrawn whenever, in the judgment of the Director, the effective administration of this part is hindered by the continuation of the variation. Where the licensee or permittee desires to employ an emergency variation, he shall submit a written application to the Director, Industry Operations for transmittal to the Director. The application shall describe the proposed variation and set forth the reasons for it. Variations may not be employed until the application is approved, except when the emergency requires immediate action to correct a situation that is threatening to life or property. Corrective action may then be taken concurrent with the filing of the application and notification of the Director via telephone.

(c) *Retention of approved variations.* The licensee or permittee shall retain, as part of his records available for examination by ATF officers, any application approved by the Director under this section.

[T.D. ATF–87, 46 FR 40384, Aug. 7, 1981, as amended by ATF 2013R–9F, 79 FR 46693, Aug. 11, 2014]

§555.23 List of explosive materials.

The Director shall compile a list of explosive materials, which shall be published and revised at least annually in the FEDERAL REGISTER. The "List of Explosive Materials" (ATF Publication 5400.8) is available at no cost upon request from the ATF Distribution Center (See §555.21).

[T.D. ATF–290, 54 FR 53054, Dec. 27, 1989, as amended by T.D. ATF–446, 66 FR 16602, Mar. 27, 2001; ATF–11F, 73 FR 57242, Oct. 2, 2008]

§555.24 Right of entry and examination.

(a) Any ATF officer may enter during business hours the premises, including places of storage, of any licensee or holder of a user permit for the purpose of inspecting or examining any records or documents required to be kept under this part, and any facilities in which explosive materials are kept or stored.

(b) Any ATF officer may inspect the places of storage for explosive materials of an applicant for a limited permit or, in the case of a holder of a limited permit, at the time of renewal of such permit.

(c) The provisions of paragraph (b) of this section do not apply to an applicant for the renewal of a limited permit if an ATF officer has, within the preceding 3 years, verified by inspection that the applicant's place of storage for explosive materials meets the requirements of subpart K of this part.

[ATF No. 1, 68 FR 13781, Mar. 20, 2003]

§555.25 Disclosure of information.

Upon receipt of written request from any State or any political subdivision of a State, the Director, Industry Operations may make available to the State or political subdivision any information which the Director, Industry Operations may obtain under the Act with respect to the identification of persons within the State or political subdivision, who have purchased or received explosive materials, together with a description of the explosive materials.

[T.D. ATF–87, 46 FR 40384, Aug. 7, 1981, as amended by ATF 2013R–9F, 79 FR 46693, Aug. 11, 2014]

§555.26 Prohibited shipment, transportation, receipt, possession, or distribution of explosive materials.

(a) *General.* No person, other than a licensee or permittee knowingly may transport, ship, cause to be transported, or receive any explosive materials: *Provided,* That the provisions of this paragraph (a) do not apply to the lawful purchase by a nonlicensee or nonpermittee of commercially manufactured black powder in quantities not to exceed 50 pounds, if the black powder is intended to be used solely for sporting, recreational, or cultural purposes in antique firearms as defined in 18 U.S.C. 921(a)(16), or in antique devices as exempted from the term "destructive device" in 18 U.S.C. 921(a)(4).

(b) *Holders of a limited permit.* No person who is a holder of a limited permit may—

(1) Transport, ship, cause to be transported, or receive in interstate or foreign commerce any explosive materials;

(2) Receive explosive materials from a licensee or permittee, whose premises are located outside the State of residence of the limited permit holder; or

(3) Receive explosive materials on more than 6 separate occasions, during the period of the permit, from one or more licensees or permittees whose premises are located within the State of residence of the limited permit holder. (See §555.105(b) for the definition of "6 separate occasions.")

(c) *Possession by prohibited persons.* No person may ship or transport any explosive material in or affecting interstate or foreign commerce or receive or possess any explosive materials which have been shipped or transported in or affecting interstate or foreign commerce who:

(1) Is under indictment or information for, or who has been convicted in any court of, a crime punishable by imprisonment for a term exceeding one year;

(2) Is a fugitive from justice;

(3) Is an unlawful user of or addicted to any controlled substance (as defined in section 102 of the Controlled Substances Act (21 U.S.C. 802) and § 555.11);

(4) Has been adjudicated as a mental defective or has been committed to a mental institution;

(5) Is an alien, other than an alien who—

(i) Is lawfully admitted for permanent residence (as that term is defined in section 101(a)(20) of the Immigration and Nationality Act (8 U.S.C. 1101)); or

(ii) Is in lawful nonimmigrant status, is a refugee admitted under section 207 of the Immigration and Nationality Act (8 U.S.C. 1157), or is in asylum status under section 208 of the Immigration and Nationality Act (8 U.S.C. 1158), and—

(A) Is a foreign law enforcement officer of a friendly foreign government, as determined by the Attorney General in consultation with the Secretary of State, entering the United States on official law enforcement business, and the shipping, transporting, possession, or receipt of explosive materials is in furtherance of this official law enforcement business;

(B) Is a person having the power to direct or cause the direction of the management and policies of a corporation, partnership, or association licensed pursuant to section 843(a) of the Act, and the shipping, transporting, possession, or receipt of explosive materials is in furtherance of such power;

(C) Is a member of a North Atlantic Treaty Organization (NATO) or other friendly foreign military force, as determined by the Attorney General in consultation with the Secretary of Defense, (whether or not admitted in a nonimmigrant status) who is present in the United States under military orders for training or other military purpose authorized by the United States, and the shipping, transporting, possession, or receipt of explosive materials is in furtherance of the military purpose; or

(D) Is lawfully present in the United States in cooperation with the Director of Central Intelligence, and the shipment, transportation, receipt, or possession of the explosive materials is in furtherance of such cooperation;

(6) Has been discharged from the armed forces under dishonorable conditions; or

(7) Having been a citizen of the United States, has renounced citizenship.

(d) *Distribution to prohibited persons.* No person may knowingly distribute explosive materials to any individual who:

(1) Is under twenty-one years of age;

(2) Is under indictment or information for, or who has been convicted in any court of, a crime punishable by imprisonment for a term exceeding one year;

(3) Is a fugitive from justice;

(4) Is an unlawful user of or addicted to any controlled substance (as defined in section 102 of the Controlled Substances Act (21 U.S.C. 802) and § 555.11);

(5) Has been adjudicated as a mental defective or has been committed to a mental institution;

(6) Is an alien, other than an alien who—

(i) Is lawfully admitted for permanent residence (as that term is defined in section 101(a)(20) of the Immigration and Nationality Act (8 U.S.C. 1101)); or

(ii) Is in lawful nonimmigrant status, is a refugee admitted under section 207 of the Immigration and Nationality Act (8 U.S.C. 1157), or is in asylum status under section 208 of the Immigration and Nationality Act (8 U.S.C. 1158), and—

(A) Is a foreign law enforcement officer of a friendly foreign government, as determined by the Attorney General in consultation with the Secretary of State, entering the United States on official law enforcement business, and the shipping, transporting, possession, or receipt of explosive materials is in furtherance of this official law enforcement business;

(B) Is a person having the power to direct or cause the direction of the management and policies of a corporation, partnership, or association licensed pursuant to section 843(a) of the Act, and the shipping, transporting, possession, or receipt of explosive materials is in furtherance of such power;

(C) Is a member of a North Atlantic Treaty Organization (NATO) or other friendly foreign military force, as determined by the Attorney General in consultation with the Secretary of Defense, (whether or not admitted in a nonimmigrant status) who is present in the United States under military orders for training or other military purpose authorized by the United States, and the shipping, transporting, possession, or receipt of explosive materials is in furtherance of the military purpose; or

(D) Is lawfully present in the United States in cooperation with the Director of Central Intelligence, and the shipment, transportation, receipt, or possession of the explosive materials is in furtherance of such cooperation;

(7) Has been discharged from the armed forces under dishonorable conditions; or

(8) Having been a citizen of the United States, has renounced citizenship.

(e) See § 555.180 for regulations concerning the prohibited manufacture, importation, exportation, shipment, transportation, receipt, transfer, or possession of plastic explosives that do not contain a detection agent.

[ATF No. 1, 68 FR 13781, Mar. 20, 2003]

§ 555.27 [Reserved]

§ 555.28 Stolen explosive materials.

No person shall receive, conceal, transport, ship, store, barter, sell, or dispose of any stolen explosive materials knowing or having reasonable cause to believe that the explosive materials were stolen.

§ 555.29 Unlawful storage.

No person shall store any explosive materials in a manner not in conformity with this part.

§ 555.30 Reporting theft or loss of explosive materials.

(a) Any licensee or permittee who has knowledge of the theft or loss of any explosive materials from his stock shall, within 24 hours of discovery, report the theft or loss by telephoning 1–800–461–8841 (nationwide toll free number) and on ATF F 5400.5 in accordance with the instructions on the form. Theft or loss of any explosive materials shall also be reported to appropriate local authorities.

(b) Any other person, except a carrier of explosive materials, who has knowledge of the theft or loss of any explosive materials from his stock shall, within 24 hours of discovery, report the theft or loss by telephoning 1–800–461–8841 (nationwide toll free number) and in writing to the nearest ATF office. Theft or loss shall be reported to appropriate local authorities.

(c) Reports of theft or loss of explosive materials under paragraphs (a) and (b) of this section must include the following information, if known:

(1) The manufacturer or brand name.

(2) The manufacturer's marks of identification (date and shift code).

(3) Quantity (applicable quantity units, such as pounds of explosives, number of detonators, etc.).

(4) Description (dynamite, blasting agents, detonators, etc.) and United Nations (UN) identification number, hazard division number, and classification letter, e.g., 1.1D, as classified by the U.S. Department of Transportation at 49 CFR 172.101 and 173.52.

(5) Size (length and diameter).

(d) A carrier of explosive materials who has knowledge of the theft or loss of any explosive materials shall, within 24 hours of discovery, report the theft or loss by telephoning 1–800–461–8841 (nationwide toll free number). Theft or loss shall also be reported to appropriate local authorities. Reports of theft or loss of explosive materials by carriers shall include the following information, if known:

(1) The manufacturer or brand name.

(2) Quantity (applicable quantity units, such as pounds of explosives, number of detonators, etc.).

(3) Description (United Nations (UN) identification number, hazard division number, and classification letter, e.g., 1.1D) as classified by the U.S. Department of Transportation at 49 CFR 172.101 and 173.52.

[T.D. ATF–87, 46 FR 40384, Aug. 7, 1981, as amended by T.D. ATF–400, 63 FR 45002, Aug. 24, 1998; ATF 2017R–21, 84 FR 13799, Apr. 8, 2019]

§ 555.31 Inspection of site accidents or fires; right of entry.

Any ATF officer may inspect the site of any accident or fire in which there is

147

reason to believe that explosive materials were involved. Any ATF officer may enter into or upon any property where explosive materials have been used, are suspected of having been used, or have been found in an otherwise unauthorized location.

§ 555.32 Special explosive devices.

The Director may exempt certain explosive actuated devices, explosive actuated tools, or similar devices from the requirements of this part. A person who desires to obtain an exemption under this section for any special explosive device, which as designed does not constitute a public safety or security hazard, shall submit a written request to the Director. Each request shall be executed under the penalties of perjury and contain a complete and accurate description of the device, the name and address of the manufacturer or importer, the purpose of and use for which it is intended, and any photographs, diagrams, or drawings as may be necessary to enable the Director to make a determination. The Director may require that a sample of the device be submitted for examination and evaluation. If it is not possible to submit the device, the person requesting the exemption shall advise the Director and designate the place where the device will be available for examination and evaluation.

§ 555.33 Background checks and clearances.

(a) *Background checks.* (1) If the Director receives from a licensee or permittee the names and appropriate identifying information of responsible persons and employees who will be authorized by the employer to possess explosive materials in the course of employment with the employer, the Director will conduct a background check in accordance with this section.

(2) The Director will determine whether the responsible person or employee is one of the persons described in any paragraph of section 842(i) of the Act (see § 555.26). In making such determination, the Director may take into account a letter or document issued under paragraph (a)(3) of this section.

(3)(i) If the Director determines that the responsible person or the employee is not one of the persons described in any paragraph of section 842(i) of the Act (see § 555.26), the Director will notify the employer in writing or electronically of the determination and issue, to the responsible person or employee, as the case may be, a letter of clearance which confirms the determination.

(ii) If the Director determines that the responsible person or employee is one of the persons described in any paragraph of section 842(i) of the Act (see § 555.26), ATF will notify the employer in writing or electronically of the determination and issue to the responsible person or the employee, as the case may be, a document that confirms the determination; explains the grounds for the determination; provides information on how the disability may be relieved; and explains how the determination may be appealed. The employer will retain the notification as part of his permanent records in accordance with § 555.121. The employer will take immediate steps to remove the responsible person from his position directing the management or policies of the business or operations as they relate to explosive materials or, as the case may be, to remove the employee from a position requiring the possession of explosive materials. Also, if the employer has listed the employee as a person authorized to accept delivery of explosive materials, as specified in § 555.103 or § 555.105, the employer must remove the employee from such list and immediately, and in no event later than the second business day after such change, notify distributors of such change.

(b) *Appeals and correction of erroneous system information*—(1) *In general.* A responsible person or employee may challenge the adverse determination set out in the letter of denial, in writing and within 45 days of issuance of the determination, by directing his or her challenge to the basis for the adverse determination, or to the accuracy of the record upon which the adverse determination is based, to the Director. The appeal request must include appropriate documentation or record(s) establishing the legal and/or factual basis for the challenge. Any record or document of a court or other

148

government entity or official furnished in support of an appeal must be certified by the court or other government entity or official as a true copy. In the case of an employee, or responsible person who did not submit fingerprints, such appeal must be accompanied by two properly completed FBI Forms FD–258 (fingerprint card). The Director will advise the individual in writing of his decision and the reasons for the decision.

(2) *Employees.* The letter of denial, among other things, will advise an employee who elects to challenge an adverse determination to submit the fingerprint cards as described above. The employee also will be advised of the agency name and address that originated the record containing the information causing the adverse determination ("originating agency"). At that time, and where appropriate, an employee is encouraged to apply to the originating agency to challenge the accuracy of the record(s) upon which the denial is based. The originating agency may respond to the individual's application by addressing the individual's specific reasons for the challenge, and by indicating whether additional information or documents are required. If the record is corrected as a result of the application to the originating agency, the individual may so notify ATF which will, in turn, verify the record correction with the originating agency and take all necessary steps to contact the agency responsible for the record system and correct the record. The employee may provide to ATF additional and appropriate documentation or record(s) establishing the legal and/or factual basis for the challenge to ATF's decision to uphold the initial denial. If ATF does not receive such additional documentation or record(s) within 45 days of the date of the decision upholding the initial denial, ATF will close the appeal.

(3) *Responsible persons.* The letter of denial, among other things, will advise a responsible person of the agency name and address which originated the record containing the information causing the adverse determination ("originating agency"). A responsible person who elects to challenge the adverse determination, where appro-

priate, is encouraged to apply to the originating agency to challenge the accuracy of the record(s) upon which the denial is based. The originating agency may respond to the individual's application by addressing the individual's specific reasons for the challenge, and by indicating whether additional information or documents are required. If the record is corrected as a result of the application to the originating agency, the individual may so notify ATF which will, in turn, verify the record correction with the originating agency and take all necessary steps to contact the agency responsible for the record system and correct the record. A responsible person may provide additional documentation or records as specified for employees in paragraph (b)(2) of this section.

(Approved by the Office of Management and Budget under control number 1140–0081)

[ATF No. 1, 68 FR 13783, Mar. 20, 2003, as amended by ATF 2017R–21, 84 FR 13799, Apr. 8, 2019]

§ 555.34 **Replacement of stolen or lost ATF Form 5400.30 (Intrastate Purchase of Explosives Coupon (IPEC)).**

When any Form 5400.30 is stolen, lost, or destroyed, the person losing possession will, upon discovery of the theft, loss, or destruction, immediately, but in all cases before 24 hours have elapsed since discovery, report the matter to the Director by telephoning 1–888–ATF–BOMB (nationwide toll free number). The report will explain in detail the circumstances of the theft, loss, or destruction and will include all known facts that may serve to identify the document. Upon receipt of the report, the Director will make such investigation as appears appropriate and may issue a duplicate document upon such conditions as the circumstances warrant.

(Approved by the Office of Management and Budget under control number 1140–0077)

[ATF No. 1, 68 FR 13783, Mar. 20, 2003]

Subpart D—Licenses and Permits

§ 555.41 **General.**

(a) [Reserved]

(b) *Licenses and permits issued on and after May 24, 2003*—(1) *In general.* (i) Each person intending to engage in business as an importer or manufacturer of, or a dealer in, explosive materials, including black powder, must, before commencing business, obtain the license required by this subpart for the business to be operated.

(ii) Each person who intends to acquire for use explosive materials within the State in which he resides on no more than 6 separate occasions during the 12-month period in which the permit is valid must obtain a limited permit under this subpart. (See § 555.105(b) for definition of "6 separate occasions.")

(iii) Each person who intends to acquire for use explosive materials from a licensee or permittee in a State other than the State in which he resides, or from a foreign country, or who intends to transport explosive materials in interstate or foreign commerce, or who intends to acquire for use explosive materials within the State in which he resides on more than 6 separate occasions during a 12-month period, must obtain a user permit under this subpart.

(iv) It is not necessary to obtain a permit if the user intends only to lawfully purchase commercially manufactured black powder in quantities not to exceed 50 pounds, intended to be used solely for sporting, recreational, or cultural purposes in antique firearms or in antique devices.

(2) *Importers, manufacturers, and dealers.* Each person intending to engage in business as an explosive materials importer, manufacturer, or dealer must file an application, with the required fee (*see* § 555.42), with ATF in accordance with the instructions on the form (*see* § 555.45). A license will, subject to law, entitle the licensee to transport, ship, and receive explosive materials in interstate or foreign commerce, and to engage in the business specified by the license, at the location described on the license. A separate license must be obtained for each business premises at which the applicant is to manufacture, import, or distribute explosive materials except under the following circumstances:

(i) A separate license will not be required for storage facilities operated by the licensee as an integral part of one business premises or to cover a location used by the licensee solely for maintaining the records required by this part.

(ii) A separate license will not be required of a licensed manufacturer with respect to his on-site manufacturing.

(iii) It will not be necessary for a licensed importer or a licensed manufacturer (for purposes of sale or distribution) to also obtain a dealer's license in order to engage in business on his licensed premises as a dealer in explosive materials. No licensee will be required to obtain a user permit to lawfully transport, ship, or receive explosive materials in interstate or foreign commerce.

(iv) A separate license will not be required of licensed manufacturers with respect to their on-site manufacture of theatrical flash powder.

(3) *Users of explosive materials.* (i) A limited permit will, subject to law, entitle the holder of such permit to receive for his use explosive materials from a licensee or permittee in his state of residence on no more than 6 separate occasions during the 12-month period in which the permit is valid. A limited permit does not authorize the receipt or transportation of explosive materials in interstate or foreign commerce. Holders of limited permits who need to receive explosive materials on more than 6 separate occasions during a 12-month period must obtain a user permit in accordance with this subpart.

(ii) Each person intending to acquire explosive materials from a licensee in a State other than a State in which he resides, or from a foreign country, or who intends to transport explosive materials in interstate or foreign commerce, must file an application for a user permit, with the required fee (*see* § 555.43), with ATF in accordance with the instructions on the form (*see* § 555.45). A user permit will, subject to law, entitle the permittee to transport, ship, and receive in interstate or foreign commerce explosive materials. Only one user permit per person is required under this part, irrespective of the number of locations relating to explosive materials operated by the holder of the user permit.

(Approved by the Office of Management and Budget under control number 1140–0083)

[ATF No. 1, 68 FR 13783, Mar. 20, 2003, as amended by ATF 5F, 70 FR 30633, May 27, 2005; ATF 2017R–21, 84 FR 13799, Apr. 8, 2019]

§ 555.42 License fees.

(a) Each applicant shall pay a fee for obtaining a three year license, a separate fee being required for each business premises, as follows:

(1) Manufacturer—$200.
(2) Importer—$200.
(3) Dealer—$200.

(b) Each applicant for a renewal of a license shall pay a fee for a three year license as follows:

(1) Manufacturer—$100.
(2) Importer—$100.
(3) Dealer—$100.

[T.D. ATF–400, 63 FR 45002, Aug. 24, 1998]

§ 555.43 Permit fees.

(a) Each applicant must pay a fee for obtaining a permit as follows:

(1) User—$100 for a three-year period.
(2) User-limited (nonrenewable)—$75.
(3) Limited—$25 for a one-year period.

(b)(1) Each applicant for renewal of a user permit must pay a fee of $50 for a three-year period.

(2) Each applicant for renewal of a limited permit must pay a fee of $12 for a one-year period.

[ATF No. 1, 68 FR 13785, Mar. 20, 2003]

§ 555.44 License or permit fee not refundable.

No refund of any part of the amount paid as a license or permit fee will be made where the operations of the licensee or permittee are, for any reason, discontinued during the period of an issued license or permit. However, the license or permit fee submitted with an application for a license or permit will be refunded if that application is denied, withdrawn, or abandoned, or if a license is cancelled subsequent to having been issued through administrative error.

§ 555.45 Original license or permit.

(a)–(b) [Reserved]

(c) Licenses and permits issued on and after May 24, 2003—(1) License. Any person who intends to engage in the business as an importer of, manufacturer of, or dealer in explosive materials, or who has not timely submitted an application for renewal of a previous license issued under this part, must file an application for License, Explosives, ATF F 5400.13, with ATF in accordance with the instructions on the form. ATF Form 5400.13 may be obtained by contacting any ATF office. The application must:

(i) Be executed under the penalties of perjury and the penalties imposed by 18 U.S.C. 844(a);

(ii) Include appropriate identifying information concerning each responsible person;

(iii) Include a photograph and fingerprints for each responsible person;

(iv) Include the names of and appropriate identifying information regarding all employees who will be authorized by the applicant to possess explosive materials by submitting ATF F 5400.28 for each employee; and

(v) Include the appropriate fee in the form of money order or check made payable to the Bureau of Alcohol, Tobacco, Firearms and Explosives.

(2) User permit and limited permit. Except as provided in § 555.41(b)(1)(iv), any person who intends to acquire explosive materials in the State in which that person resides or acquire explosive materials from a licensee or holder of a user permit in a State other than the State in which that person resides, or from a foreign country, or who intends to transport explosive materials in interstate or foreign commerce, or who has not timely submitted an application for renewal of a previous permit issued under this part, must file an application for Permit, Explosives, ATF F 5400.16 or Permit, User Limited Display Fireworks, ATF F 5400.21 with ATF in accordance with the instructions on the form. ATF Form 5400.16 and ATF Form 5400.21 may be obtained by contacting any ATF office. The application must:

(i) Be executed under the penalties of perjury and the penalties imposed by 18 U.S.C. 844(a);

(ii) Include a photograph, fingerprints, and appropriate identifying information for each responsible person;

(iii) Include the names of and appropriate identifying information regarding all employees who will be authorized by the applicant to possess explosive materials by submitting ATF F 5400.28 for each employee; and

(iv) Include the appropriate fee in the form of money order or check made payable to the Bureau of Alcohol, Tobacco, Firearms and Explosives.

(3) The Chief, Federal Explosives Licensing Center, will conduct background checks on responsible persons and employees authorized by the applicant to possess explosive materials in accordance with § 555.33. If it is determined that any responsible person or employee is described in any paragraph of section 842(i) of the Act, the applicant must submit an amended application indicating removal or reassignment of that person before the license or permit will be issued.

(Approved by the Office of Management and Budget under control number 1140–0083)

(18 U.S.C. 847 (84 Stat. 959); 18 U.S.C. 926 (82 Stat. 1226))

[T.D. ATF–200, 50 FR 10497, Mar. 15, 1985, as amended by T.D. ATF–400, 63 FR 45002, Aug. 24, 1998; ATF No. 1, 68 FR 13785, Mar. 20, 2003; ATF 2013R–9F, 79 FR 46693, Aug. 11, 2014; ATF 2017R–21, 84 FR 13799, Apr. 8, 2019]

§ 555.46 Renewal of license or permit.

(a) If a licensee or permittee intends to continue the business or operation described on a license or permit issued under this part after the expiration date of the license or permit, he shall, unless otherwise notified in writing by the Chief, Federal Explosives Licensing Center, execute and file prior to the expiration of his license or permit an application for license renewal, ATF F 5400.14 (Part III), or an application for permit renewal, ATF F 5400.15 (Part III), accompanied by the required fee, with ATF in accordance with the instructions on the form. In the event the licensee or permittee does not timely file a renewal application, he shall file an original application as required by § 555.45, and obtain the required license or permit in order to continue business or operations.

(b) A user-limited permit is not renewable and is valid for a single purchase transaction. Applications for all user-limited permits must be filed on ATF F 5400.16 or ATF F 5400.21, as required by § 555.45.

(18 U.S.C. 847 (84 Stat. 959); 18 U.S.C. 926 (82 Stat. 1226))

[T.D. ATF–87, 46 FR 40384, Aug. 7, 1981, as amended by T.D. ATF–200, 50 FR 10497, Mar. 15, 1985; T.D. ATF–290, 54 FR 53054, Dec. 27, 1989; T.D. ATF–400, 63 FR 45002, Aug. 24, 1998; ATF 2013R–9F, 79 FR 46693, Aug. 11, 2014]

§ 555.47 Insufficient fee.

If an application is filed with an insufficient fee, the application and fee submitted will be returned to the applicant.

(18 U.S.C. 847 (84 Stat. 959); 18 U.S.C. 926 (82 Stat. 1226))

[T.D. ATF–200, 50 FR 10498, Mar. 15, 1985]

§ 555.48 Abandoned application.

Upon receipt of an incomplete or improperly executed application, the applicant will be notified of the deficiency in the application. If the application is not corrected and returned within 30 days following the date of notification, the application will be considered as having been abandoned and the license or permit fee returned.

§ 555.49 Issuance of license or permit.

(a) [Reserved]

(b) *Issuance of license or permit on and after May 24, 2003.* (1) The Chief, Federal Explosives Licensing Center, will issue a license or permit if:

(i) A properly executed application for the license or permit is received; and

(ii) Through further inquiry or investigation, or otherwise, it is found that the applicant is entitled to the license or permit.

(2) The Chief, Federal Explosives Licensing Center, will approve a properly executed application for a license or permit, if:

(i) The applicant (or, if the applicant is a corporation, partnership, or association, each responsible person with respect to the applicant) is not a person described in any paragraph of section 842(i) of the Act;

(ii) The applicant has not willfully violated any provisions of the Act or this part;

(iii) The applicant has not knowingly withheld information or has not made any false or fictitious statement intended or likely to deceive, in connection with his application;

(iv) The applicant has in a State, premises from which he conducts business or operations subject to license or permit under the Act or from which he intends to conduct business or operations;

(v) The applicant has storage for the class (as described in §555.202) of explosive materials described on the application;

(vi) The applicant has certified in writing that he is familiar with and understands all published State laws and local ordinances relating to explosive materials for the location in which he intends to do business;

(vii) The applicant for a license has submitted the certificate required by section 21 of the Federal Water Pollution Control Act, as amended (33 U.S.C. 1341);

(viii) None of the employees of the applicant who will be authorized by the applicant to possess explosive materials is a person described in any paragraph of section 842(i) of the Act; and

(ix) In the case of an applicant for a limited permit, the applicant has certified in writing that the applicant will not receive explosive materials on more than 6 separate occasions during the 12-month period for which the limited permit is valid.

(3) The Chief, Federal Explosives Licensing Center, will approve or the Director, Industry Operations will deny any application for a license or permit within the 90-day period beginning on the date a properly executed application was received. However, when an applicant for license or permit renewal is a person who is, under the provisions of §555.83 or §555.142, conducting business or operations under a previously issued license or permit, action regarding the application will be held in abeyance pending the completion of the proceedings against the applicant's existing license or permit, or renewal application, or final action by the Director on an application for relief submitted under §555.142, as the case may be.

(4) The license or permit and one copy will be forwarded to the applicant, except that in the case of a user-limited permit, the original only will be issued.

(5) Each license or permit will bear a serial number and this number may be assigned to the licensee or permittee to whom issued for as long as he maintains continuity of renewal in the same region.

(Approved by the Office of Management and Budget under control number 1140–0082)

[ATF No. 1, 68 FR 13785, Mar. 20, 2003, as amended by ATF 2013R–9F, 79 FR 46693, Aug. 11, 2014; ATF 2017R–21, 84 FR 13799, Apr. 8, 2019]

§555.50 Correction of error on license or permit.

(a) Upon receipt of a license or permit issued under this part, each licensee or permittee shall examine the license or permit to insure that the information on it is accurate. If the license or permit is incorrect, the licensee or permittee shall return the license or permit to the Chief, Federal Explosives Licensing Center, with a statement showing the nature of the error. The Chief, Federal Explosives Licensing Center, shall correct the error, if the error was made in his office, and return the license or permit. However, if the error resulted from information contained in the licensee's or permittee's application for the license or permit, the Chief, Federal Explosives Licensing Center, shall require the licensee or permittee to file an amended application setting forth the correct information and a statement explaining the error contained in the application. Upon receipt of the amended application and a satisfactory explanation of the error, the Chief, Federal Explosives Licensing Center, shall make the correction on the license or permit and return it to the licensee or permittee.

(b) When the Chief, Federal Explosives Licensing Center, finds through any means other than notice from the licensee or permittee that an incorrect license or permit has been issued, (1) the Chief, Federal Explosives Licensing Center, may require the holder of the incorrect license or permit to return the license or permit for correction, and (2) if the error resulted from information contained in the licensee's or permittee's application for the license or permit, the Chief, Federal Explosives Licensing Center, shall require the licensee or permittee to file an amended application setting forth the correct information, and a statement satisfactorily explaining the error contained in the application. The Chief, Federal Explosives Licensing Center, then shall make the correction on the license or permit and return it to the licensee or permittee.

[T.D. ATF–87, 46 FR 40384, Aug. 7, 1981, as amended by T.D. ATF–290, 54 FR 53054, Dec. 27, 1989; ATF 2013R–9F, 79 FR 46693, Aug. 11, 2014]

§ 555.51 Duration of license or permit.

(a) [Reserved]

(b) *On and after May 24, 2003.* (1) An original license or user permit is issued for a period of three years. A renewal license or user permit is also issued for a period of three years. However, a user-limited permit is valid only for a single purchase transaction.

(2) A limited permit is issued for a period of one year. A renewal limited permit is also issued for a period of one year.

[ATF No. 1, 68 FR 13786, Mar. 20, 2003, as amended by ATF 2017R–21, 84 FR 13799, Apr. 8, 2019]

§ 555.52 Limitations on license or permit.

(a) The license covers the business of explosive materials specified in the license at the licensee's business premises (see § 555.41(b)).

(b) The permit is valid with respect to the type of operations of explosive materials specified in the permit.

[T.D. ATF–87, 46 FR 40384, Aug. 7, 1981, as amended by T.D. ATF–387, 62 FR 8376, Feb. 25, 1997; ATF 5F, 70 FR 30633, May 27, 2005]

§ 555.53 License and permit not transferable.

Licenses and permits issued under this part are not transferable to another person. In the event of the lease, sale, or other transfer of the business or operations covered by the license or permit, the successor must obtain the license or permit required by this part before commencing business or operations. However, for rules on right of succession, see § 555.59.

§ 555.54 Change of address.

(a) During the term of a license or permit, a licensee or permittee may move his business or operations to a new address at which he intends to regularly carry on his business or operations, without procuring a new license or permit. However, in every case, the licensee or permittee shall—

(1) Give notification of the new location of the business or operations to the Chief, Federal Explosives Licensing Center at least 10 days before the move; and

(2) Submit the license or permit to the Chief, Federal Explosives Licensing Center. The Chief, Federal Explosives Licensing Center will issue an amended license or permit, which will contain the new address (and new license or permit number, if any).

(b) Licensees and permittees whose mailing address will change must notify the Chief, Federal Explosives Licensing Center, at least 10 days before the change.

(Paragraph (b) approved by the Office of Management and Budget under control number 1140–0080)

[T.D. ATF–87, 46 FR 40384, Aug. 7, 1981, as amended by T.D. ATF–290, 54 FR 53054, Dec. 27, 1989; ATF No. 1, 68 FR 13786, Mar. 20, 2003; ATF 2013R–9F, 79 FR 46693, Aug. 11, 2014]

§ 555.56 Change in trade name.

A licensee or permittee continuing to conduct business or operations at the location shown on his license or permit is not required to obtain a new license or permit by reason of a mere change in trade name under which he conducts his business or operations. However, the licensee or permittee shall furnish his license or permit and any copies furnished with the license or permit for endorsement of the change to the Chief, Federal Explosives Licensing Center, within 30 days from the date the licensee or permittee begins his business or operations under the new trade name.

[T.D. ATF–87, 46 FR 40384, Aug. 7, 1981, as amended by T.D. ATF–290, 54 FR 53054, Dec. 27, 1989; ATF 2013R–9F, 79 FR 46693, Aug. 11, 2014]

§555.57 Change of control, change in responsible persons, and change of employees.

(a) In the case of a corporation or association holding a license or permit under this part, if actual or legal control of the corporation or association changes, directly or indirectly, whether by reason of change in stock ownership or control (in the corporation holding a license or permit or in any other corporation), by operation of law, or in any other manner, the licensee or permittee shall, within 30 days of the change, give written notification executed under the penalties of perjury, to the Chief, Federal Explosives Licensing Center. Upon expiration of the license or permit, the corporation or association shall file an ATF F 5400.13 or an ATF F 5400.16 as required by §555.45, and pay the fee prescribed in §555.42(b) or §555.43(b).

(b) Each person holding the license or permit must report to the Chief, Federal Explosives Licensing Center, any change in responsible persons or employees authorized to possess explosive materials. Such report must be submitted within 30 days of the change and must include appropriate identifying information for each responsible person. Reports relating to newly hired employees authorized to possess explosive materials must be submitted on ATF F 5400.28 for each employee.

(c) Upon receipt of a report, the Chief, Federal Explosives Licensing Center, will conduct a background check, if appropriate, in accordance with §555.33.

(d) The reports required by paragraph (b) of this section must be retained as part of a licensee's or permittee's permanent records for the period specified in §555.121.

(Approved by the Office of Management and Budget under control number 1140–0074)

[T.D. ATF–87, 46 FR 40384, Aug. 7, 1981, as amended by T.D. ATF–290, 54 FR 53054, Dec. 27, 1989; ATF 2013R–9F, 79 FR 46693, Aug. 11, 2014; ATF 2017R–21, 84 FR 13799, Apr. 8, 2019]

§555.58 Continuing partnerships.

Where, under the laws of the particular State, the partnership is not terminated on death or insolvency of a partner, but continues until the winding up of the partnership affairs is completed, and the surviving partner has the exclusive right to the control and possession of the partnership assets for the purpose of liquidation and settlement, the surviving partner may continue to conduct the business or operations under the license or permit of the partnership. If the surviving partner acquires the business or operations on completion of settlement of the partnership, he shall obtain a license or permit in his own name from the date of acquisition, as provided in §555.45. The rule set forth in this section will also apply where there is more than one surviving partner.

§555.59 Right of succession by certain persons.

(a) Certain persons other than the licensee or permittee may secure the right to carry on the same explosive materials business or operations at the same business premises for the remainder of the term of license or permit. These persons are:

(1) The surviving spouse or child, or executor, administrator, or other legal representative of a deceased licensee or permittee; and

(2) A receiver or trustee in bankruptcy, or an assignee for benefit of creditors.

(b) In order to secure the right of succession, the person or persons continuing the business or operations shall submit the license or permit and all copies furnished with the license or permit for endorsement of the succession to the Chief, Federal Explosives Licensing Center, within 30 days from the date on which the successor begins to carry on the business or operations.

[T.D. ATF–87, 46 FR 40384, Aug. 7, 1981, as amended by T.D. ATF–290, 54 FR 53054, Dec. 27, 1989; ATF 2013R–9F, 79 FR 46693, Aug. 11, 2014]

§ 555.60 Certain continuances of business or operations.

A licensee or permittee who furnishes his license or permit to the Chief, Federal Explosives Licensing Center, for correction, amendment, or endorsement, as provided in this subpart, may continue his business or operations while awaiting its return.

[T.D. ATF–87, 46 FR 40384, Aug. 7, 1981, as amended by T.D. ATF–290, 54 FR 53054, Dec. 27, 1989; ATF 2013R–9F, 79 FR 46694, Aug. 11, 2014]

§ 555.61 Discontinuance of business or operations.

Where an explosive materials business or operations is either discontinued or succeeded by a new owner, the owner of the business or operations discontinued or succeeded shall, within 30 days, furnish notification of the discontinuance or succession and submit his license or permit and any copies furnished with the license or permit to the Chief, Federal Explosives Licensing Center. (See also § 555.128.)

[T.D. ATF–87, 46 FR 40384, Aug. 7, 1981, as amended by T.D. ATF–290, 54 FR 53054, Dec. 27, 1989; ATF 2013R–9F, 79 FR 46694, Aug. 11, 2014]

§ 555.62 State or other law.

A license or permit issued under this part confers no right or privilege to conduct business or operations, including storage, contrary to State or other law. The holder of a license or permit issued under this part is not, by reason of the rights and privileges granted by that license or permit, immune from punishment for conducting an explosive materials business or operations in violation of the provisions of any State or other law. Similarly, compliance with the provisions of any State or other law affords no immunity under Federal law or regulations.

§ 555.63 Explosives magazine changes.

(a) *General.* (1) The requirements of this section are applicable to maga-zines used for other than temporary (under 24 hours) storage of explosives.

(2) A magazine is considered suitable for the storage of explosives if the construction requirements of this part are met during the time explosives are stored in the magazine.

(3) A magazine is considered suitable for the storage of explosives if positioned in accordance with the applicable table of distances as specified in this part during the time explosives are stored in the magazine.

(4) For the purposes of this section, notification of the Director, Industry Operations may be by telephone or in writing. However, if notification of the Director, Industry Operations is in writing it must be at least three business days in advance of making changes in construction to an existing magazine or constructing a new magazine, and at least five business days in advance of using any reconstructed magazine or added magazine for the storage of explosives.

(b) *Exception.* Mobile or portable type 5 magazines are exempt from the requirements of paragraphs (c) and (d) of this section, but must otherwise be in compliance with paragraphs (a) (2) and (3) of this section during the time explosives are stored in such magazines.

(c) *Changes in magazine construction.* A licensee or permittee who intends to make changes in construction of an existing magazine shall notify the Director, Industry Operations describing the proposed changes prior to making any changes. Unless otherwise advised by the Director, Industry Operations, changes in construction may commence after explosives are removed from the magazine. Explosives may not be stored in a reconstructed magazine before the Director, Industry Operations has been notified in accordance with paragraph (a)(4) of this section that the changes have been completed.

(d) *Magazines acquired or constructed after permit or license is issued.* A licensee or permittee who intends to construct or acquire additional magazines shall notify the Director, Industry Operations in accordance with paragraph (a)(4) of this section describing the additional magazines and the class and quantity of explosives to be stored in the magazine. Unless otherwise advised by the Director, Industry Operations, additional magazines may be constructed, or acquired magazines may be used for the storage of explosives. Explosives must not be stored in a magazine under construction. The Director, Industry Operations must be notified that construction has been completed.

[T.D. ATF–87, 46 FR 40384, Aug. 7, 1981, as amended by T.D. ATF–400, 63 FR 45002, Aug. 24, 1998; ATF 2013R–9F, 79 FR 46694, Aug. 11, 2014]

Subpart E—License and Permit Proceedings

§555.71 Opportunity for compliance.

Except in cases of willfulness or those in which the public interest requires otherwise, and the Director, Industry Operations so alleges in the notice of denial of an application or revocation of a license or permit, no license or permit will be revoked or renewal application denied without first calling to the attention of the licensee or permittee the reasons for the contemplated action and affording him an opportunity to demonstrate or achieve compliance with all lawful requirements and to submit facts, arguments, or proposals of adjustment. The notice of contemplated action, ATF F 5400.12, will afford the licensee or permittee 15 days from the date of receipt of the notice to respond. If no response is received within the 15 days, or if after consideration of relevant matters presented by the licensee or permittee, the Director, Industry Operations finds that the licensee or permittee is not likely to abide by the law and regulations, he will proceed as provided in §555.74.

[T.D. ATF–87, 46 FR 40384, Aug. 7 1981, as amended by T.D. ATF–446, 66 FR 16602, Mar. 27, 2001; ATF 2013R–9F, 79 FR 46694, Aug. 11, 2014]

§555.72 Denial of initial application.

Whenever the Director, Industry Operations has reason to believe that an applicant for an original license or permit is not eligible to receive a license or permit under the provisions of §555.49, he shall issue a notice of denial on ATF F 5400.11. The notice will set forth the matters of fact and law relied upon in determining that the application should be denied, and will afford the applicant 15 days from the date of receipt of the notice in which to request a hearing to review the denial. If no request for a hearing is filed within that time, a copy of the application, marked "Disapproved", will be returned to the applicant.

[T.D. ATF–87, 46 FR 40384, Aug. 7, 1981, as amended by ATF 2013R–9F, 79 FR 46694, Aug. 11, 2014]

§555.73 Hearing after initial application is denied.

If the applicant for an original license or permit desires a hearing, he shall file a request with the Director, Industry Operations within 15 days after receipt of the notice of denial. The request should include a statement of the reasons for a hearing. On receipt of the request, the Director, Industry Operations shall refer the matter to an administrative law judge who shall set a time and place (see §555.77) for a hearing and shall serve notice of the hearing upon the applicant and the Director, Industry Operations at least 10 days in advance of the hearing date. The hearing will be conducted in accordance with the hearing procedures prescribed in part 771 of this chapter (see §555.82). Within a reasonable time after the conclusion of the hearing, and as expeditiously as possible, the administrative law judge shall render his recommended decision. He shall certify to the complete record of the proceedings before him and shall immediately forward the complete certified record, together with four copies of his recommended decision, to the Director, Industry Operations for decision.

[T.D. ATF–87, 46 FR 40384, Aug. 7, 1981, as amended by ATF 2013R–9F, 79 FR 46694, Aug. 11, 2014; ATF 33F, 84 FR 64744, Nov. 25, 2019]

§555.74 Denial of renewal application or revocation of license or permit.

If following the opportunity for compliance under §555.71, or without opportunity for compliance under §555.71, as circumstances warrant, the Director, Industry Operations finds that the licensee or permittee is not likely to comply with the law or regulations or is otherwise not eligible to continue operations authorized under his license or permit, the Director, Industry Operations shall issue a notice of denial of the renewal application or revocation of the license or permit, ATF F 5400.11 or ATF F 5400.10, as appropriate. In either case, the notice will set forth the matters of fact constituting the violations specified, dates, places, and the sections of law and regulations violated. The notice will, in the case of revocation of a license or permit, specify the date on which the action is effective, which date will be on or after the date the notice is served on the licensee or permittee. The notice will also advise the licensee or permittee that he may, within 15 days after receipt of the notice, request a hearing and, if applicable, a stay of the effective date of the revocation of his license or permit.

[T.D. ATF–87, 46 FR 40384, Aug. 7, 1981, as amended by ATF 2013R–9F, 79 FR 46694, Aug. 11, 2014]

§ 555.75   Hearing after denial of renewal application or revocation of license or permit.

If a licensee or permittee whose renewal application has been denied or whose license or permit has been revoked desires a hearing, he shall file a request for a hearing with the Director, Industry Operations. In the case of the revocation of a license or permit, he may include a request for a stay of the effective date of the revocation. On receipt of the request the Director, Industry Operations shall advise the licensee or permittee whether the stay of the effective date of the revocation is granted. If the stay of the effective date of the revocation is granted, the Director, Industry Operations shall refer the matter to an administrative law judge who shall set a time and place (see § 555.77) for a hearing and shall serve notice of the hearing upon the licensee or permittee and the Director, Industry Operations at least 10 days in advance of the hearing date. If the stay of the effective date of the revocation is denied, the licensee or permittee may request an immediate hearing. In this event, the Director, Industry Operations shall immediately refer the matter to an administrative

law judge who shall set a date and place for a hearing, which date shall be no later than 10 days from the date the licensee or permittee requested an immediate hearing. The hearing will be held in accordance with the applicable provisions of part 771 of this chapter. Within a reasonable time after the conclusion of the hearing, and as expeditiously as possible, the administrative law judge shall render his decision. He shall certify to the complete record of the proceeding before him and shall immediately forward the complete certified record, together with two copies of his decision, to the Director, Industry Operations, serve one copy of his decision on the licensee or permittee or his counsel, and transmit a copy to the attorney for the Government.

[T.D. ATF–87, 46 FR 40384, Aug. 7, 1981, as amended by ATF 2013R–9F, 79 FR 46694, Aug. 11, 2014; ATF 33F, 84 FR 64744, Nov. 25, 2019]

§ 555.76   Action by Director, Industry Operations.

(a) Initial application proceedings. If, upon receipt of the record and the recommended decision of the administrative law judge, the Director, Industry Operations decides that the license or permit should be issued, the Director, Industry Operations shall cause the application to be approved, briefly stating, for the record, his reasons. If he contemplates that the denial should stand, he shall serve a copy of the administrative law judge's recommended decision on the applicant, informing the applicant of his contemplated action and affording the applicant not more than 10 days in which to submit proposed findings and conclusions or exceptions to the recommended decision with supporting reasons. If the Director, Industry Operations, after consideration of the record of the hearing and of any proposed findings, conclusions, or exceptions filed with him by the applicant, approves the findings, conclusions and recommended decision of the administrative law judge, the Director, Industry Operations shall cause the license or permit to be issued or disapproved the application accordingly. If he disapproves the findings, conclusions, and recommendation of the administrative law judge, in whole or in part, he shall by order make such findings and conclusions as in his opinion are warranted by the law and the facts in the record. Any decision of the Director, Industry Operations ordering the disapproval of an initial application for a license or permit shall state the findings and conclusions upon which it is based, including his ruling upon each proposed finding, conclusion, and exception to the administrative law judge's recommended decision, together with a statement of his findings and conclusions, and reasons or basis for his findings and conclusions, upon all material issues of fact, law or discretion presented on the record. A signed duplicate original of the decision will be served upon the applicant and the original copy containing certificate of service will be placed in the official record of the proceedings. If the decision of the Director, Industry Operations is in favor of the applicant, he shall issue the license or permit, to be effective on issuance.

(b) *Renewal application and revocation proceedings.* Upon receipt of the complete certified records of the hearing, the Director, Industry Operations shall enter an order confirming the revocation of the license or permit, or disapproving the application, in accordance with the administrative law judge's findings and decision, unless he disagrees with the findings and decision. A signed duplicate original of the order, ATF F 5400.9, will be served upon the licensee or permittee and the original copy containing certificate of service will be placed in the official record of the proceedings. If the Director, Industry Operations disagrees with the findings and decision of the administrative law judge, he shall file a petition with the Director for review of the findings and decision, as provided in §555.79. In either case, if the renewal application denial is sustained, a copy of the application marked "Disapproved" will be returned to the applicant. If the renewal application denial is reversed, a license or permit will be issued to become effective on expiration of the license or permit being renewed, or on the date of issuance, whichever is later. If the proceedings involve the revocation of a license or permit which expired before a decision is in favor of the licensee or

permittee, the Director, Industry Operations shall:

(1) If renewal application was timely filed and a stay of the effective date of the revocation was granted, cause to be issued a license or permit effective on the date of issuance;

(2) If renewal application was not timely filed but a stay of the effective date of the revocation had been granted, request that a renewal application be filed and, following that, cause to be issued a license or permit to be effective on issuance; or

(3) If a stay of the effective date of the revocation had not been granted, request that an application be filed as provided in §555.45, and process it in the same manner as for an application for an original license or permit.

(c) *Curtailment of stay of revocation effective date.* If, after approval of a request for a stay of the effective date of an order revoking a license or permit but before actions are completed under this subpart, the Director, Industry Operations finds that it is contrary to the public interest for the licensee or permittee to continue the operations or activities covered by his license or permit, the Director, Industry Operations may issue a notice of withdrawal of the approval, effective on the date of issuance. Notice of withdrawal will be served upon the licensee or permittee in the manner provided in §555.81.

[T.D. ATF–87, 46 FR 40384, Aug. 7, 1981, as amended by T.D. ATF–290, 54 FR 53054, Dec. 27, 1989; ATF 2013R–9F, 79 FR 46694, Aug. 11, 2014]

§555.77   Designated place of hearing.

The designated place of hearing set as provided in §555.73 or §555.75, will be at the location convenient to the aggrieved party.

§555.78   Representation at a hearing.

An applicant, licensee, or permittee may represent himself, or be represented by an attorney, a certified public accountant, or any other person, specifically designated in a duly executed power of attorney that shall be filed in the proceeding by the applicant, licensee, or permittee. The applicant, licensee, or permittee shall file waivers, if applicable, under the Privacy Act of 1974 and 26 U.S.C. 6103(c) (confidentiality and disclosure of returns and return information). The Director of Industry Operations may be represented in proceedings under §§ 555.73 and 555.75 by an attorney in the Office of Chief Counsel who is authorized to execute and file motions, briefs and other papers in the proceeding, on behalf of the Director of Industry Operations, in the attorney's own name as "Attorney for the Government."

[ATF 33F, 84 FR 64744, Nov. 25, 2019]

§ 555.79　Appeal on petition to the Director.

An appeal to the Director is not required prior to filing an appeal with the U.S. Court of Appeals for judicial review. An appeal may be taken by the applicant, licensee, or permittee to the Director from a decision resulting from a hearing under § 555.73 or § 555.75. An appeal may also be taken by a Director, Industry Operations from a decision resulting from a hearing under § 555.75 as provided in § 555.76(b). The appeal shall be taken by filing a petition for review on appeal with the Director within 15 days of the service of an administrative law judge's decision or an order. The petition will set forth facts tending to show action of an arbitrary nature, action without reasonable warrant in fact, or action contrary to law and regulations. A copy of the petition will be filed with the Director, Industry Operations or served on the applicant, licensee, or permittee, as the case may be. In the event of appeal, the Director, Industry Operations shall immediately forward the complete original record, by certified mail, to the Director for his consideration, review, and disposition as provided in subpart I of part 771 of this chapter. When, on appeal, the Director affirms the initial decision of the Director, Industry Operations or the administrative law judge, as the case may be, the initial decision will be final.

[T.D. ATF–87, 46 FR 40384, Aug. 7, 1981, as amended by ATF 2013R–9F, 79 FR 46694, Aug. 11, 2014; ATF 33F, 84 FR 64744, Nov. 25, 2019]

§ 555.80　Court review.

An applicant, licensee, or permittee may, within 60 days after receipt of the decision of the administrative law judge or the final order of the Director, Industry Operations or the Director, file a petition for a judicial review of the decision, with the U.S. Court of Appeals for the district in which he resides or has his principal place of business. The Director, upon notification that a petition has been filed, shall have prepared a complete transcript of the record of the proceedings. The Director, Industry Operations or the Director, as the case may be, shall certify to the correctness of the transcript of the record, forward one copy to the attorney for the Government in the review of the case, and file the original record of the proceedings with the original certificate in the U.S. Court of Appeals.

[T.D. ATF–87, 46 FR 40384, Aug. 7, 1981, as amended by ATF 2013R–9F, 79 FR 46694, Aug. 11, 2014]

§ 555.81　Service on applicant, licensee, or permittee.

All notices and other formal documents required to be served on an applicant, licensee, or permittee under this subpart will be served by certified mail or by personal delivery. Where service is by personal delivery, the signed duplicate original copy of the formal document will be delivered to the applicant, licensee, or permittee, or, in the case of a corporation, partnership, or association, by delivering it to an officer, manager, or general agent, or to its attorney of record.

§ 555.82　Rules of practice in license and permit proceedings.

Regulations governing the procedure and practice for disapproval of applications for explosives licenses and permits and for the denial of renewal or revocation of such licenses and permits under the Act are contained in part 771 of this chapter.

[ATF 33F, 84 FR 64744, Nov. 25, 2019]

§ 555.83　Operations by licensees or permittees after notice of denial or revocation.

In any case where a notice of revocation has been issued and a request for a stay of the effective date of the revocation has not been granted, the licensee or permittee shall not engage in the activities covered by the license or permit pending the outcome of proceedings under this subpart. In any case where notice of revocation has been issued but a stay of the effective date of the revocation has been granted, the licensee or permittee may continue to engage in the activities covered by his license or permit unless, or until, formally notified to the contrary: *Provided*, That in the event the license or permit would have expired before proceedings under this subpart are completed, timely renewal application must have been filed to continue the license or permit beyond its expiration date. In any case where a notice of denial of a renewal application has been issued, the licensee or permittee may continue to engage in the activities covered by the existing license or permit after the date of expiration of the license or permit until proceedings under this subpart are completed.

Subpart F—Conduct of Business or Operations

§555.101 Posting of license or user permit.

A license or user permit issued under this part, or a copy of a license or user permit, will be posted and available for inspection on the business premises at each place where explosive materials are manufactured, imported, or distributed.

[T.D. ATF–87, 46 FR 40384, Aug. 7, 1981. Redesignated by T.D. ATF–487, 68 FR 3748, Jan. 24, 2003, as amended by ATF No. 1, 68 FR 13786, Mar. 20, 2003]

§555.102 Authorized operations by permittees.

(a) *In general.* A permit issued under this part does not authorize the permittee to engage in the business of manufacturing, importing, or dealing in explosive materials. Accordingly, if a permittee's operations bring him within the definition of manufacturer, importer, or dealer under this part, he shall qualify for the appropriate license.

(b) *Distributions of surplus stocks.* Permittees are not authorized to engage in the business of sale or distribution of explosive materials. However, permit-

tees may dispose of surplus stocks of explosive materials to other licensees or permittees in accordance with §555.103 and §555.105.

[T.D. ATF–400, 63 FR 45002, Aug. 24, 1998, as amended by ATF No. 1, 68 FR 13787, Mar. 20, 2003; ATF 2017R–21, 84 FR 13799, Apr. 8, 2019]

§555.103 Transactions among licensees/permittees and transactions among licensees and holders of user permits.

(a) [Reserved]

(b) *Transactions among licensees/permittees on and after May 24, 2003*—(1) *General.* (i) A licensed importer, licensed manufacturer or licensed dealer selling or otherwise distributing explosive materials (or a holder of a user permit disposing of surplus stock to a licensee; a holder of a user permit; or a holder of a limited permit who is within the same State as the distributor) who has the certified information required by this section may sell or distribute explosive materials to a licensee or permittee for not more than 45 days following the expiration date of the distributee's license or permit, unless the distributor knows or has reason to believe that the distributee's authority to continue business or operations under this part has been terminated.

(ii) A licensed importer, licensed manufacturer or licensed dealer selling or otherwise distributing explosive materials (or a holder of a user permit disposing of surplus stock to another licensee or permittee) must verify the license or permit status of the distributee prior to the release of explosive materials ordered, as required by this section.

(iii) Licensees or permittees desiring to return explosive materials to a licensed manufacturer may do so without obtaining a certified copy of the manufacturer's license.

(2) *Verification of license/user permit.* (i) Prior to or with the first order of explosive materials, the distributee must provide the distributor a certified copy (or, in the case of a user-limited, the original) of the distributee's license or user permit. However, licensees or holders of user permits that are business organizations may (in lieu of a

certified copy of a license or user permit) provide the distributor with a certified list that contains the name, address, license or user permit number, and date of the license or user permit expiration of each location.

(ii) The distributee must also provide the distributor with a current list of the names of persons authorized to accept delivery of explosive materials on behalf of the distributee. The distributee ordering explosive materials must keep the list current and provide updated lists to licensees and holders of user permits on a timely basis. A distributor may not transfer possession of explosive materials to any person whose name does not appear on the current list of names of persons authorized to accept delivery of explosive materials on behalf of the distributee. Except as provided in paragraph (b)(3) of this section, in all instances the distributor must verify the identity of the distributee, or the employee of the distributee accepting possession of explosive materials on behalf of the distributee, by examining an identification document (as defined in § 555.11) before relinquishing possession.

(iii) A licensee or holder of a user permit ordering explosive materials from another licensee or permittee must provide to the distributor a current, certified statement of the intended use of the explosive materials, *e.g.*, resale, mining, quarrying, agriculture, construction, sport rocketry, road building, oil well drilling, seismographic research, etc.

(A) For individuals, the certified statement of intended use must specify the name, address, date and place of birth, and social security number of the distributee.

(B) For business organizations, the certified statement of intended use must specify the taxpayer identification number, the identity and the principal and local places of business.

(C) The licensee or holder of a user permit purchasing explosive materials must revise the furnished copy of the certified statement only when the information is no longer current.

(3) *Delivery of explosive materials by common or contract carrier.* When a common or contract carrier will transport explosive materials from a distributor to a distributee who is a licensee or holder of a user permit, the distributor must take the following actions before relinquishing possession of the explosive materials:

(i) Verify the identity of the person accepting possession for the common or contract carrier by examining such person's valid, unexpired driver's license issued by any State, Canada, or Mexico; and

(ii) Record the name of the common or contract carrier (*i.e.*, the name of the driver's employer) and the full name of the driver. This information must be maintained in the distributor's permanent records in accordance with § 555.121.

(4) *User-limited permit transactions.* A user-limited permit issued under the provisions of this part is valid for only a single purchase transaction and is not renewable (see § 555.51). Accordingly, at the time a user-limited permittee orders explosive materials, the licensed distributor must write on the front of the user-limited permit the transaction date, his signature, and the distributor's license number prior to returning the permit to the user-limited permittee.

(Approved by the Office of Management and Budget under control number 1140–0079)

[ATF No. 1, 68 FR 13787, Mar. 20, 2003, as amended by ATF No. 2, 68 FR 53512, Sept. 11, 2003; ATF 2017R–21, 84 FR 13799, Apr. 8, 2019]

§ 555.104 Certified copy of license or permit.

Except as provided in § 555.49(a), each person issued a license or permit under this part shall be furnished together with his license or permit a copy for his certification. If a person desires an additional copy of his license or permit for certification and for use under § 555.103, he shall:

(a) Make a reproduction of the copy of his license or permit and execute the certification on it;

(b) Make a reproduction of his license or permit, enter on the reproduction the statement: "I certify that this is a true copy of a (*insert the word license or permit*) issued to me to engage in the specified business or operations", and sign his name next to the statement; or

(c) Submit a request, in writing, for certified copies of his license or permit to the Chief, Federal Explosives Licensing Center. The request will show the name, trade name (if any), and address of the licensee or permittee and the number of copies of the license or permit desired. There is a fee of $1 for each copy of a license or permit issued by the Chief, Federal Explosives Licensing Center under this paragraph. Fee payment must accompany each request for additional copies of a license or permit. The fee must be paid by (1) cash, or (2) money order or check made payable to the Bureau of Alcohol, Tobacco, Firearms, and Explosives.

[T.D. ATF–87, 46 FR 40384, Aug. 7, 1981, as amended by T.D. ATF–290, 54 FR 53054, Dec. 27, 1989; ATF 2013R–9F, 79 FR 46694, Aug. 11, 2014]

§ 555.105 Distributions to limited permittees.

(a) [Reserved]

(b) *Distributions to holders of limited permits on and after May 24, 2003.* (1) This section will apply in any case where distribution of explosive materials to the distributee is not otherwise prohibited by the Act or this part.

(2) A licensed importer, licensed manufacturer or a licensed dealer may distribute explosive materials to a holder of a limited permit if such permittee is a resident of the same State in which the licensee's business premises are located, the holder of the limited permit presents in person or by mail ATF Form 5400.4, Limited Permittee Transaction Report (LPTR), and the licensee completes Form 5400.4 in accordance with § 555.126(b). In no event will a licensee distribute explosive materials to a holder of a limited permit unless the holder presents a Form 5400.4 with an original unaltered and unexpired Intrastate Purchase of Explosives Coupon (IPEC), ATF Form 5400.30, affixed. The coupon must bear the name, address, permit number, and the coupon number of the limited permittee seeking distribution of the explosives.

(3) A holder of a limited permit is authorized to receive explosive materials from a licensee or permittee whose premises are located in the same State of residence in which the premises of the holder of the limited permit are located on no more than 6 separate occa-

sions during the one-year period of the permit. For purposes of this section, the term "6 separate occasions" means six deliveries of explosive materials. Each delivery must—

(i) Relate to a single purchase transaction made on one ATF F 5400.4;

(ii) Be referenced on one commercial invoice or purchase order; and

(iii) Be delivered to the holder of the limited permit in one shipment delivered at the same time.

(4) A holder of a user permit may dispose of surplus stocks of explosive materials to a licensee or holder of a user permit, or a holder of a limited permit who is a resident of the same State in which the premises of the holder of the user permit are located. A holder of a limited permit may dispose of surplus stocks of explosive materials to another holder of a limited permit who is a resident of the same State in which the premises of the distributor are located, if the transaction complies with the requirements of paragraph (b)(2) of this section and § 555.126(b). A holder of a limited permit may also dispose of surplus stocks of explosive materials to a licensee or holder of a user permit if the disposition occurs in the State of residence of the holder of the limited permit. (*See* § 555.103.)

(5) Each holder of a limited permit ordering explosive materials must furnish the distributing licensee prior to or with the first order of the explosive materials a current list of the names of employees authorized to accept delivery of explosive materials on behalf of the limited permittee. The distributee ordering explosive materials must keep the list current and provide updated lists to licensees and holders of user permits on a timely basis. A licensed importer, licensed manufacturer, licensed dealer, or permittee, selling or otherwise distributing explosive materials to a holder of a limited permit must, prior to delivering the explosive materials, obtain from the limited permittee a current list of persons who are authorized to accept deliveries of explosive materials on behalf of the limited permittee. A licensee or permittee may not deliver explosive materials to a person whose name does not appear on the list.

(6)(i) *Delivery at the distributor's premises.* Where possession of explosive materials is transferred directly to the distributee at the distributor's premises, the distributor must obtain an executed Form 5400.4 in accordance with § 555.126(b) and must in all instances verify the identity of the person accepting possession on behalf of the distributee by examining an identification document (as defined in § 555.11) before relinquishing possession.

(ii) *Delivery by distributor.* Where possession of explosive materials is transferred by the distributor to the distributee away from the distributor's premises, the distributor must obtain an executed Form 5400.4 in accordance with § 555.126(b) and must in all instances verify the identity of the person accepting possession on behalf of the distributee by examining an identification document (as defined in § 555.11) before relinquishing possession.

(iii) *Delivery by common or contract carrier hired by the distributor.* Where a common or contract carrier hired by the distributor will transport explosive materials from the distributor to a holder of a limited permit:

(A) The limited permittee must, prior to delivery of the explosive materials, complete the appropriate section on Form 5400.4, affix to the Form 5400.4 one of the six IPECs he has been issued, and provide the form to the distributor in person or by mail.

(B) The distributor must, before relinquishing possession of the explosive materials to the common or contract carrier:

(*1*) Verify the identity of the person accepting possession for the common or contract carrier by examining such person's valid, unexpired driver's license issued by any State, Canada, or Mexico; and

(*2*) Record the name of the common or contract carrier (*i.e.,* the name of the driver's employer) and the full name of the driver. This information must be maintained in the distributor's permanent records in accordance with § 555.121.

(C) At the time of delivery of the explosive materials, the common or contract carrier, as agent for the distributor, must verify the identity of the person accepting delivery on behalf of the distributee, note the type and number of the identification document (as defined in § 555.11) and provide this information to the distributor. The distributor must enter this information in the appropriate section on Form 5400.4.

(iv) *Delivery by common or contract carrier hired by the distributee.* Where a common or contract carrier hired by the distributee will transport explosive materials from the distributor to a holder of a limited permit:

(A) The limited permittee must, prior to delivery of the explosive materials, complete the appropriate section on Form 5400.4, affix to the Form 5400.4 one of the six IPECs he has been issued, and provide the form to the distributor in person or by mail.

(B) Before the delivery at the distributor's premises to the common or contract carrier who will transport explosive materials to the holder of a limited permit, the distributor must:

(*1*) Verify the identity of the person accepting possession for the common or contract carrier by examining such person's valid, unexpired driver's license issued by any State, Canada, or Mexico; and

(*2*) Record the name of the common or contract carrier (*i.e.,* the name of the driver's employer) and the full name of the driver. This information must be maintained in the distributor's permanent records in accordance with § 555.121.

(7) A licensee or permittee disposing of surplus stock may sell or distribute commercially manufactured black powder in quantities of 50 pounds or less to a holder of a limited permit, nonlicensee, or nonpermittee if the black powder is intended to be used solely for sporting, recreational, or cultural purposes in antique firearms as defined in 18 U.S.C. 921(a)(16), or in antique devices as exempted from the term "destructive device" in 18 U.S.C. 921(a)(4).

(Approved by the Office of Management and Budget under control number 1140–0075)

[ATF No. 1, 68 FR 13788, Mar. 20, 2003, as amended by ATF No. 2, 68 FR 53513, Sept. 11, 2003; ATF 2017R–21, 84 FR 13799, Apr. 8, 2019]

§555.106 Certain prohibited distributions.

(a) A licensee or permittee may not distribute explosive materials to any person except—

(1) A licensee;

(2) A holder of a user permit; or

(3) A holder of a limited permit who is a resident of the State where distribution is made and in which the premises of the transferor are located.

(b) A licensee shall not distribute any explosive materials to any person:

(1) Who the licensee knows is less than 21 years of age;

(2) In any State where the purchase, possession, or use by a person of explosive materials would be in violation of any State law or any published ordinance applicable at the place of distribution;

(3) Who the licensee has reason to believe intends to transport the explosive materials into a State where the purchase, possession, or use of explosive materials is prohibited or which does not permit its residents to transport or ship explosive materials into the State or to receive explosive materials in the State; or

(4) Who the licensee has reasonable cause to believe intends to use the explosive materials for other than a lawful purpose.

(c) A licensee shall not distribute any explosive materials to any person knowing or having reason to believe that the person:

(1) Is, except as provided under §555.142 (d) and (e), under indictment or information for, or was convicted in any court of, a crime punishable by imprisonment for a term exceeding 1 year;

(2) Is a fugitive from justice;

(3) Is an unlawful user of marijuana, or any depressant or stimulant drug, or narcotic drug (as these terms are defined in the Controlled Substances Act, 21 U.S.C. 802);

(4) Was adjudicated as a mental defective or was committed to a mental institution;

(5) Is an alien, other than an alien who—

(i) Is lawfully admitted for permanent residence (as that term is defined in section 101(a)(20) of the Immigration and Nationality Act (8 U.S.C. 1101));

(ii) Is in lawful nonimmigrant status, is a refugee admitted under section 207 of the Immigration and Nationality Act (8 U.S.C. 1157), or is in asylum status under section 208 of the Immigration and Nationality Act (8 U.S.C. 1158), and—

(A) Is a foreign law enforcement officer of a friendly foreign government, as determined by the Attorney General in consultation with the Secretary of State, entering the United States on official law enforcement business, and the shipping, transporting, possession, or receipt of explosive materials is in furtherance of this official law enforcement business;

(B) Is a person having the power to direct or cause the direction of the management and policies of a corporation, partnership, or association licensed pursuant to section 843(a), and the shipping, transporting, possession, or receipt of explosive materials is in furtherance of such power;

(C) Is a member of a North Atlantic Treaty Organization (NATO) or other friendly foreign military force, as determined by the Attorney General in consultation with the Secretary of Defense, (whether or not admitted in a nonimmigrant status) who is present in the United States under military orders for training or other military purpose authorized by the United States, and the shipping, transporting, possession, or receipt of explosive materials is in furtherance of the military purpose; or

(D) Is lawfully present in the United States in cooperation with the Director of Central Intelligence, and the shipment, transportation, receipt, or possession of the explosive materials is in furtherance of such cooperation;

(6) Has been discharged from the armed forces under dishonorable conditions; or

(7) Having been a citizen of the United States, has renounced citizenship.

(d) The provisions of this section do not apply to the purchase of commercially manufactured black powder in quantities not to exceed 50 pounds, intended to be used solely for sporting, recreational, or cultural purposes in antique firearms or in antique devices, if the requirements of § 555.105(a)(7) or (b)(7) are fully met.

[T.D. ATF–87, 46 FR 40384, Aug. 7, 1981. Redesignated by T.D. ATF–487, 68 FR 3748, Jan. 24, 2003, as amended by ATF No. 1, 68 FR 13790, Mar. 20, 2003]

§ 555.107 Record of transactions.

Each licensee and permittee shall keep records of explosive materials as required by subpart G of this part.

§ 555.108 Importation.

(a) Explosive materials imported or brought into the United States by a licensed importer or holder of a user permit may be released from customs custody to the licensed importer or holder of a user permit upon proof of his status as a licensed importer or holder of a user permit. Proof of status must be made by the licensed importer or holder of a user permit furnishing to the customs officer a certified copy of his license or permit (see § 555.103).

(b) A nonlicensee or nonpermittee may import or bring into the United States commercially manufactured black powder in quantities not to exceed 50 pounds. Upon submitting to the customs officer completed ATF F 5400.3, certifying that the black powder is intended to be used solely for sporting, recreational, or cultural purposes in antique firearms or in antique devices, black powder may be released from customs custody. The disposition of the executed ATF F 5400.3 will be in accordance with the instructions on the form.

(c) The provisions of this section are in addition to, and are not in lieu of, any applicable requirement under 27 CFR Part 447.

(d) For additional requirements relating to the importation of plastic explosives into the United States on or after April 24, 1997, see § 555.183.

(e) For requirements relating to the marking of imported explosive materials, see § 555.109.

[T.D. ATF–87, 46 FR 40384, Aug. 7, 1981, as amended by T.D. ATF–387, 62 FR 8376, Feb. 25, 1997; ATF No. 1, 68 FR 13790, Mar. 20, 2003; ATF 5F, 70 FR 30633, May 27, 2005]

§ 555.109 Identification of explosive materials.

(a) *General.* Explosive materials, whether manufactured in the United States or imported, must contain certain marks of identification.

(b) *Required marks*—(1) *Licensed manufacturers.* Licensed manufacturers who manufacture explosive materials for sale or distribution must place the following marks of identification on explosive materials at the time of manufacture:

(i) The name of the manufacturer; and

(ii) The location, date, and shift of manufacture. Where a manufacturer operates his plant for only one shift during the day, he does not need to show the shift of manufacture.

(2) *Licensed importers.* (i) Licensed importers who import explosive materials for sale or distribution must place the following marks of identification on the explosive materials they import:

(A) The name and address (city and state) of the importer; and

(B) The location (city and country) where the explosive materials were manufactured, date, and shift of manufacture. Where the foreign manufacturer operates his plant for only one shift during the day, he does not need to show the shift of manufacture.

(ii) Licensed importers must place the required marks on all explosive materials imported prior to distribution or shipment for use, and in no event later than 15 days after the date of release from Customs custody.

(c) *General requirements.* (1) The required marks prescribed in this section must be permanent and legible.

(2) The required marks prescribed in this section must be in the English language, using Roman letters and Arabic numerals.

(3) Licensed manufacturers and licensed importers must place the required marks on each cartridge, bag, or other immediate container of explosive materials that they manufacture or import, as well as on any outside container used for the packaging of such explosive materials.

(4) Licensed manufacturers and licensed importers may use any method, or combination of methods, to affix the

required marks to the immediate container of explosive materials, or outside containers used for the packaging thereof, provided the identifying marks are legible, permanent, show all the required information, and are not rendered unreadable by extended periods of storage.

(5) If licensed manufacturers or licensed importers desire to use a coding system and omit printed markings on the container that show all the required information specified in paragraphs (b)(1) and (2) of this section, they must file with ATF a letterhead application displaying the coding that they plan to use and explaining the manner of its application. The Director must approve the application before the proposed coding can be used.

(d) *Exceptions*—(1) *Blasting caps.* Licensed manufacturers or licensed importers are only required to place the identification marks prescribed in this section on the containers used for the packaging of blasting caps.

(2) *Alternate means of identification.* The Director may authorize other means of identifying explosive materials, including fireworks, upon receipt of a letter application from the licensed manufacturer or licensed importer showing that such other identification is reasonable and will not hinder the effective administration of this part.

(Approved by the Office of Management and Budget under control numbers 1140–0055 and 1140–0062)

[ATF 5F, 70 FR 30633, May 27, 2005, as amended by ATF–11F, 73 FR 57242, Oct. 2, 2008]

§555.110 Furnishing of samples (Effective on and after January 24, 2003).

(a) *In general.* Licensed manufacturers and licensed importers and persons who manufacture or import explosive materials or ammonium nitrate must, when required by letter issued by the Director, furnish—

(1) Samples of such explosive materials or ammonium nitrate;

(2) Information on chemical composition of those products; and

(3) Any other information that the Director determines is relevant to the identification of the explosive materials or to identification of the ammonium nitrate.

(b) *Reimbursement.* The Director will reimburse the fair market value of samples furnished pursuant to paragraph (a) of this section, as well as reasonable costs of shipment.

(Approved by the Office of Management and Budget under control number 1140–0073)

[ATF No. 1, 68 FR 13790, Mar. 20, 2003]

Subpart G—Records and Reports

§555.121 General.

(a)(1) Licensees and permittees shall keep records pertaining to explosive materials in permanent form (i.e., commercial invoices, record books) and in the manner required in this subpart.

(2) Licensees and permittees shall keep records required by this part on the business premises for five years from the date a transaction occurs or until discontinuance of business or operations by the licensee or permittee. (See also §555.128 for discontinuance of business or operations.)

(b) ATF officers may enter the premises of any licensee or holder of a user permit for the purpose of examining or inspecting any record or document required by or obtained under this part (see §555.24). Section 843(f) of the Act requires licensees and holders of user permits to make all required records available for examination or inspection at all reasonable times. Section 843(f) of the Act also requires licensees and permittees (including holders of limited permits) to submit all reports and information relating to all required records and their contents, as the regulations in this part prescribe.

(c) Each licensee and permittee shall maintain all records of importation, production, shipment, receipt, sale, or other disposition, whether temporary or permanent, of explosive materials as the regulations in this part prescribe. Sections 842(f) and 842(g) of the Act make it unlawful for any licensee or permittee knowingly to make any false entry in, or fail to make entry in, any record required to be kept under the Act and the regulations in this part.

(Approved by the Office of Management and Budget under control number 1140–0030)

[T.D. ATF–87, 46 FR 40384, Aug. 7, 1981, as amended by T.D. ATF–172, 49 FR 14941, Apr. 16, 1984; ATF No. 1, 68 FR 13790, Mar. 20, 2003; ATF–11F, 73 FR 57242, Oct. 2, 2008]

§ 555.122 Records maintained by licensed importers.

(a) Each licensed importer shall take true and accurate physical inventories which will include all explosive materials on hand required to be accounted for in the records kept under this part. The licensed importer shall take a special inventory

(1) At the time of commencing business, which is the effective date of the license issued upon original qualification under this part;

(2) At the time of changing the location of his business to another region;

(3) At the time of discontinuing business; and

(4) At any time the Director, Industry Operations may in writing require. Each special inventory is to be prepared in duplicate, the original of which is submitted to the Director, Industry Operations, and the duplicate retained by the licensed importer. If a special inventory specified by paragraphs (a) (1) through (4) of this section has not been taken during the calendar year, at least one physical inventory will be taken. However, the record of the yearly inventory, other than a special inventory required by paragraphs (a) (1) through (4) of this section, will remain on file for inspection instead of being sent to the Director, Industry Operations. (See also § 555.127.)

(b) Each licensed importer shall, not later than the close of the next business day following the date of importation or other acquisition of explosive materials, enter the following information in a separate record:

(1) Date of importation or other acquisition.

(2) Name or brand name of manufacturer and country of manufacture.

(3) Manufacturer's marks of identification.

(4) Quantity (applicable quantity units, such as pounds of explosives, number of detonators, number of display fireworks, etc.).

(5) Description (dynamite (dyn), blasting agents (ba), detonators (det), display fireworks (df), etc.) and size (length and diameter or diameter only of display fireworks).

(c) Each licensed importer shall, not later than the close of the next business day following the date of distribution of any explosive materials to another licensee or a permittee, enter in a separate record the following information:

(1) Date of disposition.

(2) Name or brand name of manufacturer and country of manufacture.

(3) Manufacturer's marks of identification.

(4) Quantity (applicable quantity units, such as pounds of explosives, number of detonators, number of display fireworks, etc.).

(5) Description (dynamite (dyn), blasting agents (ba), detonators (det), display fireworks (df), etc.) and size (length and diameter or diameter only of display fireworks).

(6) License or permit number of licensee or permittee to whom the explosive materials are distributed.

(d) The Chief, Explosives Industry Programs Branch may authorize alternate records to be maintained by a licensed importer to record his distribution of explosive materials when it is shown by the licensed importer that alternate records will accurately and readily disclose the information required by paragraph (c) of this section. A licensed importer who proposes to use alternate records shall submit a letter application to the Chief, Explosives Industry Programs Branch and shall describe the proposed alternate records and the need for them. Alternate records are not to be employed by the licensed importer until approval is received from the Chief, Explosives Industry Programs Branch.

(e) Each licensed importer shall maintain separate records of the sales or other distribution made of explosive materials to nonlicensees or non-permittees. These records are maintained as prescribed by §555.126.

(Approved by the Office of Management and Budget under control number 1140–0030)

[T.D. ATF–87, 46 FR 40384, Aug. 7, 1981, as amended by T.D. ATF–172, 49 FR 14941, Apr. 16, 1984; T.D. ATF–293, 55 FR 3721, Feb. 5, 1990; T.D. ATF–400, 63 FR 45003, Aug. 24, 1998; ATF–11F, 73 FR 57242, Oct. 2, 2008; ATF 2013R–9F, 79 FR 46694, Aug. 11, 2014]

§555.123 Records maintained by licensed manufacturers.

(a) Each licensed manufacturer shall take true and accurate physical inventories which will include all explosive materials on hand required to be accounted for in the records kept under this part. The licensed manufacturer shall take a special inventory

(1) At the time of commencing business, which is the effective date of the license issued upon original qualification under this part;

(2) At the time of changing the location of his premises to another region;

(3) At the time of discontinuing business; and

(4) At any other time the Director, Industry Operations may in writing require. Each special inventory is to be prepared in duplicate, the original of which is submitted to the Director, Industry Operations, and the duplicate retained by the licensed manufacturer. If a special inventory required by paragraphs (a)(1) through (4) of this section has not been taken during the calendar year, at least one physical inventory will be taken. However, the record of the yearly inventory, other than a special inventory required by paragraphs (a)(1) through (4) of this section, will remain on file for inspection instead of being sent to the Director, Industry Operations. (See also §555.127.)

(b) Each licensed manufacturer shall not later than the close of the next business day following the date of manufacture or other acquisition of explosive materials, enter the following information in a separate record:

(1) Date of manufacture or other acquisition.

(2) Manufacturer's marks of identification.

(3) Quantity (applicable quantity units, such as pounds of explosives, number of detonators, number of display fireworks, etc.).

(4) Name, brand name or description (dynamite (dyn), blasting agents (ba), detonators (det), display fireworks (df), etc.) and size (length and diameter or diameter only of display fireworks).

(c) Each licensed manufacturer shall, not later than the close of the next business day following the date of distribution of any explosive materials to another licensee or a permittee, enter in a separate record the following information:

(1) Date of disposition.

(2) Name or brand name of manufacturer or name of importer, as applicable, if acquired other than by his own manufacture.

(3) Manufacturer's marks of identification.

(4) Quantity (applicable quantity units, such as pounds of explosives, number of detonators, number of display fireworks, etc.).

(5) Description (dynamite (dyn), blasting agents (ba), detonators (det), display fireworks (df), etc.) and size (length and diameter or diameter only of display fireworks).

(6) License or permit number of licensee or permittee to whom the explosive materials are distributed.

(d) Each licensed manufacturer who manufactures explosive materials for his own use shall, not later than the close of the next business day following the date of use, enter in a separate record the following information:

(1) Date of use.

(2) Quantity (applicable quantity units, such as pounds of explosives, number of detonators, number of special fireworks, etc.).

(3) Description (dynamite (dyn), blasting agents (ba), detonators (det), display fireworks (df), etc.) and size (length and diameter or diameter only of display fireworks).

Exception: A licensed manufacturer is exempt from the recordkeeping requirements of this subsection if the explosive materials are manufactured for his own use and used within a 24 hour period at the same site.

(e) The Chief, Explosives Industry Programs Branch may authorize alternate records to be maintained by a licensed manufacturer to record his distribution or use of explosive materials when it is shown by the licensed manufacturer that alternate records will accurately and readily disclose the information required by paragraph (c) of this section. A licensed manufacturer who proposes to use alternate records shall submit a letter application to the Chief, Explosives Industry Programs Branch and shall describe the proposed alternate records and the need for them. Alternate records are not to be employed by the licensed manufacturer until approval is received from the Chief, Explosives Industry Programs Branch.

(f) Each licensed manufacturer shall maintain separate records of the sales or other distribution made of explosive materials to nonlicensees or nonpermittees. These records are maintained as prescribed by § 555.126.

(Approved by the Office of Management and Budget under control number 1140–0030)

[T.D. ATF–87, 46 FR 40384, Aug. 7, 1981, as amended by T.D. ATF–172, 49 FR 14941, Apr. 16, 1984; T.D. ATF–293, 55 FR 3721, Feb. 5, 1990; T.D. ATF–400, 63 FR 45003, Aug. 24, 1998; ATF–11F, 73 FR 57242, Oct. 2, 2008; ATF 2013R–9F, 79 FR 46694, Aug. 11, 2014]

§ 555.124 Records maintained by licensed dealers.

(a) Each licensed dealer shall take true and accurate physical inventories which will include all explosive materials on hand required to be accounted for in the records kept under this part. The licensed dealer shall take a special inventory

(1) At the time of commencing business, which is the effective date of the license issued upon original qualification under this part;

(2) At the time of changing the location of his premises to another region;

(3) At the time of discontinuing business; and

(4) At any other time the Director, Industry Operations may in writing require. Each special inventory is to be prepared in duplicate, the original of which is submitted to the Director, Industry Operations, and the duplicate retained by the licensed dealer. If a special inventory required by paragraphs (a) (1) through (4) of this section has not been taken during the calendar year, at least one physical inventory will be taken. However, the record of the yearly inventory, other than a special inventory required by paragraphs (a) (1) through (4) of this section, will remain on file for inspection instead of being sent to the Director, Industry Operations. (See also § 555.127.)

(b) Each licensed dealer shall, not later than the close of the next business day following the date of purchase or other acquisition of explosive materials (except as provided in paragraph (d) of this section), enter the following information in a separate record:

(1) Date of acquisition.

(2) Name or brand name of manufacturer and name of importer (if any).

(3) Manufacturer's marks of identification.

(4) Quantity (applicable quantity units, such as pounds of explosives, number of detonators, number of display fireworks, etc.).

(5) Description (dynamite (dyn), blasting agents (ba), detonators (det), display fireworks (df), etc.) and size (length and diameter or diameter only of display fireworks).

(6) Name, address, and license or permit number of the person from whom the explosive materials are received.

(c) Each licensed dealer shall, not later than the close of the next business day following the date of use (if the explosives are used by the dealer) or the date of distribution of any explosive materials to another licensee or a permittee (except as provided in paragraph (d) of this section), enter in a separate record the following information:

(1) Date of disposition.

(2) Name or brand name of manufacturer and name of importer (if any).

(3) Manufacturer's marks of identification.

(4) Quantity (applicable quantity units, such as pounds of explosives, number of detonators, number of display fireworks, etc.).

(5) Description (dynamite (dyn), blasting agents (ba), detonators (det), display fireworks (df), etc.) and size (length and diameter or diameter only of display fireworks).

(6) License or permit number of licensee or permittee to whom the explosive materials are distributed.

(d) When a commercial record is kept by a licensed dealer showing the purchase or other acquisition information required for the permanent record prescribed by paragraph (b) of this section, or showing the distribution information required for the permanent record prescribed by paragraph (c) of this section, the licensed dealer acquiring or distributing the explosive materials may, for a period not exceeding seven days following the date of acquisition of distribution of the explosive materials, delay making the required entry into the permanent record of acquisition or distribution. However, until the required entry of acquisition or disposition is made in the permanent record, the commercial record must be (1) kept by the licensed dealer separate from other commercial documents kept by the licensee, and (2) readily available for inspection on the licensed premises.

(e) The Chief, Explosives Industry Programs Branch may authorize alternate records to be maintained by a licensed dealer to record his acquisition or disposition of explosive materials, when it is shown by the licensed dealer that alternate records will accurately and readily disclose the required information. A licensed dealer who proposes to use alternate records shall submit a letter application to the Chief, Explosives Industry Programs Branch and shall describe the proposed alternate records and the need for them. Alternate records are not to be employed by the licensed dealer until approval is received from the Chief, Explosives Industry Programs Branch.

(f) Each licensed dealer shall maintain separate records of the sales or other distribution made of explosive materials to nonlicensees or nonpermittees. These records are maintained as prescribed by §555.126.

(Approved by the Office of Management and Budget under control number 1140–0030)

[T.D. ATF–87, 46 FR 40384, Aug. 7, 1981, as amended by T.D. ATF–172, 49 FR 14941, Apr. 16, 1984; T.D. ATF–293, 55 FR 3721, Feb. 5, 1990; T.D. ATF–400, 63 FR 45003, Aug. 24, 1998; ATF–11F, 73 FR 57242, Oct. 2, 2008; ATF 2013R–9F, 79 FR 46694, Aug. 11, 2014]

§555.125 Records maintained by permittees.

(a) [Reserved]

(b) *Records maintained by permittees on and after May 24, 2003.* (1) Each holder of a user permit must take true and accurate physical inventories that will include all explosive materials on hand required to be accounted for in the records kept under this part. The permittee must take a special inventory—

(i) At the time of commencing business, which is the effective date of the permit issued upon original qualification under this part;

(ii) At the time of changing the location of his premises;

(iii) At the time of discontinuing business; and

(iv) At any other time the Director, Industry Operations may in writing require. Each special inventory is to be prepared in duplicate, the original of which is submitted to the Director, Industry Operations and the duplicate retained by the permittee. If a special inventory required by paragraphs (b)(1)(i) through (iv) of this section has not been taken during the calendar year, a permittee is required to take at least one physical inventory. The record of the yearly inventory, other than a special inventory required by paragraphs (b)(1)(i) through (iv) of this section, will remain on file for inspection instead of being sent to the Director, Industry Operations. (*See* also §555.127.)

(2) Each holder of a limited permit must take true and accurate physical inventories, at least annually, that will include all explosive materials on hand required to be accounted for in the records kept under this part.

(3) Each holder of a user permit or a limited permit must, not later than the close of the next business day following the date of acquisition of explosive materials, enter the following information in a separate record:

(i) Date of acquisition;

(ii) Name or brand name of manufacturer;

(iii) Manufacturer's marks of identification;

(iv) Quantity (applicable quantity units, such as pounds of explosives, number of detonators, number of display fireworks, etc.);

(v) Description (dynamite (dyn), blasting agents (ba), detonators (det), display fireworks (df), etc., and size (length and diameter or diameter only of display fireworks)); and

(vi) Name, address, and license number of the persons from whom the explosive materials are received.

(4) Each holder of a user permit or a limited permit must, not later than the close of the next business day following the date of disposition of surplus explosive materials to another permittee or a licensee, enter in a separate record the information prescribed in § 555.124(c).

(5) When a record book is used as a permittee's permanent record the permittee may delay entry of the required information for a period not to exceed seven days if the commercial record contains all of the required information prescribed by paragraphs (b)(3) and (b)(4) of this section. However, the commercial record may be used instead of a record book as a permanent record provided that the record contains all of the required information prescribed by paragraphs (b)(3) and (b)(4) of this section.

(6) Each holder of a user permit or a limited permit must maintain separate records of disposition of surplus stocks of explosive materials to holders of a limited permit as prescribed in § 555.126.

(7) The Chief, Explosives Industry Programs Branch may authorize alternate records to be maintained by a holder of a user permit or a limited permit to record his acquisition of explosive materials, when it is shown by the permittee that alternate records will accurately and readily disclose the required information. A permittee who proposes to use alternate records must submit a letter application to the Chief, Explosives Industry Programs Branch and must describe the proposed alternate records and the need for them. Alternate records are not to be employed by the permittee until approval is received from the Chief, Explosives Industry Programs Branch.

(Approved by the Office of Management and Budget under control number 1140–0030)

[ATF No. 1, 68 FR 13790, Mar. 20, 2003, as amended by ATF 2013R–9F, 79 FR 46694, Aug. 11, 2014; ATF 2017R–21, 84 FR 13799, Apr. 8, 2019]

§ 555.126 Limited Permittee Transaction Report for distribution of explosive materials.

(a) [Reserved]

(b) *Limited Permittee Transaction Report for distribution of explosive materials on and after May 24, 2003.* (1) A licensee or permittee may not distribute explosive materials to any person who is not a licensee or permittee. A licensee or permittee may not distribute explosive materials to a limited permittee unless the distributor records the transaction on ATF Form 5400.4, Limited Permittee Transaction Report.

(2) Before distributing explosive materials to a limited permittee, the licensee or permittee must obtain an executed Form 5400.4 from the limited permittee with an original unaltered and unexpired Intrastate Purchase of Explosives Coupon (IPEC) affixed. Except when delivery of explosive materials is made by a common or contract carrier who is an agent of the limited permittee, the licensee, permittee, or an agent of the licensee or permittee, must verify the identity of the holder of the limited permit by examining an identification document (as defined in § 555.11) and noting on the Form 5400.4 the type of document presented. The licensee or permittee must complete the appropriate section on Form 5400.4 to indicate the type and quantity of explosive materials distributed, the license or permit number of the seller, and the date of the transaction. The licensee or permittee must sign and date the form and include any other information required by the instructions on the form and the regulations in this part.

(3) One copy of Form 5400.4 must be retained by the distributor as part of his permanent records in accordance with paragraph (b)(4) of this section and for the period specified in § 555.121. The distributor must mail the other copy of Form 5400.4 to the Bureau of Alcohol, Tobacco, Firearms and Explosives in accordance with the instructions on the form.

(4) Each Form 5400.4 must be retained in chronological order by date of disposition, or in alphabetical order by name of limited permittee. A licensee may not, however, use both methods in a single recordkeeping system. Where

there is a change in proprietorship by a limited permittee, the forms may continue to be filed together after such change.

(5) The requirements of this section are in addition to any other record-keeping requirement contained in this part.

(Approved by the Office of Management and Budget under control number 1140–0078)

[T.D. ATF–87, 46 FR 40384, Aug. 7, 1981, as amended by T.D. ATF–93, 46 FR 50787, Oct. 15, 1981; T.D. ATF–172, 49 FR 14941, Apr. 16, 1984; T.D. ATF–446, 66 FR 16602, Mar. 27, 2001; ATF No. 1, 68 FR 13791, Mar. 20, 2003; ATF 2013R–9F, 79 FR 46694, Aug. 11, 2014; ATF 2017R–21, 84 FR 13800, Apr. 8, 2019]

§ 555.127 Daily summary of magazine transactions.

In taking the inventory required by §§ 555.122, 555.123, 555.124, and 555.125, a licensee or permittee shall enter the inventory in a record of daily summary transactions to be kept at each magazine of an approved storage facility; however, these records may be kept at one central location on the business premises if separate records of daily transactions are kept for each magazine. Not later than the close of the next business day, each licensee and permittee shall record by manufacturer's name or brand name, the total quantity received in and removed from each magazine during the day, and the total remaining on hand at the end of the day. Quantity entries for display fireworks may be expressed as the number and size of individual display fireworks in a finished state or as the number of packaged display segments or packaged displays. Information as to the number and size of display fireworks contained in any one packaged display segment or packaged display shall be provided to any ATF officer on request. Any discrepancy which might indicate a theft or loss of explosive materials is to be reported in accordance with § 555.30.

[T.D. ATF–293, 55 FR 3722, Feb. 5, 1990, as amended by T.D. ATF–400, 63 FR 45003, Aug. 24, 1998]

§ 555.128 Discontinuance of business.

Where an explosive materials business or operations is discontinued and succeeded by a new licensee or new permittee, the records prescribed by this subpart shall appropriately reflect such facts and shall be delivered to the successor. Where discontinuance of the business or operations is absolute, the records required by this subpart must be delivered within 30 days following the business or operations discontinuance to any ATF office located in the region in which the business was located, or to the ATF Out-of-Business Records Center, 244 Needy Road, Martinsburg, West Virginia 25405. Where State law or local ordinance requires the delivery of records to other responsible authority, the Chief, Federal Explosives Licensing Center may arrange for the delivery of the records required by this subpart to such authority. (See also, § 555.61.)

[T.D. ATF–290, 54 FR 53054, Dec. 27, 1989, as amended by T.D. ATF–446a, 66 FR 19089, Apr. 13, 2001; ATF No. 1, 68 FR 13792, Mar. 20, 2003; ATF–11F, 73 FR 57242, Oct. 2, 2008; ATF 2013R–9F, 79 FR 46694, Aug. 11, 2014]

§ 555.129 Exportation.

Exportation of explosive materials is to be in accordance with the applicable provisions of section 38 of the Arms Export Control Act (22 U.S.C. 2778) and implementing regulations. However, a licensed importer, licensed manufacturer, or licensed dealer exporting explosive materials shall maintain records showing the manufacture or acquisition of explosive materials as required by this part and records showing the quantity, the manufacturer's name or brand name of explosive materials, the name and address of the foreign consignee of the explosive materials, and the date the explosive materials were exported. See § 555.180 for regulations concerning the exportation of plastic explosives.

[T.D. ATF–87, 46 FR 40384, Aug. 7, 1981, as amended by T.D. ATF–387, 62 FR 8377, Feb. 25, 1997]

§ 555.130 [Reserved]

Subpart H—Exemptions

§ 555.141 Exemptions.

(a) *General.* Except for the provisions of §§ 555.180 and 555.181, this part does not apply to:

(1) Any aspect of the transportation of explosive materials via railroad, water, highway, or air which is regulated by the U.S. Department of Transportation and its agencies, and which pertains to safety. For example, regulations issued by the Department of Transportation addressing the security risk of aliens transporting explosives by commercial motor or railroad carrier from Canada preclude the enforcement of 18 U.S.C. 842(i)(5) against persons shipping, transporting, receiving, or possessing explosives incident to and in connection with the commercial transportation of explosives by truck or rail from Canada into the United States. Questions concerning this exception should be directed to ATF's Explosives Industry Program Branch in Washington, DC.

(2) The use of explosive materials in medicines and medicinal agents in the forms prescribed by the official United States Pharmacopeia or the National Formulary. "The United States Pharmacopeia and The National Formulary," USP and NF Compendia, are available from the United States Pharmacopeial Convention, Inc., 12601 Twinbrook Parkway, Rockville, Maryland 20852.

(3) The transportation, shipment, receipt, or importation of explosive materials for delivery to any agency of the United States or to any State or its political subdivision.

(4) Small arms ammunition and components of small arms ammunition.

(5) The manufacture under the regulation of the military department of the United States of explosive materials for, or their distribution to or storage or possession by, the military or naval services or other agencies of the United States.

(6) Arsenals, navy yards, depots, or other establishments owned by, or operated by or on behalf of, the United States.

(7) The importation, distribution, and storage of fireworks classified as UN0336, UN0337, UN0431, or UN0432 explosives by the U.S. Department of Transportation at 49 CFR 172.101 and generally known as "consumer fireworks" or "articles pyrotechnic."

(8) Gasoline, fertilizers, propellant actuated devices, or propellant actu-ated industrial tools manufactured, imported, or distributed for their intended purposes.

(9) Industrial and laboratory chemicals which are intended for use as reagents and which are packaged and shipped pursuant to U.S. Department of Transportation regulations, 49 CFR Parts 100 to 177, which do not require explosives hazard warning labels.

(10) Model rocket motors that meet all of the following criteria—

(i) Consist of ammonium perchlorate composite propellant, black powder, or other similar low explosives;

(ii) Contain no more than 62.5 grams of total propellant weight; and

(iii) Are designed as single-use motors or as reload kits capable of reloading no more than 62.5 grams of propellant into a reusable motor casing.

(b) *Black powder.* Except for the provisions applicable to persons required to be licensed under subpart D, this part does not apply with respect to commercially manufactured black powder in quantities not to exceed 50 pounds, percussion caps, safety and pyrotechnic fuses, quills, quick and slow matches, and friction primers, if the black powder is intended to be used solely for sporting, recreational, or cultural purposes in antique firearms, as defined in 18 U.S.C. 921(a)(16) or antique devices, as exempted from the term "destructive devices" in 18 U.S.C. 921(a)(4).

[T.D. ATF-87, 46 FR 40384, Aug. 7, 1981, as amended by T.D. ATF-87, 46 FR 46916, Sept. 23, 1981; T.D. ATF-293, 55 FR 3722, Feb. 5, 1990; T.D. ATF-387, 62 FR 8377, Feb. 25, 1997; T.D. ATF-400, 63 FR 45003, Aug. 24, 1998; ATF No. 1, 68 FR 13792, Mar. 20, 2003; ATF 6F, 71 FR 46101, Aug. 11, 2006; ATF 2013R-9F, 79 FR 46694, Aug. 11, 2014]

§ 555.142 Relief from disabilities.

(a) Any person prohibited from shipping or transporting any explosive in or affecting interstate or foreign commerce or from receiving or possessing any explosive which has been shipped or transported in or affecting interstate or foreign commerce may make application for relief from disabilities under section 845(b) of the Act .

(b) An application for relief from disabilities must be filed with the Director by submitting ATF Form 5400.29,

Application for Restoration of Explosives Privileges, in accordance with the instructions on the form. The application must be supported by appropriate data, including the information specified in paragraph (f) of this section. Upon receipt of an incomplete or improperly executed application for relief, the applicant will be notified of the deficiency in the application. If the application is not corrected and returned within 30 days following the date of notification, the application will be considered abandoned.

(c)(1) The Director may grant relief to an applicant if it is established to the satisfaction of the Director that the circumstances regarding the disability and the applicant's record and reputation are such that the applicant will not be likely to act in a manner dangerous to public safety and that the granting of such relief is not contrary to the public interest.

(2) Except as provided in paragraph (c)(3) of this section, the Director will not grant relief if the applicant—

(i) Has not been discharged from parole or probation for a period of at least 2 years;

(ii) Is a fugitive from justice;

(iii) Is a prohibited alien;

(iv) Is an unlawful user of or addicted to any controlled substance;

(v) Has been adjudicated a mental defective or committed to a mental institution, unless the applicant was subsequently determined by a court, board, commission, or other lawful authority to have been restored to mental competency, to be no longer suffering from a mental disorder, and to have had all rights restored; or

(vi) Is prohibited by the law of the State where the applicant resides from receiving or possessing explosive materials.

(3)(i) The Director may grant relief to aliens who have been lawfully admitted to the United States or to persons who have not been discharged from parole or probation for a period of at least 2 years if he determines that the applicant has a compelling need to possess explosives, such as for purposes of employment.

(ii) The Director may grant relief to the persons identified in paragraph (c)(2) of this section in extraordinary circumstances where the granting of such relief is consistent with the public interest.

(d) A person who has been granted relief under this section is relieved of all disabilities imposed by the Act for the disabilities disclosed in the application. The granting of relief will not affect any disabilities incurred subsequent to the date the application was filed. Relief from disabilities granted to aliens will be effective only so long as the alien retains his or her lawful immigration status.

(e)(1) A licensee or permittee who is under indictment or information for, or convicted of, a crime punishable by imprisonment for a term exceeding one year during the term of a current license or permit, or while he has pending a license or permit renewal application, shall not be barred from licensed or permit operations for 30 days after the date of indictment or information or 30 days after the date upon which his conviction becomes final. Also, if he files his application for relief under this section within such 30 day period, he may further continue licensed or permit operations while his application is pending. A licensee or permittee who does not file an application within 30 days from the date of his indictment or information, or within 30 days from the date his conviction becomes final, shall not continue licensed or permit operations beyond 30 days from the date of his indictment or information or beyond 30 days from the date his conviction becomes final.

(2) In the event the term of a license or permit of a person expires during the 30 day period following the date of indictment of information of during the 30 day period after the date upon which his conviction becomes final or while his application for relief is pending, he shall file a timely application for renewal of his license or permit in order to continue licensed or permit operations. The license or permit application is to show that the applicant has been indicted or under information for, or convicted of, a crime punishable by imprisonment for a term exceeding one year.

(3) A licensee or permittee shall not continue licensed or permit operations beyond 30 days following the date the

Director issues notification that the licensee's or permittee's application for removal of the disabilities resulting from an indictment, information or conviction has been denied.

(4) When a licensee or permittee may no longer continue licensed or permit operations under this section, any application for renewal of license of permit filed by the licensee or permittee while his application for removal of disabilities resulting from an indictment, information or conviction is pending, will be denied by the Director, Industry Operations.

(f)(1) Applications for relief from disabilities must include the following information:

(i) In the case of a corporation, or of any person having the power to direct or control the management of the corporation, information as to the absence of culpability in the offense for which the corporation, or any such person, was indicted, formally accused or convicted;

(ii) In the case of an applicant who is an individual, two properly completed FBI Forms FD–258 (fingerprint card), and a written statement from each of three references who are not related to the applicant by blood or marriage and have known the applicant for at least 3 years, recommending the granting of relief;

(iii) Written consent to examine and obtain copies of records and to receive statements and information regarding the applicant's background, including records, statements and other information concerning employment, medical history, military service, immigration status, and criminal record;

(iv) In the case of an applicant having been convicted of a crime punishable by imprisonment for a term exceeding one year, a copy of the indictment or information on which the applicant was convicted, the judgment of conviction or record of any plea of *nolo contendere* or plea of guilty or finding of guilt by the court;

(v) In the case of an applicant under indictment, a copy of the indictment or information;

(vi) In the case of an applicant who has been adjudicated a mental defective or committed to a mental institution, a copy of the order of a court,

board, commission, or other lawful authority that made the adjudication or ordered the commitment, any petition that sought to have the applicant so adjudicated or committed, any medical records reflecting the reasons for commitment and diagnoses of the applicant, and any court order or finding of a court, board, commission, or other lawful authority showing the applicant's discharge from commitment, restoration of mental competency and the restoration of rights;

(vii) In the case of an applicant who has been discharged from the Armed Forces under dishonorable conditions, a copy of the applicant's Certificate of Release or Discharge from Active Duty (Department of Defense Form 214), Charge Sheet (Department of Defense Form 458), and final court martial order;

(viii) In the case of an applicant who, having been a citizen of the United States, has renounced his or her citizenship, a copy of the formal renunciation of nationality before a diplomatic or consular officer of the United States in a foreign state or before an officer designated by the Attorney General when the United States was in a state of war (*see* 8 U.S.C. 1481(a)(5) and (6)); and

(ix) In the case of an applicant who is an alien, documentation that the applicant is an alien who has been lawfully admitted to the United States; certification from the applicant including the applicant's INS-issued alien number or admission number, country/countries of citizenship, and immigration status, and certifying that the applicant is legally authorized to work in the United States, or other purposes for which possession of explosives is required; certification from an appropriate law enforcement agency of the applicant's country of citizenship stating that the applicant does not have a criminal record; and, if applicable, certification from a Federal explosives licensee or permittee or other employer stating that the applicant is employed by the employer and must possess explosive materials for purposes of employment. These certifications must be submitted in English.

(2) Any record or document of a court or other government entity or official

required by paragraph (f)(1) of this section must be certified by the court or other government entity or official as a true copy.

(Approved by the Office of Management and Budget under control number 1140–0076)

[T.D. ATF–87, 46 FR 40384, Aug. 7, 1981. Redesignated by T.D. ATF–487, 68 FR 3748, Jan. 24, 2003, as amended by ATF No. 1, 68 FR 13792, Mar. 20, 2003; ATF 2013R–9F, 79 FR 46694, Aug. 11, 2014; ATF 2017R–21, 84 FR 13800, Apr. 8, 2019]

Subpart I—Unlawful Acts, Penalties, Seizures and Forfeitures

§555.161 Engaging in business without a license.

Any person engaging in the business of importing, manufacturing, or dealing in explosive materials without a license issued under the Act, shall be fined not more than $10,000 or imprisoned not more than 10 years, or both.

§555.162 False statement or representation.

Any person who knowingly withholds information or makes any false or fictitious oral or written statement or furnishes or exhibits any false, fictitious, or misrepresented identification, intended or likely to deceive for the purpose of obtaining explosive materials, or a license, permit, exemption, or relief from disability under the Act, shall be fined not more than $10,000 or imprisoned not more than 10 years, or both.

§555.163 False entry in record.

Any licensed importer, licensed manufacturer, licensed dealer, or permittee who knowingly makes any false entry in any record required to be kept under subpart G of this part, shall be fined not more than $10,000 or imprisoned not more than 10 years, or both.

[T.D. ATF–87, 46 FR 40384, Aug. 7, 1981, as amended by T.D. ATF–400, 63 FR 45003, Aug. 24, 1998]

§555.164 Unlawful storage.

Any person who stores any explosive material in a manner not in conformity with this part, shall be fined not more than $1,000 or imprisoned not more than one year, or both.

§555.165 Failure to report theft or loss.

(a) Any person who has knowledge of the theft or loss of any explosive materials from his stock and fails to report the theft or loss within 24 hours of discovery in accordance with §555.30, shall be fined not more than $1,000 or imprisoned not more than one year, or both.

(b) Any licensee or permittee who fails to report a theft of explosive materials in accordance with §555.30 will be fined under title 18 U.S.C., imprisoned not more than 5 years, or both.

[T.D. ATF–87, 46 FR 40384, Aug. 7, 1981, as amended by ATF No. 1, 68 FR 13793, Mar. 20, 2003; ATF 2017R–21, 84 FR 13800, Apr. 8, 2019]

§555.166 Seizure or forfeiture.

Any explosive materials involved or used or intended to be used in any violation of the Act or of this part or in any violation of any criminal law of the United States are subject to seizure and forfeiture, and all provisions of title 26, U.S.C. relating to the seizure, forfeiture, and disposition of firearms, as defined in 26 U.S.C. 5845(a), will, so far as applicable, extend to seizures and forfeitures under the Act. (See §72.27 of this title for regulations on summary destruction of explosive materials which are impracticable or unsafe to remove to a place of storage.)

[T.D. ATF–87, 46 FR 40384, Aug. 7, 1981, as amended by T.D. ATF–363, 60 FR 17449, Apr. 6, 1995]

Subpart J—Marking of Plastic Explosives

§555.180 Prohibitions relating to unmarked plastic explosives.

(a) No person shall manufacture any plastic explosive that does not contain a detection agent.

(b) No person shall import or bring into the United States, or export from the United States, any plastic explosive that does not contain a detection agent. This paragraph does not apply to the importation or bringing into the United States, or the exportation from the United States, of any plastic explosive that was imported or brought into, or manufactured in the United States prior to April 24, 1996, by or on behalf of any agency of the United States performing military or police functions (including any military reserve component) or by or on behalf of the National Guard of any State, not later than 15 years after the date of entry into force of the Convention on the Marking of Plastic Explosives with respect to the United States, *i.e.,* not later than June 21, 2013.

(c) No person shall ship, transport, transfer, receive, or possess any plastic explosive that does not contain a detection agent. This paragraph does not apply to:

(1) The shipment, transportation, transfer, receipt, or possession of any plastic explosive that was imported or brought into, or manufactured in the United States prior to April 24, 1996, by any person during the period beginning on that date and ending on April 24, 1999; or

(2) The shipment, transportation, transfer, receipt, or possession of any plastic explosive that was imported or brought into, or manufactured in the United States prior to April 24, 1996, by or on behalf of any agency of the United States performing a military or police function (including any military reserve component) or by or on behalf of the National Guard of any State, not later than 15 years after the date of entry into force of the Convention on the Marking of Plastic Explosives with respect to the United States, *i.e.,* not later than June 21, 2013.

(d) When used in this subpart, terms are defined as follows:

(1) *Convention on the Marking of Plastic Explosives* means the Convention on the Marking of Plastic Explosives for the Purposes of Detection, Done at Montreal on 1 March 1991.

(2) "Date of entry into force" of the Convention on the Marking of Plastic Explosives means that date on which the Convention enters into force with respect to the U.S. in accordance with the provisions of Article XIII of the Convention on the Marking of Plastic Explosives. The Convention entered into force on June 21, 1998.

(3) *Detection agent* means any one of the substances specified in this paragraph when introduced into a plastic explosive or formulated in such explosive as a part of the manufacturing process in such a manner as to achieve homogeneous distribution in the finished explosive, including—

(i) Ethylene glycol dinitrate (EGDN), $C_2H_4(NO_3)_2$, molecular weight 152, when the minimum concentration in the finished explosive is 0.2 percent by mass;

(ii) 2,3-Dimethyl-2,3-dinitrobutane (DMNB), $C_6H_{12}(NO_2)_2$, molecular weight 176, when the minimum concentration in the finished explosive is 0.1 percent by mass;

(iii) Para-Mononitrotoluene (p-MNT), $C_7H_7NO_2$, molecular weight 137, when the minimum concentration in the finished explosive is 0.5 percent by mass;

(iv) Ortho-Mononitrotoluene (o-MNT), $C_7H_7NO_2$, molecular weight 137, when the minimum concentration in the finished explosive is 0.5 percent by mass; and

(v) Any other substance in the concentration specified by the Director, after consultation with the Secretary of State and Secretary of Defense, that has been added to the table in Part 2 of the Technical Annex to the Convention on the Marking of Plastic Explosives.

(4) *Plastic explosive* means an explosive material in flexible or elastic sheet form formulated with one or more high explosives which in their pure form has a vapor pressure less than 10^{-4} Pa at a temperature of 25 °C, is formulated with a binder material, and is as a mixture malleable or flexible at normal room temperature. *High explosives,* as defined in § 555.202(a), are explosive materials which can be caused to detonate by means of a blasting cap when unconfined.

[T.D. ATF–387, 62 FR 8376, Feb. 25, 1997, as amended by T.D. ATF–419, 64 FR 55628, Oct. 14, 1999]

§ 555.181 Reporting of plastic explosives.

All persons, other than an agency of the United States (including any military reserve component) or the National Guard of any State, possessing any plastic explosive on April 24, 1996, shall submit a report to the Director no later than August 22, 1996. The report shall be in writing and mailed by certified mail (return receipt requested) to the Director at P.O. Box 50204, Washington, DC 20091–0204. The report shall include the quantity of plastic explosives possessed on April 24, 1996; any marks of identification on such explosives; the name and address of the manufacturer or importer; the storage location of such explosives, including the city and State; and the name and address of the person possessing the plastic explosives.

[T.D. ATF–382, 61 FR 38085, July 23, 1996, as amended by T.D. ATF–387, 62 FR 8377, Feb. 25, 1997; ATF–11F, 73 FR 57242, Oct. 2, 2008]

§ 555.182 Exceptions.

It is an affirmative defense against any proceeding involving §§ 555.180 and 555.181 if the proponent proves by a preponderance of the evidence that the plastic explosive—

(a) Consisted of a small amount of plastic explosive intended for and utilized solely in lawful—

(1) Research, development, or testing of new or modified explosive materials;

(2) Training in explosives detection or development or testing of explosives detection equipment; or

(3) Forensic science purposes; or

(b) Was plastic explosive that, by April 24, 1999, will be or is incorporated in a military device within the territory of the United States and remains an integral part of such military device, or is intended to be, or is incorporated in, and remains an integral part of a military device that is intended to become, or has become, the property of any agency of the United States performing military or police functions (including any military reserve component) or the National Guard of any State, wherever such device is located. For purposes of this paragraph, the term "military device" includes, but is not restricted to, shells, bombs, projectiles, mines, missiles, rockets, shaped charges, grenades, perforators, and similar devices lawfully manufactured exclusively for military or police purposes.

[T.D. ATF–387, 62 FR 8377, Feb. 25, 1997]

§ 555.183 Importation of plastic explosives on or after April 24, 1997.

Persons filing Form 6 applications for the importation of plastic explosives on or after April 24, 1997, shall attach to the application the following written statement, prepared in trip-

licate, executed under the penalties of perjury:

(a) "I declare under the penalties of perjury that the plastic explosive to be imported contains a detection agent as required by 27 CFR 555.180(b)"; or

(b) "I declare under the penalties of perjury that the plastic explosive to be imported is a "small amount" to be used for research, training, or testing purposes and is exempt from the detection agent requirement pursuant to 27 CFR 555.182."

[T.D. ATF–387, 62 FR 8377, Feb. 25, 1997]

§ 555.184 Statements of process and samples.

(a) A complete and accurate statement of process with regard to any plastic explosive or to any detection agent that is to be introduced into a plastic explosive or formulated in such plastic explosive shall be submitted by a licensed manufacturer or licensed importer, upon request, to the Director.

(b) Samples of any plastic explosive or detection agent shall be submitted by a licensed manufacturer or licensed importer, upon request, to the Director.

(Paragraph (a) approved by the Office of Management and Budget under control number 1140–0042)

[T.D. ATF–387, 62 FR 8378, Feb. 25, 1997, as amended by ATF–11F, 73 FR 57242, Oct. 2, 2008]

§ 555.185 Criminal sanctions.

Any person who violates the provisions of 18 U.S.C. 842(l)–(o) shall be fined under title 18, U.S.C., imprisoned for not more than 10 years, or both.

[T.D. ATF–387, 62 FR 8378, Feb. 25, 1997]

§ 555.186 Seizure or forfeiture.

Any plastic explosive that does not contain a detection agent in violation of 18 U.S.C. 842(l)–(n) is subject to seizure and forfeiture, and all provisions of 19 U.S.C. 1595a, relating to seizure, forfeiture, and disposition of merchandise introduced or attempted to be introduced into the U.S. contrary to law, shall extend to seizures and forfeitures under this subpart. See § 72.27 of this chapter for regulations on summary destruction of plastic explosives that do not contain a detection agent.

[T.D. ATF–387, 62 FR 8378, Feb. 25, 1997]

Subpart K—Storage

§ 555.201 General.

(a) Section 842(j) of the Act and § 555.29 of this part require that the storage of explosive materials by any person must be in accordance with the regulations in this part. Further, section 846 of this Act authorizes regulations to prevent the recurrence of accidental explosions in which explosive materials were involved. The storage standards prescribed by this subpart confer no right or privileges to store explosive materials in a manner contrary to State or local law.

(b) The Director may authorize alternate construction for explosives storage magazines when it is shown that the alternate magazine construction is substantially equivalent to the standards of safety and security contained in this subpart. Any alternate explosive magazine construction approved by the Director prior to August 9, 1982, will continue as approved unless notified in writing by the Director. Any person intending to use alternate magazine construction shall submit a letter application to the Director, Industry Operations for transmittal to the Director, specifically describing the proposed magazine. Explosive materials may not be stored in alternate magazines before the applicant has been notified that the application has been approved.

(c) A licensee or permittee who intends to make changes in his magazines, or who intends to construct or acquire additional magazines, shall comply with § 555.63.

(d) The regulations set forth in §§ 555.221 through 555.224 pertain to the storage of display fireworks, pyrotechnic compositions, and explosive materials used in assembling fireworks and articles pyrotechnic.

(e) [Reserved]

(f) Any person who stores explosive materials shall notify the authority having jurisdiction for fire safety in the locality in which the explosive materials are being stored of the type, magazine capacity, and location of each site where such explosive materials are stored. Such notification shall be made orally before the end of the day on which storage of the explosive materials commenced and in writing within 48 hours from the time such storage commenced.

(Paragraph (f) approved by the Office of Management and Budget under control number 1140–0071)

[T.D. ATF–87, 46 FR 40384, Aug. 7, 1981, as amended by T.D. ATF–293, 55 FR 3722, Feb. 5, 1990; T.D. ATF–400, 63 FR 45003, Aug. 24, 1998; ATF–11F, 73 FR 57242, Oct. 2, 2008; ATF 2013R–9F, 79 FR 46694, Aug. 11, 2014; ATF 2017R–21, 84 FR 13800, Apr. 8, 2019]

§ 555.202 Classes of explosive materials.

For purposes of this part, there are three classes of explosive materials. These classes, together with the description of explosive materials comprising each class, are as follows:

(a) *High explosives.* Explosive materials which can be caused to detonate by means of a blasting cap when unconfined, (for example, dynamite, flash powders, and bulk salutes).

(b) *Low explosives.* Explosive materials which can be caused to deflagrate when confined (for example, black powder, safety fuses, igniters, igniter cords, fuse lighters, and "display fireworks" classified as UN0333, UN0334, or UN0335 by the U.S. Department of Transportation regulations at 49 CFR 172.101, except for bulk salutes).

(c) *Blasting agents.* (For example, ammonium nitrate-fuel oil and certain water-gels (see also § 555.11).

[T.D. ATF–87, 46 FR 40384, Aug. 7, 1981, as amended by T.D. ATF–293, 55 FR 3722, Feb. 5, 1990; T.D. ATF–400, 63 FR 45003, Aug. 24, 1998; ATF 2017R–21, 84 FR 13800, Apr. 8, 2019]

§ 555.203 Types of magazines.

For purposes of this part, there are five types of magazines. These types, together with the classes of explosive materials, as defined in § 555.202, which will be stored in them, are as follows:

(a) *Type 1 magazines.* Permanent magazines for the storage of high explosives, subject to the limitations prescribed by §§ 555.206 and 555.213. Other classes of explosive materials may also be stored in type 1 magazines.

(b) *Type 2 magazines.* Mobile and portable indoor and outdoor magazines for the storage of high explosives, subject to the limitations prescribed by §§ 555.206, 555.208(b), and 555.213. Other classes of explosive materials may also be stored in type 2 magazines.

(c) *Type 3 magazines.* Portable outdoor magazines for the temporary storage of high explosives while attended (for example, a "day-box"), subject to the limitations prescribed by §§ 555.206 and 555.213. Other classes of explosives materials may also be stored in type 3 magazines.

(d) *Type 4 magazines.* Magazines for the storage of low explosives, subject to the limitations prescribed by §§ 555.206(b), 555.210(b), and 555.213. Blasting agents may be stored in type 4 magazines, subject to the limitations prescribed by §§ 555.206(c), 555.211(b), and 555.213. Detonators that will not mass detonate may also be stored in type 4 magazines, subject to the limitations prescribed by §§ 555.206(a), 555.210(b), and 555.213.

(e) *Type 5 magazines.* Magazines for the storage of blasting agents, subject to the limitations prescribed by §§ 555.206(c), 555.211(b), and 555.213.

§ 555.204 Inspection of magazines.

Any person storing explosive materials shall inspect his magazines at least every seven days. This inspection need not be an inventory, but must be sufficient to determine whether there has been unauthorized entry or attempted entry into the magazines, or unauthorized removal of the contents of the magazines.

§ 555.205 Movement of explosive materials.

All explosive materials must be kept in locked magazines meeting the standards in this subpart unless they are:

(a) In the process of manufacture;

(b) Being physically handled in the operating process of a licensee or user;

(c) Being used; or

(d) Being transported to a place of storage or use by a licensee or permittee or by a person who has lawfully acquired explosive materials under § 555.106.

§ 555.206 Location of magazines.

(a) Outdoor magazines in which high explosives are stored must be located no closer to inhabited buildings, passenger railways, public highways, or other magazines in which high explosives are stored, than the minimum distances specified in the table of distances for storage of explosive materials in § 555.218.

(b) Outdoor magazines in which low explosives are stored must be located no closer to inhabited buildings, passenger railways, public highways, or other magazines in which explosive materials are stored, than the minimum distances specified in the table of distances for storage of low explosives in § 555.219, except that the table of distances in § 555.224 shall apply to the storage of display fireworks. The distances shown in § 555.219 may not be reduced by the presence of barricades.

(c)(1) Outdoor magazines in which blasting agents in quantities of more than 50 pounds are stored must be located no closer to inhabited buildings, passenger railways, or public highways than the minimum distances specified in the table of distances for storage of explosive materials in § 555.218.

(2) Ammonium nitrate and magazines in which blasting agents are stored must be located no closer to magazines in which high explosives or other blasting agents are stored than the minimum distances specified in the table of distances for the separation of ammonium nitrate and blasting agents in § 555.220. However, the minimum distances for magazines in which explosives and blasting agents are stored from inhabited buildings, etc., may not be less than the distances specified in the table of distances for storage of explosives materials in § 555.218.

[T.D. ATF–87, 46 FR 40384, Aug. 7, 1981, as amended by T.D. ATF–293, 55 FR 3722, Feb. 5, 1990; T.D. ATF–400, 63 FR 45003, Aug. 24, 1998]

§ 555.207 Construction of type 1 magazines.

A type 1 magazine is a permanent structure: a building, an igloo or "Army-type structure", a tunnel, or a dugout. It is to be bullet-resistant, fire-resistant, weather-resistant, theft-resistant, and ventilated.

(a) *Buildings.* All building type magazines are to be constructed of masonry, wood, metal, or a combination of these materials, and have no openings except for entrances and ventilation. The ground around building magazines must slope away for drainage or other adequate drainage provided.

(1) *Masonry wall construction.* Masonry wall construction is to consist of brick, concrete, tile, cement block, or cinder block and be not less than 6 inches in thickness. Hollow masonry units used in construction must have all hollow spaces filled with well-tamped, coarse, dry sand or weak concrete (at least a mixture of one part cement and eight parts of sand with enough water to dampen the mixture while tamping in place). Interior walls are to be constructed of, or covered with, a nonsparking material.

(2) *Fabricated metal wall construction.* Metal wall construction is to consist of sectional sheets of steel or aluminum not less than number 14-gauge, securely fastened to a metal framework. Metal wall construction is either lined inside with brick, solid cement blocks, hardwood not less than four inches thick, or will have at least a six inch sand fill between interior and exterior walls. Interior walls are to be constructed of, or covered with, a nonsparking material.

(3) *Wood frame wall construction.* The exterior of outer wood walls is to be covered with iron or aluminum not less than number 26-gauge. An inner wall of, or covered with nonsparking material will be constructed so as to provide a space of not less than six inches between the outer and inner walls. The space is to be filled with coarse, dry sand or weak concrete.

(4) *Floors.* Floors are to be constructed of, or covered with, a nonsparking material and shall be strong enough to bear the weight of the maximum quantity to be stored. Use of pallets covered with a nonsparking material is considered equivalent to a floor constructed of or covered with a nonsparking material.

(5) *Foundations.* Foundations are to be constructed of brick, concrete, cement block, stone, or wood posts. If piers or posts are used, in lieu of a continuous foundation, the space under the buildings is to be enclosed with metal.

(6) *Roof.* Except for buildings with fabricated metal roofs, the outer roof is to be covered with no less than number 26-guage iron or aluminum, fastened to at least 7⁄8 inch sheathing.

(7) *Bullet-resistant ceilings or roofs.* Where it is possible for a bullet to be fired directly through the roof and into the magazine at such an angle that the bullet would strike the explosives within, the magazine is to be protected by one of the following methods:

(i) A sand tray lined with a layer of building paper, plastic, or other nonporous material, and filled with not less than four inches of coarse, dry sand, and located at the tops of inner walls covering the entire ceiling area, except that portion necessary for ventilation.

(ii) A fabricated metal roof constructed of 3⁄16-inch plate steel lined with four inches of hardwood. (For each additional 1⁄16 inch of plate steel, the hardwood lining may be decreased one inch.)

(8) *Doors.* All doors are to be constructed of not less than 1⁄4 inch plate steel and lined with at least two inches of hardwood. Hinges and hasps are to be attached to the doors by welding, riveting or bolting (nuts on inside of door). They are to be installed in such a manner that the hinges and hasps cannot be removed when the doors are closed and locked.

(9) *Locks.* Each door is to be equipped with (i) two mortise locks; (ii) two padlock fastened in separate hasps and staples; (iii) a combination of a mortise lock and a padlock; (iv) a mortise lock that requires two keys to open; or (v) a three-point lock. Padlocks must have at least five tumblers and a case-hardened shackle of at least 3⁄8 inch diameter. Padlocks must be protected with not less than 1⁄4 inch steel hoods constructed so as to prevent sawing or lever action on the locks, hasps, and staples. These requirements do not apply to magazine doors that are adequately secured on the inside by means of a bolt, lock, or bar that cannot be actuated from the outside.

(10) *Ventilation.* Ventilation is to be provided to prevent dampness and heating of stored explosive materials.

Ventilation openings must be screened to prevent the entrance of sparks. Ventilation openings in side walls and foundations must be offset or shielded for bullet-resistant purposes. Magazines having foundation and roof ventilators with the air circulating between the side walls and the floors and between the side walls and the ceiling must have a wooden lattice lining or equivalent to prevent the packages of explosive materials from being stacked against the side walls and blocking the air circulation.

(11) *Exposed metal.* No sparking material is to be exposed to contact with the stored explosive materials. All ferrous metal nails in the floor and side walls, which might be exposed to contact with explosive materials, must be blind nailed, countersunk, or covered with a nonsparking lattice work or other nonsparking material.

(b) *Igloos, "Army-type structures", tunnels, and dugouts.* Igloo, "Army-type structure", tunnel, and dugout magazines are to be constructed of reinforced concrete, masonry, metal, or a combination of these materials. They must have an earthmound covering of not less than 24 inches on the top, sides and rear unless the magazine meets the requirements of paragraph (a)(7) of this section. Interior walls and floors must be constructed of, or covered with, a nonsparking material. Magazines of this type are also to be constructed in conformity with the requirements of paragraph (a)(4) and paragraphs (a)(8) through (11) of this section.

§555.208 Construction of type 2 magazines.

A type 2 magazine is a box, trailer, semitrailer, or other mobile facility.

(a) *Outdoor magazines—(1) General.* Outdoor magazines are to be bullet-resistant, fire-resistant, weather-resistant, theft-resistant, and ventilated. They are to be supported to prevent direct contact with the ground and, if less than one cubic yard in size, must be securely fastened to a fixed object. The ground around outdoor magazines must slope away for drainage or other adequate drainage provided. When unattended, vehicular magazines must have wheels removed or otherwise effectively immobilized by kingpin locking devices or other methods approved by the Director.

(2) *Exterior construction.* The exterior and doors are to be constructed of not less than ¼-inch steel and lined with at least two inches of hardwood. Magazines with top openings will have lids with water-resistant seals or which overlap the sides by at least one inch when in a closed position.

(3) *Hinges and hasps.* Hinges and hasps are to be attached to doors by welding, riveting, or bolting (nuts on inside of door). Hinges and hasps must be installed so that they cannot be removed when the doors are closed and locked.

(4) *Locks.* Each door is to be equipped with (i) two mortise locks; (ii) two padlocks fastened in separate hasps and staples; (iii) a combination of a mortise lock and a padlock; (iv) a mortise lock that requires two keys to open; or (v) a three-point lock. Padlocks must have at least five tumblers and a case-hardened shackle of at least ⅜-inch diameter. Padlocks must be protected with not less than ¼-inch steel hoods constructed so as to prevent sawing or lever action on the locks, hasps, and staples. These requirements do not apply to magazine doors that are adequately secured on the inside by means of a bolt, lock, or bar that cannot be actuated from the outside.

(b) *Indoor magazines—(1) General.* Indoor magazines are to be fire-resistant and theft-resistant. They need not be bullet-resistant and weather-resistant if the buildings in which they are stored provide protection from the weather and from bullet penetration. No indoor magazine is to be located in a residence or dwelling. The indoor storage of high explosives must not exceed a quantity of 50 pounds. More than one indoor magazine may be located in the same building if the total quantity of explosive materials stored does not exceed 50 pounds. Detonators must be stored in a separate magazine (except as provided in §555.213) and the total quantity of detonators must not exceed 5,000.

(2) *Exterior construction.* Indoor magazines are to be constructed of wood or metal according to one of the following specifications:

183

(i) Wood indoor magazines are to have sides, bottoms and doors constructed of at least two inches of hardwood and are to be well braced at the corners. They are to be covered with sheet metal of not less than number 26-gauge (.0179 inches). Nails exposed to the interior of magazines must be countersunk.

(ii) Metal indoor magazines are to have sides, bottoms and doors constructed of not less than number 12-gauge (.1046 inches) metal and be lined inside with a nonsparking material. Edges of metal covers must overlap sides at least one inch.

(3) *Hinges and hasps.* Hinges and hasps are to be attached to doors by welding, riveting, or bolting (nuts on inside of door). Hinges and hasps must be installed so that they cannot be removed when the doors are closed and locked.

(4) *Locks.* Each door is to be equipped with (i) two mortise locks; (ii) two padlocks fastened in separate hasps and staples; (iii) a combination of a mortise lock and a padlock; (iv) a mortise lock that requires two keys to open; or (v) a three-point lock. Padlocks must have at least five tumblers and a case-hardened shackle of at least ⅜-inch diameter. Padlocks must be protected with not less than ¼-inch steel hoods constructed so as to prevent sawing or lever action on the locks, hasps, and staples. Indoor magazines located in secure rooms that are locked as provided in this subparagraph may have each door locked with one steel padlock (which need not be protected by a steel hood) having at least five tumblers and a case-hardened shackle of at least ⅜-inch diameter, if the door hinges and lock hasp are securely fastened to the magazine. These requirements do not apply to magazine doors that are adequately secured on the inside by means of a bolt, lock, or bar that cannot be actuated from the outside.

(c) *Detonator boxes.* Magazines for detonators in quantities of 100 or less are to have sides, bottoms and doors constructed of not less than number 12-gauge (.1046 inches) metal and lined with a nonsparking material. Hinges and hasps must be attached so they cannot be removed from the outside. One steel padlock (which need not be protected by a steel hood) having at

least five tumblers and a case-hardened shackle of at least ⅜-inch diameter is sufficient for locking purposes.

§ 555.209 Construction of type 3 magazines.

A type 3 magazine is a "day-box" or other portable magazine. It must be fire-resistant, weather-resistant, and theft-resistant. A type 3 magazine is to be constructed of not less than number 12-gauge (.1046 inches) steel, lined with at least either ½-inch plywood or ½-inch Masonite-type hardboard. Doors must overlap sides by at least one inch. Hinges and hasps are to be attached by welding, riveting or bolting (nuts on inside). One steel padlock (which need not be protected by a steel hood) having at least five tumblers and a case-hardened shackle of at least ⅜-inch diameter is sufficient for locking purposes. Explosive materials are not to be left unattended in type 3 magazines and must be removed to type 1 or 2 magazines for unattended storage.

§ 555.210 Construction of type 4 magazines.

A type 4 magazine is a building, igloo or "Army-type structure", tunnel, dugout, box, trailer, or a semitrailer or other mobile magazine.

(a) *Outdoor magazines—*(1) *General.* Outdoor magazines are to be fire-resistant, weather-resistant, and theft-resistant. The ground around outdoor magazines must slope away for drainage or other adequate drainage be provided. When unattended, vehicular magazines must have wheels removed or otherwise be effectively immobilized by kingpin locking devices or other methods approved by the Director.

(2) *Construction.* Outdoor magazines are to be constructed of masonry, metal-covered wood, fabricated metal, or a combination of these materials. Foundations are to be constructed of brick, concrete, cement block, stone, or metal or wood posts. If piers or posts are used, in lieu of a continuous foundation, the space under the building is to be enclosed with fire-resistant material. The walls and floors are to be constructed of, or covered with, a nonsparking material or lattice work. The doors must be metal or solid wood covered with metal.

(3) *Hinges and hasps.* Hinges and hasps are to be attached to doors by welding, riveting, or bolting (nuts on inside of door). Hinges and hasps must be installed so that they cannot be removed when the doors are closed and locked.

(4) *Locks.* Each door is to be equipped with (i) two mortise locks; (ii) two padlocks fastened in separate hasps and staples; (iii) a combination of a mortise lock and a padlock; (iv) a mortise lock that requires two keys to open; or (v) a three-point lock. Padlocks must have at least five tumblers and case-hardened shackle of at least ⅜ inch diameter. Padlocks must be protected with not less than ¼ inch steel hoods constructed so as to prevent sawing or lever action on the locks, hasps, and staples. These requirements do not apply to magazine doors that are adequately secured on the inside by means of a bolt, lock, or bar that cannot be actuated from the outside.

(b) *Indoor magazine—(1) General.* Indoor magazines are to be fire-resistant and theft-resistant. They need not be weather-resistant if the buildings in which they are stored provide protection from the weather. No indoor magazine is to be located in a residence or dwelling. The indoor storage of low explosives must not exceed a quantity of 50 pounds. More than one indoor magazine may be located in the same building if the total quantity of explosive materials stored does not exceed 50 pounds. Detonators that will not mass detonate must be stored in a separate magazine and the total number of electric detonators must not exceed 5,000.

(2) *Construction.* Indoor magazines are to be constructed of masonry, metal-covered wood, fabricated metal, or a combination of these materials. The walls and floors are to be constructed of, or covered with, a nonsparking material. The doors must be metal or solid wood covered with metal.

(3) *Hinges and hasps.* Hinges and hasps are to be attached to doors by welding, riveting, or bolting (nuts on inside of door). Hinges and hasps must be installed so that they cannot be removed when the doors are closed and locked.

(4) *Locks.* Each door is to be equipped with (i) two mortise locks; (ii) two padlocks fastened in separate hasps and staples; (iii) a combination of a mortise

lock and padlock; (iv) a mortise lock that requires two keys to open; or (v) a three-point lock. Padlocks must have at least five tumblers and a case-hardened shackle of at least ⅜ inch diameter. Padlocks must be protected with not less than ¼ inch steel hoods constructed so as to prevent sawing or lever action on the locks, hasps, and staples. Indoor magazines located in secure rooms that are locked as provided in this subparagraph may have each door locked with one steel padlock (which need not be protected by a steel hood) having at least five tumblers and a case-hardened shackle of at least ⅜ inch diameter, if the door hinges and lock hasp are securely fastened to the magazine. These requirements do not apply to magazine doors that are adequately secured on the inside by means of a bolt, lock, or bar that cannot be actuated from the outside.

§555.211 Construction of type 5 magazines.

A type 5 magazine is a building, igloo or "Army-type structure", tunnel, dugout, bin, box, trailer, or a semitrailer or other mobile facility.

(a) *Outdoor magazines—(1) General.* Outdoor magazines are to be weather-resistant and theft-resistant. The ground around magazines must slope away for drainage or other adequate drainage be provided. When unattended, vehicular magazines must have wheels removed or otherwise be effectively immobilized by kingpin locking devices or other methods approved by the Director.

(2) *Construction.* The doors are to be constructed of solid wood or metal.

(3) *Hinges and hasps.* Hinges and hasps are to be attached to doors by welding, riveting, or bolting (nuts on inside of door). Hinges and hasps must be installed so that they cannot be removed when the doors are closed and locked.

(4) *Locks.* Each door is to be equipped with (i) two mortise locks; (ii) two padlocks fastened in separate hasps and staples; (iii) a combination of a mortise lock and a padlock; (iv) a mortise lock that requires two keys to open; or (v) a three-point lock. Padlocks must have at least five tumblers and a case-hardened shackle of at least ⅜ inch diameter. Padlocks must be protected with

not less than ¼ inch steel hoods constructed so as to prevent sawing or lever action on the locks, hasps, and staples. Trailers, semitrailers, and similar vehicular magazines may, for each door, be locked with one steel padlock (which need not be protected by a steel hood) having at least five tumblers and a case-hardened shackle of at least ⅜ inch diameter, if the door hinges and lock hasp are securely fastened to the magazine and to the door frame. These requirements do not apply to magazine doors that are adequately secured on the inside by means of a bolt, lock, or bar that cannot be actuated from the outside.

(5) *Placards.* The placards required by Department of Transportation regulations at 49 CFR part 172, subpart F, for the transportation of blasting agents shall be displayed on all magazines.

(b) *Indoor magazines*—(1) *General.* Indoor magazines are to be theft-resistant. They need not be weather-resistant if the buildings in which they are stored provide protection from the weather. No indoor magazine is to be located in a residence or dwelling. Indoor magazines containing quantities of blasting agents in excess of 50 pounds are subject to the requirements of § 555.206 of this subpart.

(2) *Construction.* The doors are to be constructed of wood or metal.

(3) *Hinges and hasps.* Hinges and hasps are to be attached to doors by welding, riveting, or bolting (nuts on inside). Hinges and hasps must be installed so that they cannot be removed when the doors are closed and locked.

(4) *Locks.* Each door is to be equipped with (i) two mortise locks; (ii) two padlocks fastened in separate hasps and staples; (iii) a combination of a mortise lock and a padlock; (iv) a mortise lock that requires two keys to open; or (v) a three-point lock. Padlocks must have at least five tumblers and a case-hardened shackle of at least ⅜ inch diameter. Padlocks must be protected with not less than ¼ inch steel hoods constructed so as to prevent sawing or lever action on the locks, hasps, and staples. Indoor magazines located in secure rooms that are locked as provided in this subparagraph may have each door locked with one steel padlock (which need not be protected by a steel

hood) having at least five tumblers and a case-hardened shackle of at least ⅜ inch diameter, if the door hinges and lock hasps are securely fastened to the magazine and to the door frame. These requirements do not apply to magazine doors that are adequately secured on the inside by means of a bolt, lock, or bar that cannot be actuated from the outside.

[T.D. ATF–87, 46 FR 40384, Aug. 7, 1981, as amended by T.D. ATF–298, 55 FR 21863, May 30, 1990]

§ 555.212   Smoking and open flames.

Smoking, matches, open flames, and spark producing devices are not permitted:

(a) In any magazine;

(b) Within 50 feet of any outdoor magazine; or

(c) Within any room containing an indoor magazine.

§ 555.213   Quantity and storage restrictions.

(a) Explosive materials in excess of 300,000 pounds or detonators in excess of 20 million are not to be stored in one magazine unless approved by the Director.

(b) Detonators are not to be stored in the same magazine with other explosive materials, except under the following circumstances:

(1) In a type 4 magazine, detonators that will not mass detonate may be stored with electric squibs, safety fuse, shock tube, igniters, and igniter cord.

(2) In a type 1 or type 2 magazine, detonators may be stored with delay devices and any of the items listed in paragraph (b)(1) of this section.

[T.D. ATF–487, 68 FR 3748, Jan. 24, 2003, as amended by ATF 15F, 75 FR 3163, Jan. 20, 2010]

§ 555.214   Storage within types 1, 2, 3, and 4 magazines.

(a) Explosive materials within a magazine are not to be placed directly against interior walls and must be stored so as not to interfere with ventilation. To prevent contact of stored explosive materials with walls, a non-sparking lattice work or other nonsparking material may be used.

(b) Containers of explosive materials are to be stored so that marks are visible. Stocks of explosive materials are to be stored so they can be easily counted and checked upon inspection.

(c) Except with respect to fiberboard or other nonmetal containers, containers of explosive materials are not to be unpacked or repacked inside a magazine or within 50 feet of a magazine, and must not be unpacked or repacked close to other explosive materials. Containers of explosive materials must be closed while being stored.

(d) Tools used for opening or closing containers of explosive materials are to be of nonsparking materials, except that metal slitters may be used for opening fiberboard containers. A wood wedge and a fiber, rubber, or wooden mallet are to be used for opening or closing wood containers of explosive materials. Metal tools other than nonsparking transfer conveyors are not to be stored in any magazine containing high explosives.

§555.215   Housekeeping.

Magazines are to be kept clean, dry, and free of grit, paper, empty packages and containers, and rubbish. Floors are to be regularly swept. Brooms and other utensils used in the cleaning and maintenance of magazines must have no spark-producing metal parts, and may be kept in magazines. Floors stained by leakage from explosive materials are to be cleaned according to instructions of the explosives manufacturer. When any explosive material has deteriorated it is to be destroyed in accordance with the advice or instructions of the manufacturer. The area surrounding magazines is to be kept clear of rubbish, brush, dry grass, or trees (except live trees more than 10 feet tall), for not less than 25 feet in all

directions. Volatile materials are to be kept a distance of not less than 50 feet from outdoor magazines. Living foliage which is used to stabilize the earthen covering of a magazine need not be removed.

§555.216   Repair of magazines.

Before repairing the interior of magazines, all explosive materials are to be removed and the interior cleaned. Before repairing the exterior of magazines, all explosive materials must be removed if there exists any possibility that repairs may produce sparks or flame. Explosive materials removed from magazines under repair must be (a) placed in other magazines appropriate for the storage of those explosive materials under this subpart, or (b) placed a safe distance from the magazines under repair where they are to be properly guarded and protected until the repairs have been completed.

§555.217   Lighting.

(a) Battery-activated safety lights or battery-activated safety lanterns may be used in explosives storage magazines.

(b) Electric lighting used in any explosives storage magazine must meet the standards prescribed by the "National Electrical Code," (National Fire Protection Association, NFPA 70–81), for the conditions present in the magazine at any time. All electrical switches are to be located outside of the magazine and also meet the standards prescribed by the National Electrical Code.

(c) Copies of invoices, work orders or similar documents which indicate the lighting complies with the National Electrical Code must be available for inspection by ATF officers.

§555.218   Table of distances for storage of explosive materials.

Quantity of explosives		Distances in feet							
		Inhabited buildings		Public highways with traffic volume of 3000 or fewer vehicles/day		Passenger railways—public highways with traffic volume of more than 3,000 vehicles/day		Separation of magazines	
Pounds over	Pounds not over	Barricaded	Unbarricaded	Barricaded	Unbarricaded	Barricaded	Unbarricaded	Barricaded	Unbarricaded
0	5	70	140	30	60	51	102	6	12
5	10	90	180	35	70	64	128	8	16

Quantity of explosives		Distances in feet							
Pounds over	Pounds not over	Inhabited buildings		Public highways with traffic volume of 3000 or fewer vehicles/day		Passenger railways—public highways with traffic volume of more than 3,000 vehicles/day		Separation of magazines	
		Barricaded	Unbarricaded	Barricaded	Unbarricaded	Barricaded	Unbarricaded	Barricaded	Unbarricaded
10	20	110	220	45	90	81	162	10	20
20	30	125	250	50	100	93	186	11	22
30	40	140	280	55	110	103	206	12	24
40	50	150	300	60	120	110	220	14	28
50	75	170	340	70	140	127	254	15	30
75	100	190	380	75	150	139	278	16	32
100	125	200	400	80	160	150	300	18	36
125	150	215	430	85	170	159	318	19	38
150	200	235	470	95	190	175	350	21	42
200	250	255	510	105	210	189	378	23	46
250	300	270	540	110	220	201	402	24	48
300	400	295	590	120	240	221	442	27	54
400	500	320	640	130	260	238	476	29	58
500	600	340	680	135	270	253	506	31	62
600	700	355	710	145	290	266	532	32	64
700	800	375	750	150	300	278	556	33	66
800	900	390	780	155	310	289	578	35	70
900	1,000	400	800	160	320	300	600	36	72
1,000	1,200	425	850	165	330	318	636	39	78
1,200	1,400	450	900	170	340	336	672	41	82
1,400	1,600	470	940	175	350	351	702	43	86
1,600	1,800	490	980	180	360	366	732	44	88
1,800	2,000	505	1,010	185	370	378	756	45	90
2,000	2,500	545	1,090	190	380	408	816	49	98
2,500	3,000	580	1,160	195	390	432	864	52	104
3,000	4,000	635	1,270	210	420	474	948	58	116
4,000	5,000	685	1,370	225	450	513	1,026	61	122
5,000	6,000	730	1,460	235	470	546	1,092	65	130
6,000	7,000	770	1,540	245	490	573	1,146	68	136
7,000	8,000	800	1,600	250	500	600	1,200	72	144
8,000	9,000	835	1,670	255	510	624	1,248	75	150
9,000	10,000	865	1,730	260	520	645	1,290	78	156
10,000	12,000	875	1,750	270	540	687	1,374	82	164
12,000	14,000	885	1,770	275	550	723	1,446	87	174
14,000	16,000	900	1,800	280	560	756	1,512	90	180
16,000	18,000	940	1,880	285	570	786	1,572	94	188
18,000	20,000	975	1,950	290	580	813	1,626	98	196
20,000	25,000	1,055	2,000	315	630	876	1,752	105	210
25,000	30,000	1,130	2,000	340	680	933	1,866	112	224
30,000	35,000	1,205	2,000	360	720	981	1,962	119	238
35,000	40,000	1,275	2,000	380	760	1,026	2,000	124	248
40,000	45,000	1,340	2,000	400	800	1,068	2,000	129	258
45,000	50,000	1,400	2,000	420	840	1,104	2,000	135	270
50,000	55,000	1,460	2,000	440	880	1,140	2,000	140	280
55,000	60,000	1,515	2,000	455	910	1,173	2,000	145	290
60,000	65,000	1,565	2,000	470	940	1,206	2,000	150	300
65,000	70,000	1,610	2,000	485	970	1,236	2,000	155	310
70,000	75,000	1,655	2,000	500	1,000	1,263	2,000	160	320
75,000	80,000	1,695	2,000	510	1,020	1,293	2,000	165	330
80,000	85,000	1,730	2,000	520	1,040	1,317	2,000	170	340
85,000	90,000	1,760	2,000	530	1,060	1,344	2,000	175	350
90,000	95,000	1,790	2,000	540	1,080	1,368	2,000	180	360
95,000	100,000	1,815	2,000	545	1,090	1,392	2,000	185	370
100,000	110,000	1,835	2,000	550	1,100	1,437	2,000	195	390
110,000	120,000	1,855	2,000	555	1,110	1,479	2,000	205	410
120,000	130,000	1,875	2,000	560	1,120	1,521	2,000	215	430
130,000	140,000	1,890	2,000	565	1,130	1,557	2,000	225	450
140,000	150,000	1,900	2,000	570	1,140	1,593	2,000	235	470
150,000	160,000	1,935	2,000	580	1,160	1,629	2,000	245	490
160,000	170,000	1,965	2,000	590	1,180	1,662	2,000	255	510
170,000	180,000	1,990	2,000	600	1,200	1,695	2,000	265	530
180,000	190,000	2,010	2,010	605	1,210	1,725	2,000	275	550
190,000	200,000	2,030	2,030	610	1,220	1,755	2,000	285	570
200,000	210,000	2,055	2,055	620	1,240	1,782	2,000	295	590
210,000	230,000	2,100	2,100	635	1,270	1,836	2,000	315	630
230,000	250,000	2,155	2,155	650	1,300	1,890	2,000	335	670
250,000	275,000	2,215	2,215	670	1,340	1,950	2,000	360	720

Quantity of explosives		Distances in feet							
Pounds over	Pounds not over	Inhabited buildings		Public highways with traffic volume of 3000 or fewer vehicles/day		Passenger railways— public highways with traffic volume of more than 3,000 vehicles/day		Separation of magazines	
		Barricaded	Unbarricaded	Barricaded	Unbarricaded	Barricaded	Unbarricaded	Barricaded	Unbarricaded
275,000	300,000	2,275	2,275	690	1,380	2,000	2,000	385	770

TABLE: AMERICAN TABLE OF DISTANCES FOR STORAGE OF EXPLOSIVES (DECEMBER 1910), AS REVISED AND APPROVED BY THE INSTITUTE OF MAKERS OF EXPLOSIVES—JUNE 1991.

Notes to the Table of Distances for Storage of Explosives

(1) Terms found in the table of distances for storage of explosive materials are defined in § 555.11.

(2) When two or more storage magazines are located on the same property, each magazine must comply with the minimum distances specified from inhabited buildings, railways, and highways, and, in addition, they should be separated from each other by not less than the distances shown for "Separation of Magazines," except that the quantity of explosives contained in cap magazines shall govern in regard to the spacing of said cap magazines from magazines containing other explosives. If any two or more magazines are separated from each other by less than the specified "Separation of Magazines" distances, then such two or more magazines, as a group, must be considered as one magazine, and the total quantity of explosives stored in such group must be treated as if stored in a single magazine located on the site of any magazine of the group, and must comply with the minimum of distances specified from other magazines, inhabited buildings, railways, and highways.

(3) All types of blasting caps in strengths through No. 8 cap should be rated at 1½ lbs. (1.5 lbs.) of explosives per 1,000 caps. For strengths higher than No. 8 cap, consult the manufacturer.

(4) For quantity and distance purposes, detonating cord of 50 or 60 grains per foot should be calculated as equivalent to 9 lbs. of high explosives per 1,000 feet. Heavier or lighter core loads should be rated proportionately.

[T.D. ATF–87, 46 FR 40384, Aug. 7, 1981, as amended by T.D. ATF–400, 63 FR 45003, Aug. 24, 1998; T.D. ATF–446, 66 FR 16602, Mar. 27, 2001; T.D. ATF–446a, 66 FR 19089, Apr. 13, 2001; ATF 2017R–21, 84 FR 13800, Apr. 8, 2019]

§ 555.219 Table of distances for storage of low explosives.

Pounds		From inhabited building distance (feet)	From public railroad and highway distance (feet)	From above ground magazine (feet)
Over	Not over			
0	1,000	75	75	50
1,000	5,000	115	115	75
5,000	10,000	150	150	100
10,000	20,000	190	190	125
20,000	30,000	215	215	145
30,000	40,000	235	235	155
40,000	50,000	250	250	165
50,000	60,000	260	260	175
60,000	70,000	270	270	185
70,000	80,000	280	280	190
80,000	90,000	295	295	195
90,000	100,000	300	300	200
100,000	200,000	375	375	250
200,000	300,000	450	450	300

TABLE: DEPARTMENT OF DEFENSE AMMUNITION AND EXPLOSIVES STANDARDS, TABLE 5–4.1 EXTRACT; 4145.27 M, MARCH 1969

[T.D. ATF–87, 46 FR 40384, Aug. 7, 1981, as amended by ATF 2017R–21, 84 FR 13800, Apr. 8, 2019]

§ 555.220 Table of separation distances of ammonium nitrate and blasting agents from explosives or blasting agents.

Donor weight (pounds)		Minimum separation distance of acceptor from donor when barricaded (ft.)		Minimum thickness of artificial barricades (in.)
Over	Not over	Ammonium nitrate	Blasting agent	
....	100	3	11	12
100	300	4	14	12
300	600	5	18	12
600	1,000	6	22	12
1,000	1,600	7	25	12
1,600	2,000	8	29	12
2,000	3,000	9	32	15
3,000	4,000	10	36	15
4,000	6,000	11	40	15
6,000	8,000	12	43	20
8,000	10,000	13	47	20
10,000	12,000	14	50	20
12,000	16,000	15	54	25
16,000	20,000	16	58	25
20,000	25,000	18	65	25

Donor weight (pounds)		Minimum separation distance of acceptor from donor when barricaded (ft.)		Minimum thickness of artificial barricades (in.)
Over	Not over	Ammonium nitrate	Blasting agent	
25,000	30,000	19	68	30
30,000	35,000	20	72	30
35,000	40,000	21	76	30
40,000	45,000	22	79	35
45,000	50,000	23	83	35
50,000	55,000	24	86	35
55,000	60,000	25	90	35
60,000	70,000	26	94	40
70,000	80,000	28	101	40
80,000	90,000	30	108	40
90,000	100,000	32	115	40
100,000	120,000	34	122	50
120,000	140,000	37	133	50
140,000	160,000	40	144	50
160,000	180,000	44	158	50
180,000	200,000	48	173	50
200,000	220,000	52	187	60
220,000	250,000	56	202	60
250,000	275,000	60	216	60
275,000	300,000	64	230	60

TABLE: NATIONAL FIRE PROTECTION ASSOCIATION (NFPA) OFFICIAL STANDARD NO. 492, 1968

Notes of Table of Separation Distances of Ammonium Nitrate and Blasting Agents From Explosives or Blasting Agents

(1) This table specifies separation distances to prevent explosion of ammonium nitrate and ammonium nitrate-based blasting agents by propagation from nearby stores of high explosives or blasting agents referred to in the table as the "donor." Ammonium nitrate, by itself, is not considered to be a donor when applying this table. Ammonium nitrate, ammonium nitrate-fuel oil or combinations thereof are acceptors. If stores of ammonium nitrate are located within the sympathetic detonation distance of explosives or blasting agents, one-half the mass of the ammonium nitrate is to be included in the mass of the donor.

(2) When the ammonium nitrate and/or blasting agent is not barricaded, the distances shown in the table must be multiplied by six. These distances allow for the possibility of high velocity metal fragments from mixers, hoppers, truck bodies, sheet metal structures, metal containers, and the like which may enclose the "donor." Where explosives storage is in bullet-resistant magazines or where the storage is protected by a bullet-resistant wall, distances and barricade thicknesses in excess of those prescribed in the table in § 555.218 are not required.

(3) These distances apply to all ammonium nitrate with respect to its separation from stores of high explosives and blasting agents. Ammonium nitrate explosive mixtures that are high explosives pursuant to § 555.202(a) or are defined as a blasting agent pursuant to

§ 555.11 are subject to the table of distances for storage of explosive materials in § 555.218 and to the table of separation distances of ammonium nitrate and blasting agents from explosives or blasting agents in this section.

(4) These distances apply to blasting agents which pass the insensitivity test prescribed in regulations of the U.S. Department of Transportation (49 CFR part 173).

(5) Earth or sand dikes, or enclosures filled with the prescribed minimum thickness of earth or sand are acceptable artificial barricades. Natural barricades, such as hills or timber of sufficient density that the surrounding exposures which require protection cannot be seen from the "donor" when the trees are bare of leaves, are also acceptable.

(6) For determining the distances to be maintained from inhabited buildings, passenger railways, and public highways, use the table in § 555.218.

[T.D. ATF–87, 46 FR 40384, Aug. 7, 1981, as amended by ATF 2017R–21, 84 FR 13800, Apr. 8, 2019; ATF 2002R–226F, 84 FR 12097, Apr. 1, 2019]

§ 555.221 Requirements for display fireworks, pyrotechnic compositions, and explosive materials used in assembling fireworks or articles pyrotechnic.

(a) Display fireworks, pyrotechnic compositions, and explosive materials used to assemble fireworks and articles pyrotechnic shall be stored at all times as required by this Subpart unless they are in the process of manufacture, assembly, packaging, or are being transported.

(b) No more than 500 pounds (227 kg) of pyrotechnic compositions or explosive materials are permitted at one time in any fireworks mixing building, any building or area in which the pyrotechnic compositions or explosive materials are pressed or otherwise prepared for finishing or assembly, or any finishing or assembly building. All pyrotechnic compositions or explosive materials not in immediate use will be stored in covered, non-ferrous containers.

(c) The maximum quantity of flash powder permitted in any fireworks process building is 10 pounds (4.5 kg).

(d) All dry explosive powders and mixtures, partially assembled display fireworks, and finished display fireworks shall be removed from fireworks process buildings at the conclusion of a day's operations and placed in approved magazines.

[T.D. ATF–293, 55 FR 3722, Feb. 5, 1990, as amended by T.D. ATF–400, 63 FR 45004, Aug. 24, 1998]

§555.222 Table of distances between fireworks process buildings and between fireworks process and fireworks nonprocess buildings.

Net weight of fireworks[1] (pounds)	Display fireworks[2] (feet)	Consumer fireworks[3] (feet)
0–100	57	37
101–200	69	37
201–300	77	37
301–400	85	37
401–500	91	37
Above 500	Not permitted[4][5]	Not permitted[4][5]

[1] Net weight is the weight of all pyrotechnic compositions, and explosive materials and fuse only.

[2] The distances in this column apply only with natural or artificial barricades. If such barricades are not used, the distances must be doubled.

[3] While consumer fireworks or articles pyrotechnic in a finished state are not subject to regulation, explosive materials used to manufacture or assemble such fireworks or articles are subject to regulation. Thus, fireworks process buildings where consumer fireworks or articles pyrotechnic are being processed shall meet these requirements.

[4] A maximum of 500 pounds of in-process pyrotechnic compositions, either loose or in partially-assembled fireworks, is permitted in any fireworks process building. Finished display fireworks may not be stored in a fireworks process building.

[5] A maximum of 10 pounds of flash powder, either in loose form or in assembled units, is permitted in any fireworks process building. Quantities in excess of 10 pounds must be kept in an approved magazine.

[T.D. ATF–293, 55 FR 3723, Feb. 5, 1990, as amended by T.D. ATF–400, 63 FR 45004, Aug. 24, 1998]

§555.223 Table of distances between fireworks process buildings and other specified areas.

DISTANCE FROM PASSENGER RAILWAYS, PUBLIC HIGHWAYS, FIREWORKS PLANT BUILDINGS USED TO STORE CONSUMER FIREWORKS AND ARTICLES PYROTECHNIC, MAGAZINES AND FIREWORKS SHIPPING BUILDINGS, AND INHABITED BUILDINGS.[3][4][5]

Net weight of fireworks[1] (pounds)	Display fireworks[1] (feet)	Consumer fireworks[2] (feet)
0–100	200	25
101–200	200	50
201–300	200	50
301–400	200	50
401–500	200	50

DISTANCE FROM PASSENGER RAILWAYS, PUBLIC HIGHWAYS, FIREWORKS PLANT BUILDINGS USED TO STORE CONSUMER FIREWORKS AND ARTICLES PYROTECHNIC, MAGAZINES AND FIREWORKS SHIPPING BUILDINGS, AND INHABITED BUILDINGS.[3][4][5]—Continued

Net weight of fireworks[1] (pounds)	Display fireworks[1] (feet)	Consumer fireworks[2] (feet)
Above 500	Not permitted	Not permitted.

[1] Net weight is the weight of all pyrotechnic compositions, and explosive materials and fuse only.

[2] While consumer fireworks or articles pyrotechnic in a finished state are not subject to regulation, explosive materials used to manufacture or assemble such fireworks or articles are subject to regulation. Thus, fireworks process buildings where consumer fireworks or articles pyrotechnic are being processed shall meet these requirements.

[3] This table does not apply to the separation distances between fireworks process buildings (see §555.222) and between magazines (see §§555.218 and 555.224).

[4] The distances in this table apply with or without artificial or natural barricades or screen barricades. However, the use of barricades is highly recommended.

[5] No work of any kind, except to place or move items other than explosive materials from storage, shall be conducted in any building designated as a warehouse. A fireworks plant warehouse is not subject to §555.222 or this section, tables of distances.

[T.D. ATF–293, 55 FR 3723, Feb. 5, 1990, as amended by T.D. ATF–400, 63 FR 45004, Aug. 24, 1998]

§555.224 Table of distances for the storage of display fireworks (except bulk salutes).

Net weight of firework[1] (pounds)	Distance between magazine and inhabited building, passenger railway, or public highway[3][4] (feet)	Distance between magazines[2][3] (feet)
0–1000	150	100
1001–5000	230	150
5001–10000	300	200
Above 10000	Use table §555.218	

[1] Net weight is the weight of all pyrotechnic compositions, and explosive materials and fuse only.

[2] For the purposes of applying this table, the term "magazine" also includes fireworks shipping buildings for display fireworks.

[3] For fireworks storage magazines in use prior to March 7, 1990, the distances in this table may be halved if properly barricaded between the magazine and potential receptor sites (55 FR 3717).

[4] This table does not apply to the storage of bulk salutes. Use table at §555.218.

[T.D. ATF–293, 55 FR 3723, Feb. 5, 1990, as amended by T.D. ATF–400, 63 FR 45004, Aug. 24, 1998; ATF 2017R–21, 84 FR 13800, Apr. 8, 2019]

SUBCHAPTER D—MISCELLANEOUS REGULATIONS RELATING TO ALCOHOL AND TOBACCO

PART 646—CONTRABAND CIGARETTES

GENERAL

Sec.
646.141 Scope of part.
646.142 Territorial extent.
646.143 Meaning of terms.

RECORDS

646.146 General requirements.
646.147 Required information.
646.150 Retention of records.

OTHER PROVISIONS RELATING TO THE DISTRIBUTION OF CIGARETTES

646.153 Authority of appropriate ATF officers to enter business premises.

PENALTIES AND FORFEITURES

646.154 Penalties.
646.155 Forfeitures.

AUTHORITY: 18 U.S.C. 2341–2346, unless otherwise noted.

SOURCE: 45 FR 48612, July 21, 1980, unless otherwise noted. Redesignated by T.D. ATF–487, 68 FR 3753, Jan. 24, 2003.

EDITORIAL NOTE: Nomenclature changes to part 646 appear by T.D. ATF–487, 68 FR 4753, Jan. 24, 2003.

GENERAL

§ 646.141 Scope of part.

The regulations in this subpart relate to the distribution of cigarettes in excess of 60,000 in a single transaction.

§ 646.142 Territorial extent.

The provisions of the regulations in this part apply in the several States of the United States, the District of Columbia, the Commonwealth of Puerto Rico, and the Virgin Islands.

§ 646.143 Meaning of terms.

When used in this part, terms are defined as follows in this section. Words in the plural shall include the singular, and vice versa. Words indicating the masculine gender shall include the feminine. The terms "includes" and "including" do not exclude other things not named which are in the same general class or are otherwise within the scope of the term defined.

Appropriate ATF officer. An officer or employee of the Bureau of Alcohol, Tobacco, Firearms, and Explosives (ATF) authorized to perform any functions relating to the administration or enforcement of this part by ATF Order 1130.28, Delegation of the Director's Authorities in 27 CFR Parts 45 and 646.

Business premises. When used with respect to a distributor, the property on which the cigarettes are kept or stored. The business premises includes the property where the records of a distributor are kept.

Common or contract carrier. A carrier holding a certificate of convenience and necessity, a permit for contract carrier by motor vehicle, or other valid operating authority under the Interstate Commerce Act, or under equivalent operating authority from a regulatory agency of the United States or of any State.

Contraband cigarettes. Any quantity of cigarettes in excess of 60,000, if—

(a) The cigarettes bear no evidence of the payment of applicable State cigarette taxes in the State where the cigarettes are found;

(b) The State in which the cigarettes are found requires a stamp, impression, or other indication to be placed on packages or other containers of cigarettes to evidence payment of cigarette taxes; and

(c) The cigarettes are in the possession of any person other than an exempted person.

Disposition. The movement of cigarettes from a person's business premises, wherever situated, by shipment or other means of distribution.

Distribute. To sell, ship, issue, give, transfer, or otherwise dispose of.

Distributor. Any person who distributes more than 60,000 cigarettes in a single transaction.

Exempted person. Any person who is—

(a) Holding a permit issued pursuant to Chapter 52 of the Internal Revenue Code of 1954 as a manufacturer of tobacco products or as an export warehouse proprietor;

(b) Operating a customs bonded warehouse pursuant to section 311 or 555 of the Tariff Act of 1930 (19 U.S.C. 1311 or 1555);

(c) An agent of a tobacco products manufacturer, an export warehouse proprietor, or an operator of a customs bonded warehouse;

(d) A common or contract carrier transporting the cigarettes involved under a proper bill of lading or freight bill which states the quantity, source, and destination of the cigarettes;

(e) Licensed or otherwise authorized by the State, in which he possesses cigarettes, to account for and pay cigarette taxes imposed by that State; and who has complied with the accounting and payment requirements relating to his license or authorization with respect to the cigarettes involved; or

(f) An agent of the United States, of an individual State, or of a political subdivision of a State and having possession of cigarettes in connection with the performance of official duties.

(g) Operating within a foreign-trade zone established under 19 U.S.C., section 81b, when the cigarettes involved have been entered into the zone under zone-restricted status or, in respect to foreign cigarettes, have been admitted into the zone but have not been entered in the United States.

Person. Any individual, corporation, company, association, firm, partnership, society, or joint stock company.

State. A State of the United States, the District of Columbia, the Commonwealth of Puerto Rico, or the Virgin Islands.

[45 FR 48612, July 21, 1980, as amended by T.D. ATF–472, 67 FR 8881, Feb. 27, 2002; ATF 2013R–9F, 79 FR 46694, Aug. 11, 2014]

RECORDS

§646.146 General requirements.

Each distributor of cigarettes shall keep copies of invoices, bills of lading, or other suitable commercial records relating to each disposition of more than 60,000 cigarettes. Dividing a single agreement for the disposition of more than 60,000 cigarettes into the delivery of smaller components of 60,000 cigarettes or less does not exempt the distributor from the recordkeeping requirements of this part. The dis-

tributor shall include the information prescribed in §646.147 in his commercial records of disposition.

§646.147 Required information.

(a) *Distributors who are exempted persons.* Each distributor who is an exempted person as defined in §646.143 shall show the following information in his commercial records.

(1) For each disposition of more than 60,000 cigarettes to an exempted person; or for each disposition of more than 60,000 cigarettes to a person who is not an exempted person and which is delivered by the distributor to the recipient's place of business, the distributor shall show on dated records—

(i) The full name of the purchaser (or the recipient if there is no purchaser);

(ii) The street address (including city and state) to which the cigarettes are destined; and

(iii) The quantity of cigarettes disposed of.

(2) For each disposition of more than 60,000 cigarettes, other than the dispositions specified in paragraph (a)(1) of this section, the distributor shall show on dated records—

(i) The full name of the purchaser (if any);

(ii) The name, address (including city and state), and signature of the person receiving the cigarettes;

(iii) The street address (including city and state) to which the cigarettes are destined;

(iv) The quantity of cigarettes disposed of;

(v) The driver's license number of the individual receiving the cigarettes;

(vi) The license number of the vehicle in which the cigarettes are removed from the distributor's business premises;

(vii) A declaration by the individual receiving the cigarettes of the specific purpose of receipt (such as personal use, resale, delivery to another person, etc.); and

(viii) A declaration by the person receiving the cigarettes of the name and address of his principal when he is acting as an agent.

(b) *Distributors who are not exempted persons.* Each distributor who is not an exempted person as defined in §646.143 shall show on dated commercial records the information specified in paragraphs (a)(2) (i) through (viii) of this section for each disposition of more than 60,000 cigarettes.

(Approved by the Office of Management and Budget under control number 1512–0391)

[45 FR 48612, July 21, 1980, as amended by T.D. ATF–172, 49 FR 14943, Apr. 16, 1984]

§ 646.150 Retention of records.

(a) *General.* Each distributor of cigarettes shall retain the records required by §§ 646.146 and 646.147 for three years following the close of the year in which the records are made. The distributor shall keep the required records on his business premises.

(b) *Shorter retention periods.* The appropriate ATF officer may, pursuant to an application submitted by a distributor, approve a shorter retention period where—

(1) The distributor requesting the shorter retention period is an agent of a tobacco products manufacturer;

(2) The tobacco products manufacturer will keep the required record for each disposition of more than 60,000 cigarettes from the agent's premises for the full retention period specified in paragraph (a) of this section; and

(3) The approval of a shorter retention period will not unduly hinder the administration of enforcement of this subpart.

(c) *Application requirements.* Each distributor proposing to employ a shorter retention period shall submit a written application, in duplicate, to the appropriate ATF officer. A distributor may not employ a shorter retention period until approval is received from the appropriate ATF officer. Each application should indicate the duration of the proposed retention period and should include the information required by paragraph (b) of this section.

[45 FR 48612, July 21, 1980, as amended by T.D. ATF–472, 67 FR 8880, 8881, Feb. 27, 2002]

OTHER PROVISIONS RELATING TO THE DISTRIBUTION OF CIGARETTES

§ 646.153 Authority of appropriate ATF officers to enter business premises.

Any appropriate ATF officer may enter the business premises of any distributor of cigarettes to inspect the records required by §§ 646.146 through 646.147 or to inspect any cigarettes stored on the premises—

(a) Pursuant to duly issued search warrant or an administrative inspection warrant; or

(b) Upon the consent of the distributor to enter his premises.

[45 FR 48612, July 21, 1980, as amended by T.D. ATF–472, 67 FR 8881, Feb. 27, 2002]

PENALTIES AND FORFEITURES

§ 646.154 Penalties.

(a) Any person who knowingly ships, transports, receives, possesses, sells, distributes, or purchases contraband cigarettes shall be fined not more than $100,000 or imprisoned not more than five years, or both.

(b) Any person who knowingly violates any regulation contained in this part or makes any false statement or misrepresentation with respect to the information required to be recorded by this part shall be fined not more than $5,000 or imprisoned not more than three years, or both.

§ 646.155 Forfeitures.

(a) Any contraband cigarettes involved in any violation of the provisions of 18 U.S.C. chapter 114 shall be subject to seizure and forfeiture. All provisions of the Internal Revenue Code of 1954 (title 26 U.S.C.) relating to the seizure, forfeiture, and disposition of firearms, as defined in section 5845(a) of that Code, shall, so far as applicable, extend to seizures and forfeitures of contraband cigarettes under the provisions of 18 U.S.C. chapter 114.

(b) Any vessel, vehicle or aircraft used to transport, carry, convey, or conceal or possess any contraband cigarettes with respect to which there has been committed any violation of any provision of 18 U.S.C. chapter 114 or the regulations in this subpart shall be subject to seizure and forfeiture under the Customs laws, as provided by the Act of August 9, 1939 (49 U.S.C. 781–788).

(18 U.S.C. 2344; 53 Stat. 1291 (49 U.S.C. 782))

PARTS 647–699 [RESERVED]

SUBCHAPTER E—EXPLOSIVE LICENSE AND PERMIT PROCEEDINGS

PARTS 700–770 [RESERVED]

PART 771—RULES OF PRACTICE IN EXPLOSIVE LICENSE AND PERMIT PROCEEDINGS

Subpart A—Scope and Construction of Regulations

Sec.
771.1   Scope of part.
771.2   Liberal construction.
771.3   Forms prescribed.

Subpart B—Definitions

771.5   Meaning of terms.

Subpart C—General

771.25   Communications and pleadings.
771.26   Service on applicant, licensee, or permittee.
771.27   Service on the Director of Industry Operations or Director.

TIME

771.28   Computation.
771.29   Continuances and extensions.

REPRESENTATION AT HEARINGS

771.30   Personal representation.
771.31   Attorneys and other representatives.

Subpart D—Compliance and Settlement

771.35   Opportunity for compliance.
771.36   Settlement.
771.37   Notice of contemplated action.
771.38   Licensee's or permittee's failure to meet requirements within reasonable time.
771.39   Authority of Director of Industry Operations to proceed with revocation or denial action.

Subpart E—Revocation or Denial

771.40   Denial of initial application.
771.41   Denial of renewal application or revocation of license or permit.
771.42   Grounds for revocation of licenses or permits.
771.43   Grounds for denial of applications for licenses or permits.

Subpart F—Hearing Procedure

NOTICES

771.55   Content.

771.56   Forms.
771.57   Execution and disposition.
771.58   Designated place of hearing.

REQUEST FOR HEARING

771.59   Initial application proceedings.
771.60   Revocation or denial of renewal proceedings.
771.61   Notice of hearing.

NON-REQUEST FOR HEARING

771.62   Initial application.
771.63   Revocation or denial of renewal.

RESPONSES TO NOTICES

771.64   Answers.
771.65   Responses admitting facts.
771.66   Initial conferences.

FAILURE TO APPEAR

771.67   Initial applications.
771.68   Revocation or denial of renewal.

WAIVER OF HEARING

771.69   Withdrawal of request for hearing.
771.70   Adjudication based upon written submissions.

SURRENDER OF LICENSE OR PERMIT

771.71   Before citation.
771.72   After citation.

MOTIONS

771.73   General.
771.74   Prior to hearing.
771.75   At hearing.

HEARING

771.76   General.
771.77   Initial applications.
771.78   Revocation or denial of renewal.

BURDEN OF PROOF

771.79   Initial applications.
771.80   Revocation or denial of renewal.

GENERAL

771.81   Stipulations at hearing.
771.82   Evidence.
771.83   Closing of hearings; arguments, briefs, and proposed findings.
771.84   Reopening of the hearing.

RECORD OF TESTIMONY

771.85   Stenographic record.
771.86   Oath of reporter.

Subpart G—Administrative Law Judges

771.95   Responsibilities of administrative law judges.
771.96   Disqualification.
771.97   Powers.
771.98   Separation of functions.
771.99   Conduct of hearing.
771.100 Unavailability of administrative law judge.

Subpart H—Decisions

771.105 Administrative law judge's findings and recommended decision.
771.106 Certification and transmittal of record and decision.

ACTION BY DIRECTOR OF INDUSTRY OPERATIONS

771.107 Initial application proceedings.
771.108 Director of Industry Operations' decision.
771.109 Revocation or denial of renewal proceedings.
771.110 Revocation or denial of renewal.
771.111 Proceedings involving violations not within the division of issuance of license or permit.

Subpart I—Review

771.120 Appeal on petition to the Director.
771.121 Review by Director.
771.122 Denial of renewal or revocation.
771.123 Court review.

Subpart J—Miscellaneous

771.124 Depositions.
771.125 Witnesses and fees.
771.126 Discovery.
771.127 Privileges.

RECORD

771.135 What constitutes record.
771.136 Availability.

AUTHORITY: 18 U.S.C. 843, 847.

SOURCE: 84 FR 64744, Nov. 25, 2019, unless otherwise noted.

Subpart A—Scope and Construction of Regulations

§ 771.1   Scope of part.

Regulations in this part govern procedures and practices for disapproving applications for licenses and permits and denying renewal of or revocation of such licenses or permits under 18 U.S.C. chapter 40.

§ 771.2   Liberal construction.

Regulations in this part shall be liberally construed to secure just, expeditious, and efficient determination of the issues presented. The Rules of Civil Procedure for the U.S. District Courts (28 U.S.C. appendix) are not controlling, but may act as a guide in any situation not provided for or controlled by this part and shall be liberally construed or relaxed when necessary.

§ 771.3   Forms prescribed.

(a) The Director is authorized to prescribe all forms required by this part. All of the information called for in each form shall be furnished as indicated by the headings on the form and the instructions on or pertaining to the form. In addition, information called for in each form shall be furnished as required by this part.

(b) Requests for forms should be made to the ATF Distribution Center or through the ATF website at *http://www.atf.gov.*

Subpart B—Definitions

§ 771.5   Meaning of terms.

When used in this part and in forms prescribed under this part, where not otherwise distinctly expressed or manifestly incompatible with the intent thereof, terms shall have the meaning provided in this subpart. Words in the plural form shall include the singular, and *vice versa*, and words importing the masculine gender shall include the feminine.

Administrative law judge. The person appointed pursuant to 5 U.S.C. 3105, designated to preside over any administrative proceedings under this part.

Applicant. Any person who has filed an application for a license or permit under 18 U.S.C. chapter 40.

Application. Any application for a license or permit, including renewal applications, under 18 U.S.C. chapter 40.

ATF. The Bureau of Alcohol, Tobacco, Firearms, and Explosives, Department of Justice.

Attorney for the Government. An attorney in the ATF Office of Chief Counsel authorized to represent the Director of Industry Operations in the proceeding.

CFR. The Code of Federal Regulations.

Contemplated notice. Includes any notice contemplating the revocation or denial of renewal of a license or permit.

Director. The Director, Bureau of Alcohol, Tobacco, Firearms, and Explosives, Department of Justice.

Director of Industry Operations. The principal ATF official in a Field Operations division responsible for administering regulations in this part.

Ex parte communication. An oral or written communication not on the public record with respect to which reasonable prior notice to all parties is not given, but not including requests for status reports.

Initial decision. The decision of the Director of Industry Operations in a proceeding concerning the revocation of, denial of renewal of, or denial of application for a license or permit. This decision becomes the agency's final decision in the absence of an appeal.

Final decision. The definitive decision of ATF, *e.g.*, the agency's decision in the absence of an appeal or the Director's decision following an appeal to the Director.

License. Subject to applicable law, entitles the licensee to transport, ship, and receive explosive materials in interstate or foreign commerce, and to engage in the business specified by the license, at the location described on the license.

Licensee. Any importer, manufacturer, or dealer licensed under the provisions of 18 U.S.C. chapter 40 and 27 CFR part 555.

Limited permit. A permit issued to a person authorizing him to receive for his use explosive materials from a licensee or permittee in his State of residence on no more than six occasions during the 12-month period in which the permit is valid. A limited permit does not authorize the receipt or transportation of explosive materials in interstate or foreign commerce.

Other term. Any other term defined in the Federal explosives laws (18 U.S.C. chapter 40), the regulations promulgated thereunder (27 CFR part 555), or the Administrative Procedure Act (5 U.S.C. 551 *et seq.*), where used in this part, shall have the meaning assigned to it therein.

Permittee. Any user of explosives for a lawful purpose who has obtained either a user permit or a limited permit under 18 U.S.C. chapter 40 and 27 CFR part 555.

Person. Any individual, corporation, company, association, firm, partnership, society, or joint stock company.

Recommended decision. The advisory decision of the administrative law judge in any proceeding regarding the revocation of, denial of renewal of, or denial of application for a license or permit. ATF must act on a recommended decision with its own initial or final decision.

User-limited permit. A user permit valid only for a single purchase transaction. Recipients of a user-limited permit must obtain a new permit for any subsequent purchase transaction.

User permit. A permit issued to a person authorizing him to—

(1) Acquire for his own use explosive materials from a licensee in a State other than the State in which he resides or from a foreign country; and

(2) Transport explosive materials in interstate or foreign commerce.

Willfulness. The plain indifference to, or purposeful disregard of, a known legal duty. Willfulness may be demonstrated by, but does not require, repeat violations involving a known legal duty.

Subpart C—General

§771.25 Communications and pleadings.

(a) All communications to the Government regarding the procedures set forth in this part and all pleadings, such as answers, motions, requests, or other papers or documents required or permitted to be filed under this part, relating to a proceeding pending before an administrative law judge, shall be addressed to the administrative law judge at his post of duty and the Attorney for the Government. Communications concerning proceedings not pending before an administrative law judge should be addressed to the Director of Industry Operations or Director, as the case may be.

(b) Except to the extent required for the disposition of ex parte matters as authorized by law, no ex parte communications shall be made to or from the administrative law judge concerning the merits of the adjudication. If the administrative law judge receives or makes an ex parte communication not authorized by law, the administrative law judge shall place on the record of the proceeding:

(1) All such written communications;

(2) Memoranda stating the substance of all such oral communications; and

(3) All written responses and memoranda stating the substance of all oral responses to paragraphs (b)(1) and (2) of this section.

§ 771.26 Service on applicant, licensee, or permittee.

All orders, notices, motions, and other formal documents required to be served under the regulations in this part may be served by mailing a signed, original copy thereof to the designated representative of the applicant, licensee, or permittee by certified mail, with request for return receipt card, at the representative's business address, by personal service, or as otherwise agreed to by the parties. If the applicant, licensee, or permittee has not yet designated a representative, all orders, notices, motions, and other formal documents required to be served under the regulations in this part may be served by mailing a signed, original copy thereof to the applicant, licensee, or permittee at the address stated on his application, license, or permit, or at his last known address, or by delivery of such original copy to the applicant, licensee, or permittee personally, or in the case of a corporation, partnership, or other unincorporated association, by delivering the same to an officer, or manager, or general agent thereof, or to its attorney of record. Such personal service may be made by any employee of the Department of Justice designated by the Attorney General or by any employee of ATF. A certificate of mailing and the return receipt card, or certificate of service signed by the person making such service, shall be filed as a part of the record.

§ 771.27 Service on the Director of Industry Operations or Director.

Pleadings, motions, notices, and other formal documents may be served by certified mail, by personal service, or as otherwise agreed to by the parties, on the Director of Industry Operations (or upon the Attorney for the Government on behalf of the Director of Industry Operations), or on the Director, if the proceeding is before him for review on appeal.

TIME

§ 771.28 Computation.

In computing any period of time prescribed or allowed by this part, the day of the act, event, or default after which the designated period of time is to run is not to be included. The last day of the period to be computed is to be included, unless it is a Saturday, Sunday, or Federal holiday, in which event the period runs until the next day that is not a Saturday, Sunday, or Federal holiday. Pleadings, requests, or other papers or documents required or permitted to be filed under this part must be received for filing at the appropriate office within the time limits, if any, for such filing.

§ 771.29 Continuances and extensions.

For good cause shown, the administrative law judge, Director, or Director of Industry Operations, as the case may be, may grant continuances and, as to all matters pending before him, extend any time limit prescribed by the regulations in this part (except where the time limit is statutory).

REPRESENTATION AT HEARINGS

§ 771.30 Personal representation.

Any individual or member of a partnership may appear for himself, or for such partnership, and a corporation or association may be represented by a bona fide officer of such corporation or association, upon showing of adequate authorization.

§ 771.31 Attorneys and other representatives.

An applicant, licensee, or permittee may represent himself, or be represented by an attorney, a certified public accountant, or any other person, specifically designated in a duly executed power of attorney that shall be filed in the proceeding by the applicant, licensee, or permittee. The applicant, licensee, or permittee shall file waivers, if applicable, under the Privacy Act of 1974 and 26 U.S.C. 6103(c) (confidentiality and disclosure of returns and return information). The Director of Industry Operations may be represented in proceedings by an attorney in the Office of Chief Counsel who is authorized to execute and file motions, briefs, and other papers in the proceeding on behalf of the Director of Industry Operations, in the attorney's own name as "Attorney for the Government."

Subpart D—Compliance and Settlement

§ 771.35 Opportunity for compliance.

No license or permit shall be revoked or denied renewal unless, prior to the institution of proceedings, facts or conduct warranting such action shall have been called to the attention of the licensee or permittee by the Director of Industry Operations in writing in a contemplated notice, and the licensee or permittee shall have been accorded an opportunity to demonstrate or achieve compliance with all lawful requirements as set forth in section 9(b) of the Administrative Procedure Act. In cases in which the Director of Industry Operations alleges in his contemplated notice, with supporting reasons, willful violations or that the public interest requires otherwise, this section does not apply and the issuance of a contemplated notice is unnecessary.

§ 771.36 Settlement.

Any proposals of settlement should be made to the Director of Industry Operations, but may be made through the Attorney for the Government. Where necessary, the date of the hearing may be postponed pending consideration of such proposals when they are made in good faith and not for the purpose of delay. If proposals of settlement are submitted, and they are considered unsatisfactory, the Director of Industry Operations may reject the proposals

and may, either directly or through the Attorney for the Government, inform the licensee or permittee of any conditions on which the alleged violations may be settled. If the proposals of settlement are considered satisfactory to the Director of Industry Operations, the licensee or permittee shall be notified thereof and the proceeding shall be dismissed.

§ 771.37 Notice of contemplated action.

Where the Director of Industry Operations has not ascertained whether the licensee or permittee has willfully violated the Federal explosives laws and where he believes the matter has the potential to be settled informally, *i.e.,* without formal administrative proceedings, he shall, in accordance with section 5(b) of the Administrative Procedure Act, prior to the issuance of a notice of revocation or denial of renewal, give the licensee or permittee a contemplated notice of such action and an opportunity to show why the license or permit should not be revoked or denied renewal. The notice should inform the licensee or permittee of the charges on which the notice would be based, if issued, and afford him a period of 15 days from the date of the notice, or such longer period as the Director of Industry Operations deems necessary, in which to submit proposals of settlement to the Director of Industry Operations. Where informal settlement is not reached promptly because of inaction by the applicant, licensee, or permittee or proposals are made for the purpose of delay, a notice shall be issued in accordance with § 771.42 or § 771.43, as appropriate. The issuance of a notice of contemplated action does not entitle the recipient to a hearing before an administrative law judge.

§ 771.38 Licensee's or permittee's failure to meet requirements within reasonable time.

If the licensee or permittee fails to meet the requirements of applicable laws and regulations in this part within such reasonable time as may be specified by the Director of Industry Operations, proceedings for revocation or denial of renewal of the license or permit shall be initiated.

§ 771.39 Authority of Director of Industry Operations to proceed with revocation or denial action.

Where the evidence is conclusive and the nature of the violation is such as to preclude any settlement, the violation is of a continuing character that necessitates immediate action to protect the public interest, or the Director of Industry Operations believes that any informal settlement of the alleged violation.will not ensure future compliance with applicable laws and regulations in this part, or in any similar case where the circumstances are such as to clearly preclude informal settlement, and the Director of Industry Operations so finds and states the reasons therefor in the notice, the Director of Industry Operations may proceed with the revocation or denial of renewal.

Subpart E—Revocation or Denial

§ 771.40 Denial of initial application.

Whenever the Director of Industry Operations has reason to believe that an applicant for an original license or permit is not eligible to receive a license or permit under the provisions of § 555.49 of this chapter, the Director of Industry Operations shall issue a notice of denial on ATF Form 5400.11 (Notice of Denial of Application for License or Permit) (F 5400.11). The notice will set forth the matters of fact and law relied upon in determining that the application should be denied and will afford the applicant 15 days from the date of receipt of the notice in which to request a hearing to review the denial. If no request for a hearing is filed within that time, a copy of the application, marked "Disapproved," will be returned to the applicant.

§ 771.41 Denial of renewal application or revocation of license or permit.

If, following the opportunity for compliance under § 555.71 of this chapter, or without opportunity for compliance under § 555.71 of this chapter as circumstances warrant, the Director of Industry Operations finds that the licensee or permittee is not likely to comply with applicable laws or regulations in this part or is otherwise not eligible to continue operations authorized under his license or permit, the Di-

rector of Industry Operations shall issue a notice of denial of the renewal application or revocation of the license or permit, ATF F 5400.11 (Notice of Denial of Application for License or Permit) or ATF Form 5400.10 (Notice of Revocation of License or Permit) (F 5400.10), as appropriate. The notice will set forth the matters of fact constituting the violations specified, dates, places, and the sections of law and regulations violated. In the case of the revocation of a license or permit, the notice will specify the date on which the action is effective, which date will be on or after the date the notice is served on the licensee or permittee. The notice will also advise the licensee or permittee that he may, within 15 days after receipt of the notice, request a hearing and, if applicable, a stay of the effective date of the revocation of his license or permit.

§ 771.42 Grounds for revocation of licenses or permits.

Whenever the Director of Industry Operations has reason to believe that any holder of a license or permit has willfully violated any provision of 18 U.S.C. chapter 40 or 27 CFR part 555 or has become ineligible to continue operations authorized under the license or permit, the Director of Industry Operations shall issue a notice for the revocation of such license or permit, as the case may be.

§ 771.43 Grounds for denial of applications for licenses or permits.

If, upon examination of any application (including a renewal application) for a license or permit, the Director of Industry Operations has reason to believe that the applicant is not entitled to such license or permit, the Director of Industry Operations shall issue a denial of the application. An applicant is not eligible for a license or permit if he fails to meet the requirements of 18 U.S.C. 843(b) and § 555.49 of this chapter.

Subpart F—Hearing Procedure

NOTICES

§ 771.55 Content.

(a) Notices for the revocation or denial of renewal of a license or permit shall be promptly issued by the Director of Industry Operations and shall set forth:

(1) The sections of law and regulations relied upon for authority and jurisdiction;

(2) The specific grounds upon which the revocation or denial is based, *i.e.*, the matters of fact constituting the violations specified, dates, places, and sections of law and regulations violated;

(3) In the case of a revocation, the date on which the action is effective; and

(4) That the licensee or permittee has 15 days from receipt of the notice within which to request a hearing before an administrative law judge.

(b) Notices for the denial of an initial application for a license or permit shall set forth:

(1) The sections of law and regulations relied upon for authority and jurisdiction;

(2) The specific grounds upon which the denial is based, *i.e.*, the matters of fact and law relied upon for the disapproval of the application; and

(3) That the application will be disapproved unless a hearing is requested within 15 days from receipt of the notice.

§ 771.56 Forms.

Notices shall be issued on the following forms:

(a) ATF Form 5400.9, "Order After Denial or Revocation Hearing," for all revocations or denials of renewal of licenses or permits pursuant to 18 U.S.C. chapter 40 after a hearing has been held and a Recommended Decision has been issued by the administrative law judge;

(b) Form 5400.10, "Notice of Revocation for License or Permit," for all revocations of licenses or permits pursuant to 18 U.S.C. chapter 40, except as provided for in paragraph (a) of this section;

(c) Form 5400.11, "Notice of Denial of Application for License or Permit," for the denial of renewal or original applications for licenses or permits pursuant to 18 U.S.C. chapter 40, except as provided for in paragraph (a) of this section;

(d) Form 5400.12, "Notice of Contemplated Denial or Revocation of License or Permit," for the contemplated revocation or denial of renewal application of licenses or permits pursuant to 18 U.S.C. chapter 40; or

(e) Such other forms as the Director may prescribe.

§ 771.57 Execution and disposition.

A signed original of the applicable form shall be served on the licensee or permittee. If a hearing is requested, a copy shall be sent to the administrative law judge designated to conduct the hearing. Any remaining copies shall be retained for the office of the Director of Industry Operations.

§ 771.58 Designated place of hearing.

The designated place of hearing shall be determined by the administrative law judge, taking into consideration the convenience and necessity of the parties and their representatives.

REQUEST FOR HEARING

§ 771.59 Initial application proceedings.

(a) If the applicant for an initial license or permit desires a hearing, he shall file a request in writing with the Director of Industry Operations within 15 days after receipt of notice of the disapproval, in whole or in part, of the application.

(b) On receipt of the request, the Director of Industry Operations shall forward a copy of the request, together with a copy of the notice, to the Office of Chief Counsel for the assignment of an administrative law judge.

(c) After the Office of Chief Counsel notifies the Director of Industry Operations or the Attorney for the Government of the assignment of an administrative law judge, the Director of Industry Operations shall notify the licensee or permittee of the assignment, if the administrative law judge has not already done so.

§ 771.60 Revocation or denial of renewal proceedings.

(a) If the licensee or permittee desires a hearing, he shall file a request, in writing, with the Director of Industry Operations within 15 days after receipt of the notice or within such time as the Director of Industry Operations may allow.

· (b) Where a licensee or permittee requests a hearing, the Director of Industry Operations shall forward a copy of the request, together with a copy of the notice, to the Office of Chief Counsel for the assignment of an administrative law judge.

(c) After the Office of Chief Counsel notifies the Director of Industry Operations or the Attorney for the Government of the assignment of an administrative law judge, the Director of Industry Operations shall notify the licensee or permittee of the assignment, if the administrative law judge has not already done so.

(d) In the case of a revocation, a licensee or permittee may include a request for a stay of the effective date of revocation with the request for a hearing.

(e) On receipt of a request for a stay of the effective date of a revocation, the Director of Industry Operations shall timely advise the licensee or permittee whether the stay is granted.

(1) If the stay is granted, the matter shall be referred to an administrative law judge pursuant to paragraph (b) of this section.

(2) If the stay is denied, the licensee or permittee may request an immediate hearing. In this event, the Director of Industry Operations shall immediately refer the matter to the Office of Chief Counsel for the assignment of an administrative law judge, who shall set a date and place for hearing, which date shall be no later than 10 days from the date the licensee or permittee requested the immediate hearing.

§ 771.61 Notice of hearing.

Once a request for a hearing has been referred to the administrative law judge, the administrative law judge shall set a time and place for a hearing and shall serve notice thereof upon the parties at least 10 days in advance of the hearing date.

NON-REQUEST FOR HEARING

§ 771.62 Initial application.

In the case of an initial application, if the applicant does not request a hearing within 15 days, or within such additional time as the Director of Industry Operations may in his discretion allow, the Director of Industry Operations will return a copy of the application, marked "Disapproved," to the applicant, accompanied by a brief statement including the findings upon which the denial is based.

§ 771.63 Revocation or denial of renewal.

In the case of a revocation or denial of renewal of an application, if the licensee or permittee does not request a hearing within 15 days, or within such additional time as the Director of Industry Operations may in his discretion allow, the Director of Industry Operations shall make the initial decision in the case pursuant to § 771.78(b).

RESPONSES TO NOTICES

§ 771.64 Answers.

(a) Where the licensee or permittee requests a hearing in accordance with §§ 771.59 and 771.60, a written response to the relevant notice may be filed with the administrative law judge and served on the Director of Industry Operations within 15 days after the licensee or permittee receives service of the designation of the administrative law judge.

(b) Where no hearing is requested, the licensee or permittee may file a written answer to the relevant notice with the Director of Industry Operations within 15 days after service of the notice.

(c) An answer shall contain a concise statement of the facts that constitute the grounds for defense. A hearing, if requested, may be limited to the issues contained in the notice and the answer. The administrative law judge or Director of Industry Operations, as the case may be, may, as a matter of discretion, waive any requirement of this section.

(d) Answers need not be filed in initial application proceedings.

§ 771.65 Responses admitting facts.

If the licensee or permittee desires to waive the hearing on the allegations of fact set forth in the notice and does not contest the facts, the answer may consist of a statement that the licensee or permittee admits all material allegations of fact charged in the notice to be true. The Director of Industry Operations shall base the decision on the notice and such answer, although such an answer shall not affect the licensee's or permittee's right to submit proposed findings of fact and conclusions of law or right to appeal.

§ 771.66 Initial conferences.

(a) In any proceeding, the administrative law judge, upon his own motion or upon the motion of one of the parties or their qualified representatives, may in the administrative law judge's discretion direct the parties or their qualified representatives to appear at a specified time and place for a conference to consider:

(1) Simplification of the issues;

(2) The necessity of amendments to the pleadings;

(3) The possibility of obtaining stipulations, admissions of facts, and documents;

(4) The possibility of both parties exchanging information or scheduling discovery;

(5) A date on which both parties will simultaneously submit lists of proposed hearing exhibits;

(6) Limiting the number of expert witnesses;

(7) Identifying and, if practicable, scheduling all witnesses to be called; however, there is no requirement in these proceedings for the parties to submit pre-hearing statements or statements of proposed testimony by witnesses; and

(8) Such other matters as may aid in the disposition of the proceeding.

(b) As soon as practicable after such conference, the administrative law judge shall issue an order that recites the action taken, the amendments allowed to the pleadings, and the agreements made by the parties or their qualified representatives as to any of the matters considered. The order shall also limit the issues for hearing to those not disposed of by admission or agreement. Such order shall control the subsequent course of the proceedings, unless modified for good cause by a subsequent order. After discovery is complete, the order may be amended or supplemented if necessary.

§ 771.67 Initial applications.

Where the applicant on an initial application for a license or permit has requested a hearing and does not appear at the appointed time and place, evidence has not been offered to refute or explain the grounds upon which disapproval of the application is contemplated, and no good cause has been shown for the failure to appear, the applicant shall be considered to have waived the hearing. When such waiver occurs, a default judgment against the applicant will be entered and the administrative law judge shall recommend disapproval of said application.

§ 771.68 Revocation or denial of renewal.

If, on the date set for a hearing concerning the revocation or denial of renewal of a license or permit, the licensee or permittee does not appear, no evidence has been offered, and no good cause has been shown for the failure to appear, the Attorney for the Government will proceed ex parte and offer for the record sufficient evidence to make a *prima facie* case. At such hearing, documents, statements, and affidavits may be submitted in lieu of testimony of witnesses.

§ 771.69 Withdrawal of request for hearing.

At any time prior to the assignment of an administrative law judge, the licensee or permittee may, by filing written notice with the Director of Industry Operations, withdraw his request for a hearing. If such a notice is filed after assignment to the administrative law judge and prior to issuance of his recommended decision the Director of Industry Operations shall move the administrative law judge to dismiss the proceedings as moot. If such a notice is filed either after issuance of a notice of denial or notice of revocation and before assignment of the administrative law judge, or after issuance by the administrative law judge of his recommended decision and prior to the Director of Industry Operations' order disapproving the application or denying the renewal of or revoking the license or permit, the Director of Industry Operations shall, by order, dismiss the proceeding.

§ 771.70 Adjudication based upon written submissions.

The licensee or permittee may waive the hearing before the administrative law judge and stipulate that the matter will be adjudicated by the Director of Industry Operations based upon written submissions. Written submissions may include stipulations of law or facts, proposed findings of fact and conclusions of law, briefs, or any other documentary material. The pleadings, together with the written submissions of both the licensee or permittee and the attorney for the Government, shall constitute the record on which the initial decision shall be based. The election to contest the denial or revocation without a hearing under this section does not affect the licensee's or permittee's right to appeal to the Director pursuant to § 555.79 of this chapter or to the United States Court of Appeals for the circuit in which the licensee or permittee resides or has his principle place of business pursuant to § 555.80 of this chapter.

SURRENDER OF LICENSE OR PERMIT

§ 771.71 Before citation.

If a licensee or permittee surrenders the license or permit before the notice of revocation or denial of renewal, the Director of Industry Operations may accept the surrender. But if the evidence, in the opinion of the Director of Industry Operations, warrants issuance of a notice for revocation or denial of renewal, the surrender shall be refused and the Director of Industry Operations shall issue the notice.

§ 771.72 After citation.

If a licensee or permittee surrenders the license or permit after notice, but prior to the referral to an administrative law judge and prior to an initial decision, the Director of Industry Operations may accept the surrender of the license or permit and dismiss the proceeding as moot. If a licensee or permittee surrenders the license or permit

after notice and after the referral to the administrative law judge, but prior to the issuance of a recommended decision, the Director of Industry Operations may accept the surrender of the license or permit and shall move the administrative law judge to dismiss the proceedings as moot. In either case, if, in the opinion of the Director of Industry Operations, the evidence is such as to warrant revocation or denial of renewal, as the case may be, the surrender of the license or permit shall be refused, and the proceeding shall continue.

MOTIONS

§ 771.73 General.

All motions shall be made and addressed to the administrative law judge before whom the proceeding is pending, and copies of all motion papers shall be served upon the other party or parties. The administrative law judge may dispose of any motion without oral argument, but he may, if he so desires, set it down for hearing and request argument. The administrative law judge may dispose of such motion prior to the hearing on the merits or he may postpone the disposition until the hearing on the merits. No appeal may be taken from any ruling on a motion until the whole record is certified for review. Examples of typical motions may be found in the Rules of Civil Procedure referred to in § 771.2.

§ 771.74 Prior to hearing.

All motions that should be made prior to the hearing, such as a motion directed to the sufficiency of the pleadings or of preliminary orders, shall be filed in writing with the Director of Industry Operations or the administrative law judge if the matter has been referred to him, and shall briefly state the order or relief applied for and the grounds for such motion.

§ 771.75 At hearing.

Motions at the hearing may be made in writing to the administrative law judge or stated orally on the record.

§771.76 General.

If a hearing is requested, it shall be held at the time and place stated in the notice of hearing unless otherwise ordered by the administrative law judge.

§771.77 Initial applications.

(a) The administrative law judge who presides at the hearing on initial applications shall recommend a decision to the Director of Industry Operations. The administrative law judge shall certify the complete record of the proceedings before him and shall immediately forward the complete certified record to the Director of Industry Operations. The administrative law judge shall also send one copy of his recommended decision to the applicant or the applicant's representative, one copy to the Attorney for the Government, and one copy to the Director of Industry Operations, who shall make the initial decision as provided in §771.107. The applicant may be directed by the Director of Industry Operations to produce such records as may be deemed necessary for examination. All hearings on applications shall be open to the public subject to such restrictions and limitations as may be consistent with orderly procedure.

(b) If no hearing is requested, the return of the application marked "Disapproved" is the Director of Industry Operations' initial decision.

§771.78 Revocation or denial of renewal.

(a) The administrative law judge who presides at the hearing in proceedings for the revocation or denial of renewal of licenses or permits shall make a recommended decision to the Director of Industry Operations. The administrative law judge shall certify the complete record of the proceedings before him and shall immediately forward the complete certified record to the Director of Industry Operations. The administrative law judge shall also send one copy of his recommended decision to the licensee or permittee or the licensee's or permittee's representative, one copy to the Attorney for the Government, and one copy to the Director of Industry Operations, who shall make

the initial decision as provided in §771.109.

(b) If no hearing is requested, the Director of Industry Operations shall make the initial decision.

§771.79 Initial applications.

In hearings on the initial denial of applications, the burden of proof is on the Government to show by a preponderance of the evidence that the Director of Industry Operations had reason to believe that the applicant is not entitled to a permit or license.

§771.80 Revocation or denial of renewal.

In hearings on the revocation or denial of renewal of a license or permit, the burden of proof is on the Government to show that the Director of Industry Operations had reason to believe that the licensee or permittee is not entitled to a permit or license, as may be the case. The Government must meet this proof by a preponderance of the evidence.

§771.81 Stipulations at hearing.

If there has been no initial conference under §771.66, the administrative law judge may at the beginning of the hearing require that the parties attempt to arrive at such stipulations as will eliminate the necessity of taking evidence with respect to allegations of fact about which there is no substantial dispute. The administrative law judge should take similar action, where appropriate, throughout the hearing and should call and conduct any conferences that he deems advisable with a view to the simplification, clarification, and disposition of any of the issues involved in the hearing.

§771.82 Evidence.

The Federal Rules of Evidence are not binding on these proceedings. However, any relevant evidence that would be admissible under the rules of evidence governing civil proceedings in matters not involving trial by jury in the Courts of the United States shall be admissible. The administrative law judge may relax such rules in any hearing when in his judgment such relaxation would not impair the rights of either party and would more speedily conclude the hearing or would better serve the ends of justice. However, the administrative law judge shall provide for the exclusion of irrelevant, immaterial, or unduly repetitious evidence. Every party shall have the right to present his case or defense by oral or documentary evidence, depositions, or duly authenticated copies of records and documents; to submit rebuttal evidence; and to conduct such reasonable cross-examination as may be required for a full and true disclosure of the facts.

(a) *Witnesses.* The administrative law judge shall have the right in his discretion to limit the number of witnesses whose testimony may be merely cumulative and shall, as a matter of policy, not only exclude irrelevant, immaterial, or unduly repetitious evidence but shall also limit the cross-examination of witnesses to that required for a full and true disclosure of the facts so as not to unnecessarily prolong the hearing and unduly burden the record. Opinion or expert testimony shall be admitted when the administrative law judge is satisfied that the witness is properly qualified as defined by Federal Rules of Evidence 701 or 702.

(b) *Documentary evidence.* Material and relevant evidence shall not be excluded because it is not the best evidence unless its authenticity is challenged, in which case reasonable time shall be given to establish its authenticity. When only portions of a document are to be relied upon, the offering party shall prepare the pertinent excerpts, adequately identified, and shall supply copies of such excerpts, together with a statement indicating the purpose for which such materials will be offered, to the administrative law judge and to the other parties. Only the excerpts, so prepared and submitted, shall be received in the record. However, the whole of the original document should be made available for examination and for use by opposing counsel for purposes of cross-examination. Compilations, charts, summaries of data, and photocopies of documents may be admitted in evidence if the proceedings will thereby be expedited, and if the material upon which they are based is available for examination by the parties. Objections to the evidence shall be in short form, stating the grounds relied upon. The transcript shall not include argument or debate on objections, except as ordered by the administrative law judge, but shall include the rulings thereon. Where official notice is taken of a material fact not appearing in the evidence in the record, any party shall, on timely request, be afforded an opportunity to controvert such fact.

(c) *Hearsay.* Probative, material, and reliable hearsay evidence is admissible in proceedings under this subpart.

§ 771.83 Closing of hearings; arguments, briefs, and proposed findings.

Before closing a hearing, the administrative law judge shall inquire of each party whether the party has any further evidence to offer, which inquiry and the response thereto shall be shown in the record. The administrative law judge may hear arguments of counsel and the administrative law judge may limit the time of such arguments at his discretion. The administrative law judge may, in his discretion, allow briefs to be filed on behalf of either party but shall closely limit the time within which the briefs for both parties shall be filed, so as to avoid unreasonable delay. The administrative law judge shall also ascertain whether the parties desire to submit proposed findings and conclusions, together with supporting reasons, and, if so, a period of not more than 15 days (unless extended by the administrative law judge)—after the close of the hearing or receipt of a copy of the record, if one is requested—will be allowed for such purpose.

§ 771.84 Reopening of the hearing.

The Director, the Director of Industry Operations, or the administrative law judge, as the case may be, may, as to all matters pending before him, in his discretion reopen a hearing—

(a) In case of default under § 771.67 or § 771.68 where the applicant, licensee, or permittee failed to request a hearing or to appear after one was set, upon petition setting forth reasonable grounds for such failure; and

(b) Where any party desires leave to adduce additional evidence upon petition summarizing such evidence, establishing its materiality, and stating reasonable grounds why such party with due diligence was unable to produce such evidence at the hearing.

RECORD OF TESTIMONY

§771.85 Stenographic record.

A stenographic record shall be made of the testimony and proceedings, including stipulations, admissions of fact, and arguments of counsel in all proceedings. A transcript of the evidence and proceedings at the hearing shall be made in all cases.

§771.86 Oath of reporter.

The reporter making the stenographic record shall subscribe an oath before the administrative law judge, to be filed in the record of the case, that he will truly and correctly report the oral testimony and proceedings at such hearing and accurately transcribe the same to the best of his ability.

Subpart G—Administrative Law Judges

§771.95 Responsibilities of administrative law judges.

In hearings under this subpart, administrative law judges must apply all governing agency rulings and governing agency precedent. They shall be responsible for the conduct of hearings and shall render their decisions as soon as is reasonably possible after the hearing is closed. Administrative law judges shall also be responsible for the preparation, certification, and forwarding of the complete record of proceedings and the administrative work relating thereto and, by arrangement with Directors of Industry Operations and representatives of the Office of Chief Counsel shall have access to facilities and temporary use of personnel at such times and places as are needed in the prompt dispatch of official business.

§771.96 Disqualification.

An administrative law judge shall, at any time, withdraw from any proceeding if he deems himself disqualified. Upon the filing in good faith by the applicant, licensee, permittee, or Attorney for the Government of a timely and sufficient affidavit of facts showing personal bias or otherwise warranting the disqualification of any administrative law judge, if the administrative law judge fails to disqualify himself, the Director shall upon appeal, as provided in §771.120, determine the matter as a part of the record and decision in the proceeding. If the Director decides the administrative law judge should have deemed himself disqualified, the Director will remand the record for hearing de novo before another administrative law judge. If the Director should decide against the disqualification of the administrative law judge, the proceeding will be reviewed on its merits by the original administrative law judge. The burden is upon the party seeking disqualification to set forth evidence sufficient to overcome the presumption of the administrative law judge's honesty and integrity.

§771.97 Powers.

Administrative law judges shall have authority to:

(a) Administer oaths and affirmations;

(b) Issue subpoenas as authorized by law;

(c) Rule upon offers of proof and receive relevant evidence;

(d) Take or cause depositions to be taken whenever the ends of justice would be served thereby;

(e) Regulate the course of the hearing;

(f) Hold conferences for the settlement or simplification of the issues by consent of the parties;

(g) Require the attendance at such conferences of at least one representative of each party who has the authority to negotiate concerning resolution of issues in controversy;

(h) Dispose of procedural requests or similar matters;

(i) Render recommended decisions in proceedings on applications for licenses and permits and on revocation or denial of renewal of licenses or permits;

(j) Call, examine, and cross-examine witnesses, including hostile or adverse witnesses, when the administrative law judge deems such action to be necessary to a just disposition of the case, and introduce into the record documentary or other evidence; and

(k) Take any other action authorized by rule of the Bureau of Alcohol, Tobacco, Firearms, and Explosives consistent with the Administrative Procedure Act. *See* 5 U.S.C. 556(c) and 18 U.S.C. 843.

§ 771.98 Separation of functions.

Administrative law judges shall perform no functions inconsistent with their duties and responsibilities. The Director may assign administrative law judges duties not inconsistent with the performance of their functions as administrative law judges. Except to the extent required for the disposition of ex parte matters as required by law, no administrative law judge shall consult any person or party as to any fact in issue unless there has been notice and opportunity for all parties to participate. The functions of the administrative law judge shall be entirely separated from the general investigative functions of the agency. No officer, employee, or agent engaged in the performance of investigative or prosecuting functions in any proceeding shall, in that proceeding or a factually related proceeding, participate or advise in the administrative law judge's or Director's decision, or in the agency review on appeal, except as a witness or counsel in the proceedings. The administrative law judge may not informally obtain advice or opinions from the parties or their counsel, or from any officer or employee of the ATF, as to the facts or the weight or interpretation to be given to the evidence. The administrative law judge may, however, informally obtain advice on matters of law or procedure in a proceeding from officers or employees who were not engaged in the performance of investigative or prosecuting functions in that proceeding or a factually related proceeding. The administrative law judge may, at any time, consult with

and obtain instructions from the Director on questions of law and policy. Furthermore, it is not a violation of the separation of functions for the administrative law judge to participate in the questioning of witnesses, where the questioning is for clarification or to move the proceedings along, and where the questioning is not so extensive as to place the administrative law judge in the position of a prosecuting officer.

§ 771.99 Conduct of hearing.

The administrative law judge is charged with the duty of conducting a fair and impartial hearing and of maintaining order in form and manner consistent with the dignity of a court proceeding. In the event that counsel or any person or witness in any proceeding shall refuse to obey the orders of the administrative law judge, or be guilty of disorderly or contemptuous language or conduct in connection with any hearing, the administrative law judge may, for good cause stated in the record, suspend the hearing and, in the case of disorderly or contemptuous language or conduct by an attorney, report the matter to the Department of Justice, Office of Professional Responsibility. *See* 28 CFR 0.39a(a)(9). The refusal of a witness to answer any question that has been ruled to be proper shall be considered by the administrative law judge in determining the weight to be given all the testimony of that witness.

§ 771.100 Unavailability of administrative law judge.

In the event that the administrative law judge designated to conduct a hearing becomes unavailable before the filing of his findings and recommended decision, the Director may assign the case to another administrative law judge for the continuance of the proceeding, in accordance with the regulations in this part in the same manner as if he had been designated administrative law judge at the commencement of the proceeding.

Subpart H—Decisions

§771.105 Administrative law judge's findings and recommended decision.

Within a reasonable time after the conclusion of the hearing, and as expeditiously as possible, the administrative law judge shall render his recommended decision. All decisions shall become a part of the record and, if proposed findings and conclusions have been filed, shall show the administrative law judge's ruling upon each of such proposed findings and conclusions. Decisions shall consist of:

(a) A brief statement of the issues of fact involved in the proceeding;

(b) The administrative law judge's findings and conclusions, as well as the reasons or basis therefor with record references, upon all the material issues of fact, law, or discretion presented on the record (including, when appropriate, comment as to the credibility and demeanor of the witnesses); and

(c) The administrative law judge's recommended determination as to the revocation or denial at issue.

§771.106 Certification and transmittal of record and decision.

After reaching his decision, the administrative law judge shall certify the complete record of the proceeding before him and shall immediately forward the complete certified record together with one copy of the administrative law judge's recommended decision to the Director of Industry Operations for initial decision, one copy of the recommended decision to the applicant or the applicant's representative, and one copy of the recommended decision to the Attorney for the Government.

ACTION BY DIRECTOR OF INDUSTRY OPERATIONS

§771.107 Initial application proceedings.

(a) *Accepting the recommended decision.* If the Director of Industry Operations, after consideration of the record of the hearing and of any proposed findings, conclusions, or exceptions filed with him by the applicant, accepts the recommended decision of the administrative law judge, the Director of Industry Operations shall by order approve or disapprove of the application in accordance with the recommended decision. If the Director of Industry Operations approves the application, he shall briefly state for the record his reasons therefor. However, if the Director of Industry Operations disapproves of the applications, he shall serve a copy of the administrative law judge's recommended decision on the applicant, informing the applicant of the Director of Industry Operations' contemplated action and affording the applicant not more than 10 days in which to submit proposed findings and conclusions or exceptions to the recommended decision with reasons in support thereof.

(b) *Rejecting the recommended decision.* If, after such consideration referenced in paragraph (a) of this section, the Director of Industry Operations rejects the recommended decision of the administrative law judge, in whole or in part, the Director of Industry Operations shall by order make such findings and conclusions as in his opinion are warranted by the law and facts in the record. Any decision of the Director of Industry Operations ordering the disapproval of an application for a permit shall state the findings and conclusions upon which it is based, including his ruling upon each proposed finding, conclusion, and exception to the administrative law judge's recommended decision, together with a statement of the administrative law judge's findings, conclusions, and reasons or basis therefor, upon all material issues of fact, law, or discretion presented on the record. A signed original of the decision of the Director of Industry Operations shall be served upon the applicant and the original copy containing a certificate of service shall be placed in the official record of the proceeding.

§771.108 Director of Industry Operations' decision.

When the Director of Industry Operations issues an initial decision in accordance with §771.77 or §771.107 the decision shall become a part of the record. The decision shall consist of:

(a) A brief statement of the issues involved in the proceedings;

(b) The Director of Industry Operations' findings and conclusions, as well as the reasons therefor; and

(c) The Director of Industry Operations' determination on the record.

§ 771.109 Revocation or denial of renewal proceedings.

(a) *Accepting the recommended decision.* After consideration of the complete certified record of the hearing, if the Director of Industry Operations agrees with the recommended decision of the administrative law judge, the Director of Industry Operations shall enter an order revoking or denying the renewal of the license or permit or dismissing the proceedings in accordance with the administrative law judge's recommended decision.

(b) *Rejecting the recommended decision.* After consideration of the complete certified record of the hearing, if the Director of Industry Operations disagrees with the recommended decision of the administrative law judge, he may file a petition with the Director for review of the recommended decision, as provided in § 771.120. If the Director of Industry Operations files such a petition, he shall withhold issuance of the order pending the decision of the Director, upon receipt of which he shall issue the order in accordance with the Director's decision. A signed original of the order of the Director of Industry Operations shall be served upon the licensee or permittee or his representative and the original copy containing a certificate of service shall be placed in the official record of the proceeding.

(c) *Decisions pursuant to § 771.78(b).* In a case where the initial decision is made by the Director of Industry Operations in accordance with § 771.78(b), the Director of Industry Operations shall also issue an order revoking or denying the renewal of the license or permit, or dismissing the proceedings in accordance with his initial decision. A signed original of the decision and order of the Director of Industry Operations shall be served upon the licensee or permittee or his representative and the original copy placed in the official record of the proceeding.

§ 771.110 Revocation or denial of renewal.

Pursuant to § 771.109(a), when the Director of Industry Operations issues an order revoking or denying the renewal of a license or permit, he shall furnish a copy of the order and of the recommended decision on which it is based to the Director. Should such order be subsequently set aside on review by the courts, the Director of Industry Operations will so advise the Director.

§ 771.111 Proceedings involving violations not within the division of issuance of license or permit.

In the event violations occurred at a place not within the field division where the licensee or permittee is located, the Director of Industry Operations of the field division where the licensee or permittee is located will take jurisdiction over any proceeding and will take appropriate action in accordance with this subpart, including issuing the relevant notice.

Subpart I—Review

§ 771.120 Appeal on petition to the Director.

(a) An appeal to the Director may be made by the applicant, licensee, or permittee, or by the Director of Industry Operations (DIO). For the applicant, licensee, or permittee, such appeal shall be made by filing a petition for review on appeal with the Director within 15 days of the service of the adverse initial decision by the Director of Industry Operations. For the Director of Industry Operations, such appeal shall be taken by filing a petition for review on appeal with the Director within 15 days of the issuance of the administrative law judge's decision recommending against revocation or denial of renewal. The petitioning applicant, licensee, or permittee must submit arguments showing that the Director of Industry Operations' initial decision, and if applicable the underlying administrative law judge's recommended decision, was without reasonable warrant in fact or contrary to law and regulations. The petitioning DIO must submit arguments showing the administrative law judge's recommended decision was without reasonable warrant in fact or contrary to law and regulations. Nothing in this part shall limit the authority of the Director to review the administrative law judge's decision exercising all the powers that he would have in making the recommended decision.

(b) A copy of the petition shall be filed with the Director of Industry Operations or served on the applicant, licensee, or permittee, as the case may be. In the event of an appeal, the Director of Industry Operations shall immediately certify and forward the complete original record, by certified mail, to the Director, for his consideration and review.

§771.121   Review by Director.

(a) *Modification or reversal.* On appeal, the Director shall afford a reasonable opportunity for the submission of proposed findings, conclusions, or exceptions with reasons in support thereof and an opportunity for oral argument. The Director may alter or modify any finding of the administrative law judge (or of the Director of Industry Operations as the case may be) and may affirm, reverse, or modify the recommended decision of the administrative law judge, or the initial decision of the Director of Industry Operations, or may remand the case for further hearing, but shall not consider evidence that is not a part of the record.

(b) *Affirmance.* Except in the case of a remand, when, on appeal, the Director affirms the initial decision of the Director of Industry Operations or the recommended decision of the administrative law judge, as the case may be, such decision shall be the agency's final decision.

(c) *Recusal.* Appeals and petitions for review shall not be decided by the Director in any proceeding in which the Director has engaged in an investigation or prosecution and in such event the Director shall so state his disqualification in writing and refer the record to the Deputy Director for appropriate action. The Deputy Director may designate an Assistant Director or one of the Deputy Director's principal aides to consider any proceeding instead of the Director. The original copy of the decision on review shall be placed in the official record of the proceeding, a signed duplicate original shall be served upon the applicant, licensee, or permittee, and a copy shall be transmitted to the Director of Industry Operations.

§771.122   Denial of renewal or revocation.

If the Director orders the denial of an application, a copy of the application marked "Disapproved" will be returned to the applicant by the Director of Industry Operations. If the Director orders a revocation of a license of permit, any stay of revocation will be withdrawn and the revocation will become effective upon the order of the Director of Industry Operations. After the issuance of a denial of a renewal application or a revocation, and pending the final determination of a timely appeal, the licensee or permittee may continue operations, if at all, pursuant to §555.83 of this chapter.

§771.123   Court review.

(a) If an applicant, licensee, or permittee files an appeal in the United States Court of Appeals for the circuit in which he resides or has his principle place of business, within 60 days after the receipt of the Director's decision, the Director, upon notification that an appeal has been taken, shall prepare the record for submission to the court in accordance with applicable court rules.

(b) If an applicant, licensee, or permittee does not seek review with the Director, but instead seeks review within 60 days after the receipt of the initial decision of the Director of Industry Operations pursuant to §771.109, the Director of Industry Operations, upon notification that an appeal has been taken, shall prepare the record for submission to the court in accordance with applicable court rules. The Director of Industry Operations shall notify the Director if such an appeal is taken.

(c) The Director, or the Director of Industry Operations, as the case may be, shall certify the correctness of the transcript of the record, forward one copy to the attorney for the Government in the review of the case, and file the original record of the proceedings with the original certificate in the appropriate United States Court of Appeals.

Subpart J—Miscellaneous

§ 771.124 Depositions.

The administrative law judge may take or order the taking of depositions by either party to the proceeding at such time and place as the administrative law judge may designate before a person having the power to administer oaths, upon application therefor and notice to the parties to the action. The testimony shall be reduced to writing by the person taking the deposition, or a person under his direction, and the deposition shall be subscribed by the deponent unless subscribing thereof is waived in writing by the parties.

§ 771.125 Witnesses and fees.

Witnesses summoned before the administrative law judge may be paid the same fees and mileage that are paid witnesses in the courts of the United States, and witnesses whose depositions are taken and the persons taking the same shall severally be entitled to the same fees as are paid for like services in the courts of the United States. Witness fees and mileage shall be paid by the party at whose instance the witnesses appear and the person taking the deposition shall be paid by the party at whose instance the deposition is taken.

§ 771.126 Discovery.

The discovery provisions of the Federal Rules of Civil Procedure and the Federal Rules of Criminal Procedure are not controlling with respect to agency proceedings under this part.

However, fundamental fairness requires a party be given the opportunity to know what evidence is offered and a chance to rebut such evidence. Either party may petition the administrative law judge . for non-burdensome discovery if the party can demonstrate that the interests of justice require disclosure of these materials.

§ 771.127 Privileges.

The Administrative Procedure Act, 5 U.S.C. 559, provides that, except as otherwise required by law, privileges relating to procedure or evidence apply equally to agencies and persons. Therefore, an agency may rely on judicially-approved privileges to resist production of its files where appropriate.

RECORD

§ 771.135 What constitutes record.

The transcript of testimony, pleadings, exhibits, all papers and requests filed in the proceeding, and all findings, decisions, and orders, shall constitute the exclusive record. Where the decision rests on official notice of material fact not appearing in the record, the administrative law judge shall so state in his findings and any party shall, on timely request, be afforded an opportunity to show facts to the contrary.

§ 771.136 Availability.

A copy of the record shall be available for inspection or copying by the parties to the proceedings during business hours at the office of the administrative law judge or the Director of Industry Operations or, pending administrative review, at the Office of the Director.

PARTS 772–799 [RESERVED]

FINDING AIDS

A list of CFR titles, subtitles, chapters, subchapters and parts and an alphabetical list of agencies publishing in the CFR are included in the CFR Index and Finding Aids volume to the Code of Federal Regulations which is published separately and revised annually.

Table of CFR Titles and Chapters
Alphabetical List of Agencies Appearing in the CFR
List of CFR Sections Affected

Table of CFR Titles and Chapters

(Revised as of April 1, 2023)

Title 1—General Provisions

I   Administrative Committee of the Federal Register (Parts 1—49)
II   Office of the Federal Register (Parts 50—299)
III   Administrative Conference of the United States (Parts 300—399)
IV   Miscellaneous Agencies (Parts 400—599)
VI   National Capital Planning Commission (Parts 600—699)

Title 2—Grants and Agreements

SUBTITLE A—OFFICE OF MANAGEMENT AND BUDGET GUIDANCE FOR GRANTS AND AGREEMENTS

I   Office of Management and Budget Governmentwide Guidance for Grants and Agreements (Parts 2—199)
II   Office of Management and Budget Guidance (Parts 200—299)

SUBTITLE B—FEDERAL AGENCY REGULATIONS FOR GRANTS AND AGREEMENTS

III   Department of Health and Human Services (Parts 300—399)
IV   Department of Agriculture (Parts 400—499)
VI   Department of State (Parts 600—699)
VII   Agency for International Development (Parts 700—799)
VIII   Department of Veterans Affairs (Parts 800—899)
IX   Department of Energy (Parts 900—999)
X   Department of the Treasury (Parts 1000—1099)
XI   Department of Defense (Parts 1100—1199)
XII   Department of Transportation (Parts 1200—1299)
XIII   Department of Commerce (Parts 1300—1399)
XIV   Department of the Interior (Parts 1400—1499)
XV   Environmental Protection Agency (Parts 1500—1599)
XVIII   National Aeronautics and Space Administration (Parts 1800—1899)
XX   United States Nuclear Regulatory Commission (Parts 2000—2099)
XXII   Corporation for National and Community Service (Parts 2200—2299)
XXIII   Social Security Administration (Parts 2300—2399)
XXIV   Department of Housing and Urban Development (Parts 2400—2499)
XXV   National Science Foundation (Parts 2500—2599)
XXVI   National Archives and Records Administration (Parts 2600—2699)

Title 2—Grants and Agreements—Continued

Chap.

XXVII	Small Business Administration (Parts 2700—2799)
XXVIII	Department of Justice (Parts 2800—2899)
XXIX	Department of Labor (Parts 2900—2999)
XXX	Department of Homeland Security (Parts 3000—3099)
XXXI	Institute of Museum and Library Services (Parts 3100—3199)
XXXII	National Endowment for the Arts (Parts 3200—3299)
XXXIII	National Endowment for the Humanities (Parts 3300—3399)
XXXIV	Department of Education (Parts 3400—3499)
XXXV	Export-Import Bank of the United States (Parts 3500—3599)
XXXVI	Office of National Drug Control Policy, Executive Office of the President (Parts 3600—3699)
XXXVII	Peace Corps (Parts 3700—3799)
LVIII	Election Assistance Commission (Parts 5800—5899)
LIX	Gulf Coast Ecosystem Restoration Council (Parts 5900—5999)
LX	Federal Communications Commission (Parts 6000—6099)

Title 3—The President

| I | Executive Office of the President (Parts 100—199) |

Title 4—Accounts

| I | Government Accountability Office (Parts 1—199) |

Title 5—Administrative Personnel

I	Office of Personnel Management (Parts 1—1199)
II	Merit Systems Protection Board (Parts 1200—1299)
III	Office of Management and Budget (Parts 1300—1399)
IV	Office of Personnel Management and Office of the Director of National Intelligence (Parts 1400—1499)
V	The International Organizations Employees Loyalty Board (Parts 1500—1599)
VI	Federal Retirement Thrift Investment Board (Parts 1600—1699)
VIII	Office of Special Counsel (Parts 1800—1899)
IX	Appalachian Regional Commission (Parts 1900—1999)
XI	Armed Forces Retirement Home (Parts 2100—2199)
XIV	Federal Labor Relations Authority, General Counsel of the Federal Labor Relations Authority and Federal Service Impasses Panel (Parts 2400—2499)
XVI	Office of Government Ethics (Parts 2600—2699)
XXI	Department of the Treasury (Parts 3100—3199)
XXII	Federal Deposit Insurance Corporation (Parts 3200—3299)
XXIII	Department of Energy (Parts 3300—3399)
XXIV	Federal Energy Regulatory Commission (Parts 3400—3499)
XXV	Department of the Interior (Parts 3500—3599)

Title 5—Administrative Personnel—Continued

XXVI   Department of Defense (Parts 3600—3699)
XXVIII   Department of Justice (Parts 3800—3899)
XXIX   Federal Communications Commission (Parts 3900—3999)
XXX   Farm Credit System Insurance Corporation (Parts 4000—4099)
XXXI   Farm Credit Administration (Parts 4100—4199)
XXXIII   U.S. International Development Finance Corporation (Parts 4300—4399)
XXXIV   Securities and Exchange Commission (Parts 4400—4499)
XXXV   Office of Personnel Management (Parts 4500—4599)
XXXVI   Department of Homeland Security (Parts 4600—4699)
XXXVII   Federal Election Commission (Parts 4700—4799)
XL   Interstate Commerce Commission (Parts 5000—5099)
XLI   Commodity Futures Trading Commission (Parts 5100—5199)
XLII   Department of Labor (Parts 5200—5299)
XLIII   National Science Foundation (Parts 5300—5399)
XLV   Department of Health and Human Services (Parts 5500—5599)
XLVI   Postal Rate Commission (Parts 5600—5699)
XLVII   Federal Trade Commission (Parts 5700—5799)
XLVIII   Nuclear Regulatory Commission (Parts 5800—5899)
XLIX   Federal Labor Relations Authority (Parts 5900—5999)
L   Department of Transportation (Parts 6000—6099)
LII   Export-Import Bank of the United States (Parts 6200—6299)
LIII   Department of Education (Parts 6300—6399)
LIV   Environmental Protection Agency (Parts 6400—6499)
LV   National Endowment for the Arts (Parts 6500—6599)
LVI   National Endowment for the Humanities (Parts 6600—6699)
LVII   General Services Administration (Parts 6700—6799)
LVIII   Board of Governors of the Federal Reserve System (Parts 6800—6899)
LIX   National Aeronautics and Space Administration (Parts 6900—6999)
LX   United States Postal Service (Parts 7000—7099)
LXI   National Labor Relations Board (Parts 7100—7199)
LXII   Equal Employment Opportunity Commission (Parts 7200—7299)
LXIII   Inter-American Foundation (Parts 7300—7399)
LXIV   Merit Systems Protection Board (Parts 7400—7499)
LXV   Department of Housing and Urban Development (Parts 7500—7599)
LXVI   National Archives and Records Administration (Parts 7600—7699)
LXVII   Institute of Museum and Library Services (Parts 7700—7799)
LXVIII   Commission on Civil Rights (Parts 7800—7899)
LXIX   Tennessee Valley Authority (Parts 7900—7999)
LXX   Court Services and Offender Supervision Agency for the District of Columbia (Parts 8000—8099)
LXXI   Consumer Product Safety Commission (Parts 8100—8199)

217

Title 5—Administrative Personnel—Continued

Chap.

LXXIII   Department of Agriculture (Parts 8300—8399)

LXXIV   Federal Mine Safety and Health Review Commission (Parts 8400—8499)

LXXVI   Federal Retirement Thrift Investment Board (Parts 8600—8699)

LXXVII   Office of Management and Budget (Parts 8700—8799)

LXXX   Federal Housing Finance Agency (Parts 9000—9099)

LXXXIII   Special Inspector General for Afghanistan Reconstruction (Parts 9300—9399)

LXXXIV   Bureau of Consumer Financial Protection (Parts 9400—9499)

LXXXVI   National Credit Union Administration (Parts 9600—9699)

XCVII   Department of Homeland Security Human Resources Management System (Department of Homeland Security—Office of Personnel Management) (Parts 9700—9799)

XCVIII   Council of the Inspectors General on Integrity and Efficiency (Parts 9800—9899)

XCIX   Military Compensation and Retirement Modernization Commission (Parts 9900—9999)

C   National Council on Disability (Parts 10000—10049)

CI   National Mediation Board (Parts 10100—10199)

CII   U.S. Office of Special Counsel (Parts 10200—10299)

CIV   Office of the Intellectual Property Enforcement Coordinator (Part 10400—10499)

Title 6—Domestic Security

I   Department of Homeland Security, Office of the Secretary (Parts 1—199)

X   Privacy and Civil Liberties Oversight Board (Parts 1000—1099)

Title 7—Agriculture

SUBTITLE A—OFFICE OF THE SECRETARY OF AGRICULTURE (PARTS 0—26)

SUBTITLE B—REGULATIONS OF THE DEPARTMENT OF AGRICULTURE

I   Agricultural Marketing Service (Standards, Inspections, Marketing Practices), Department of Agriculture (Parts 27—209)

II   Food and Nutrition Service, Department of Agriculture (Parts 210—299)

III   Animal and Plant Health Inspection Service, Department of Agriculture (Parts 300—399)

IV   Federal Crop Insurance Corporation, Department of Agriculture (Parts 400—499)

V   Agricultural Research Service, Department of Agriculture (Parts 500—599)

VI   Natural Resources Conservation Service, Department of Agriculture (Parts 600—699)

VII   Farm Service Agency, Department of Agriculture (Parts 700—799)

Title 7—Agriculture—Continued

Chap.

VIII   Agricultural Marketing Service (Federal Grain Inspection Service, Fair Trade Practices Program), Department of Agriculture (Parts 800—899)

IX   Agricultural Marketing Service (Marketing Agreements and Orders; Fruits, Vegetables, Nuts), Department of Agriculture (Parts 900—999)

X   Agricultural Marketing Service (Marketing Agreements and Orders; Milk), Department of Agriculture (Parts 1000—1199)

XI   Agricultural Marketing Service (Marketing Agreements and Orders; Miscellaneous Commodities), Department of Agriculture (Parts 1200—1299)

XIV   Commodity Credit Corporation, Department of Agriculture (Parts 1400—1499)

XV   Foreign Agricultural Service, Department of Agriculture (Parts 1500—1599)

XVI   [Reserved]

XVII   Rural Utilities Service, Department of Agriculture (Parts 1700—1799)

XVIII   Rural Housing Service, Rural Business-Cooperative Service, Rural Utilities Service, and Farm Service Agency, Department of Agriculture (Parts 1800—2099)

XX   [Reserved]

XXV   Office of Advocacy and Outreach, Department of Agriculture (Parts 2500—2599)

XXVI   Office of Inspector General, Department of Agriculture (Parts 2600—2699)

XXVII   Office of Information Resources Management, Department of Agriculture (Parts 2700—2799)

XXVIII   Office of Operations, Department of Agriculture (Parts 2800—2899)

XXIX   Office of Energy Policy and New Uses, Department of Agriculture (Parts 2900—2999)

XXX   Office of the Chief Financial Officer, Department of Agriculture (Parts 3000—3099)

XXXI   Office of Environmental Quality, Department of Agriculture (Parts 3100—3199)

XXXII   Office of Procurement and Property Management, Department of Agriculture (Parts 3200—3299)

XXXIII   Office of Transportation, Department of Agriculture (Parts 3300—3399)

XXXIV   National Institute of Food and Agriculture (Parts 3400—3499)

XXXV   Rural Housing Service, Department of Agriculture (Parts 3500—3599)

XXXVI   National Agricultural Statistics Service, Department of Agriculture (Parts 3600—3699)

XXXVII   Economic Research Service, Department of Agriculture (Parts 3700—3799)

XXXVIII   World Agricultural Outlook Board, Department of Agriculture (Parts 3800—3899)

XLI   [Reserved]

Title 7—Agriculture—Continued

Chap.

XLII   Rural Business-Cooperative Service and Rural Utilities Service, Department of Agriculture (Parts 4200—4299)

L   Rural Business-Cooperative Service, and Rural Utilities Service, Department of Agriculture (Parts 5000—5099)

Title 8—Aliens and Nationality

I   Department of Homeland Security (Parts 1—499)

V   Executive Office for Immigration Review, Department of Justice (Parts 1000—1399)

Title 9—Animals and Animal Products

I   Animal and Plant Health Inspection Service, Department of Agriculture (Parts 1—199)

II   Agricultural Marketing Service (Fair Trade Practices Program), Department of Agriculture (Parts 200—299)

III   Food Safety and Inspection Service, Department of Agriculture (Parts 300—599)

Title 10—Energy

I   Nuclear Regulatory Commission (Parts 0—199)

II   Department of Energy (Parts 200—699)

III   Department of Energy (Parts 700—999)

X   Department of Energy (General Provisions) (Parts 1000—1099)

XIII   Nuclear Waste Technical Review Board (Parts 1300—1399)

XVII   Defense Nuclear Facilities Safety Board (Parts 1700—1799)

XVIII   Northeast Interstate Low-Level Radioactive Waste Commission (Parts 1800—1899)

Title 11—Federal Elections

I   Federal Election Commission (Parts 1—9099)

II   Election Assistance Commission (Parts 9400—9499)

Title 12—Banks and Banking

I   Comptroller of the Currency, Department of the Treasury (Parts 1—199)

II   Federal Reserve System (Parts 200—299)

III   Federal Deposit Insurance Corporation (Parts 300—399)

IV   Export-Import Bank of the United States (Parts 400—499)

V   [Reserved]

VI   Farm Credit Administration (Parts 600—699)

VII   National Credit Union Administration (Parts 700—799)

VIII   Federal Financing Bank (Parts 800—899)

IX   (Parts 900—999)[Reserved]

Title 12—Banks and Banking—Continued

Chap.

X Consumer Financial Protection Bureau (Parts 1000—1099)

XI Federal Financial Institutions Examination Council (Parts 1100—1199)

XII Federal Housing Finance Agency (Parts 1200—1299)

XIII Financial Stability Oversight Council (Parts 1300—1399)

XIV Farm Credit System Insurance Corporation (Parts 1400—1499)

XV Department of the Treasury (Parts 1500—1599)

XVI Office of Financial Research, Department of the Treasury (Parts 1600—1699)

XVII Office of Federal Housing Enterprise Oversight, Department of Housing and Urban Development (Parts 1700—1799)

XVIII Community Development Financial Institutions Fund, Department of the Treasury (Parts 1800—1899)

Title 13—Business Credit and Assistance

I Small Business Administration (Parts 1—199)

III Economic Development Administration, Department of Commerce (Parts 300—399)

IV Emergency Steel Guarantee Loan Board (Parts 400—499)

V Emergency Oil and Gas Guaranteed Loan Board (Parts 500—599)

Title 14—Aeronautics and Space

I Federal Aviation Administration, Department of Transportation (Parts 1—199)

II Office of the Secretary, Department of Transportation (Aviation Proceedings) (Parts 200—399)

III Commercial Space Transportation, Federal Aviation Administration, Department of Transportation (Parts 400—1199)

V National Aeronautics and Space Administration (Parts 1200—1299)

VI Air Transportation System Stabilization (Parts 1300—1399)

Title 15—Commerce and Foreign Trade

SUBTITLE A—OFFICE OF THE SECRETARY OF COMMERCE (PARTS 0—29)

SUBTITLE B—REGULATIONS RELATING TO COMMERCE AND FOREIGN TRADE

I Bureau of the Census, Department of Commerce (Parts 30—199)

II National Institute of Standards and Technology, Department of Commerce (Parts 200—299)

III International Trade Administration, Department of Commerce (Parts 300—399)

IV Foreign-Trade Zones Board, Department of Commerce (Parts 400—499)

VII Bureau of Industry and Security, Department of Commerce (Parts 700—799)

221

Title 15—Commerce and Foreign Trade—Continued

Chap.

VIII   Bureau of Economic Analysis, Department of Commerce (Parts 800—899)

IX   National Oceanic and Atmospheric Administration, Department of Commerce (Parts 900—999)

XI   National Technical Information Service, Department of Commerce (Parts 1100—1199)

XIII   East-West Foreign Trade Board (Parts 1300—1399)

XIV   Minority Business Development Agency (Parts 1400—1499)

XV   Office of the Under-Secretary for Economic Affairs, Department of Commerce (Parts 1500—1599)

SUBTITLE C—REGULATIONS RELATING TO FOREIGN TRADE AGREEMENTS

XX   Office of the United States Trade Representative (Parts 2000—2099)

SUBTITLE D—REGULATIONS RELATING TO TELECOMMUNICATIONS AND INFORMATION

XXIII   National Telecommunications and Information Administration, Department of Commerce (Parts 2300—2399) [Reserved]

Title 16—Commercial Practices

I   Federal Trade Commission (Parts 0—999)

II   Consumer Product Safety Commission (Parts 1000—1799)

Title 17—Commodity and Securities Exchanges

I   Commodity Futures Trading Commission (Parts 1—199)

II   Securities and Exchange Commission (Parts 200—399)

IV   Department of the Treasury (Parts 400—499)

Title 18—Conservation of Power and Water Resources

I   Federal Energy Regulatory Commission, Department of Energy (Parts 1—399)

III   Delaware River Basin Commission (Parts 400—499)

VI   Water Resources Council (Parts 700—799)

VIII   Susquehanna River Basin Commission (Parts 800—899)

XIII   Tennessee Valley Authority (Parts 1300—1399)

Title 19—Customs Duties

I   U.S. Customs and Border Protection, Department of Homeland Security; Department of the Treasury (Parts 0—199)

II   United States International Trade Commission (Parts 200—299)

III   International Trade Administration, Department of Commerce (Parts 300—399)

IV   U.S. Immigration and Customs Enforcement, Department of Homeland Security (Parts 400—599) [Reserved]

222

Title 20—Employees' Benefits

Chap.

I   Office of Workers' Compensation Programs, Department of Labor (Parts 1—199)

II   Railroad Retirement Board (Parts 200—399)

III   Social Security Administration (Parts 400—499)

IV   Employees' Compensation Appeals Board, Department of Labor (Parts 500—599)

V   Employment and Training Administration, Department of Labor (Parts 600—699)

VI   Office of Workers' Compensation Programs, Department of Labor (Parts 700—799)

VII   Benefits Review Board, Department of Labor (Parts 800—899)

VIII   Joint Board for the Enrollment of Actuaries (Parts 900—999)

IX   Office of the Assistant Secretary for Veterans' Employment and Training Service, Department of Labor (Parts 1000—1099)

Title 21—Food and Drugs

I   Food and Drug Administration, Department of Health and Human Services (Parts 1—1299)

II   Drug Enforcement Administration, Department of Justice (Parts 1300—1399)

III   Office of National Drug Control Policy (Parts 1400—1499)

Title 22—Foreign Relations

I   Department of State (Parts 1—199)

II   Agency for International Development (Parts 200—299)

III   Peace Corps (Parts 300—399)

IV   International Joint Commission, United States and Canada (Parts 400—499)

V   United States Agency for Global Media (Parts 500—599)

VII   U.S. International Development Finance Corporation (Parts 700—799)

IX   Foreign Service Grievance Board (Parts 900—999)

X   Inter-American Foundation (Parts 1000—1099)

XI   International Boundary and Water Commission, United States and Mexico, United States Section (Parts 1100—1199)

XII   United States International Development Cooperation Agency (Parts 1200—1299)

XIII   Millennium Challenge Corporation (Parts 1300—1399)

XIV   Foreign Service Labor Relations Board; Federal Labor Relations Authority; General Counsel of the Federal Labor Relations Authority; and the Foreign Service Impasse Disputes Panel (Parts 1400—1499)

XV   African Development Foundation (Parts 1500—1599)

XVI   Japan-United States Friendship Commission (Parts 1600—1699)

XVII   United States Institute of Peace (Parts 1700—1799)

223

Title 23—Highways

Chap.

I   Federal Highway Administration, Department of Transportation (Parts 1—999)

II   National Highway Traffic Safety Administration and Federal Highway Administration, Department of Transportation (Parts 1200—1299)

III   National Highway Traffic Safety Administration, Department of Transportation (Parts 1300—1399)

Title 24—Housing and Urban Development

SUBTITLE A—OFFICE OF THE SECRETARY, DEPARTMENT OF HOUSING AND URBAN DEVELOPMENT (PARTS 0—99)

SUBTITLE B—REGULATIONS RELATING TO HOUSING AND URBAN DEVELOPMENT

I   Office of Assistant Secretary for Equal Opportunity, Department of Housing and Urban Development (Parts 100—199)

II   Office of Assistant Secretary for Housing-Federal Housing Commissioner, Department of Housing and Urban Development (Parts 200—299)

III   Government National Mortgage Association, Department of Housing and Urban Development (Parts 300—399)

IV   Office of Housing and Office of Multifamily Housing Assistance Restructuring, Department of Housing and Urban Development (Parts 400—499)

V   Office of Assistant Secretary for Community Planning and Development, Department of Housing and Urban Development (Parts 500—599)

VI   Office of Assistant Secretary for Community Planning and Development, Department of Housing and Urban Development (Parts 600—699) [Reserved]

VII   Office of the Secretary, Department of Housing and Urban Development (Housing Assistance Programs and Public and Indian Housing Programs) (Parts 700—799)

VIII   Office of the Assistant Secretary for Housing—Federal Housing Commissioner, Department of Housing and Urban Development (Section 8 Housing Assistance Programs, Section 202 Direct Loan Program, Section 202 Supportive Housing for the Elderly Program and Section 811 Supportive Housing for Persons With Disabilities Program) (Parts 800—899)

IX   Office of Assistant Secretary for Public and Indian Housing, Department of Housing and Urban Development (Parts 900—1699)

X   Office of Assistant Secretary for Housing—Federal Housing Commissioner, Department of Housing and Urban Development (Interstate Land Sales Registration Program) (Parts 1700—1799) [Reserved]

XII   Office of Inspector General, Department of Housing and Urban Development (Parts 2000—2099)

XV   Emergency Mortgage Insurance and Loan Programs, Department of Housing and Urban Development (Parts 2700—2799) [Reserved]

224

Title 24—Housing and Urban Development—Continued
Chap.

XX   Office of Assistant Secretary for Housing—Federal Housing Commissioner, Department of Housing and Urban Development (Parts 3200—3899)

XXIV   Board of Directors of the HOPE for Homeowners Program (Parts 4000—4099) [Reserved]

XXV   Neighborhood Reinvestment Corporation (Parts 4100—4199)

Title 25—Indians

I   Bureau of Indian Affairs, Department of the Interior (Parts 1—299)

II   Indian Arts and Crafts Board, Department of the Interior (Parts 300—399)

III   National Indian Gaming Commission, Department of the Interior (Parts 500—599)

IV   Office of Navajo and Hopi Indian Relocation (Parts 700—899)

V   Bureau of Indian Affairs, Department of the Interior, and Indian Health Service, Department of Health and Human Services (Part 900—999)

VI   Office of the Assistant Secretary, Indian Affairs, Department of the Interior (Parts 1000—1199)

VII   Office of the Special Trustee for American Indians, Department of the Interior (Parts 1200—1299)

Title 26—Internal Revenue

I   Internal Revenue Service, Department of the Treasury (Parts 1—End)

Title 27—Alcohol, Tobacco Products and Firearms

I   Alcohol and Tobacco Tax and Trade Bureau, Department of the Treasury (Parts 1—399)

II   Bureau of Alcohol, Tobacco, Firearms, and Explosives, Department of Justice (Parts 400—799)

Title 28—Judicial Administration

I   Department of Justice (Parts 0—299)

III   Federal Prison Industries, Inc., Department of Justice (Parts 300—399)·

V   Bureau of Prisons, Department of Justice (Parts 500—599)

VI   Offices of Independent Counsel, Department of Justice (Parts 600—699)

VII   Office of Independent Counsel (Parts 700—799)

VIII   Court Services and Offender Supervision Agency for the District of Columbia (Parts 800—899)

IX   National Crime Prevention and Privacy Compact Council (Parts 900—999)

Title 28—Judicial Administration—Continued

Chap.

XI   Department of Justice and Department of State (Parts 1100—1199)

Title 29—Labor

SUBTITLE A—OFFICE OF THE SECRETARY OF LABOR (PARTS 0—99)

SUBTITLE B—REGULATIONS RELATING TO LABOR

I   National Labor Relations Board (Parts 100—199)

II   Office of Labor-Management Standards, Department of Labor (Parts 200—299)

III   National Railroad Adjustment Board (Parts 300—399)

IV   Office of Labor-Management Standards, Department of Labor (Parts 400—499)

V   Wage and Hour Division, Department of Labor (Parts 500—899)

IX   Construction Industry Collective Bargaining Commission (Parts 900—999)

X   National Mediation Board (Parts 1200—1299)

XII   Federal Mediation and Conciliation Service (Parts 1400—1499)

XIV   Equal Employment Opportunity Commission (Parts 1600—1699)

XVII Occupational Safety and Health Administration, Department of Labor (Parts 1900—1999)

XX   Occupational Safety and Health Review Commission (Parts 2200—2499)

XXV   Employee Benefits Security Administration, Department of Labor (Parts 2500—2599)

XXVII Federal Mine Safety and Health Review Commission (Parts 2700—2799)

XL   Pension Benefit Guaranty Corporation (Parts 4000—4999)

Title 30—Mineral Resources

I   Mine Safety and Health Administration, Department of Labor (Parts 1—199)

II   Bureau of Safety and Environmental Enforcement, Department of the Interior (Parts 200—299)

IV   Geological Survey, Department of the Interior (Parts 400—499)

V   Bureau of Ocean Energy Management, Department of the Interior (Parts 500—599)

VII   Office of Surface Mining Reclamation and Enforcement, Department of the Interior (Parts 700—999)

XII   Office of Natural Resources Revenue, Department of the Interior (Parts 1200—1299)

Title 31—Money and Finance: Treasury

SUBTITLE A—OFFICE OF THE SECRETARY OF THE TREASURY (PARTS 0—50)

SUBTITLE B—REGULATIONS RELATING TO MONEY AND FINANCE

Title 31—Money and Finance: Treasury—Continued

_{Chap.}

I   Monetary Offices, Department of the Treasury (Parts 51—199)

II   Fiscal Service, Department of the Treasury (Parts 200—399)

IV   Secret Service, Department of the Treasury (Parts 400—499)

V   Office of Foreign Assets Control, Department of the Treasury (Parts 500—599)

VI   Bureau of Engraving and Printing, Department of the Treasury (Parts 600—699)

VII   Federal Law Enforcement Training Center, Department of the Treasury (Parts 700—799)

VIII   Office of Investment Security, Department of the Treasury (Parts 800—899)

IX   Federal Claims Collection Standards (Department of the Treasury—Department of Justice) (Parts 900—999)

X   Financial Crimes Enforcement Network, Department of the Treasury (Parts 1000—1099)

Title 32—National Defense

SUBTITLE A—DEPARTMENT OF DEFENSE

I   Office of the Secretary of Defense (Parts 1—399)

V   Department of the Army (Parts 400—699)

VI   Department of the Navy (Parts 700—799)

VII   Department of the Air Force (Parts 800—1099)

SUBTITLE B—OTHER REGULATIONS RELATING TO NATIONAL DEFENSE

XII   Department of Defense, Defense Logistics Agency (Parts 1200—1299)

XVI   Selective Service System (Parts 1600—1699)

XVII   Office of the Director of National Intelligence (Parts 1700—1799)

XVIII   National Counterintelligence Center (Parts 1800—1899)

XIX   Central Intelligence Agency (Parts 1900—1999)

XX   Information Security Oversight Office, National Archives and Records Administration (Parts 2000—2099)

XXI   National Security Council (Parts 2100—2199)

XXIV   Office of Science and Technology Policy (Parts 2400—2499)

XXVII   Office for Micronesian Status Negotiations (Parts 2700—2799)

XXVIII   Office of the Vice President of the United States (Parts 2800—2899)

Title 33—Navigation and Navigable Waters

I   Coast Guard, Department of Homeland Security (Parts 1—199)

II   Corps of Engineers, Department of the Army, Department of Defense (Parts 200—399)

IV   Great Lakes St. Lawrence Seaway Development Corporation, Department of Transportation (Parts 400—499)

227

Title 34—Education

Chap.

SUBTITLE A—OFFICE OF THE SECRETARY, DEPARTMENT OF EDUCATION (PARTS 1—99)

SUBTITLE B—REGULATIONS OF THE OFFICES OF THE DEPARTMENT OF EDUCATION

I   Office for Civil Rights, Department of Education (Parts 100—199)

II   Office of Elementary and Secondary Education, Department of Education (Parts 200—299)

III   Office of Special Education and Rehabilitative Services, Department of Education (Parts 300—399)

IV   Office of Career, Technical, and Adult Education, Department of Education (Parts 400—499)

V   Office of Bilingual Education and Minority Languages Affairs, Department of Education (Parts 500—599) [Reserved]

VI   Office of Postsecondary Education, Department of Education (Parts 600—699)

VII   Office of Educational Research and Improvement, Department of Education (Parts 700—799) [Reserved]

SUBTITLE C—REGULATIONS RELATING TO EDUCATION

XI   [Reserved]

XII   National Council on Disability (Parts 1200—1299)

Title 35 [Reserved]

Title 36—Parks, Forests, and Public Property

I   National Park Service, Department of the Interior (Parts 1—199)

II   Forest Service, Department of Agriculture (Parts 200—299)

III   Corps of Engineers, Department of the Army (Parts 300—399)

IV   American Battle Monuments Commission (Parts 400—499)

V   Smithsonian Institution (Parts 500—599)

VI   [Reserved]

VII   Library of Congress (Parts 700—799)

VIII   Advisory Council on Historic Preservation (Parts 800—899)

IX   Pennsylvania Avenue Development Corporation (Parts 900—999)

X   Presidio Trust (Parts 1000—1099)

XI   Architectural and Transportation Barriers Compliance Board (Parts 1100—1199)

XII   National Archives and Records Administration (Parts 1200—1299)

XV   Oklahoma City National Memorial Trust (Parts 1500—1599)

XVI   Morris K. Udall Scholarship and Excellence in National Environmental Policy Foundation (Parts 1600—1699)

Title 37—Patents, Trademarks, and Copyrights

I   United States Patent and Trademark Office, Department of Commerce (Parts 1—199)

II   U.S. Copyright Office, Library of Congress (Parts 200—299)

Title 37—Patents, Trademarks, and Copyrights—Continued

Chap.

III Copyright Royalty Board, Library of Congress (Parts 300—399)

IV National Institute of Standards and Technology, Department of Commerce (Parts 400—599)

Title 38—Pensions, Bonuses, and Veterans' Relief

I Department of Veterans Affairs (Parts 0—199)

II Armed Forces Retirement Home (Parts 200—299)

Title 39—Postal Service

I United States Postal Service (Parts 1—999)

III Postal Regulatory Commission (Parts 3000—3099)

Title 40—Protection of Environment

I Environmental Protection Agency (Parts 1—1099)

IV Environmental Protection Agency and Department of Justice (Parts 1400—1499)

V Council on Environmental Quality (Parts 1500—1599)

VI Chemical Safety and Hazard Investigation Board (Parts 1600—1699)

VII Environmental Protection Agency and Department of Defense; Uniform National Discharge Standards for Vessels of the Armed Forces (Parts 1700—1799)

VIII Gulf Coast Ecosystem Restoration Council (Parts 1800—1899)

IX Federal Permitting Improvement Steering Council (Part 1900)

Title 41—Public Contracts and Property Management

SUBTITLE A—FEDERAL PROCUREMENT REGULATIONS SYSTEM [NOTE]

SUBTITLE B—OTHER PROVISIONS RELATING TO PUBLIC CONTRACTS

50 Public Contracts, Department of Labor (Parts 50–1—50–999)

51 Committee for Purchase From People Who Are Blind or Severely Disabled (Parts 51–1—51–99)

60 Office of Federal Contract Compliance Programs, Equal Employment Opportunity, Department of Labor (Parts 60–1—60–999)

61 Office of the Assistant Secretary for Veterans' Employment and Training Service, Department of Labor (Parts 61–1—61–999)

62—100 [Reserved]

SUBTITLE C—FEDERAL PROPERTY MANAGEMENT REGULATIONS SYSTEM

101 Federal Property Management Regulations (Parts 101–1—101–99)

102 Federal Management Regulation (Parts 102–1—102–299)

103—104 [Reserved]

105 General Services Administration (Parts 105–1—105–999)

Title 41—Public Contracts and Property Management—Continued

Chap.

109   Department of Energy Property Management Regulations (Parts 109–1—109–99)

114   Department of the Interior (Parts 114–1—114–99)

115   Environmental Protection Agency (Parts 115–1—115–99)

128   Department of Justice (Parts 128–1—128–99)

129—200   [Reserved]

SUBTITLE D—FEDERAL ACQUISITION SUPPLY CHAIN SECURITY

201   Federal Acquisition Security Council (Parts 201–1—201–99).

SUBTITLE E [RESERVED]

SUBTITLE F—FEDERAL TRAVEL REGULATION SYSTEM

300   General (Parts 300–1—300–99)

301   Temporary Duty (TDY) Travel Allowances (Parts 301–1—301–99)

302   Relocation Allowances (Parts 302–1—302–99)

303   Payment of Expenses Connected with the Death of Certain Employees (Part 303–1—303–99)

304   Payment of Travel Expenses from a Non-Federal Source (Parts 304–1—304–99)

Title 42—Public Health

I   Public Health Service, Department of Health and Human Services (Parts 1—199)

II—III   [Reserved]

IV   Centers for Medicare & Medicaid Services, Department of Health and Human Services (Parts 400—699)

V   Office of Inspector General-Health Care, Department of Health and Human Services (Parts 1000—1099)

Title 43—Public Lands: Interior

SUBTITLE A—OFFICE OF THE SECRETARY OF THE INTERIOR (PARTS 1—199)

SUBTITLE B—REGULATIONS RELATING TO PUBLIC LANDS

I   Bureau of Reclamation, Department of the Interior (Parts 400—999)

II   Bureau of Land Management, Department of the Interior (Parts 1000—9999)

III   Utah Reclamation Mitigation and Conservation Commission (Parts 10000—10099)

Title 44—Emergency Management and Assistance

I   Federal Emergency Management Agency, Department of Homeland Security (Parts 0—399)

IV   Department of Commerce and Department of Transportation (Parts 400—499)

Title 45—Public Welfare

Subtitle A—Department of Health and Human Services (Parts 1—199)

Subtitle B—Regulations Relating to Public Welfare

II   Office of Family Assistance (Assistance Programs), Administration for Children and Families, Department of Health and Human Services (Parts 200—299)

III   Office of Child Support Enforcement (Child Support Enforcement Program), Administration for Children and Families, Department of Health and Human Services (Parts 300—399)

IV   Office of Refugee Resettlement, Administration for Children and Families, Department of Health and Human Services (Parts 400—499)

V   Foreign Claims Settlement Commission of the United States, Department of Justice (Parts 500—599)

VI   National Science Foundation (Parts 600—699)

VII   Commission on Civil Rights (Parts 700—799)

VIII   Office of Personnel Management (Parts 800—899)

IX   Denali Commission (Parts 900—999)

X   Office of Community Services, Administration for Children and Families, Department of Health and Human Services (Parts 1000—1099)

XI   National Foundation on the Arts and the Humanities (Parts 1100—1199)

XII   Corporation for National and Community Service (Parts 1200—1299)

XIII   Administration for Children and Families, Department of Health and Human Services (Parts 1300—1399)

XVI   Legal Services Corporation (Parts 1600—1699)

XVII   National Commission on Libraries and Information Science (Parts 1700—1799)

XVIII   Harry S. Truman Scholarship Foundation (Parts 1800—1899)

XXI   Commission of Fine Arts (Parts 2100—2199)

XXIII   Arctic Research Commission (Parts 2300—2399)

XXIV   James Madison Memorial Fellowship Foundation (Parts 2400—2499)

XXV   Corporation for National and Community Service (Parts 2500—2599)

Title 46—Shipping

I   Coast Guard, Department of Homeland Security (Parts 1—199)

II   Maritime Administration, Department of Transportation (Parts 200—399)

III   Coast Guard (Great Lakes Pilotage), Department of Homeland Security (Parts 400—499)

IV   Federal Maritime Commission (Parts 500—599)

Title 47—Telecommunication

Chap.

I   Federal Communications Commission (Parts 0—199)

II   Office of Science and Technology Policy and National Security Council (Parts 200—299)

III   National Telecommunications and Information Administration, Department of Commerce (Parts 300—399)

IV   National Telecommunications and Information Administration, Department of Commerce, and National Highway Traffic Safety Administration, Department of Transportation (Parts 400—499)

V   The First Responder Network Authority (Parts 500—599)

Title 48—Federal Acquisition Regulations System

1   Federal Acquisition Regulation (Parts 1—99)

2   Defense Acquisition Regulations System, Department of Defense (Parts 200—299)

3   Department of Health and Human Services (Parts 300—399)

4   Department of Agriculture (Parts 400—499)

5   General Services Administration (Parts 500—599)

6   Department of State (Parts 600—699)

7   Agency for International Development (Parts 700—799)

8   Department of Veterans Affairs (Parts 800—899)

9   Department of Energy (Parts 900—999)

10   Department of the Treasury (Parts 1000—1099)

12   Department of Transportation (Parts 1200—1299)

13   Department of Commerce (Parts 1300—1399)

14   Department of the Interior (Parts 1400—1499)

15   Environmental Protection Agency (Parts 1500—1599)

16   Office of Personnel Management, Federal Employees Health Benefits Acquisition Regulation (Parts 1600—1699)

17   Office of Personnel Management (Parts 1700—1799)

18   National Aeronautics and Space Administration (Parts 1800—1899)

19   Broadcasting Board of Governors (Parts 1900—1999)

20   Nuclear Regulatory Commission (Parts 2000—2099)

21   Office of Personnel Management, Federal Employees Group Life Insurance Federal Acquisition Regulation (Parts 2100—2199)

23   Social Security Administration (Parts 2300—2399)

24   Department of Housing and Urban Development (Parts 2400—2499)

25   National Science Foundation (Parts 2500—2599)

28   Department of Justice (Parts 2800—2899)

29   Department of Labor (Parts 2900—2999)

30   Department of Homeland Security, Homeland Security Acquisition Regulation (HSAR) (Parts 3000—3099)

34   Department of Education Acquisition Regulation (Parts 3400—3499)

51   Department of the Army Acquisition Regulations (Parts 5100—5199) [Reserved]

52   Department of the Navy Acquisition Regulations (Parts 5200—5299)

53   Department of the Air Force Federal Acquisition Regulation Supplement (Parts 5300—5399) [Reserved]

54   Defense Logistics Agency, Department of Defense (Parts 5400—5499)

57   African Development Foundation (Parts 5700—5799)

61   Civilian Board of Contract Appeals, General Services Administration (Parts 6100—6199)

99   Cost Accounting Standards Board, Office of Federal Procurement Policy, Office of Management and Budget (Parts 9900—9999)

Title 49—Transportation

SUBTITLE A—OFFICE OF THE SECRETARY OF TRANSPORTATION (PARTS 1—99)

SUBTITLE B—OTHER REGULATIONS RELATING TO TRANSPORTATION

I   Pipeline and Hazardous Materials Safety Administration, Department of Transportation (Parts 100—199)

II   Federal Railroad Administration, Department of Transportation (Parts 200—299)

III   Federal Motor Carrier Safety Administration, Department of Transportation (Parts 300—399)

IV   Coast Guard, Department of Homeland Security (Parts 400—499)

V   National Highway Traffic Safety Administration, Department of Transportation (Parts 500—599)

VI   Federal Transit Administration, Department of Transportation (Parts 600—699)

VII   National Railroad Passenger Corporation (AMTRAK) (Parts 700—799)

VIII   National Transportation Safety Board (Parts 800—999)

X   Surface Transportation Board (Parts 1000—1399)

XI   Research and Innovative Technology Administration, Department of Transportation (Parts 1400—1499) [Reserved]

XII   Transportation Security Administration, Department of Homeland Security (Parts 1500—1699)

Title 50—Wildlife and Fisheries

I   United States Fish and Wildlife Service, Department of the Interior (Parts 1—199)

II   National Marine Fisheries Service, National Oceanic and Atmospheric Administration, Department of Commerce (Parts 200—299)

III   International Fishing and Related Activities (Parts 300—399)

IV   Joint Regulations (United States Fish and Wildlife Service, Department of the Interior and National Marine Fisheries Service, National Oceanic and Atmospheric Administration, Department of Commerce); Endangered Species Committee Regulations (Parts 400—499)

  V   Marine Mammal Commission (Parts 500—599)

VI   Fishery Conservation and Management, National Oceanic and Atmospheric Administration, Department of Commerce (Parts 600—699)

Alphabetical List of Agencies Appearing in the CFR

(Revised as of April 1, 2023)

Agency	CFR Title, Subtitle or Chapter
Administrative Conference of the United States	1, III
Advisory Council on Historic Preservation	36, VIII
Advocacy and Outreach, Office of	7, XXV
Afghanistan Reconstruction, Special Inspector General for	5, LXXXIII
African Development Foundation	22, XV
Federal Acquisition Regulation	48, 57
Agency for International Development	2, VII; 22, II
Federal Acquisition Regulation	48, 7
Agricultural Marketing Service	7, I, VIII, IX, X, XI; 9, II
Agricultural Research Service	7, V
Agriculture, Department of	2, IV; 5, LXXIII
Advocacy and Outreach, Office of	7, XXV
Agricultural Marketing Service	7, I, VIII, IX, X, XI; 9, II
Agricultural Research Service	7, V
Animal and Plant Health Inspection Service	7, III; 9, I
Chief Financial Officer, Office of	7, XXX
Commodity Credit Corporation	7, XIV
Economic Research Service	7, XXXVII
Energy Policy and New Uses, Office of	2, IX; 7, XXIX
Environmental Quality, Office of	7, XXXI
Farm Service Agency	7, VII, XVIII
Federal Acquisition Regulation	48, 4
Federal Crop Insurance Corporation	7, IV
Food and Nutrition Service	7, II
Food Safety and Inspection Service	9, III
Foreign Agricultural Service	7, XV
Forest Service	36, II
Information Resources Management, Office of	7, XXVII
Inspector General, Office of	7, XXVI
National Agricultural Library	7, XLI
National Agricultural Statistics Service	7, XXXVI
National Institute of Food and Agriculture	7, XXXIV
Natural Resources Conservation Service	7, VI
Operations, Office of	7, XXVIII
Procurement and Property Management, Office of	7, XXXII
Rural Business-Cooperative Service	7, XVIII, XLII
Rural Development Administration	7, XLII
Rural Housing Service	7, XVIII, XXXV
Rural Utilities Service	7, XVII, XVIII, XLII
Secretary of Agriculture, Office of	7, Subtitle A
Transportation, Office of	7, XXXIII
World Agricultural Outlook Board	7, XXXVIII
Air Force, Department of	32, VII
Federal Acquisition Regulation Supplement	48, 53
Air Transportation Stabilization Board	14, VI
Alcohol and Tobacco Tax and Trade Bureau	27, I
Alcohol, Tobacco, Firearms, and Explosives, Bureau of	27, II
AMTRAK	49, VII
American Battle Monuments Commission	36, IV
American Indians, Office of the Special Trustee	25, VII
Animal and Plant Health Inspection Service	7, III; 9, I
Appalachian Regional Commission	5, IX
Architectural and Transportation Barriers Compliance Board	36, XI

Agency	CFR Title, Subtitle or Chapter
Arctic Research Commission	45, XXIII
Armed Forces Retirement Home	5, XI; 38, II
Army, Department of	32, V
Engineers, Corps of	33, II; 36, III
Federal Acquisition Regulation	48, 51
Benefits Review Board	20, VII
Bilingual Education and Minority Languages Affairs, Office of	34, V
Blind or Severely Disabled, Committee for Purchase from People Who Are	41, 51
Federal Acquisition Regulation	48, 19
Career, Technical, and Adult Education, Office of	34, IV
Census Bureau	15, I
Centers for Medicare & Medicaid Services	42, IV
Central Intelligence Agency	32, XIX
Chemical Safety and Hazard Investigation Board	40, VI
Chief Financial Officer, Office of	7, XXX
Child Support Enforcement, Office of	45, III
Children and Families, Administration for	45, II, III, IV, X, XIII
Civil Rights, Commission on	5, LXVIII; 45, VII
Civil Rights, Office for	34, I
Coast Guard	33, I; 46, I; 49, IV
Coast Guard (Great Lakes Pilotage)	46, III
Commerce, Department of	2, XIII; 44, IV; 50, VI
Census Bureau	15, I
Economic Affairs, Office of the Under-Secretary for	15, XV
Economic Analysis, Bureau of	15, VIII
Economic Development Administration	13, III
Emergency Management and Assistance	44, IV
Federal Acquisition Regulation	48, 13
Foreign-Trade Zones Board	15, IV
Industry and Security, Bureau of	15, VII
International Trade Administration	15, III; 19, III
National Institute of Standards and Technology	15, II; 37, IV
National Marine Fisheries Service	50, II, IV
National Oceanic and Atmospheric Administration	15, IX; 50, II, III, IV, VI
National Technical Information Service	15, XI
National Telecommunications and Information Administration	15, XXIII; 47, III, IV
National Weather Service	15, IX
Patent and Trademark Office, United States	37, I
Secretary of Commerce, Office of	15, Subtitle A
Commercial Space Transportation	14, III
Commodity Credit Corporation	7, XIV
Commodity Futures Trading Commission	5, XLI; 17, I
Community Planning and Development, Office of Assistant Secretary for	24, V, VI
Community Services, Office of	45, X
Comptroller of the Currency	12, I
Construction Industry Collective Bargaining Commission	29, IX
Consumer Financial Protection Bureau	5, LXXXIV; 12, X
Consumer Product Safety Commission	5, LXXI; 16, II
Copyright Royalty Board	37, III
Corporation for National and Community Service	2, XXII; 45, XII, XXV
Cost Accounting Standards Board	48, 99
Council on Environmental Quality	40, V
Council of the Inspectors General on Integrity and Efficiency	5, XCVIII
Court Services and Offender Supervision Agency for the District of Columbia	5, LXX; 28, VIII
Customs and Border Protection	19, I
Defense, Department of	2, XI; 5, XXVI; 32, Subtitle A; 40, VII
Advanced Research Projects Agency	32, I
Air Force Department	32, VII
Army Department	32, V; 33, II; 36, III; 48, 51
Defense Acquisition Regulations System	48, 2
Defense Intelligence Agency	32, I

Agency	CFR Title, Subtitle or Chapter
Defense Logistics Agency	32, I, XII; 48, 54
Engineers, Corps of	33, II; 36, III
National Imagery and Mapping Agency	32, I
Navy, Department of	32, VI; 48, 52
Secretary of Defense, Office of	2, XI; 32, I
Defense Contract Audit Agency	32, I
Defense Intelligence Agency	32, I
Defense Logistics Agency	32, XII; 48, 54
Defense Nuclear Facilities Safety Board	10, XVII
Delaware River Basin Commission	18, III
Denali Commission	45, IX
Disability, National Council on	5, C; 34, XII
District of Columbia, Court Services and Offender Supervision Agency for the	5, LXX; 28, VIII
Drug Enforcement Administration	21, II
East-West Foreign Trade Board	15, XIII
Economic Affairs, Office of the Under-Secretary for	15, XV
Economic Analysis, Bureau of	15, VIII
Economic Development Administration	13, III
Economic Research Service	7, XXXVII
Education, Department of	2, XXXIV; 5, LIII
Bilingual Education and Minority Languages Affairs, Office of	34, V
Career, Technical, and Adult Education, Office of	34, IV
Civil Rights, Office for	34, I
Educational Research and Improvement, Office of	34, VII
Elementary and Secondary Education, Office of	34, II
Federal Acquisition Regulation	48, 34
Postsecondary Education, Office of	34, VI
Secretary of Education, Office of	34, Subtitle A
Special Education and Rehabilitative Services, Office of	34, III
Educational Research and Improvement, Office of	34, VII
Election Assistance Commission	2, LVIII; 11, II
Elementary and Secondary Education, Office of	34, II
Emergency Oil and Gas Guaranteed Loan Board	13, V
Emergency Steel Guarantee Loan Board	13, IV
Employee Benefits Security Administration	29, XXV
Employees' Compensation Appeals Board	20, IV
Employees Loyalty Board	5, V
Employment and Training Administration	20, V
Employment Policy, National Commission for	1, IV
Employment Standards Administration	20, VI
Endangered Species Committee	50, IV
Energy, Department of	2, IX; 5, XXIII; 10, II, III, X
Federal Acquisition Regulation	48, 9
Federal Energy Regulatory Commission	5, XXIV; 18, I
Property Management Regulations	41, 109
Energy, Office of	7, XXIX
Engineers, Corps of	33, II; 36, III
Engraving and Printing, Bureau of	31, VI
Environmental Protection Agency	2, XV; 5, LIV; 40, I, IV, VII
Federal Acquisition Regulation	48, 15
Property Management Regulations	41, 115
Environmental Quality, Office of	7, XXXI
Equal Employment Opportunity Commission	5, LXII; 29, XIV
Equal Opportunity, Office of Assistant Secretary for	24, I
Executive Office of the President	3, I
Environmental Quality, Council on	40, V
Management and Budget, Office of	2, Subtitle A; 5, III, LXXVII; 14, VI; 48, 99
National Drug Control Policy, Office of	2, XXXVI; 21, III
National Security Council	32, XXI; 47, II
Presidential Documents	3
Science and Technology Policy, Office of	32, XXIV; 47, II
Trade Representative, Office of the United States	15, XX

237

Agency	CFR Title, Subtitle or Chapter
Export-Import Bank of the United States	2, XXXV; 5, LII; 12, IV
Family Assistance, Office of	45, II
Farm Credit Administration	5, XXXI; 12, VI
Farm Credit System Insurance Corporation	5, XXX; 12, XIV
Farm Service Agency	7, VII, XVIII
Federal Acquisition Regulation	48, 1
Federal Acquisition Security Council	41, 201
Federal Aviation Administration	14, I
Commercial Space Transportation	14, III
Federal Claims Collection Standards	31, IX
Federal Communications Commission	2, LX; 5, XXIX; 47, I
Federal Contract Compliance Programs, Office of	41, 60
Federal Crop Insurance Corporation	7, IV
Federal Deposit Insurance Corporation	5, XXII; 12, III
Federal Election Commission	5, XXXVII; 11, I
Federal Emergency Management Agency	44, I
Federal Employees Group Life Insurance Federal Acquisition Regulation	48, 21
Federal Employees Health Benefits Acquisition Regulation	48, 16
Federal Energy Regulatory Commission	5, XXIV; 18, I
Federal Financial Institutions Examination Council	12, XI
Federal Financing Bank	12, VIII
Federal Highway Administration	23, I, II
Federal Home Loan Mortgage Corporation	1, IV
Federal Housing Enterprise Oversight Office	12, XVII
Federal Housing Finance Agency	5, LXXX; 12, XII
Federal Labor Relations Authority	5, XIV, XLIX; 22, XIV
Federal Law Enforcement Training Center	31, VII
Federal Management Regulation	41, 102
Federal Maritime Commission	46, IV
Federal Mediation and Conciliation Service	29, XII
Federal Mine Safety and Health Review Commission	5, LXXIV; 29, XXVII
Federal Motor Carrier Safety Administration	49, III
Federal Permitting Improvement Steering Council	40, IX
Federal Prison Industries, Inc.	28, III
Federal Procurement Policy Office	48, 99
Federal Property Management Regulations	41, 101
Federal Railroad Administration	49, II
Federal Register, Administrative Committee of	1, I
Federal Register, Office of	1, II
Federal Reserve System	12, II
Board of Governors	5, LVIII
Federal Retirement Thrift Investment Board	5, VI, LXXVI
Federal Service Impasses Panel	5, XIV
Federal Trade Commission	5, XLVII; 16, I
Federal Transit Administration	49, VI
Federal Travel Regulation System	41, Subtitle F
Financial Crimes Enforcement Network	31, X
Financial Research Office	12, XVI
Financial Stability Oversight Council	12, XIII
Fine Arts, Commission of	45, XXI
Fiscal Service	31, II
Fish and Wildlife Service, United States	50, I, IV
Food and Drug Administration	21, I
Food and Nutrition Service	7, II
Food Safety and Inspection Service	9, III
Foreign Agricultural Service	7, XV
Foreign Assets Control, Office of	31, V
Foreign Claims Settlement Commission of the United States	45, V
Foreign Service Grievance Board	22, IX
Foreign Service Impasse Disputes Panel	22, XIV
Foreign Service Labor Relations Board	22, XIV
Foreign-Trade Zones Board	15, IV
Forest Service	36, II
General Services Administration	5, LVII; 41, 105
Contract Appeals, Board of	48, 61
Federal Acquisition Regulation	48, 5

Agency	CFR Title, Subtitle or Chapter
Federal Management Regulation	41, 102
Federal Property Management Regulations	41, 101
Federal Travel Regulation System	41, Subtitle F
General	41, 300
Payment From a Non-Federal Source for Travel Expenses	41, 304
Payment of Expenses Connected With the Death of Certain Employees	41, 303
Relocation Allowances	41, 302
Temporary Duty (TDY) Travel Allowances	41, 301
Geological Survey	30, IV
Government Accountability Office	4, I
Government Ethics, Office of	5, XVI
Government National Mortgage Association	24, III
Grain Inspection, Packers and Stockyards Administration	7, VIII; 9, II
Great Lakes St. Lawrence Seaway Development Corporation	33, IV
Gulf Coast Ecosystem Restoration Council	2, LIX; 40, VIII
Harry S. Truman Scholarship Foundation	45, XVIII
Health and Human Services, Department of	2, III; 5, XLV; 45, Subtitle A
Centers for Medicare & Medicaid Services	42, IV
Child Support Enforcement, Office of	45, III
Children and Families, Administration for	45, II, III, IV, X, XIII
Community Services, Office of	45, X
Family Assistance, Office of	45, II
Federal Acquisition Regulation	48, 3
Food and Drug Administration	21, I
Indian Health Service	25, V
Inspector General (Health Care), Office of	42, V
Public Health Service	42, I
Refugee Resettlement, Office of	45, IV
Homeland Security, Department of	2, XXX; 5, XXXVI; 6, I; 8, I
Coast Guard	33, I; 46, I; 49, IV
Coast Guard (Great Lakes Pilotage)	46, III
Customs and Border Protection	19, I
Federal Emergency Management Agency	44, I
Human Resources Management and Labor Relations Systems	5, XCVII
Immigration and Customs Enforcement Bureau	19, IV
Transportation Security Administration	49, XII
HOPE for Homeowners Program, Board of Directors of	24, XXIV
Housing and Urban Development, Department of	2, XXIV; 5, LXV; 24, Subtitle B
Community Planning and Development, Office of Assistant Secretary for	24, V, VI
Equal Opportunity, Office of Assistant Secretary for	24, I
Federal Acquisition Regulation	48, 24
Federal Housing Enterprise Oversight, Office of	12, XVII
Government National Mortgage Association	24, III
Housing—Federal Housing Commissioner, Office of Assistant Secretary for	24, II, VIII, X, XX
Housing, Office of, and Multifamily Housing Assistance Restructuring, Office of	24, IV
Inspector General, Office of	24, XII
Public and Indian Housing, Office of Assistant Secretary for	24, IX
Secretary, Office of	24, Subtitle A, VII
Housing—Federal Housing Commissioner, Office of Assistant Secretary for	24, II, VIII, X, XX
Housing, Office of, and Multifamily Housing Assistance Restructuring, Office of	24, IV
Immigration and Customs Enforcement Bureau	19, IV
Immigration Review, Executive Office for	8, V
Independent Counsel, Office of	28, VII
Independent Counsel, Offices of	28, VI
Indian Affairs, Bureau of	25, I, V
Indian Affairs, Office of the Assistant Secretary	25, VI
Indian Arts and Crafts Board	25, II

Agency	CFR Title, Subtitle or Chapter
Indian Health Service	25, V
Industry and Security, Bureau of	15, VII
Information Resources Management, Office of	7, XXVII
Information Security Oversight Office, National Archives and Records Administration	32, XX
Inspector General	
Agriculture Department	7, XXVI
Health and Human Services Department	42, V
Housing and Urban Development Department	24, XII, XV
Institute of Peace, United States	22, XVII
Intellectual Property Enforcement Coordinator, Office of	5, CIV
Inter-American Foundation	5, LXIII; 22, X
Interior, Department of	2, XIV
American Indians, Office of the Special Trustee	25, VII
Endangered Species Committee	50, IV
Federal Acquisition Regulation	48, 14
Federal Property Management Regulations System	41, 114
Fish and Wildlife Service, United States	50, I, IV
Geological Survey	30, IV
Indian Affairs, Bureau of	25, I, V
Indian Affairs, Office of the Assistant Secretary	25, VI
Indian Arts and Crafts Board	25, II
Land Management, Bureau of	43, II
National Indian Gaming Commission	25, III
National Park Service	36, I
Natural Resource Revenue, Office of	30, XII
Ocean Energy Management, Bureau of	30, V
Reclamation, Bureau of	43, I
Safety and Environmental Enforcement, Bureau of	30, II
Secretary of the Interior, Office of	2, XIV; 43, Subtitle A
Surface Mining Reclamation and Enforcement, Office of	30, VII
Internal Revenue Service	26, I
International Boundary and Water Commission, United States and Mexico, United States Section	22, XI
International Development, United States Agency for	22, II
Federal Acquisition Regulation	48, 7
International Development Cooperation Agency, United States	22, XII
International Development Finance Corporation, U.S.	5, XXXIII; 22, VII
International Joint Commission, United States and Canada	22, IV
International Organizations Employees Loyalty Board	5, V
International Trade Administration	15, III; 19, III
International Trade Commission, United States	19, II
Interstate Commerce Commission	5, XL
Investment Security, Office of	31, VIII
James Madison Memorial Fellowship Foundation	45, XXIV
Japan–United States Friendship Commission	22, XVI
Joint Board for the Enrollment of Actuaries	20, VIII
Justice, Department of	2, XXVIII; 5, XXVIII; 28, I, XI; 40, IV
Alcohol, Tobacco, Firearms, and Explosives, Bureau of	27, II
Drug Enforcement Administration	21, II
Federal Acquisition Regulation	48, 28
Federal Claims Collection Standards	31, IX
Federal Prison Industries, Inc.	28, III
Foreign Claims Settlement Commission of the United States	45, V
Immigration Review, Executive Office for	8, V
Independent Counsel, Offices of	28, VI
Prisons, Bureau of	28, V
Property Management Regulations	41, 128
Labor, Department of	2, XXIX; 5, XLII
Benefits Review Board	20, VII
Employee Benefits Security Administration	29, XXV
Employees' Compensation Appeals Board	20, IV
Employment and Training Administration	20, V
Federal Acquisition Regulation	48, 29

240

Agency	CFR Title, Subtitle or Chapter
Federal Contract Compliance Programs, Office of	41, 60
Federal Procurement Regulations System	41, 50
Labor-Management Standards, Office of	29, II, IV
Mine Safety and Health Administration	30, I
Occupational Safety and Health Administration	29, XVII
Public Contracts	41, 50
Secretary of Labor, Office of	29, Subtitle A
Veterans' Employment and Training Service, Office of the Assistant Secretary for	41, 61; 20, IX
Wage and Hour Division	29, V
Workers' Compensation Programs, Office of	20, I, VI
Labor-Management Standards, Office of	29, II, IV
Land Management, Bureau of	43, II
Legal Services Corporation	45, XVI
Libraries and Information Science, National Commission on	45, XVII
Library of Congress	36, VII
Copyright Royalty Board	37, III
U.S. Copyright Office	37, II
Management and Budget, Office of	5, III, LXXVII; 14, VI; 48, 99
Marine Mammal Commission	50, V
Maritime Administration	46, II
Merit Systems Protection Board	5, II, LXIV
Micronesian Status Negotiations, Office for	32, XXVII
Military Compensation and Retirement Modernization Commission	5, XCIX
Millennium Challenge Corporation	22, XIII
Mine Safety and Health Administration	30, I
Minority Business Development Agency	15, XIV
Miscellaneous Agencies	1, IV
Monetary Offices	31, I
Morris K. Udall Scholarship and Excellence in National Environmental Policy Foundation	36, XVI
Museum and Library Services, Institute of	2, XXXI
National Aeronautics and Space Administration	2, XVIII; 5, LIX; 14, V
Federal Acquisition Regulation	48, 18
National Agricultural Library	7, XLI
National Agricultural Statistics Service	7, XXXVI
National and Community Service, Corporation for	2, XXII; 45, XII, XXV
National Archives and Records Administration	2, XXVI; 5, LXVI; 36, XII
Information Security Oversight Office	32, XX
National Capital Planning Commission	1, IV, VI
National Counterintelligence Center	32, XVIII
National Credit Union Administration	5, LXXXVI; 12, VII
National Crime Prevention and Privacy Compact Council	28, IX
National Drug Control Policy, Office of	2, XXXVI; 21, III
National Endowment for the Arts	2, XXXII
National Endowment for the Humanities	2, XXXIII
National Foundation on the Arts and the Humanities	45, XI
National Geospatial-Intelligence Agency	32, I
National Highway Traffic Safety Administration	23, II, III; 47, VI; 49, V
National Imagery and Mapping Agency	32, I
National Indian Gaming Commission	25, III
National Institute of Food and Agriculture	7, XXXIV
National Institute of Standards and Technology	15, II; 37, IV
National Intelligence, Office of Director of	5, IV; 32, XVII
National Labor Relations Board	5, LXI; 29, I
National Marine Fisheries Service	50, II, IV
National Mediation Board	5, CI; 29, X
National Oceanic and Atmospheric Administration	15, IX; 50, II, III, IV, VI
National Park Service	36, I
National Railroad Adjustment Board	29, III
National Railroad Passenger Corporation (AMTRAK)	49, VII
National Science Foundation	2, XXV; 5, XLIII; 45, VI
Federal Acquisition Regulation	48, 25
National Security Council	32, XXI; 47, II

Agency	CFR Title, Subtitle or Chapter
National Technical Information Service	15, XI
National Telecommunications and Information Administration	15, XXIII; 47, III, IV, V
National Transportation Safety Board	49, VIII
Natural Resource Revenue, Office of	30, XII
Natural Resources Conservation Service	7, VI
Navajo and Hopi Indian Relocation, Office of	25, IV
Navy, Department of	32, VI
Federal Acquisition Regulation	48, 52
Neighborhood Reinvestment Corporation	24, XXV
Northeast Interstate Low-Level Radioactive Waste Commission	10, XVIII
Nuclear Regulatory Commission	2, XX; 5, XLVIII; 10, I
Federal Acquisition Regulation	48, 20
Occupational Safety and Health Administration	29, XVII
Occupational Safety and Health Review Commission	29, XX
Ocean Energy Management, Bureau of	30, V
Oklahoma City National Memorial Trust	36, XV
Operations Office	7, XXVIII
Patent and Trademark Office, United States	37, I
Payment From a Non-Federal Source for Travel Expenses	41, 304
Payment of Expenses Connected With the Death of Certain Employees	41, 303
Peace Corps	2, XXXVII; 22, III
Pennsylvania Avenue Development Corporation	36, IX
Pension Benefit Guaranty Corporation	29, XL
Personnel Management, Office of	5, I, IV, XXXV; 45, VIII
Federal Acquisition Regulation	48, 17
Federal Employees Group Life Insurance Federal Acquisition Regulation	48, 21
Federal Employees Health Benefits Acquisition Regulation	48, 16
Human Resources Management and Labor Relations Systems, Department of Homeland Security	5, XCVII
Pipeline and Hazardous Materials Safety Administration	49, I
Postal Regulatory Commission	5, XLVI; 39, III
Postal Service, United States	5, LX; 39, I
Postsecondary Education, Office of	34, VI
President's Commission on White House Fellowships	1, IV
Presidential Documents	3
Presidio Trust	36, X
Prisons, Bureau of	28, V
Privacy and Civil Liberties Oversight Board	6, X
Procurement and Property Management, Office of	7, XXXII
Public and Indian Housing, Office of Assistant Secretary for	24, IX
Public Contracts, Department of Labor	41, 50
Public Health Service	42, I
Railroad Retirement Board	20, II
Reclamation, Bureau of	43, I
Refugee Resettlement, Office of	45, IV
Relocation Allowances	41, 302
Research and Innovative Technology Administration	49, XI
Rural Business-Cooperative Service	7, XVIII, XLII, L
Rural Development Administration	7, XLII
Rural Housing Service	7, XVIII, XXXV, L
Rural Utilities Service	7, XVII, XVIII, XLII, L
Safety and Environmental Enforcement, Bureau of	30, II
Science and Technology Policy, Office of	32, XXIV; 47, II
Secret Service	31, IV
Securities and Exchange Commission	5, XXXIV; 17, II
Selective Service System	32, XVI
Small Business Administration	2, XXVII; 13, I
Smithsonian Institution	36, V
Social Security Administration	2, XXIII; 20, III; 48, 23
Soldiers' and Airmen's Home, United States	5, XI
Special Counsel, Office of	5, VIII
Special Education and Rehabilitative Services, Office of	34, III
State, Department of	2, VI; 22, I; 28, XI

242

Agency	CFR Title, Subtitle or Chapter
Federal Acquisition Regulation	48, 6
Surface Mining Reclamation and Enforcement, Office of	30, VII
Surface Transportation Board	49, X
Susquehanna River Basin Commission	18, VIII
Tennessee Valley Authority	5, LXIX; 18, XIII
Trade Representative, United States, Office of	15, XX
Transportation, Department of	2, XII; 5, L
Commercial Space Transportation	14, III
Emergency Management and Assistance	44, IV
Federal Acquisition Regulation	48, 12
Federal Aviation Administration	14, I
Federal Highway Administration	23, I, II
Federal Motor Carrier Safety Administration	49, III
Federal Railroad Administration	49, II
Federal Transit Administration	49, VI
Great Lakes St. Lawrence Seaway Development Corporation	33, IV
Maritime Administration	46, II
National Highway Traffic Safety Administration	23, II, III; 47, IV; 49, V
Pipeline and Hazardous Materials Safety Administration	49, I
Secretary of Transportation, Office of	14, II; 49, Subtitle A
Transportation Statistics Bureau	49, XI
Transportation, Office of	7, XXXIII
Transportation Security Administration	49, XII
Transportation Statistics Bureau	49, XI
Travel Allowances, Temporary Duty (TDY)	41, 301
Treasury, Department of the	2, X; 5, XXI; 12, XV; 17, IV; 31, IX
Alcohol and Tobacco Tax and Trade Bureau	27, I
Community Development Financial Institutions Fund	12, XVIII
Comptroller of the Currency	12, I
Customs and Border Protection	19, I
Engraving and Printing, Bureau of	31, VI
Federal Acquisition Regulation	48, 10
Federal Claims Collection Standards	31, IX
Federal Law Enforcement Training Center	31, VII
Financial Crimes Enforcement Network	31, X
Fiscal Service	31, II
Foreign Assets Control, Office of	31, V
Internal Revenue Service	26, I
Investment Security, Office of	31, VIII
Monetary Offices	31, I
Secret Service	31, IV
Secretary of the Treasury, Office of	31, Subtitle A
Truman, Harry S. Scholarship Foundation	45, XVIII
United States Agency for Global Media	22, V
United States and Canada, International Joint Commission	22, IV
United States and Mexico, International Boundary and Water Commission, United States Section	22, XI
U.S. Copyright Office	37, II
U.S. Office of Special Counsel	5, CII
Utah Reclamation Mitigation and Conservation Commission	43, III
Veterans Affairs, Department of	2, VIII; 38, I
Federal Acquisition Regulation	48, 8
Veterans' Employment and Training Service, Office of the Assistant Secretary for	41, 61; 20, IX
Vice President of the United States, Office of	32, XXVIII
Wage and Hour Division	29, V
Water Resources Council	18, VI
Workers' Compensation Programs, Office of	20, I, VII
World Agricultural Outlook Board	7, XXXVIII

List of CFR Sections Affected

All changes in this volume of the Code of Federal Regulations (CFR) that were made by documents published in the FEDERAL REGISTER since January 1, 2018 are enumerated in the following list. Entries indicate the nature of the changes effected. Page numbers refer to FEDERAL REGISTER pages. The user should consult the entries for chapters, parts and subparts as well as sections for revisions.

For changes to this volume of the CFR prior to this listing, consult the annual edition of the monthly List of CFR Sections Affected (LSA). The LSA is available at *www.govinfo.gov*. For changes to this volume of the CFR prior to 2001, see the "List of CFR Sections Affected, 1949–1963, 1964–1972, 1973–1985, and 1986–2000" published in 11 separate volumes. The "List of CFR Sections Affected 1986-2000" is available at *www.govinfo.gov*.

2018

27 CFR

83 FR Page

Chapter II
447.11	Amended	66553
478.11	Amended	66554
479.11	Amended	66554

2019

27

84 FR Page

Chapter II
447	Policy statement	9239
478	Policy statement	9239
478.40	Removed	12094
478.40a	Removed	12094
478.57	(b) and (c) removed; (a) redesignated as undesignated text	12094
478.76	Revised	64743
478.92	Heading revised; (a)(3) and (c) removed	12094
478.95	Amended	12094
478.116	Amended	12094
478.119	Removed	12094
478.132	Removed	12094
478.153	Removed	12094
478.171	Amended	12094, 60334
479	Policy statement	9239
479.32	(a) and (c) removed; (b) redesignated as undesignated text	12094
555.11	Amended	13799
555.27	Removed	13799

27—Continued

84 FR Page

Chapter II—Continued
555.30	(a), (b), and (d) introductory text amended	13799
555.33	Heading amended	13799
555.41	(a) removed	13799
555.45	(a) and (b) removed	13799
555.49	(a) removed	13799
555.51	(a) removed	13799
555.57	(b) amended	13799
555.73	Amended	64744
555.75	Amended	64744
555.78	Revised	64744
555.79	Amended	64744
555.82	Revised	64744
555.102	(b)(1), (2) designation, and (b)(2) heading removed	13799
555.103	(a) removed	13799
555.105	Heading amended; (a) removed	13799
555.125	(a) removed	13799
555.126	Heading amended; (a) removed	13800
555.142	Heading amended	13800
555.165	(b) amended	13800
555.201	(e) removed	13800
555.202	(a) amended	13800
555.218	Table amended	13800
555.219	Table amended	13800
555.220	Table amended; eff. 5-31-19	12097
555.220	Table amended	13800
555.224	Table amended	13800

27—Continued

84 FR
Page

Chapter II—Continued
771.1—771.136 (Subchapter E)
  Added.......................................64744

2020-2021

(No regulations published)

2022

27 CFR

87 FR
Page

Chapter II
447.11 Amended..............................24734
447.42 (a)(1)(iv)(A) amended 24734
447.45 (a)(2)(ii) amended................24734
478 Authority citation revised 193
478.11 Amended......................193, 24734
478.11 Correction: Amended 51249
478.12 Added 24735
478.12 Correction: (a)(1) revised;
  (a)(3) amended 51249
478.12 Correction: (a)(4)(iv), (d),
  and (f)(2) amended....................51250
478.47 (a) amended 24741
478.50 (a) amended 24741
478.73 (a) amended...........................193
478.92 (a) revised; (c) added 24741
478.92 Correction: (a)(1)(iii)
  amended.................................51250
478.104 Added 193
478.122 Revised 24743

27 CFR—Continued

87 FR
Page

Chapter II—Continued
478.123 Revised 24744
478.124 (c)(4) revised; (b) and (f)
  amended.................................24744
478.125 (e), (f), and, (i) revised.........24745
478.125 Correction: (i) amended 51250
478.125a (a)(4) amended; (a)(4)
  table redesignated as (a)(4)
  Table 1 and revised....................24746
478.129 (b), (d) and (e) revised 24746
479.11 Amended.............................24747
479.11 Correction: Amended 51250
479.102 Revised 24747
479.102 Correction: (a)(3)(A)
  through (C) redesignated as
  (a)(3)(i) through (iii); (b)(3)(A)
  through (C) redesignated as
  (b)(3)(i) through (iii);(a)(6)
  amended.................................51250
479.103 Amended 24749

2023

(Regulations published from January 1,
2023, through April 1, 2023)

27 CFR

88 FR
Page

Chapter II
478.11 Amended 6574
479.11 Amended 6575

○